What reviewers have said:

Words for a Deaf Daughter

"A heartbreaking, lyrical account of his 'retarded' daughter whose strange and beautiful presence in the world compelled her father to rethink and resee his own relation to the natural and human universe." —Saul Maloff, *Newsweek*

"A rare celebration of the human spirit that will move thousands of readers. . . . West has probably never written with such affirmative eloquence as in this beautiful and moving book. . . . It is, without mawkishness, a masterpiece." —*Publishers Weekly*

"Paul West uses the language with a combined ingenuity and precision. If one does not pay strict attention, this book will break the heart." —Jean Stafford, *Washington Post Book World*

"It is a work of art. Mr. West has written a long and complicated poem here, at once wild and funny and beautiful and loving and mad." —*New Yorker*

"What is so remarkable, what I envy Mr. West, is what he has done with the pain. It is not just that he loves his child, and describes with poetic passion (he is a born writer) what it means to help her gain speech and some genuine exchange with the world around her. It is rather that he has discovered his vocation, and through and with Mandy seems to be finding out everything worth knowing. . . . Mr. West writes with a soaring, inexplicable joyousness . . . which makes everything most of us worry about look pretty cheap. . . . A revelation." —*The Guardian*

"Extraordinary, brilliant and most fascinating . . . a masterpiece of the imagination . . . an inspired, super-intelligent, poetically sensitive rambling letter of love." —Monica Dickens, *Boston Globe*

"A work of art, the vision of the loved object widening beyond adoration into new ways of seeing the world. The beauty of *Words for a Deaf Daughter* is the truth of its form." —R. Z. Sheppard, *Time*

"There are descriptive passages in this book that burn themselves into the mind . . . a stunning feat of writing . . . a song of life in the midst of calamity." —Chaim Potok, *New York Times Book Review*

"A triumphant book." —*Times Literary Supplement*

"Likely to wrench your heart, then fill it with joy. Poetic and passionate, but unsentimental." —*Christian Century*

"Magnificent eloquence . . . a brilliant and joyful book . . . his language is intense and special." —*Harper's*

"The courage, wisdom, and bittersweet joy conveyed should provide more help to those whose lives revolve around a disabled person than a stack of psychology handbooks." —*Library Journal*

"This account is one of hope and energy and joy . . . written with something of Mandy's plunging exuberance." —Mary Sullivan, *The Listener*

Gala

"West shines best when he dares to invade those close to home and heart. *Gala*, a novel in which he attempts to jimmy the lock on his deaf daughter Mandy's closed world, tells of their joint attempt to build a basement model of the Milky Way. From this domestic conceit West launches headlong into the more rarified precincts of brain biochemistry, astrophysics, and linguistics, yet the sum is anything but dry meditation; his prose burns with the incandescent passion only a parent could muster." —Albert Mobilio, *Voice Literary Supplement*

"*Gala* outshines, outlaughs and outthinks any other novel I've read this year." —Ronald Christ, *Commonweal*

"The sky was man's first picture book and in West's punchy prose all its images and colors spin, retract, implode (West, you'll remember, is something of a wizard with words) . . . a cosmic high-wire trip." —*Kirkus Reviews*

"This is a beautiful novel." —J. D. O'Hara, *Washington Post*

ALSO BY PAUL WEST

FICTION

Love's Mansion
The Women of Whitechapel and Jack the Ripper
Lord Byron's Doctor
The Place in Flowers Where Pollen Rests
The Universe, and Other Fictions
Rat Man of Paris
The Very Rich Hours of Count von Stauffenberg
Caliban's Filibuster
Colonel Mint
Bela Lugosi's White Christmas
I'm Expecting to Live Quite Soon
Alley Jaggers
Tenement of Clay

NONFICTION

James Ensor
Portable People
Sheer Fiction I & II
Out of My Depths: A Swimmer in the Universe
I, Said the Sparrow
The Wine of Absurdity
Byron and the Spoiler's Art

POETRY

The Snow Leopard
The Spellbound Horses

PAUL WEST

Words for a Deaf Daughter
and
Gala

with a new preface by the author

Dalkey Archive Press

First Dalkey Archive edition, November 1993

Library of Congress Cataloging-in-Publication Data

West, Paul, 1930-
 [Words for a deaf daughter]
 Words for a deaf daughter; and, Gala / Paul West with a new preface
by the author. — 1st Dalkey Archive one-vol. ed.
 1. West, Paul, 1930-   —Biography—Family. 2. Children, Deaf—
United States—Family relationships. 3. Fathers and daughters—United
States—Biography. 4. Authors, American—20th century—Biography.
5. Fathers and daughters—Fiction. I. West, Paul, 1930-   Gala. 1993.
II. Title: Words for a deaf daughter. III. Title: Gala.
PS3573.E8247Z468   1993   813.54—dc20   93-18997
[B]
ISBN 1-56478-036-8

Partially funded by grants from The National Endowment for the Arts
and The Illinois Arts Council

Dalkey Archive Press
Fairchild Hall
Illinois State University
Normal, IL 61790-4241

*Printed on permanent/durable acid-free paper and bound in the United
States of America.*

Preface

Although the subject of *Words for a Deaf Daughter* could not read the book while I was writing it, and still has been unable to read it some twenty years later, she did participate in the writing, by which I mean she sat on my knee, or nearby, while I wrote. It suited her especially that I was writing on the backs of envelopes slit open; something homespun and undignified in that appealed to her, not least because it was on such paper that she did her own extraordinary daubs and composed what passed with her for prose. The original manuscript sits in a steel drawer in a university library now, an uncouth bundle of pencilled, ball-pointed, crayoned handwriting joined, quite often, by Mandy's scrawls and squiggles: a garish obbligato in the margin, sometimes on the middle of the page. Often enough, in her ecstatically ebullient way, she would snatch a page from me and run away with it, giggling.

She knew what was going on was about her, and she

even staged a barbaric correspondence with my editor at Harper and Row (as the house called itself then). When the book first came out, she carried a copy to school and made a nuisance of herself, not quoting but brandishing the thing at her teachers. After all, her picture appeared in it, and some of her drawings (one of which graces this new edition's cover). It is moving to contemplate such a view of the book, a view that maintains and perpetuates Book as a mysterious item, forever to be fingered and pondered, never wholly to be fathomed. I have nothing to add to the record its pages keep; the experience of writing such a book while its invoked recipient messed about with it fed into the book's subject all along, and I know that, because she nudged me or grabbed a sheet, I lost phrases, had to terminate sentences prematurely, and literally forgot what she'd done ten minutes earlier in favor of some escapade more recent. My familiar, equipped as always with brush and crayon, pencil and fountain pen, was an unquiet host, but also an inexhaustible object of contemplation. The book trembled like mercury as she breathed on it, skewed away sideways as she tormented its author, and mutated second after second. What I really needed was a team of accomplices, to divert her and steady me, but she and I fudged it up alone during alert mornings, and fuzzy afternoons when we both inclined to doze; if you look at the holograph you can see where we goofed and the handwriting kept pace, index to fatigue. It was the most frustrating writing experience of my life, but unique in that the writing provoked into happening things that slid straight into the book, like molten ore settling into a mold at unthinkable speed. It kept being over before it had begun, and it kept beginning again before it had started. An experiment, it was a hectic transcription, and I sometimes pretended I was Busoni, shifting Bach organ music into music for piano; certainly living by my wits, a monster of diabolical balance. I could have written my book after midnight, as I do nowadays, filling its chalice during a dead calm; but that would have been too serene a performance, minus the badgering, the torment, the impromptu brilliance of Amanda herself, gadfly, angel, the most preposterous of all persons from Porlock.

Since then, *Words* has had various incarnations and some embarrassing jackets, though its numerous reviews have been astounding. It has become a teaching text and a manual for parents (though, I would think, an erratic and expressionistic one). It began as an essay in the now defunct *New American Review*, chosen by Theodore Solotaroff (who turned the book down for New American Library, which was when Frances McCullough of Harper and Row glommed on to it). The copy I sent off to Gollancz in London was that rarity, a carbon copy of the typescript, and a smudgy one at that. I still feel, for obvious reasons, an addiction to the physical artifact of those two hundred messy handwritten pages tied together with string: an ideal bundle for Thomas Carlyle's housemaid to light the fire with. Emotion drenches those pages as it does any rereading—this, however, isn't one of the books I tug out of the shelf in the small hours to see how I was writing in those days. It has turned out to be the record of a heyday, of her finest hours.

After twenty years, the voluminous correspondence has tapered off; I had never realized how many people out there had been in the same fix and needed to share their findings. Yet, to me, the book ranks not as useful or epistemological, but as art, verbal art, creating and exploiting that special form of the epistle which seems dramatic: the letter to someone who will never read it, although the rest of the world can. That knife's edge scores me still, because you have to write with passionate scrupulosity, knowing the world has the advantage of the person addressed, whose effability exposes her literal "infancy"—which is the state of not being able to speak. To write in and about such a situation or emergency requires unflinching sensitivity, and I fault myself for not having been unflinching and sensitive enough. I set down what I could, determined to set something down, much in the mood of the German composer Stockhausen, whose "Out of the Seven Days" tells what it was like to live alone in his house for a week with nothing but water to sustain him. *Existenz-musik,* I would call it. Perhaps *Words* is *Existenz-prose.* Is-ness barography. Whatever it is, it cannot be read or judged by conventional standards and requires a generous adjustment in taste, going as it does toward the cry, the shout, the incessant appalled murmur we all emit but fail to heed.

Only the other day, I heard (significant verb) how American Sign Language expresses the word "pasteurize": by passing your hand *past your eyes.* That, like many ingenuities of the handicapped, enthralls me and makes my world wider.

When I finished *Gala,* six years after *Words,* Harper and Row asked me for a brief preface, but not without first asking me if I would classify *Gala* as nonfiction, which it is not. I refused, although offered more money for misdescribing my book. Only to me, perhaps, was it vital to insist on minute distinctions.

Readers will recognize, or think they recognize, two of the characters in *Gala,* and rightly. But Milk and Deulius, as such, exist only within *Gala*'s pages, whereas whom and what I extrapolated them from exist nonfictionally, as do others of the novel's characters, while yet others are outright imaginary. The mix, as sidewalk colorists say, is all my own work, a tapestry or mosaic that was in my head long before I wrote either book. Both books came out of the same ferment, and *Gala,* in its different register, is a true emotional sequel to the other. What I do in it is to stage the scenario of a wish-fulfillment; the wish abides, and the book partly fulfills it on the level of imagination. I have often thought that one should be able not only to describe something but also to recover (or create) anticipations of it. If there were life forms on Mars, unknown, one should be able to imagine them correct in every detail. *Gala* is a planet indeed, a pipedream rendered into prose, perhaps under the auspices of Thomas de Quincey, whose "The Affliction of Childhood" afflicts me yet.

As I wrote in 1976, the traditional prefatory note to a work of fiction denies that the characters resemble people living or dead. In this case I am obliged, selectively, both to deny it and admit it, and to add that some of those who were alive in 1976 are now dead. The reaper has been through my squad. All I can add is that I tried to invade imaginatively situations I know quite well, and in doing so to win or exact some freedom of response, of conjecture and intrusive epitome, of license to transpose or combine, otherwise illicit. That is in part what art is for, as well as being a means of trying to create something perfect. I think of this book, as Mark Seinfelt reminded me the other day, as an "autofiction": its stimulus, or occasion, I know profoundly at first hand; its pattern, much noticed by scientists, is a dream that I signed.

Drawing the star charts in color was a soothing joy, but I have never been able to find them since; their spring binder must have carried them off among those very stars for verification by the synod of the galaxies. I still search, but in vain. Like so many treasure islands, that binder of pleasure has floated away. In my 1976 preface, I wrote that any sequel to *Gala* would "probably be neither memoir nor novel but a prose poem dense as a neutron star, one flake of which, metaphorically speaking, would weigh a million tons and cut through any of us as if we were air." Perhaps when I find the binder I will write the sequel to the sequel. Or, when I write the sequel to the sequel, the binder will come back to hand. The two books together are intended to state that I and others were here, and our imaginations too.

P.W., 1993

Words for a Deaf Daughter

Contents

1. Walk Don't Run

Coming into this room for the first time, they all flinch and stare at what hangs from the eight-foot cord stretched between the bay window and the inside one of frosted glass that flanks the hallway, admitting light but throwing faces into distorted silhouette.

The second and third times they still flinch and stare, but not as frightened. And even we, coming in from the dusk when it is too dark to see the leaves on the low branches your toes flick when you ride high on your swing, wince at the gallery of hanged midgets swaying in non-unison as our arrival disturbs the air around them. Hush. Whisper who dares: Christopher Robin *refuses* to say his prayers.

From left to right this is the present complement (although not the constant one, for any day you might substitute a paratrooper, a dog, or an ordinary doll):

one golliwog, crayoned in black on white paper, attached with Scotch tape having holly and berries on it—a round, vacant smile fixed since last Christmas;

a silver girl who is you bathing in a canary-yellow bath with red taps;

a hugged-shabby golliwog, three-dimensional and not scissored out of cardboard—back of head toward us and maybe no face remaining;

then, big as you, Nosferatu, adapted from an early Dracula movie but modified to fit your own unspoken but explicit preferences and so meriting a sentence to himself. His face is a yellow canvas Halloween mask with thin black mandarin mustache smeared on in charcoal; one eyehole spills lipstick blood down the side of his nose and the other is plugged with a cognac cork; the forehead wrinkles are weals lined with—what was it?—mascara or eyebrow pencil; the rest of him, corrugated cardboard pieces which once enveloped books on Galápagos birds and a whole miniature farm, we painted either with ink (his royal-blue coat) or in mauve and green stripes of poster color (the drainpipe trousers encasing those rickety legs that don't exist), letting him dry out before affixing five crimson buttons, four square floral coasters for pockets, an outsize pacifier against his right kneecap, a six-coil winding of string about his left leg, a hearing aid in each ear (like you) made of spare wire and a plastic bottle cap, and—at the extremities of each limb—white paper claws, curling and tipped red with nail varnish. He broods and leers, the major presence on the line; and no wonder, actually, for I think you force-dried him at the fire while I was out of the house hunting supplies.

That makes *two* sentences, I know. Saying it makes three.

And he is smoking a real, stubbed-out cigarette in a rolled-paper holder resembling a spent firework.

Four sentences, you see. Five. Never mind: someone who is no respecter of appearances has stuck a face of arsenical green against his right shoulder, so he looks both beheaded and not, the one head not quite underneath his arm (but tilting that way, so he *could* if he wished walk the Bloody Tower like him in the song), the other head erect in a sentinel's aloofness, banana-yellow-bald. If we sit beneath him on the sofa that isn't near enough the wall to catch windfalls from the line, which happen when the Scotch tape has dried out, the claws on his right foot float against the backs of our heads. When you yourself sit, they float above you like hooks ready to hoist you up to join the figures in the air. But you never go, in spite of your passion for standing on window sills, riding escalators to the top of every building, sitting voluptuously at the tops of slides. You are content to have them over you, watching, presiding, eavesdropping perhaps; guardian angels, furies, and gargoyles all in one; paper-edge sharp, paper-frail, paint- or crayon-static; household gods always in need of repair and whom, from time to time, you console for their thinness by adding a real golly or two to the line.

Interrupting myself, if I may, I know that in school at this very moment you'll be matching and naming colors in the room whose door bears the imperative, in the ITA spelling, WAUK. And some of them tell you not to run, the doors I mean. I'm certainly moving through your household gods at *wauk*ing speed but, then, you and I do our fair share of running when you come home, and I, doing my best to contort my face into a likeness of Nosferatu's, have to chase you up the stairs or round the apple trees, both eaters and cookers.

Back now to where *I* was. Next there's a crew-cut golliwog painted in garish quarters, then a multi-spotted clown superimposed over a golliwog in baggy breeches (like the Dutch boys in your books who stuck their fingers in the dike to keep the sea back). For eight inches, now, the line holds nothing save a transparent slip of Scotch tape like

8mm film hung blankly out to dry; on this, once, hung the clown who now, hooked into a string loop by his egregious head horn, blots out the Dutch golliwog. There follow five more creations: an eager, alert golliwog in red-striped shirt but minus feet; a pike-nosed Japanese fighter plane called the Kawasaki Hien, camouflaged green and gray and cut out from the lid of the box the kit came in, the decals like blood moons; another golliwog, also Dutch, with an oafish grin and, stuck on his left leg like a cannibal trophy, a mustached man in military uniform; a lime-green clown whose legs come trunking out from the base of his neck, and whose face is a skull; and an armless purple gorilla in vermilion jeans. At the line's end hangs your own contribution, a red triangle trimmed with white fluff—a Santa Claus's hat on which you stuck a miniature of Santa himself, whom you call "Beard." A quick look down and we find your print, in a frame, of "Boy with Dove" (Picasso, born 1881, eighty years before you), the boy's face emptied of emotion as he looks into the middle or the far distance with the dove at his chin. Last, the budgerigar in his cage and the sliding glass partition you once butted with your corn-haired head and smashed.

Why tell you what you know? Maybe the reasons are selfish; but when, if ever, you read this, you will have forgotten your years of infant *Sturm und Drang* as well as the comparative idyll of this, your second year in school. A year ago, after you had been at school only a month, they divided you up for the annual report issued in the month of birth (and found you baffling). Here it is, including the by now almost classical reference to your right convergent squint, especially when looking into cameras. Your lip-reading rubric has this beneath it: *Understands familiar words through lip-reading and hearing. Span of attention for assimilating new vocabulary is still short.* Yes, and I know

4

you can be incorrigibly frivolous about new words, few of which you ever seem to think you need; but I have also seen you checking through your physiognomy at a mirror, saying the words loudly and almost correctly while the bits of head they denote remain in place. As they say in the report under Speech Aptitude, you imitate *many sounds very well, with an accurate reproduction of intonation too;* but they go on to note how you are *easily distracted from concentrated speech work* (so was I, if it's any comfort to you, until about twenty-five). Always, you have taken or left speech, as you thought fit; and no bribe or coercion will work, but only a counter-distraction equivalent to gold over silver, radioactivity over magnetism, Samarkand over Acapulco, or—if things are really bad—*sambur,* the Indian elk, over such familiars as a plastic mouse and a double-jointed toy poodle, hose pipe over water pistol, a foot-long pencil made of rock candy (disguised as an umbrella) over anything that writes. The house is crammed with gaudy attention getters we used to use, both at home and at the audiology clinic, just to get you to *look*—and as soon as you looked we, they, took the baubles away in order to work with what attention you gave while it lasted. Which often wasn't long: time for a word, a plosive, a round O, concessions you perfunctorily made to the word-obsessed rest of the world.

Next among your school souvenirs-to-come (their souvenirs of you) I find something beguilingly titled Kindergarten Occupations ("including Pre-Reading and Elementary Numbers," which according to a Harvard seminar that includes a few brilliant children is arbitrary anyway). Here again you have a good beginning, as I well know, having seen you mount an insensate fury because I had drawn a figure with only one leg, or, more refinedly provoking, only one eyebrow: *Discrimination,* I read, *between shapes, colors, and*

5

*sizes is accurate and she draws meaning from simple pic-
tures but not yet from the written word, nor yet from numbers, spoken or written.* As for your Manual Skills—you
who paint astounding abstracts, which you sometimes populate with people who are globeheads on single stems—you
come out well: *Controls scissors, pencils, and brushes well
and manipulates small parts of constructional toys. Paintings show an interest in color and her drawings a liking for
pattern.* They may not know it, they may not remember it
(but I think they *were* told): your interest in color used to
extend to painting your whole face green with eye shadow,
thus converting yourself into something between a chloro-
phyll goblin and a fugitive from a horror film. Also, you
painted windows, daubed walls, both inside and out, and
laughingly improvised pigments from anything at hand—
instant coffee plus plaster of Paris plus Ajax cleanser plus
ink, all for windows and walls and carpets, the top of my
desk, the mail and papers as they arrived. And soot! Let's
be kind to each other and forget about soot. Of pattern, all
I'll say is that your passion for design and symmetry would
have done credit to a medieval theologian. Somewhere in
your head you kept a kind of DNA pattern of the attitudes
and millimetrical relationships in which you wanted things
to be—slippers, cutlery, cushions, curtains, rugs, and pok-
ers, all such. I have seen you rage because, somewhere in
the house, there was a bottle with an imperfectly replaced
top, or because someone was engorging with the wrong
spoon. If there is to be an argument from design, then at
some point you must surely have been dispatched to earth
as a special proof.

Let's look at Physical Education. They say—in what
strikes me as consummate understatement—that you are
energetic, which is like calling the cheetah not backward
in moving forward or the elephant heavier than air. Or, say,

a laser beam equal to the chore of wax melting. A compulsive, rapid, and exquisitely coordinated mover, you have overrun us all while working out of your system something that you inhale back again with each breath; and so, on it goes, this unquenchable agitation of your legs and arms that never quite matches the rhythm of your high-pitched, looping call. You never lose balance, trip, skid, misjudge a distance, or cannon into things you don't in any case intend to wreck. Throwing, though, you use both your arms and legs and then throw backward with a lovely inconsequentiality it is hard to mimic (though we try, wanting to know how it feels). In this case, movement is all, and destination is as much beside the point as the parabola the thrown thing makes. School found you enjoyed P.E., but also that you tend to keep to familiar apparatus; then they added, *Does not comprehend Musical Movement, but joins in when encourage.* But you rock, when consoling yourself, in a perfect rhythm, just like the Olympic flip-jumper Dick Fosbury when he is preparing to take off. It's only when you try to dance that you settle for dynamic cavort in lieu of the specific timing and pattern that most mortals—for reasons which I confess have always eluded me—try to move to. You—well, let's say you are closer to Nijinsky or Zorba the Greek than to Fred Astaire.

The report's concluding long entry comments on your Social Development, an aspect of your life which—because people would never let their children play with you for reasons you never knew about—only began with school. Up to then, you played with adults and aped adult ways. *Plays happily,* the report says, *alongside other children but does not enter into their play, nor join in easily with group activities, although her interest in what the other children are doing is increasing.* Simply, you had never had any practice, had not realized that suddenly you were permitted to play

7

with other children. I have never seen you refuse to play with any consenting adult in private or in public; but, of course, then you played exceeding rough, and only the hardiest among the adults consented a second time. Torn hair, bashed nose, rent lapels, fingernailed eyes, and brutalized privates, these were the stigmata you bestowed. I remember the playing and the mythologies it suggested: a commando course supervised by an overwhelming midget; *Götterdämmerung* written in mud, rain, and your own bland wee; Herculean tests in the presence of a three-foot warbling Zeus whose fists pounded us further and further into muscle-snapping contortions until we felt we had lived in the Augean stables since the year One, the venue always liberally swilled by yourself with floods of water or littered with hillocks of refuse. Given knowledge, strength, and time, you would certainly have converted any aircraft hangar into a play area approximating—by what your own ideals were then—a diluvial hell, a-bulge with alligators which paradoxically sang like linnets, adults who melted at the first hit of your spit (and then weirdly remanifested themselves as gigantic umbrellas with big rancid lettuce leaves for fabric); eagles and buzzards (whose appearance you seemed to fancy in your picture books) and herring gulls (which you bared your teeth at and, maybe, expected one day to fight on even terms, having taken off while running like the wind beneath them). Those things certainly would be part of any master plan of yours, but also—if I'm getting it right—coal, sand, polyunsaturated oil, and broken glass, hammers and shovels and knives, mayonnaise to slick your eel body with and soft nougat to plaster down your spilling hair.

The last comment on you reads, with bleak simplicity: *Difficult to assess. (Brain damage?)*. The question mark sums up a great deal of the considerable amount said about you over the past years and either canceled out or left dubiously standing. It is clear that, more often than occasionally, something in your head doesn't work as it ought to; something that seems tied up with your hearing's poorness. What? I wish I knew. The words that crop up—brain damage, middle-brain damage, nerve deafness, autism, dyslexia, etc.—give us no more than an illusion of command, or of knowing, yet I know of parents who, wanting passionately to have their child diagnosed, refuse the specific label when it comes. In the semi-dark of not knowing, we go ahead and treat you as only deaf and encourage you to progress at a speed that doesn't compound your difficulties. Whatever might be the total or the explanation of the things wrong with you, let me tell you—in case, maybe, you've been too busy to realize it—exuberant play and emphatic response have worked minor wonders with you already; so has school, and so has (I presume) the battery of tiny rituals you've evolved in play. *Ee-ya,* you say when things are going well, a gentle rocking sound which, made under the roof of your mouth, announces you are happy and intend to prolong that condition by repeating its vocal signal.

And *ee-ya* we ourselves have got into the habit of saying, even when you're not around. I wouldn't waste such a *trouvaille* for worlds; but, then, I couldn't really write you a whole letter of *ee-ya,* even when that sound expresses the mood I usually feel. Hence, all these words, a surprise package for you and your introduction to people who'd want to know you. You wake each day, uncertain if the world is still there: you check the garden to see if your slide has survived the darkness or merely several hours of your not having used it; you do much the same when you come home from school. In fact, without our knowing it, you probably check a dozen treasures in a whole burst of intermittent apprehension; so thank goodness things don't move of their

9

own accord, slides dissolve in rain, swings work themselves up overnight and lunge off above the trees in elated orbit. Your love of pattern comes from—it's obvious, isn't it?—your deep sense of precariousness in a world of near silence. You're both the tyrant and the victim of categories, locations, and Mercator fixes. Not only do you want everything in its place; you even devise new places for things whose places didn't seem sure enough: the gray velvet elephant kneeling in the window you have thrust forward upon his trunk, and there in that position he must stay; he used to stand straight elsewhere, but *where* you have brainwashed us into forgetting. So too with the alarm clocks, which you have appropriated to your bedside table, asserting a multiple claim not so much on time itself (of which you are almost heedless) as on rattling bells held repeatedly against your right ear, the one through which a little contraband-like sound comes in. Somehow, if things are where you think they ought to be, they do better than otherwise what they are supposed to do.

And yet, and yet (I would be more confident deciphering some ancient stone whose writings use an unknown alphabet), once you have set in order and in place all you think that matters, you shower it with your own special confetti of toffee wrappers, popsicle sticks, ripped newspapers, string, rubber bands, hair clips, and crayon shavings, as well as small items of potato salad, breakfast cereal, and unfinished vanilla ices. It's as if, having designed and erected Stonehenge or seen the ground plan of Leptis Magna, you can happily ignore weeds that thrive or sand that amasses. You don't, as they say, pick up after you; but, with your geometer's knowledge of where things are under or among the clutter (assuming no creep has interfered with them), you race over and round and among them with batlike accuracy, only occasionally reversing to bestow a heel tap of delicate acknowledgment—for being there to be circumvented at all, but, having been circumvented, having to be gone back to out of a kind of Rube Goldberg civility mixed with collector's pride. (You'd have understood Samuel Johnson's *having* to touch all the hitching posts as he went down Fleet Street.) Courier, acrobat and pirouetting elf in one, you pay daily homage to the just-so-ness man can achieve. You have little idea, yet, of surname, and none of address, city and country, but you know where the *wun, tω, thrεε* counting chart belongs, which coat goes on which hook, which hair clip is missing from which side of your head. *Oi-ya!* you howl when things have been displaced, a cry that climbs until it seems to rend our skulls and then dives in curt exasperation. *Ee-ya,* you coo when things have been set where they belong, when the matching hair clip has been reinstalled; and there you are in a contained ecstasy that finds all planets behaving well around your sun and passes meteors by without a glance.

An "exceptional" child (to use a term whose very precision wins a bonus from the word's conventional link with cleverness), you astound me as jugglers and mystics and astronauts do. You didn't seem unusual—not to mention exceptional—until you were two. Up to then you fooled everyone, including the doctor and your observant big sister; your excellent lip-reading carried you that far, and I salute the tremendous and spontaneous effort you made in thus responding to the only normality you knew. A tiny girl, you self-helped yourself to somewhere just below average until the colossal odds against you showed you up. Slow to speak, you were cautious about starting to walk; but once you had walked you ran like a bird preparing to take off. You fell in love, as well, with water and umbrellas, and in the presence of either orated vehemently (although non-verbally) to yourself. Water you preferred

11

in puddles on the living-room floor or in baths, but you also liked it in rainspouts, saucepans, and lavatory basins. Umbrellas—which, I think, exerted the stronger spell—you collected with casual relentlessness. You never had fewer than a dozen. They were your trees, really: a plastic-leaved, tin-branched orchard of them, which every night had to be rolled up firm and laid across your bed, and every morning landed in a cascade on ours when you came heavy-footedly in, hooting for them to be opened. Then, with half-blind eyes, down to the living room where we spread them over the floor like Pan and Company afforesting a bare mountain while you, red-cheeked with elation, danced among them, catching occasionally the beads on the rib ends and skimming the canopies half round, but never trampling the handles or ramming a fist through the fabric.

You would stand, do a preliminary skip to get your timing right—a one-two-three with your big toes creased downward as if to scratch earth—and then flow into a joyous high-kneed pounding, your long hair a flash, your arms providing you with a tightrope walker's balance, your eyes unobtainably fixed on an upper corner of the room, where you saw what no one else saw. You looked and smiled, and danced the more wildly for it, fueling your semi-tarantella from the presence in the vacancy. *Fred,* we began to say, domesticating the ghost: *it's Fred again.* And so, each morning, with a flim and a flam, and a flim again, followed by a swift series of flim-flams, you danced spread-eagled, lithe and bony, chirping on an empty stomach.

It was winter when we flew you to the university clinic in a Viscount which lurched through the rain above the heaving, pumice-gray sea. At each plunge or sideslip you let out a birdcall of delight. Born on the island, home of witches, banshees, and temperamental goblins, you had never been off it. And now, leaving it for the first time,

you seemed isolated in a new way. Your three words—
baba, more, and *ish-ish*—you had used heroically, intend-
ing meanings we missed and being credited with others that
we invented. I listened to the lax, feathered whine of the
engines, wondering what noise they made to you as you sat
smiling into the clouds through the tall oval of the window.
I'd heard, I told myself, on humid days the squeak of my
sinuses filling, and then a pop of contraction on a day of
high pressure, with all the sinews and membranes tugging
and fluctuating in a mucous orchestration. But that was
nothing to what I imagined for your own head: a tinnitus
of bad bells, a frying noise, which in combination drove
you to cup a hand over your right ear and rock heavily to
that side as if trying to shake something loose or back into
place or—thought ended: the two-foot doll, bathed with
you every night in the bathroom and brought with you on
the plane, slipped sideways from your casual hug, and a
cache of bath water spilled into your lap. *My* fault, I said:
you can't blame a stark-naked doll.

When we landed, you whooped down the steps from the
plane. It was still raining, but we had two umbrellas, both
yours. The only trouble was that you didn't want them open
or up; they had to be carried before us like totems, one red,
the other green, every loose fold clamped tight by a rubber
band. Two umbrellas kept from being wet made good folk
stare; but good folk knew nothing of umbrellas, water, and
you. In the taxi, however, you opened up the red umbrella
and sat in an indifferent silence, an erect-sitting being of
utter trustfulness, heedless of the roof lining you might
puncture, and with no more idea of where you were going
than of where you had come from. Out of the taxi, you
insisted, with a plangent squeak, on the umbrella's being
folded again and rebound in its rubber band. Then you
were ready to march with us past the porter's lodge (empty),

wrongly up steps to the Department of Law and down again, and finally into a waiting room stocked with heavy, ridable toys, and equipped with tiny toilets whose still water you inspected and approved.

Called for, we went left into the laboratory (one wall of which was a one-way window facing a lecture room). You stared at the people, the things, and, it seemed, at Fred, whom you have always been able to find anywhere. You grew busy and began to chirp. When, to your exact satisfaction, you had arranged the umbrellas and the doll on a low table, you turned to the experts with a patronizing smile. We sat and watched—your mother at one end of the room, myself (still feeling damp) at the other—helpless on the perimeter and unable to smoke. There was some tinkering with a green box, all dials, and a chart. The door snicked open, admitting an authoritative face which beamed and vanished. Then testing began with overtures of friendship from the studious-mannered man whose trousers looked as if he kneeled a lot. The calm woman in patent-leather high heels clicked a tiny clicker, but you did not turn. They gave you a doll then and tried you from behind with a duck quack, a whistle of low pitch, several rattles, then a small tom-tom. Abruptly, not having turned, you ran to the table, slammed one doll alongside the other and hooted, with finger pointed, for the red umbrella to be opened. There were nods; the umbrella opened, sprang taut, was set in your hands, and you squatted, drawing it down over your head as if sheltering under a thin, frail mushroom, slipping out a hand to adjust a downslid sock, and beginning to make again the birdcall (as if a curlew tried to bleat) which had driven countless local dogs into emulative frenzy, provoked birds into surpassing themselves (searching for a bird, they never saw *you*), and scared all the cats away.

Private under the panels of vinyl, you sang with mounting fervor, the umbrella stem between your legs. No one moved. It was clear that you were going to be given your leisure, allowed to collect yourself. In succession you fluted your voice upward in an ecstatic trill, twirled the umbrella like a color disc without once catching the rim or the plastic against your face (a perfect, sheltering fit it was), peeped out to giggle just a bit fearfully, hoisted the umbrella up and away behind you in a pose from *The Mikado,* and then hid again beneath it. We had seen your face shining with heat, seen you only long enough for that.

Now they tapped on your roof, flicked middle finger hard off thumb against the fabric, and brought their mouths close to the surface, calling your name. Out you came, astounded at something heard: not your name, because you didn't know it then, but something—a retaliating and envious dog, a curlew weary of being competed with, a cat returning to venture a duet—amplified and vibrating in the umbrella above you, but only faces and maneuvering mouths to make it. Us. Us only; so you concealed yourself again, tilting the canopy forward.

What brought you out again and kept you out was the xylophone. You abandoned the umbrella for it, fondled it a while, then beat the living decibels out of it, a Lionel Hampton Lilliputian who struck away and then canted your ear close to the trembling bars, your eyes widening in half-piqued recognition that *this* was what we'd flown you across the sea for. You banged on it with the wooden hammer a few times more and let it fall the two and a half feet to the parquet, wincing once in the wrong direction as it hit.

After calls, hums, hisses, pops, buzzes, barks, bays, and several indeterminate ululations, all from behind you, they did the left side while you smiled at a distracting monkey puppet over on the right. My hands were holding each other too tightly; your mother, twelve yards down the room, looked pale, her maternity shut painfully off and her own hands beginning gestures that ended halfway, the fingers tongue-tied.

"Now," said the studious kneeling man, his kindly face tense, and snapped two wooden bars together. A slapstick, I thought, like the split lath of the harlequin. But whatever was going on, it wasn't low comedy. What he said next, after a fractional shake of his head to the woman in heels— the professional pair's exchange of glances crossing the parental one—sounded like:

"Right down the track." The headshake was a zero in mime.

You smiled at the puppet, offering your hand to put inside it. They let you, working through all the modes of sound, but not to a crescendo, only to a punctuational drum tap, which you ignored. And then, as the light waned— that legendary dank Manchester light swollen with soot and rain and absorbed by tons on tons of Victorian brick and tile—they switched sides, this time beguiling you with a model farm at which you sat, cantankerously checking the cows for udders (as a country girl should) and stationing Clydesdale horses at the water trough. Brilliants of wet formed along your nose and you heard not the snap-crack of the wooden bars; not the first time, anyway. But when it came from a yard closer—these testers gliding about the room like prankish Druids—you flinched, directed an offended stare in a vaguely right-hand direction, and went back to your farm. Again and again they worked from the right, varying the angle and the sound. Again and again, with just a few moments of preoccupied indifference, you jerked your head sideways, beginning to be cheerful as you discovered the routine: beginning to play.

Suddenly there was no farm. It went into a gray steel cabinet against which you kicked and at which you took a running kick as your eyes began to pour (tears whopping enough, I thought, to merit nostrils for conduits) and your birdcall harshened. As you swung, both-handed, the xylophone at the locked handle of the door, I got up, stuck out a hand as I half-fell in a skid on the polish, and took a tonic sol-fa smack in the forehead as you swung the instrument backward again, farther than before, the better to mangle the steel between you and the authentic cows, the horses a-thirsting.

"Ap," I sort of said through the plong and the blank crash, not seeing well. "You might as well get it out again."

"Naughty girl," your mother said unconvincedly as you laugh-cried, pitching the xylophone over your shoulder without so much as a look. I have seen you dispose in the same way of bus tickets, mail, money, books, food, scissors, and plates. The oubliette is anywhere behind you.

"She'll soon—" I heard, but the rest was drowned by a scream of unmitigated anger while you pounded the cabinet with both fists.

"Strong!" called the man who kneeled a lot, busying himself with earphones attached to the many-dialed machine. "She's a grand temper."

"You've seen nothing," I told him. "Yet." I knew how, in the Cleopatra-Clytemnestra rages to which you entitled and still entitle yourself, you could butt your head through a firm window (one so far, without bloodshed, but there were long blond hairs on the splinters of glass). Or pound your uncallused hand down through the crisp and warm pulp of a loaf not long out of the oven, once burying your hand and bringing your arm up with a bread mallet wedged on your wrist, crying, "Ish! Ish!" which is anthem, plea, and threat in one.

But it wasn't *Ish* you came out with this time; it was the first of your calls, *Baba—babababa,* uttered with pauses only

17

long enough for everyone present to shout the same phonemes back at you. If we didn't, you increased the volume,
blustering and raucous. It was the most comprehensive aural
version of yourself. So the clinic room, soundproof of course
(there is even a sign just inside the entrance requesting silence), became a barnyard for a while. Turning wet-eyed,
grime-faced, to each of us in turn, you babbled at us, coerc-
ing, commanding, appealing; and in turn and sometimes in
unison we babbled and brayed back, short only of a cock-a-
doodle-doo, the hymn of a pig wallowing or even farrow-
ing in hot lava, and a moose drowning in a swamp of caviar.
This, so that the testing could go on: one farmyard for another.

In the beginning is the test, and in the end comes a remedy of sorts. But how, I wondered, can they even begin—
overworked but obliged not to rush; never short of children
to work with, one in six hundred being somehow deaf and
usually not deaf only—until they too have run their fingers
across the crowns of the blunt, curiously thick, small teeth
you had then, have seen you dance a full hour among the
umbrellas, have night after night studied your fanatical
attention to the placing of your slippers within an invisible
outline which is there and symmetrical for you beneath the
chest of drawers in your bedroom. . . . As you were then:
now you have new teeth, you dance less among umbrellas
and fuss less about slippers; but how I felt hasn't gone at all.

"You haven't—" I began to say on our third trip to the
clinic, seen her do the living things: give Creation a run
for its money. Not at home. They hadn't seen you, like a
gross Ophelia, distribute around the house—on the window
ledges, in the wardrobe between two decent suits or dresses,
on the rim of the letter box, on the Christmas tree itself—
pork sausages on butcher's hooks or threaded on wire coat
hangers. Or eat the sausage raw, oblivious of worms. Or, in

18

hydrodynamic delight, rip off shoes and socks to plant your bare feet on the TV screen whenever it showed water. Or (I stopped: they were calling your name again and you weren't ever going to answer) sit naked and warbling for an hour in a washbasin of cold water. Or green your face, eat nail varnish, coat the windows with lavender furniture polish, jump down five stairs fearlessly, mimic (by waving a stiffened arm) men carrying umbrellas, chant into a toilet pedestal after choking it with a whole roll of tissue, chew cigarettes, cover yourself with Band-aids when there wasn't a scratch in sight, climb any ladder and refuse to descend, slide pencils up your nose, use a rubber hammer on the doctor's private parts, drink from your potty, wade into a sewer-inspection chamber the plumber had opened, eat six bananas in six minutes, wind and play those alarm clocks at your right ear again and again, shave your face and arms and legs with instant lather and bladeless razor, threaten enormous dogs by advancing upon them with a reed in hand, cut your own hair at random, dissolve soap in a tin basin, rock so hard that your hair touched the floor on either side, sit motionless and rapt in front of a mirror, voluminously autograph walls, tear samples from the dictionary or a book of Picasso prints, stare unblinking into 150-watt bulbs, run, run, run everywhere, heedless of gesticulating and half-felled adults and the sanity of drivers. Exclusive, you even collected and threw away all the keys in the house. . . .

"Mandy . . . *Mandy* . . . MANDY," said the folk at the clinic, upping the volume as you gazed from them to the red finger spinning across the dial and back again. When you heard them, your expression changed, fixing in atavistic wonder. It was as if we were watching the face of sound itself while you, flushed and nervous, heard something visible. After an interval they let you use the micro-

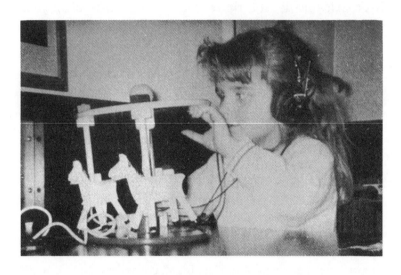

"watching the face of sound itself . . ."

phone yourself, and you began to boom and call in an almost continuous orgy of sound, confronted for the first time with your own share of the missing continent: a Columbus of euphony dumbfoundedly exclaiming at the glories of exclamation itself, every bit like the man in Xenophon who kept shouting *thalassa!* when he saw the sea. I myself felt a bit like shouting; I'd never heard anyone hearing before. And since then I've known a good many firsts with you— things which, up to then, I'd done without really experiencing them, or which you yourself thought up and I myself had never dreamed of doing. Some of the latter are grotesque and sometimes rather revolting as well; I try not to do them, but usually you prevail, imperious queen with your dithering court. I do as I am told. Most people would, just as unquestioningly as Louis XIV's courtiers at Versailles asked for admission by scraping on the door with the elongated nail of the little finger otherwise used for ear cleaning.

It's four years since that first visit to the clinic when powerlessness hit home to us. The strain told on you too. You fetched a shovel from the garden to destroy with: lighting fixtures, windows, crockery, clocks. Strong always, you lifted and swung it with ease, pouting with birdcall. It took you two years to reject the shovel, to change from indefatigable and destructive hobgoblin into a girl who, gaining a word a month only to lose it the month after, developed big, Nordic, luminously beautiful features. Capable, without warning, of histrionic graciousness of manner (as if all the pressures lifted at once and the noises in your head stopped), you enjoyed your increasingly frequent visits to the clinic (toys, earphones, EEG apparatus), ate mightily, hardly ever caught a cold, thumped obliviously past staring or derisive children, and rebaffled the experts. Deaf, yes; "stone" deaf (in that melodramatic inversion of the pathetic fallacy) in the left ear; autistic, perhaps, but that's a vague word like "romantic"; brain damage not ruled out; amblyopia mentioned, with an ophthalmologist joining your team.

At five, blasé by now about Viscounts, you went to live near the clinic and the school associated with it (*one* of the schools, I should say). I signed out a speech trainer, on which you had a daily lesson, dealing sometimes in words, sometimes in sheer noise. You did your jigsaws like an impatient robot, began to lip-read, and gradually built up and kept a tiny vocabulary enunciated with almost coy preciosity, intoning "more" like an aria, raising "hair" into "har," curtailing "mouth" into "mou," lengthening "nose" into a three-second sound, but all the same *talking* although you still didn't know your name. Nicknames accumulated, but not in your presence: Moo, from Mandy-Moo; Birdie, from your call; Tish, from *ish-ish;* Lulu, developed cunningly from the two-syllable, high-pitched call with which your mother called you in and still does; Yee, which sound you yourself substituted for Baba; Proof, from the condition called Manda-proof, you being the only thing or person invulnerable to yourself, or so we said; and, strangest of all to strangers, Boat, your own word for water—until you got *worbar*—shouted while paddling your feet on the TV screen.

Epic formulae, these, while you went incognito; but, since then, other nicknames—names which augment you, eke you out as the dictionary puts it—have come and gone, while you have been busy learning and retaining your real name. Boula came from a mellow little incantation of your own (usually *boula-boo*) rhyming with "howler." Tadpole, sounding disrespectful, was and is a term of endearment somehow expressing the larval, strangely vulnerable innocence that floods across your face at times, and Spider, sounding even worse, describes you when you are all flicking legs, impossible to hold, and certain to pinch or nip, bite or scratch. East (or *The* East) is the logical extension of your contrariness (as in East West) and, in fact, brought after it the mock title of East-Priest, you being the hierophant of contrariness (if you don't mind my saying so).

Most recently, on account of the magnificent exhilaration with which you bump around in the world of home and school, we have begun to call you Jaunty, a word not much used these days but having some connection with *gentil* or *genteel* and certainly the right one for your special fusion of "easy sprightliness" with "airy self-satisfaction" (that's what the dictionary says). I'd almost forgotten your true middle name, Klare, which we reserve for you when the hair is pulled back off your forehead, thus exposing the most babylike feature you have: *Klare without the hair,* that's what we say when your bangs are back, but also when you're being several years less than your age. Then there's Bertie, via Birdie, for when you're being unduly tomboyish;

and I mustn't forget Mandy Brella, called in from the name reserves when your umbrella obsession takes you over for a whole day, and Mrs. Manda, the indefatigable, havoc-creating automaton of housework who washes wallpaper and swills down the kitchen floor with many bucketfuls of water as if it is the stony, bloodied, slippery underfoot of a slaughterhouse.

Fun for us, of course, all that; but learning who you truly were was grim for you. During one spell (I mean phase, but spell suggests also the primitive power that seemed to hold you in thrall), you averaged only three hours' sleep a night, erupting at midnight with umbrella and jigsaws, then fetching a guitar, one mechanical top, several model baths, a dish brimming with soap dissolved, a length of rusty iron piping and a purloined fruit knife, with all of which to while away the night until you could go out. And always wet. You became frenetic, twitched more than ever, during this waiting period: all that soothed you was running water, the swing in the garden, and the ghoulish faces I pulled while pursuing you—as usual—up the stairs. You partnered everyone at the lavatory, exclaiming "Oh" in exaggerative dismay at anyone's being under the vile necessity and then seeking to examine the deposit. But, we noticed, your *Yee* (or *Ee*) was less strident, less insistent; a month later, it had become a delicate, diffident greeting to be answered just as quietly, and you became drier, banged your head less, were less captivated by the grotesque or the effluvial, gave up rending the day's newspaper, lost your passion for knives, began to draw faces and bodies that had two eyes, not one, with two legs instead of a barbed-wire entanglement of blue ballpoint. You even drew a bath—always the long throne of your joy—with a Mandy in it.

You took the intelligence test and managed well before, after forty minutes' concentration, you flung the next puzzle across the room and began a blue-ribbon tantrum. The children's hospital lost your file, and two starch-bosomed nurses lost their cool when you screamed twenty minutes solid because they took from you the model jet kept to calm little boys during EEG tests. You thought it was a present—you think anything is a present (every salesman who arrives at the door with a case of samples has brought you a case of presents).

"I'll buy it," I shouted against the screams. "It's worth it." No, that was out of the question; it was part of the equipment, it was HOSPITAL PROPERTY. You vanished into the pathology lab, and were there found admiring fetuses, tumors, and cysts in their quiet jars, a true humanist explaining to you what was what. We got you a jet at the airport, and, later, a helicopter, a new model bath, a miniature cooking set in Bavarian iron, building blocks, card games, a thousand candy cigarettes, as many lollipops and ices: a surplus for purposes of habilitation, no matter what got smashed, lost, torn, or wasted, no matter what melted or disappeared into the trapped water in the lavatory.

Out of the clutter you have come a girl who can make beds (sometimes six sheets to a bed), bake bread black, fry bacon tin-hard, iron and fold clothes with all the finesse of a weight lifter, Hoover the carpets, mow the lawn, more or less set a table, adjust the TV, fell apples from the tree by swatting it with a tennis racquet, tune your own hearing aids, on your best days butter bread and on most days recite your first name. You cried and shuffled not at all when you began at the school for the deaf, a day girl, almost six. You have become unoffendably gregarious, have learned to hold hands. You look through illustrated magazines with an almost clinical gravity. You have discovered how *No* doubles your range of concepts, and you see Fred, I realize, less and less. The Martian we sometimes call you, or Miss Ra-

24

belais (two more names!). Photogenic, long and agile, you have a vocabulary, a schoolbag and a homework book, which is all penumbra to the darkness of one small girl invading the house with a big shovel, sometimes a coal hammer, and that unfailing drooped-eyelid leer.

One special thing left a new light shining (and there have been others since). Your class of nine children, working by the loop that amplifies sound identically for you all, whichever way you all turn, was told to draw a spider's web. All drew but you, who sat abstractedly apart, aloof from this planet. No one saw you move—and, being thoroughly ambidextrous at that time, you could have done it with either hand—but when your teacher reached you, you were *yee*-ing gently beside a perfectly delineated web, all done in one unbroken line, with a spider at center. Just a few smudges. It went up on the classroom wall, a prized exhibit, and is now in the big roll of all your drawings, not (where I think you meant it to go) in your crate of junk in which, I once thought, you meant to bury us all, outclassed by your energy, thwarted by your privacy, heartsick at Nature's misbehavior, and as short of new expedients as of sleep.

And now, having gone this long (and having cheated by including something I'd written about, instead of to, you, on a previous occasion), I'm going to stop; there'll be more later, after later. In the meantime, here's a peace offering, to be accepted in the same spirit as it's made in. When, from time to time, I take a rest, I'll stand you one of these— nothing much but something, *some things,* to keep you going and maybe gentle you a little. Fyodor Dostoevsky, when a student of engineering at the military school, once drew up an admirable design for a fortress; but, and here's the offering, he forgot to provide it with entrances and exits.

2. All the Grades of Sandpaper

Back to you now, if you're still receiving me. I'd thought of starting, one, two, three, thirty, umpteen, but that's not how to balance; that's not how to count the blessings compared with the cost. It's better bookkeeping to tell you that you quicken in us the sense of life and make us grateful for what's usually taken for granted. A handicap so severe as yours (and maybe I should be using the plural for its multiple kind) drives a parent through fury, then through an empty, vengeful indignation, to two points: first, when in the absence of explanations medical and reasons cosmic, he ignores the handicap *to make it go away;* second, nearer to common sense, when he welcomes it in as your special gift and, while trying to eliminate it, learns its nature by heart as a caution to himself and studies the voracious subtlety of your compensations—as when you, unlike most of us, smell at a pencil newly sharpened, inhaling from the beechwood its own soot-sour bouquet, or trace with addicted fingers the corrugations on the flat of a halved cabbage before eating it raw with the same naturalness with which you drink vinegar, steak sauce, and mayonnaise, and sniff glue. I too, now, have tasted ink (a flavor of charred toenail), coal (a rotted iron-and-yeast pill), bark (woolly and bland, suggesting vulcanized crab meat), leather (a taste here not of the meat or the fat next the hide but of the fur once outside it and of seaweed iodine).

Tasting—testing—with you, I have found new ways into the world. You discover what you discover because you have lost what you've lost; or, rather, you recover what men have lost precisely because they neglect to use something which you never even had and therefore could not "lose." I tag along on your voyages of exploration, and together we sneak into the randomness, the arbitrariness, of the universe as distinct from its patterns. Without you— although I have in my time delighted in *The Compleat Angler*'s bald and mild arcana, in insect books and fungus books, in Jean Rostand's reports on tadpoles and toads— I don't think I would be delving, as I now am, with strangely relevant irrelevance, into the behavior of slugs, mushrooms, cicadas, and flesh-eating plants. Because you brandished it at a big dog, I found out about great reed mace (*Typha latifolia*), often wrongly called the bulrush, but rightly, I reckon, thought almost human. The black six-foot stem is a long cheroot, topped by a yellow spike, and, as my *Observer's Book of Wild Flowers* says, "the closely packed pistillate flowers forming the 'mace' consist of a stalked ovary, with a slender style and a one-sided, narrow stigma, and enveloped in tufts of soft, brownish hairs." A tall woman of a flower—but you can argue that one with me when you come to it in your own time.

I keep two books, one for what *you* do, one for what I find out while waiting for our first conversation. You ate a dandelion flower some time back; one day I'll try you (the genial sense) with the leaves in oil and vinegar, that good salad. I have a lot to tell you which, thank goodness, I've been late in learning; so it's fresh. The hyena isn't quite the scavenger he's supposed to be, whereas the almost extinct American bald eagle is a scavenger out and out. And so on: it's a question, really, of finding a life style, of opening up for myself a universe into which you fit. So I try to devise for you the biggest memberships possible, now and then blundering from wishful thinking into wishful biology, but at other times enrolling you in majestic clans you'd stare at if you knew about them, just as some of the inhumanly ordinary on the earth have stared at you—and still do, themselves suffering a vicarious penalty and, with their frowns, wondering why such children as you aren't put apart. . . .

To get back. Take the shark, created perpetually with two inexplicable handicaps: it has no swim bladder, so must keep on the move or sink; its fixed, paired fins have hardly any braking effect and no motive power, which means that it finds difficulty stopping or reversing. A shark, therefore, is compulsive and a bit helpless; no one knows why. Or take the bulbul bird, the fruit-eating bat, the guinea pig, and man, who alone among known species cannot make their own vitamin C; the reason for this inborn metabolic flaw no one knows. But *all* sharks and bulbul birds and fruit-eating bats and guinea pigs and men are handicapped in these respective ways, whereas what I'm casting around for is a handicap not just inexplicable but also affecting just a few specimens only.

Trying again, I come up with the Mexican amphibian, the axolotl, which instead of becoming a salamander and emerging from water onto land remains an amphibian-to-be and stays in its aquatic larval form. One probable cause of this arrested development is a lack of thyroxine, the hormone secreted by the thyroid gland; for if an axolotl is given thyroid gland extracted from cattle or iodine (an essential component of thyroxine) it turns into a salamander instead of living out its days as a full-grown juvenile, a Peter Pan whose problem is akin to that of humans with goiter. (In Wyoming and the Rocky Mountains, in fact, tiger salamanders often don't assume adult form and humans are liable to goiter, and the reason is lack of iodine in the water.) But it has also been suggested that the axolotl remains aquatic because the lakes it inhabits don't dry up, whereas the surrounding land—the axolotl being found wild only in certain lakes around Mexico City—is barren and dry. Life is easier, securer, in the lake; but, should the lakes dry up, the axolotl could still (I gather) change into a salamander, thus, it seems, having an option to which iodine is irrelevant. Further, an axolotl being transported to a laboratory or a dealer will change into an adult soon after having arrived!

So here is your axolotl, a full-grown juvenile able to breed, which doesn't grow up because either (1) its diet is incomplete or (2) it is programmed for survival, no matter what form it survives in or how incomplete its diet continues to be or (3) it's a bit sluggish and needs a jolt. How to reconcile these three explanations or evaluate them one against the others I don't know; but, clearly, in the axolotl the zoological spring fails to unwind, underwound by diet, overwound by exceptional caution, or just stuck. Just think: a bump equals a drought which equals iodine! And for all axolotls, who are surely better off, with their three chances, than sharks, which cannot easily stop and would sink if they did, and those species which have to get their vitamin C from outside sources. The self-protective axolotl (the name means "water sport" or "servant of water") does not go in search of what makes him develop until he's developed, which only iodine, or shocks ecological or transportational, can bring about. Small wonder that axolotls in aquaria spend most of their time on the bottom of the tank (cause or effect?) and when they muster enough energy to squabble can regenerate bitten-off gills, feet, and chunks of tail. Somebody up there has a soft spot for these stay-at-home amphibians *manqués,* and so too have the residents of Mexico City, who catch them to roast. What you yourself would do if you had one and he turned into a salamander because of a bump you'd given him (a highly probable occurrence), I can only half imagine; but he would almost certainly have to go, for axolotls keep easily while salamanders do not (and that is to ignore altogether their supposed passion for inhabiting fire).

Trying again, I come up with even more specialized flaws. The barracudina, for example, unlike most deep-sea fishes, has no light-emitting organs (most species of barracudina anyway) and so is in some difficulty swimming as fast as it does at depths of down to two miles. Its embarrassment, in the impersonally functional sense of being incommoded and handicapped, is surely worse than that of all hummels, those inexplicably hornless cattle and stags who nonetheless give a good account of themselves when competing with the horned; or of those species of army ants which, being averse to light, have to bore tunnels parallel to the march of the main body; or of those brown-lipped snails whose rim lips are white and those white-lipped snails whose rim lips are brown; or of hens that grow wattles, begin to crow, yet still lay an occasional egg; or of so-called "waltzing" mice, which have an abnormality of that part of the inner ear concerned with balance. Or consider such other samples as these of a partly mismanaged universe: the hereditary deafness found in white dogs like Dalmatians and bull terriers; *Gentiana acaulis,* which for reasons unknown refuses to flower in good soil but does well where the acid and lime counts are high; holly, whose greenish flowers are sometimes bisexual, although sometimes male and female flowers exist on *separate* plants (which is why they tell people to plant hollies in groups); uranium 235, old faithful of an unstable and vulnerable isotope which is as it is because it isn't otherwise ("We're here because we're here," they used to sing in World War One, rejoicing at minds gone blank); the particle for which, it seems, there is no anti-particle; flawed crystals in which one atom is where another should be or where no atom ought to be at all; the so-called incoherence of natural light, traveling as it does in brief packets of energy in random directions at uncorrelated times, compared with the light from an optical maser; acridines, believed to produce mutations which consist in the deletion or addition of a base or bases from the DNA chain. Such is the beginning of my list, over your head and before your time but nonetheless your alibi—not so much an excuse (the popular sense) as your being genuinely elsewhere while the universe put a foot wrong with that mouse or this crystal, but suffering a similar misadministration that relates you more closely than most people to Nature; a Nature I never really noticed until it bungled.

As a factory, Nature—the more familiar end of the universe—is more reliable than the best baseball pitcher ever, but less reliable than the London Underground. To be sure, where it falters it sometimes lowers its guard usefully: U-235 gives us the chain reaction, or at least the possibility of it; the misbehaving particle may teach us something about the "elementariness" of particles (e.g., are two different particles equally fundamental or is one merely an "excited" state of the other?). The imperfect crystal tells physicists a great deal about the mechanical properties of solids. And the deaf, or deaf because brain-damaged, child, from whom

I wander only to hunt out some peers and analogues, is equally instructive. I mean, someone such as you would prepare anyone for the next phase, in which we find what I will call the superior intricacy of one deaf-blind child I know of: a child born without eyes or ears and with all internal organs so garbled that sex cannot be determined. Yet he/she knows how to get angry (why not?), is eager to sniff at things and people alike. Something on the lines of "Age 6—80 decibel hearing loss—IQ 75 on the Leiter International Performance Scale" says nothing much if you are willing to learn something more; neither does "Age 7— hearing nil—sight nil—sex?—IQ minimal" if you, and I mean other people as well as you, have a passion to learn (and that ambiguity I intend). How a parent himself proceeds from the statistics depends on who and what he is, how much of Nature he is willing to look at; but, pretty certainly, there will be some desperation in his proceeding. Which, given such standard desirables as warmth, light, and some health, may not be a bad thing. It's a bit like writing the prospective novel—being a prospector for fiction in uncharted areas—inasmuch as the parent doesn't know where he will end up or how.

To put it topically, locally: the parents run the home around the child; we around you. We learn your ignorances until they are ours. We steal your condition (steal *into* it) by means of risky analogies, like the mystic borrowing the lover's terms, the lover borrowing the mystic's. We glut you with smellables, tangibles, edibles, and visibles: all the perfumes of Arabia; all the grades of sandpaper, leading up to a feel at an elephant; all the fluents from goat's milk to mercury; all the spices from cinnamon to chili; all the zoos, parades, Dufys, flags, unwanted *National Geographics,* French colonial stamps, travel posters, and rainbows we can muster. Always a color camera, preferably Polaroid, because you don't like to wait.

Against all this—your stark handicap and any voluptuously zany sharing in it—set a thought, neither apocalyptic nor original. Ten years after the atomic explosion on Bikini atoll, fishes were living in the trees and birds were sitting on sterile eggs; turtles, instead of going back to the sea after laying their own eggs, pressed on to the island's interior, where they died of thirst. Their skeletons remain, thousands of them, evidence of a gratuitous handicap we might have had the brains to do without. Speaking of brains, each brain having ten trillion cells of which most people bring only a fifth into play, I wonder how and when we shall be able to shift into dialogue and I can really (if you'll pardon the metaphor) bend your ear and no longer one-sidedly sound off into an interim that might last forever or, if it ends, end just short of enabling you to read these words. Even a serious brain injury can't kill off all ten trillion cells and an indefatigable effort can bring into action millions of cells that otherwise might never have been used at all. If the main highway is blocked off, we can try going through the side roads; which, surely, is why they were provided in the first place. (Or do they merely represent an inscrutable, pleonastic, French *ne?* I hope not.)

I find, anyway, an analogy which, although too picturesque to be medically proper, might appeal to you: water, so much a comfort to you that I sometimes think *you* amphibian, begins by following the original slopes and inequalities of whatever surface has newly formed or been upraised from the sea floor, but soon divides up into river systems, each river deepening and widening its valley as best it can—soft rock here, hard rock there; here a steep slope, there a shallow one; one river enlarging its drainage area

33

at the expense of another in that slow but exciting-sounding maneuver called river capture. The rivers look after their own interests, and good for the rivers! At the end of the Ice Age, for example, when owing to the melting of ice from the St. Lawrence Valley the waters from the lakes flowed northeast again, the stream from Lake Erie plunged over the edge of a steep limestone escarpment, and, ever since, because of erosion, as a waterfall has cut its way further and further upstream. After the ice left the Baltic (we're traveling again), the Vistula and Oder rivers had a northward outlet and, in fact, broke through the line of the Baltic Heights. In Australia the waters of the Darling-Murray river system, slowing up as they reach the plains, deposit rock waste they no longer have the speed to carry; the beds and banks get higher and higher, and, in fact, in some places the rivers flow several feet above the level of the surrounding land. But flow they do, whereas the plateau of Mexico, from parts of which there is no outlet, abounds in saline depressions and great accumulations of debris.

There isn't *always* a way through; but, looking as I now am at two diagrams of drainage areas (before and after a shift of the Divide) which in a rudimentary way resemble drawings of the brain, I'll trust in Nature's capacity to change, in man's willingness to give Nature a helping hand. One river in Brazil has been made to flow upward; the Institute for the Achievement of Human Potential in Philadelphia floods brain-damaged children's senses with impressions, prescribes crawling in slatted boxes, eye exercises done with a flashlight, breathing masks to increase carbon-dioxide intake, minimum intake of liquids, and no music (for music stimulates the subdominant hemisphere of the brain). You yourself, like so many brain-damaged children (you may or may not be among these), were for years neither right- nor left-handed, a condition the Philadelphia patterning is meant to rectify—jogging Nature into going one way or the other (as it did when you began to use your left hand increasingly). This is to make Nature do what is within Nature's compass, whereas we can't, as far as I know, engineer the river of the mind uphill; the child who is psychotic or whose brain is defective—sickness or incompleteness—isn't handicapped but utterly disqualified.

You see, I'm getting classroomishly serious, not laughing as often as you, in your ebulliently hectic way, would like—how abandoned you are when there is loud laughter you can hear and which you can join in. Behind those increasingly frequent neat and tender smiles of yours, you stockpile guffaws of an exquisite timbre that topple and mount at speed over a whole octave. You have taught us the virtue in play for play's sake and, as it were, have commandeered our senses, so that we hoard impressions and bits of offbeat information on your behalf, longing to tell you and hoping that, one day, we will.

Just because these things are so, and not otherwise, like U-235, we memorize the brown bear of the Arctic who eats female salmon only (for the succulent roe), the guillemot who on a narrow cliff ledge arranges its one egg heavy end inward; the bone needle, the size of a paper clip, and thirteen thousand years old, found twenty feet from where the Marmes Man's remains were uncovered in Washington State; the romantic-looking balconies which, jutting out over the canal from the weathered stone of the house walls in Guanajuato, Mexico, are really toilets built over an open sewer; triclad worms which live in the underparts of horseshoe crabs; sea pansies and sea wasps; the DNA of a pigmy virus created from inert chemicals; or, nearer your own stomping grounds, the published finding that autistic children are the only children who don't like school holidays (any more than you do, who always plead for "kool")—I

35

know of one Oxford don's child who insists on crossing the Bodleian quadrangle in the same way time after time, into and out of the same two entrances. We're also saving for you the new center, in Pamplona of the bulls, for brain-damaged children; the deaf actors from Gallaudet College, Washington, D.C., performing Euripides' *Iphigenia in Aulis* with an eloquent wealth of hand movements which, one critic said, "seemed to chisel emotions out of the air"; a party of twelve deaf children who, traveling from Derby in England to Dortmund in Germany, were *en route* for almost twenty-four hours and, thanks to British Railways (who set up the itinerary), had to change trains five times; or, some-thing in your future—although not for the born deaf, so I might rescript it—Exercise 35 in the Compound Consonant *dr* in a lip-reading primer: a surrealistic, sinister-bland non-conversation in which suburban propriety suffuses a Geor-gian hangover, with the only thing missing being a postilion struck dead, dumb, or deaf, by lightning. How's this?

> Do you prefer *dr*ama or farce?
> *Dr*aw on your private bank account for the amount.
> He *dr*ew out his savings and spent them.
> Old Tom was a *dr*over in the early days.
> What a *dr*eary prospect!
> The roll of a *dr*um is stirring.
> I think he's had a *dr*op too much.
> We *dr*ank to their health and happiness.
> Do we *dr*ess for dinner?
> *Dr*ink to me only with thine eyes.
> Is this a *dr*y area?
> The *dr*ains need attention.
> Some people *dr*own their sorrows in *dr*ink.

Drrrrr! It has, I think, to be deciphered like Linear B; but, clearly, if there is a hidden story, somebody blew his total pelf to sit in the first row at a happening in which an old shepherd called Drake (an ex-drummer) got so pixillated he fell in his best tuxedo down an open manhole and broke his neck on the encrusted geranium-tinted brick, there being no water to cushion his fall.

What I was getting ready to say, before I went off into a verbal equivalent of one of the sudden romps with which we rupture the days' even processes, was this: not only do you transform those close to you into Autolycuses, snappers-up of unconsidered trifles; you acquaint us, as much through what you miss as through what you discover, with the pageantry of life's incidentals: the texture of matters of fact, of the matter-of-fact. *Must tell Manda that,* we murmur but mostly we can't, unless there's a nonverbal way, lurid, preferably, and strong-smelling, with a surface rich in corrugations like the halved cabbages and an assertive taste. The sea, writes Rupert Brooke in one of his letters, "was 〰〰," which corrugation might not signify choppy (or whatever it did mean) to you, but resembles the mid-air scribble you do while asking for *kool* and, could you but transpose it from sea-green blackboard to wine-dark sea, would surely match how the British Channel felt to you the day you crossed by Condor Hydrofoil at about thirty-five knots from Jersey in the Channel Islands to Saint-Malo in France, your vulnerably white hands clamped on a rail and your face the color of porridge. And without being sick, on either the outward or the return trip, but gamely—with that stiff-lipped aghastness you reserve for the most trying trials in your trial-haunted childhood—tagging on while the cheap liquor that honor demands one buy was bought. *La belle France* was where you couldn't even muster the heart to sneer at an omelet.

But the bottle—ah, the bottle! GUARANTEED SAME QUALITY THROUGHOUT THE WORLD, it says just under the prancing boots of that jolly Regency buck (or whatever he is) in

37

the red coat and the white drainpipes, himself sort-of-hydrofoiling a tenth of an inch above the blacklettered strip of Kilmarnock self-congratulation. I would guarantee *you* in the same terms, THROUGHOUT THE WORLD, not merely because one of your nicknames happens to be Proof, but because gold labels become you, as you have so often proved by affixing them to your forehead and arms with status-giving spit. And if, like this Scotch, you had been honored in Sydney in 1880, only a century after Captain Cook sailed along the green eastern coast of Australia, or in Paris in 1885 (4 triumphal arches to shelter under, one Eiffel Tower 985 feet high to gape at, millions of big umbrellas to sit and sip under), or in Jamaica in 1891 (from where I still remember the sordor and stench of French Town in Kingston, big landslides of molten chocolate in the crammed rain forests, Rastafarians with golliwog hair working in slow motion on the narrow hill roads, banked flowers on the university campus like a hundred gaudy burial mounds, drums at night out of the far trees while I bit on overcooked British mutton, hummingbirds frozen in midair)—if you had been there, if you had just *been,* you would surely have been By Appointment to Whatever Majesty it was that ruled the time: court jester extraordinary, mistress of the royal sausage rolls, keeper-finder-polisher-tester of all Majestical ear trumpets. Or, given chance, you would have been Ludwig van Beethoven's bedmaker (he being the one who, in his Heiligenstadt Testament, furiously confessed, "I must live like an exile," though I reckon what he called his "fiery, impulsive temperament, sensible, even, to the distractions of social life" had nothing on yours; after six years of deafness, both you and he, you at six and he at twenty-eight, are level. "Compelled early in my life," he cries, "to isolate myself, to spend my life in solitude. . . . Already

38

in my 28th year I have been compelled to become a philosopher; this is no easy matter").

Already, he says. As you already know, and as I myself realize from those bleak, expressionless faces you sometimes wear—confronting yourself with something you don't know as a hurt or a riddle but which doesn't feel right—there's an answer we cannot find to a question you can't formulate: *Must it be?* The whys and wherefores belong to a Sphinx whom we, reversing the Greek myth, would strangle for riddling with us in the first place. Clever Oedipus, recognizing man as the being which, "having only one voice, has sometimes two feet, sometimes three, and sometimes four and is weakest when it has most," clever Oedipus got the Sphinx to throw herself to death; but, confronted with a being which, having only one voice, has sometimes two ears, sometimes four, and is weakest when it is spoken to, might never have won the prize of the Theban throne. Answering right, he earned the right to stick Jocasta's pin into his eyes; answering wrong, he would have been strangled by the Sphinx on her rock. Either way, a setup: no quarter given, none asked; no buddy spared even a dime, none panhandled for. If there is a quick way to Colonus, where Oedipus spent his last hours under the favorable auspices of the Eumenides, we never hear of it. Art, for the Victorians, was the quickest way out of Manchester; but there is no quick way with the riddle of your handicap. I see you in a portable ghetto you carry round with you, the only inhabitant, and sometimes—when busyness and distractions and horseplay fail and you submit to the pure silence of your birthright—you are as forlorn as Beethoven pleading, one month before his death, for "old, white Rhine or Moselle wine." His bottles, Rüdesheimer Berg, 1806, arrived two days before his death. As the Abbé Stadler said when blessing him the year before, *"Hilft's nix, schadt's nix"* (Does no good, does no harm)—so let's talk our way back to our own bottles. Complaining might do harm; does no good.

The last of the "Highest Awards" the Scotch won—or so it seems from the gold label—was Brisbane in 1897. Nothing in our own century? *Nothing?* Skip it, here's the Wolfschmidt vodka (70 Proof in Britain, 80 in the States) which came in a tiny *sabot* from a creaky dark wineshop in St. Helier, an unfancy bottle but having a label resplendent with tiny gold medallions (thirty-four overlapping like grape bunches), two coats of arms with, beneath one, in minuscules, MOSCOW plus indecipherable date, and, beneath the other, NOVGOROD (I think) plus an equally indecipherable date. It also says "Original Genuine Vodka since 1847." Before Scotch, that is, which has congeners in it, whereas vodka hasn't. Packed into the small rear label in the tiny print you're always supposed to read in contracts and insurance policies, there's a roll call of cities (or towns) where Wolfschmidt has won *diplômes d'honneur* and medals that are bronze, silver, or gold (a bibulous Olympics): just imagine, all this ritual delectable bibbing wove its way in between the wars and the earthquakes and the plagues, all the way from the year in which Grant became President (1869) while they were disestablishing the Irish Church and opening formally the Suez Canal, to the year (Berne, 1954) when, at Bikini atoll, the first American hydrogen bomb went off, messing up the animal and bird life there (as we've said), and food rationing ended in Britain and I, back from Columbia University, began my military service in a coarse blue battledress (gear for peace) that chafed the inside of my thighs. Good old Wolfschmidt, whose honor roll of places-won-at would have delighted Marlowe's Tamburlaine himself and twice, anyway, won appointment to the Imperial House of Romanoff. *Romanoff?* Off—

40

Off we go, here we go, round and into and through the year, no years, YEAR-Z, 1869–70, ST. PETERSBURG! the Russian one, where Peter the Great issued a ukase ordering his entire court to learn to dance and where Nijinsky, in 1900, was chosen for the Imperial School because he had extraordinary thighs. St. Petersburg, *Peters——burg!*

Bur, you say, evoking the female hop catkin, some person who can't be shaken off, *burr,* a winter shiver, *brrr.* Let's try the next vodka victory, nearer your mouth. The clearing house of the world, London. *Lon——don.*

Lon, you whisper. I'll add Chaney, both of whose parents were deaf, which is how he learned to mime.

Now Riga, ice-blocked in winter (isn't it?): *Ree. Ga.*

Ree! Drrr, *drrr,* you made a thin, cold sound, like an icicle going up a silver-tongued mockingbird's nostril!

Vienna, a big wheel, round and round, roundabout.

You say it without hesitating. *Rounabou. Roun.*

Vienna, I tell you. *Vee. Enn.*

Ben, percussively. *Ben, ben.*

Benissimo. Try Jelgava, on the river Aa—you pick up the last word and give it full voice, your own special sound for histrionic pity when one or the other of us nicks his finger or you've rammed the umbrella spike into our tender zones and the urgent, pretend cables go out to—oh, where? —Karachi, Tokyo, Timbuctoo: WOUNDED IN FRONT AGAIN, which is where James Boswell said one *should* have been wounded to be a man at all. What? Oh, nothing. Try Paris. PAR——EE.

And, of course, effortlessly as this making you a present of my own mentality, you come out with *EE,* meaning "Please forgive me that hostile act, we are friends and playmates and henchmen again, aren't we, you *will* be around for me to do it to again?" *EE?* My girl, there's no right speech out of Paris town, which Frankie Villon, a pop singer from way back, said against the chill wind of his luck: arguing his case for staying there, see, in spite of burglaries and thefts and jail and two near hangings until it took a whole Parliament to banish him, the rascal with snow on the brain. Whereas Moscow, where, wouldn't you know it? they serve iced drinks and ivory ice cream in the railway station on the most freezing nights and nothing else; Moscow's an immovable feast, and I don't here give a damn about the mute *e* so long as we don't get a mute you. *Moss——Go.*

And you say Mo, as in Moses.

Try Bordeaux, on all those bottles of mine you like to paw.

Beau, you seem to say, uttering good and valid and pertinent French which is utterly beautiful except you mean "escalator." So let's go on to Naples, where Lady Hamilton, espying Nelson come all the way from Alexandria in the shattered *Vanguard,* yelled, "O God! Is it possible!" and fell into his arms in a faint. NAY——PL.

You agree with me and say your *Nay.*

Amsterdam! Where, for breakfast, they eat strawberry sandwiches! OM-STER-DOM. Said with a king-sized strawberry in the mouth. OM-STER-DOMM.

Om, you say, half of Omsk, which is not on the list of vodka triumphs.

Grazie, try Nice, amber and ultramarine and bony, sunny white, klaxons and Caravelles and whipping rainbow pennants. Dufy. NEECE. And, lo and untold, you have it perfectly, needling the vowel and surreptitiously tapping your tongue against the sibilant. *Neece, th.* And so, regarding ANTWERP LIVERPOOL EDINBURGH BRUSSELS TIFLIS CHICAGO, all those illustr—

oops, *gung,* your plastic Hong Kong hammer in my eye, gosh—*illustrious.* I said it. *Cities.* I got it out. Half the cone-

42

tents—ha, leave it, I like the idea of *cone*tents however accidentally come by—of this house come from Hong Kong, where typhoons almost but not quite float out to sea those thousands of sweat-laboring human snails who assemble all that gaudy, therapeutic, polythene trash in overgrown kennels flung and stuck on the sides of the hills many social niches below, but uphill-toiling niches above, Kai Man Book Store and Wah Kiu STUDIO, classy ports of call for you know who—

You know Hoo?

Hoo who?

Hoo Flung.

Hoo Flung What? That celluloid mallet into my eye, all that already caking plaster of Paris against the outside of the kitchen window; maybe some Optine will help both. Let's have a song, girl; a song, girl, while we wait for normal vision to resume:

> You've two big teeth,
> You've two big teeth
> Right up there in the front,
> And spanking chopping new,
> But no teeth at the side.

Don't ever, please, wrench off bottle caps with those. *Eeeee.*

And so—no, that's too conciliatory a transition. Better to say: Now, about the oval-framed blue-tinted passport picture of Marie Brizard on the Cherry Brandy from Bordeaux (*Marie Brizard et Roger,* it says actually, but Roger is not, as they say, in evidence). Two clumps of cherries on the label seem to be held in space by a complex of goldwire curlicues resembling treble clefs on their sides, like inebriated signatures. 24° it says to their left, 70 cl. to their right. *Maison fondée en 1755,* before vodka, before Scotch, *hein?* and, on the aluminum cap, DEVISSEZ three times, which is roughly what *you* mean when you say "wind" when applied to clocks, or, by extension, to peeling the black masking paper off a Polaroid photograph. So: you wind—unwind— the top, snapping these seven threads of frail metal but only, if we believe the arrows, counter-clockwise. If you go with the clock, you screw home the cap for all eternity and the only way in is to smash the bottle with your favorite length of iron piping. You love, I know, the raised lettering in the bottle's glass, running your fingers over it like Braille, and with the same humming hoot that gives you away when, after maximum logistical stealth, you have filched and opened a flip-top can of beer and are pouring onto the ice cubes in your tumbler a cold, golden, quick one such as you always take in the kitchen, your own version of a *distingué.* One cube in your mouth cools the froth as it lingers after the beer has gone, and the can ring goes on your finger, the wedge-shaped metal flap being the precious stone. Or semi-precious talisman.

Your actual birthstone, my *Executive's Data Book* tells me, happens to be opal or tourmaline, from Latin *opalus* from Sanskrit *upala,* which is for "gem," and from Singhalese *toramalli* (what next?). One is "hydrous silica" with sometimes changing colors: milk-white or bluish with greens, yellows, reds, while the other is a mineral of various colors, comes out of granite, and has "electric properties." I sometimes think that if you asked all the questions I imagine you might if things were otherwise we'd go into the dictionary and never come out: live in there, I mean, hitching our way from word to word as if words were inns and explaining ourselves with *Oh, we're fun-ologists* (like Marilyn Monroe saying, *I'm a chant-ooze*), and all the time hunting derivations down through cognate forms and guessing Scotch–Vodka–Marie Brizard guesses when it said [?] or "etym. dub." Why, we'd even find out why Sanskrit's called San-

44

skrit and Singhalese Singhalese; and, who knows, Etym. Dub. would keep us fairly constant company like a worldly wise, cautious great white hunter until he went off with [?] or was supplanted by Erron. Flynn or Sl. (Slim the Trim Gun) or Unexpl. (which is a word with a *pl* in it, which is plane to you, which proves you can harbor a Boeing or a VC-10 in a very small, unnoticed, suffix of a hangar indeed). *Pl!* you call, as if to friends, as they bluster over in their tunnel-throated landing approaches, wheels down and all lights winking in the daylight. And then you go on with your household chores at the sink or on the grass: either washing the alarm clocks in a deep detergent foam with a stiff brush, stacking plates with maenad abandon (tossing each one from you at least two feet with nerve-testing crashes you don't hear), and shampooing the fire irons, poker, tongs, hearth brush and all; or brushing the grass, weeding the garden by uprooting all the genuine flowers, and jumping up and down in the garbage cans to pack things tight.

To please you (because we draw with our fiber or felt pens on the same rough surface), I'm writing this on the insides of the larger envelopes that arrive in the mail, containing catalogues from Blackwell's and the college departments of eager publishing houses: one long slit, then a short, and we have an approximately quarto sheet on which to draw slides, baths, planes, and even such bizarre things as words and, always, unless we are playing truant by tinkering with Japanese, spelling in the Initial Teaching Alphabet. *Wauk, doent run.* Or, maybe, instead of either, *Fly!* I see you've already helped yourself to the picture, in yesterday's newspaper, of E. S. Kraus's 250-seat airbus whose fuselage is shaped like a trout and the Hindenburg and R 100 airships (rather than the cylindrical Zeppelins of World War One). It reminds me of Crescent II, the little glider I designed when I was fourteen and submitted, as plans, to the

Aeromodeller: my first publication, bringing my first check. "This glider," the Unabashed Young Designer noted in the bottom corner of the gratuitously intricate drawing, "is for free soaring flight only and flies fast—will hold thermals. Performance: 1st, 24 secs, 2nd, 31 secs, 3rd, 32.5," and up and up until sublime anoxia cancels all. It was wartime, so for certain parts (except the trim tab) I specified copper instead of aluminum, this being unobtainable because, as Spitfires, it was demolishing the Nazi formations over our heads, or, as Lancasters, plastering German cities with ten-ton bombs that converted them into something less than the ash on a Churchill cigar. In the sky the aluminum saucepans of yesterday found a lasting incarnation. Or in wreckage in dank fields and through the roofs of cowsheds and among the small shops of cities, subjected to a final scorch beyond all heat of cooking, and with men in them.

A good saucepan outlives any of us, doesn't it? Whereas even a good plane doesn't, and, nowadays, is obsolescent after five years, finished after ten. The longest lasters, I suppose, have been the Avro Ansons (in some of which I toured around above the British Isles, once dramatically identifying Cambridge as North London) and the DC3's: thirty years apiece, which sounds impossibly dogged in times when the Navy, in the TV guides, proclaims "Our New Navy's All Muscle And It Needs Men! Missiles That Punch Aircraft Out Of The Sky . . . Cut The Coupon. You Can Join At Fifteen." In return you get a fifty-two-page booklet that woos even further all young Nelsons and John Paul Joneses whose chins are pimply. In these days the gun barrel goes up with the projectile, the horn accompanies its own seed. . . . Sorry, this is out of your ken so far, although I know the boys at school ascend the lavatory partitions to watch you girls. Let's just agree that we don't want *any* aircraft punched out of the sky, and risk the death-delivering ones. Death? Oh, I'll save a postscript for it; a blank thing, it blanks us out, and there are some things which, along with William Ralph Inge, "the gloomy Dean," I "could not bring myself to say in English . . . about our little girl" (instead, on the loss of his daughter, he wrote verses in Latin). Or, for that matter, bring myself to say *to* you who have, even if you don't know it, known one death in the family.

Strange, though: out of some preternatural tact, you do not grieve over absences; you accept. You have no metaphysics, no cosmic worries, but just an assumption of your own shrill perpetuality, a busy insouciance that's near-Olympian. When a leper's thumb fell into his bowl, the Buddha ate it—and that's your sort of conduct too; you retrieve and immediately munch all of your food that falls and all—carpet whiskers, fluff, dirt, cigarette ash—that comes with it. Except (there are so many yous) you'll never touch cheese, chocolate, or fish (saving only the humble brisling in tomato sauce and the smallest shrimps).

Where, I keep saying, where were we? Having already communicated our personalities to each other (a loving tug-of-peace both raucous and casual), we fumble when in words. Too much to tell you all at once and I can't say it all out in one word, much as I would like to. Silence may be golden and older, closer to Eden, than speech; but *our* near-silence lasts too long. I'm all for an age of silver in which, wearing the vowels down, we open our bird's-eyes, view the last third of this century, and then happily slither over the edge into yapping decadence: all wings clipped from young chickens since modern breeds of poultry never fly and they're easier to pack that way; all sculpture done in plastic tubing; all music tape-recorded in aviaries; all painting done in mine-dark rooms; all writing done by verbal roulette; all talk by reading thoughts; all procreation by registered test tube; all leisure psychedelic and not feet-up lazy; all human odor vanquished by on-squirted processed musk of animals; all tobacco mentholated; all rivers stale with inspissated industrial filth; all sunlight held off by the atmosphere; all buffalo, otter, and bald eagles extinct; all roads jammed with stationary, unmovable, and rusting cars; all coffee and wheat burned to raise the price, and all hogs buried; all food in cans stacked under dead fields in colossal silos; all disease and dying done away with and the healthy crammed fifty to a room while the fallout flakes endlessly down; all breath taking suspended until the success of the project to abolish saliva. . . . Apropos of nothing—almost but not quite—did you know that Robinson Crusoe's real name was Kreutznaer? He tells us in his second sentence.

But enough of him; I am told how a few days ago you set the school on its ear by mounting your A1 De Luxe Pullman Top Person Jetstream squeal in the playground. A button was missing from your new nylon blouse and you sustained the siren of your SOS until the matron found a replacement and sewed it in place. At once you fell quiet, beamed, and they all—matron, your teacher, and her assistant—felt they had been released from some monstrous visitation which nonetheless carried within it the germ of an amnesty. Could such an awful keening have been emitted by this same genial, poised, smiling face? Only that morning, your teacher and the other children in your class had been admiring your new blue-and-white outfit; pretty, they said, *pre'ee,* so the loss of a button hit you doubly hard.

You surprise only those people for whom your bravura neatness (in some things) isn't an accepted part of day-to-day living. Your socks must be, literally, up tight, with no disfiguring wrinkles or twists, and the tops must be folded down exactly the right amount. Two hair clips on one side of your head must have counterparts in identical position on the other side, holding your hair in the same degree of tension. The same goes for hair ribbons, which must bind punitively, and for the rubber bands under them, which must never snap; for you know the difference at once, no matter how tight the ribbon stays over the break. Curtains open or closed must match. When one of us lifts a cup or takes off a shoe or a slipper, so do you. When one of us crosses legs, so do you, and with the same leg uppermost (you watch only one at a time, otherwise your legs would be like windmills while you tried to fit all positions into one ensemble). When we eat, it is perilous to set down all the tools at once: you abominate unclean platters, tools not in action, and, given a chance, remove them to the kitchen forthwith, heedless of pauses for breath or rest. Given your own way, you would clear the table before the meal began; one brief glimpse of a hissing steak, one sniff of steaming vegetables, and you would clear the decks. Sometimes, even, when you are especially enraged or merely want to be extra-emphatic, you remove plate and uneaten portion in one fluent dispatch to the garbage can outside. At all costs be tidy (Kreutznaer-Crusoe was, too): except that you yourself dawdle over most of your meals and, in the evenings especially, lie flat on the carpet or pedal your legs in the air while your slippers dangle by their heels from your toes. Something Roman wins out in you eventually, so that you trough in indolent disregard of whatever clothes you have on: marinara sauce is the insignia most usually to be found on your blouses; butter in your hair, oil along your arms, bits of ham in your shoes, and, as often as not, your plate and the knife you use as a spoon (if you aren't eating with your hands) are marooned in a pool of milk.

Gobbling or nibbling, you preposterously feed both of the girls within you: the precisionist and the hooligan, the one creating exquisite designs for the other to wreck, the

49

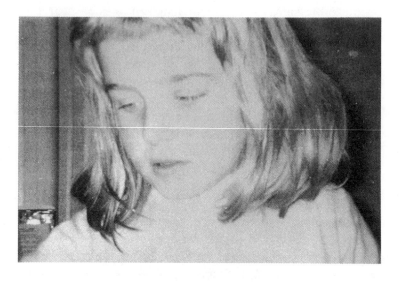

"both of the girls within you . . ."

other manufacturing a chaos which the precisionist is tempted to remedy until the very last moment, when she chickens out. Only special untidinesses bother you; all others you ignore. I sometimes think you would happily live in ankle-deep mud so long as your stocking tops showed straight above the surface and your hair was lashed tight, with nothing straying.

So, we tell your teacher, if certain treasures break, repair at once with anything at hand: Scotch tape, chewing gum, stamp edging. Or be prepared to have both eardrums bombarded into singing numbness by the most belligerent plea in the world: *Oi-ya!* For that is the kind of girl you are. A banshee-mandrake lurks behind your substantial, protein-glowing beauty, ever ready to coerce the world into righting tiny errors in arrangement, even when, say, you are in a mood of gracious repose with your legs spread wide before a winter fire to warm your vitals. *Cuishing,* the Manx call it, having a *cuish;* and that's part of your birthright too. Your blood runs faster with the heat from the fire and fuels your vocal organs until, I think, you could rival the howl of a gale off that Irish sea in a bad March. But summer heat knocks you out, driving you to quite voluntary siestas on your bed or, on torrid days, into moments of amok brandishing of sharp things followed by an almost catatonic hour or two, during which the heat seems to possess and annul you as no freeze of winter can. Cold, I gather, you almost enjoy although it insults your ears and chest; heat you loathe and must be sheltered from.

But whatever the protective garb—anorak or straw hat in the Caribbean style—it has to be colorful and chic, a touch *outré* perhaps, and this is clearest when you choose in stores with that unfailing eye for the most expensive item and the newest mode. And whatever is can be made more so with badges, the lions and castle of Saint-Malo, the three-legged Manx swastika, the Penn State mountain lion, to all three of which we must be adding an Oxford ox and, those family arms you gain on your mother's side, the dove with olive branch and the comprehensive-sounding phrase, *deus et pax.* So you'll never have to have your line researched to see if you're entitled to a family crest or need to transact with that old Air Force colleague of mine who, when last heard of, was selling coats of arms to American tourists under the title of herald *poursuivant,* with letters patent as befitted him and a set of red silk doctoral robes for an honorary degree he'd somehow omitted to acquire. We sympathize, don't we? with his helpless desire for pageantry, for the gorgeous. We come into the world, *out of mother,* as a child wrote in a poem I read somewhere, *and a giant smacks us.* Who, after that, if he could remember it, wouldn't want to be a peacock in a splendid wrapper?

3. Birds

Cuffed or overreaching from some rain spout choked with leaves, mold, rust, and the caked soot of industrial fallout, one fledgling sparrow hit the concrete lightly as a balled-up Kleenex:

a weathered-looking thing, mousy and mudthumbed, pessimistic black match-head eyes saying *fnint, fnint,*

puny chirp, clover-soft claws like commas on the ends of the leatherette leg stems,

and tuft wings only.

So you took it, him, her, in and coaxed the wildness out of (let's say) him, versed him in your wordless way in plate-rim perching, on-your-shoulder standing, inside-your-blouse-hiding against the unspoiled skin which, at first, goose-pimpled at his touch. Unabashed, he reconnoitered the house, shelves and pelmets and all the undusted places, and flipped tiny pellets of meat eater's lime behind him as he went. He soon lost his cuffed-out look and delivered regular morning huzzas with a baby-avian accent. Knew where his meal ticket was, troughed on wriggling mealworms specially procured. But was not averse to minced steak, a flake of ham, a tiny strip of nerveless clipped-off cuticle, or —as I discover from his kind in general as they infest the lawn day after day—the carcass of a roasted chicken with parsley-sage stuffing smudged against the transparent bones of what's left. Go he had to, rejoining his squadron through an upper downstairs window, Goliath-strong, Alice-innocent, Thumbelina-unreal. And never came back or tried to, thus leaving a gap behind him for the bird in your life, a gap we have filled so far with two successive specimens of *Melopsittacus undulatus,* these being budgerigars first-named Orry I and II after a mythical Gaelic king, but whom you dub *boid* and who thus has become *Boyd,* a real name to drop in company. Boyd I survived a week only; the vet yanked his neck hard and blood spilled, then seeped, from the beak. Boyd II you knew wasn't Boyd I, and you stared at him with all the squinting gravity of a tourist being conned in a bazaar but not really knowing how to counter. You saw the same iridescent green, yes; the same flimsy egg-shaped trunk, the same parsonically clownish face, the same cage. But you held back, no doubt in the belief that he who marks time knows it the second time round: no plucking at the Chagall-blue tail feathers, no cupped hand around the plump nothing of his belly with your elbow resting on the wire drawbridge of the cage door; no flicks at the dowel and wire swing suspended from the inside of the top of the cage. And, for a time, you didn't even offer to clean out the tray in the bottom.

Need finally ousted memory as it usually does if we talk to you with exaggerated hand gestures and the Three Stooges faces that are standard in this house—all for the purpose of distracting you until you concentrate on what you actually need and not on what you used to have. They say Nijinsky

53

was built like a bird and had webbed feet, which is why he could jump so high, stay up there as long as it takes to blow a nose. *Tell you anything so long as you know you are being talked to.* And so, with Boyd II in mind, we go, go, go: *TELL ME TELL ME TELL ME! OI-YA! O-O-I-I—YA! TELLTELLTELL!*

This is a four-guinea orange slubbed Cecil Gee roll-neck shirt which I'm wearing, an export special. STOP-STOP? HOW *can* I STOP?

An old Good-King-Wenceslas, King-Lear-Canute-type statue has been removed from the Palace of Westminster and is for sale along with his neighbors the gryphons and unicorns and a queen fidgeting with the Anston stone braid of her robe and a praying other king (Edward the Confessor?) whose hands are drooping low. Want a statue for the garden, a soap box for bird orators, an outsize peg to hang a balloon on? STOP

What if Nosferatu met Robinson Crusoe-Kreutznaer? Alone, the pair of them, on an island, hungry and mighty irritable? STOP   OI-YA OI-YA STOP

They've just dynamited the Most Beautiful Hotel In The World, the Royal Picardy at Le Touquet, the hotel with the aerated water in its pool and having its own airport STOP OI-YA

Palomar astronomers are studying a radio source called 3C9 receding at four-fifths the speed of light and already nine billion light years away: almost a light year for each cell, used or unused, in your brain STOP

In Micronesia, as soon as a boy child is born, they plant coconut trees for him; and boy and trees grow up together, and they keep him in food and drink, liquor and skin lotion, buttons, butter, slippers, soap, rope and rugs, plastic and pickles, thread and timber. He drinks the sun and inhales the moon and does not know he lives on an island perched on the summit of a submerged mountain as high as Everest, an island propped up into the air by the accumulated skeletons of tiny sea creatures STOP OI—STOP

There is, going into the Congo, soap collected by Quakers from Philadelphia hotels STOP   OI-YA YA YA YA YA YA!

The Viet Cong give reporters souvenirs in the form of aluminum combs made from shot-down American planes STOP   OOOOOIIIII-YAH!

In Florida, Greek sponge divers who get the bends are packed in ice STOP

Someone claims to have seen Don Quixote on Wall Street STOP

Blind, Frederick Delius was carried in his chair to the top of a hill so he could feel the dawn STOP

Someone says a white polar bear once quoted Virgil STOP

Al-Siyuti, never mind who, tells how Zubaydah, alias Creamkin, once crammed a poet's mouth with jewels which he sold for twenty thousand dinars STOP

One apprentice bull fighter, a *novillero,* keeps a whole ham hanging in his Mercedes and in his private plane to remind him of his early poverty STOP

In A.D. 700, passengers sailing to Byzantium were forbidden to fry fish STOP

Sigurd the Volsung scalded his fingers with boiling blood and thrust them into his mouth to cool; as soon as the blood touched his tongue he understood the language of birds STOP

Boa constrictor is tough eating, grain-fed rats are tasty, iguanas suit those whose stomachs "soar above all prejudices" (Charles Darwin said it), giant tortoises STOP STOP

You are beginning to scream *Eeeeeeeeeeeeeeee,* it is still the wrong bird, not the wrong topic or set of gestures, not the weather or your stomach or even the ragged trim of your socks or the bent Space Patrol sugar cigarette stranded

55

between the fingers of your left hand, *oi-ya, eeeeeeeee,* it is just the wrong one out of all the grass parakeets in the world. Call them what we will—Australian lovebirds or *melo*-etcetera—this is the one one you don't want. Something-instead-of-a-sparrow you took, although with your own patented sick-grinning bad grace that says how letdown and foul you'd feel even if things were suddenly to come right. But a changeling demolishes the steady frieze you count upon and maybe even implies loathsome finalities beyond, say, the last of today's ice cream, the ball-point gone dry and having to be thrown away because it isn't designed for a refill, the apple core upon which you cannot graft the crisp flesh again. Mini-ends, these, which you heed with eyes as calibrating as a gunsmith's. It would be the same if you'd had a Biscay bull or a lava lizard. You would prefer, I reckon, to lick the same popsicle day in, day out, if only one would last that long—the same steak, the same loaf, the identical gob of mustard; all your paintings on the same sheet of paper, all baths with the same cake of soap, all rest with the same sleep, all EEEEEE*eeeeee*eeeeee— eee- eee- (ee): your scream has diminished into a plaintive hoot.

Boyd irrevocably is the generic specific particular, the one word for that *boid*. I'll bite my tongue, but that won't alter the facts of succession for you, who want—oh, complicatedly perverse and sly desire—a static, monist universe in whose laundry sameness you have a perfect place provided you yourself don't change. Henry James's "special radiance of disconnection" has no appeal to you; instead, you want a special radiance of supreme forms—graffiti in the margins of Genesis which no hack with mop and pail can efface and no after-hours renegade numen modify. Your vocabulary has no plurals, so you're entitled, aren't you, to your brash, ecstatic singularity which requires all birds to be one and the same? I watch a jet through the window that curls and flexes like a worm as it moves past a flaw in the glass and then resumes its shape again, never having changed at all. I'm glad *you* didn't see it, because, of that phenomenon, there is absolutely no explaining I could offer you. Time out now, just a few minutes.

There arrived in the mail the other day a book containing studies of such children as you (you undiffidently, as usual, thought the package was for you, and in a profound sense it was). One contribution is by one of the medical men who tried to diagnose you, and he says, "After experience" (as the poet W. D. Snodgrass would put it), "preoccupation with tried and familiar things and repetition of stereotyped pieces of behaviour brings and maintains relief from anxiety at the expense of progress in learning and adaptation." *Wow,* you say, *what on earth*—but he did see how you clung to and clamored for the miniature bath. What he says bears also on this refusal of the second budgerigar and, I think, on its refined converse in your attitude to a discarded, very elegant black umbrella of your mother's which has a loose spike I have attached by means of a short, tapered inch of hexagonal pencil fitted through it. Every day you pull off the spike and bring it to me, along with the big screwdriver and the claw hammer, to have it reaffixed, thus maintaining the umbrella in a state of permanent intermittent disrepair. The only thing you can do about one bird's succeeding another is to adjust mentally, which you sometimes find as easy as opening up a pharaoh's tomb with a pin, whereas the umbrella—umbrellas being time-honored objects in your defensive anthology of the world—you can take liberties with, playing fast and loose with it against the certainty of its never becoming like Humpty Dumpty. You modify its condition only to reassert its durable identity (like a tiny Maud Bodkin with an archetypal pattern). And when, after some puzzling and some crude handiwork with a penknife, I plug the spike back on, you hold the umbrella vertical before you, shivering with an ecstasy we all might envy and chanting, with an awestruck lilt, *brella, brella, brella!* The Holy Grail, the Shield of Achilles, the brand Excalibur coming up out of the lake could give no greater joy, no more captivating a glimpse of the reticent *Logos,* than this contraption of torn waterproofed cloth and disintegrating stays. You hang it, dead center, with patient accuracy, on the crossbar of the hanger holding a suit, an offering infinitely more pleasing to me than the links of raw sausage you once habitually hung in the same spot.

You impress me, for not only do you now try to repair the umbrella yourself on this very desk I'm at, hammering and puffing and scraping with the knife and then squinting down the shaft like a billiards player with a faulty cue; you have even reconciled yourself to Boyd II who, I agree, is less tame and less intimately sociable than his predecessor. Sit on your shoulder like the sparrow and Boyd I? Not he. At most, when you rest your hand on one of the four perches flimsily installed in his cage, he'll set a claw on your knuckles, and you, you hold your breath impossibly long. Big exhalation, then, which ruffles his green fluff but not enough to make him shift his claw. He doesn't—

I'm sorry, I've forgotten what: a nicely spoken lady has just been at the door offering, as "a member of a group representing all religions" (*all?*), to discuss, of all things, religion: that which *binds,* hey? Honk, honk. Madam, if the Lulu were at home and not elsewhere pursuing her studies in ballistics, boys, and the breast stroke, I would have you in to wrestle like Job with her: best of three falls, Rabelaisian angel *versus* proselytizer; one of God's sports *versus* one of God's PR itinerants; handicap *versus* the Light of the World. There are in this lighted world so very many beautifully spoken ladies whose only handicap is an un-manured gentility gleaned from taste, good books, and a nice upbringing. Faith, they preach, some of them, and even more of them culture. Some of them, having no knowledge, counsel. Some of them, because they hate the body, become—ironic term—mistresses in girls' schools. And there are gentlemen who, lacking gentleness and gentility as well as a passable intellect, discover an outlet for their malevolence among young males. One such, at my old school, had to be sacked for breaking a meter rule across the spine of a boy prone on a table in an empty staff room. Another such, headmaster of the same school, went from my mind altogether after I left his vicinity but recrudesced, when I was twenty and entering Oxford, with a character assassination addressed to the rector of my college-to-be; who read it aloud to me, grinned, and tore it up. A doctor of divinity and therefore exceptionally equipped for dealing with rowdy teenagers in an undistinguished secondary school, he had also been severely gassed in World War One (in which my father lost his left eye and almost the right). San Quentin, we said in our callous way, would have made a better job of things; but, surviving as he did, this quasi-hieratic *Gauleiter* of Divinity in a gown that reeked of mothballs and putrescent kipper, developed remarkable expertise in what I call distributing the shit.

Still a bit of anger left, you see! How anyone can enjoy school I do not know, not when that's how they treat some of the non-handicapped in some of the places. You, I'm sure, will fare much better; it takes a lot of selfless dedication to teach in such a school as yours, where the important thing is not rigmarole and parroting and punishment, but the human potential of individual children who, some of them, may never be able to speak conventionally as long as they live. Your teachers are the sort of people who are grateful for what can be, not the sort who specialize in being petulant about what cannot.

O.K.: end of extra-curricular seminar; back to faith and culture, one excellent test of which is to help you up the stairs while cupping with one hand (so it won't fall and like soft oil paint smear stockings, shoes, rug) the Polish boiling sausage which you have involuntarily shifted into your blue school panties. Always, when you, child of Nature, squat while playing, atavistic habit has a chance of taking over. I have seen you take the delicious—because deliberate—liberty of flooding your slide from the top platform just as if you were a grizzled prospector in the Sierra Madre sluicing for gold. And then, all conscience and giggling regret, you fetch bucket and mop and swab the full length of the metal runway with hot water and a foaming cleanser, having restaked your claim with a picric libation.

But the excremental's only the beginning, isn't it? The freshman bit. Later courses in faith and culture would entail trying to explain to you why we, against whose ears you sometimes thrust your rattling alarm clocks, never wear hearing aids; where anywhere is; what money is; what a surname is for; which day is which by date; that you will grow into a woman; and what God is reckoned to be by people who, through argument or ritualistic fawning, would "save" you. I quote from the 1838 annual report of the Ulster Institution for the Deaf and Dumb and the Blind, Belfast:

A little mute, in his 8th year, a day scholar, was unfortunately killed at one of the Factories before he could have known the revealed will of God. Very different, however, were the circumstances of a poor blind boy, who died about the same age. He was delicate and deformed; but during a lingering and painful illness he discovered a vigour of mind, an eagerness for spiri-

60

"an 'earth-ecstatic' . . ."

tual instruction, a meekness of disposition, which gave satisfactory evidence of a saving change of heart.

Kindly do not be meek, that's all I ask of you. At school assembly, which is gratifyingly casual, those who are present clap hands above their heads; the fun supplication I call it when I'm not, as sometimes, brooding on the variously handicapped giving thanks for incapacities that render them immune to theological coercion or asking for apocalyptic favors. No, your own ebullient joy in being alive makes you, in one of Edna St. Vincent Millay's better phrases, an "earth-ecstatic," pleased by your own hallucinations (Fred, say, or when you look down to where the wall meets the floor and delightedly shout *ice, ice!*) and asking pitifully little out of life—although that little, being specially and unvaryingly eclectic, wears out those around you. I've drawn for you, and cut out with scissors, I don't know how many baths and slides; finishing one is the best reason for doing another.

The French psychologist Zazzo has pointed out—and with the force of a revelation because no one before him had thought about so obvious a fact—that children such as you, being slow to progress scholastically, often tend to be at a particular stage longer than other children and therefore become reluctant to move on even when they are ready for it mentally. They don't want to do the necessary unlearning, exchange life belt for water wings and these for scuba outfit, and so on. That you recently did so, graduating from kindergarten to junior school with none of the tumult we expected, but with elated voracity, is a small marvel—brought about in part by your first teacher, whose sympathetic determination won you over and made you learn. Her name you still don't know, any more than you know the names of the children in your new class; but her face and general appearance you flung yourself toward with plunging affection. Say her name here: Mrs. Standeven, the name itself like an allegorical promise from the "new wave" of teachers, a wave in which you surfrode when, in fact, you might have gone under or simply refused to get wet. It is well known that the first teacher determines a great deal of the handicapped child's future progress. How fortunate, then, you were. During your last week in the kindergarten, she drew the junior building in your homework book and, underneath, a poignant sketch of the children who were remaining with her: "Mandy sez bie-bie tω evrybody."

And now you have a special new book which, with its chic wallpaper cover, looks like a pamphlet of poems from a private press; but inside it has the new faces, one to a page, and the trunks and the arms and the legs, all in vivid colors. Here you are too, the tallest of the eight, your head a bunker of beribboned saffron supported by your elastic neck and those never-still legs. Your grin is giddy, which it always is when not diffidently gentle, and I suspect you have all the qualifications to become the class's clown. Already you have trespassed onto the high-school slide in an individualistic sortie that might have won you a broken neck; already, confronted with a student teacher in a trendy blouse and a crimson mini-skirt, you have shown your importunate passion for pretty clothes by leaping upon the girl and embracing her outfit, joyfully wetting yourself in the act.

Oo, you cry in the presence of what you find beautiful, *oo-oo!* "She is a girl," your new head teacher said of you, "with a mind of her own." Yes: the more we read your mind, the more we realize whose it is—not any of ours, not school's, not teacher's, not Karen's, Adrian's, Katrina's, Derek's, Lyn's, Mel's or Mike's, although like all of them in the baroque gallery in the homework book you clutch a red-and-yellow striped popsicle big as a ping-pong bat. Getting very sociable, you are; and yet—raw source of energy that you also are, given to using the bodies of others as mattresses or launching pads, and homing intimately in as you do on people's recent injuries and vulnerable parts— you remain just a bit the autist of the breakfast table, gifted with a knack for stark concentration, for looking into the essence of an umbrella or a bird cage, for outstaring brightest indirect sunlight. On the one hand, at the local library, on the same day as you impassively studied the little Thalidomide boy whose hands jutted from the fringes of his shoulders like fingered wings and walked on twelve-inch-square platforms of inch-thick wood for balance, you impulsively wheeled away the old man sitting reading in his wheelchair, thinking he needed a ride, I suppose, *un petit tour,* a bit of mothering, maybe. On the other hand, you sit in trances, interrupting yourself only to hoot *byebye!* and point violently away, which is where we should go. To pester you further is to incur what I these last few days have watched seachange and bloom: a putrid-looking bruise, the signature of an impersonally delivered karate-type punch—not to hurt anyone but to fend off irrelevance, to divide what you want from what you don't.

Captivated bafflement has therefore become our mode of life, caught as we are between your compulsive sociability, your animal high spirits, and your Garbo remotenesses, your Zen-disciplined immobility. And we guess a lot: play you (pardon the idiom) by ear. It's always something of a relief to find you doing something ordinary, something neither calisthenic nor separatist, something which doesn't reinforce what I call the Manda-effect, which is a double phenomenon: numbed eardrums from the volume of your coloratura self-accompaniment while romping; and anticlimactic pinging when you desist, as if, like Pascal, we have discovered the silence of all space and feel frightened by it.

Boyd you now care for with enigmatic gentleness. You shout to him (in warning?) and then, with those powerful wiry arms, lift down his cage and set it centrally on the coffee table. It is high, so you stand on a chair to get it, as you do when ferreting after stogies to snap in half, nail varnish to tint your toenails with, a new toilet air freshener to sniff at. Yank down the wire door, thrust your arm into the cage in preliminary greeting, and then to work. Lift out the balsa-wood-light chunk of cuttlefish bone which is for calcium, then the spray of millet, while Boyd vaults and flutters in routine panic. Now the four dung-sullied perches and the ladder of white round rods. Slide out the tray with its sandpaper carpet, bear it gingerly to the back door of the house and tip on the grass the old grit, the spilled seed, and the accumulated bird lime. At once the sparrows come down on the debris like Assyrians. The sandpaper you leave where it falls and the tray you bring in after giving it a summary knock against the wall and, for good measure in the very act of walking back, bang it like a gong with your fist. Rinse in hot water and dry it with the special cloth. Lay Boyd's fresh floor (the sandpaper is limp, feels oily on the back) and slide the tray back in, giving it a slam if it sticks. Flap the millet against your wrist and set it back on the sandpaper. Over the waste basket, rub the cuttlefish bone with a handful of tissues and then reinstall while Boyd in the corner near his round red-rimmed mirror stares at himself with self-conscious nervousness. Next the abandonedly scattered sand and Tonic Grit (the makers claim it "acts as teeth to the bird" and "is free from any harmful decaying matter"). Flinging this stuff, you look like Marianne who sows on old French stamps: *la française,* but she, assuredly, would never try to make Boyd *eat* his sand or grit. A gay sprinkle across the room—we find it later in the toes of our shoes, in our hair, and sometimes in the butter, so mysteriously you make it travel—and you are done.

Lift out, always in this order, the pot of birdseed and the pot of water, which both clip behind the end bars, and march with the first to the back door again, there to puff off the husks while stirring the contents with a forefinger and squinting your eyes against the lifted chaff. Back in the kitchen, refill with Golden Life Birdseed, which is "super-enriched with six extra ingredients including iodine, vitamins, and lysine, and ensures brighter cere—perfection of claw and beak—a longer, happier, healthy life." (G. L. Birdseed provides an advisory service too and we, I suppose, should provide Boyd with such extras as chickweed, watercress, and dandelion leaf.) Now slip the seed pot back and then the replenished water one. Boyd moves not at all during this (mostly, anyway).

All that remains is to wash-wipe the perches and the ladder, replace them, which you do with much magenta-faced grunting while your hair tumbles and flows with your body's motion, and then, after a quick stroke along the crossbar of the non-removable wire swing, attend to Boyd's luxury item, the honey cone shaped like a bell and made of honey-coated seeds—which he prefers to seed that's plain, no matter how "Golden." Boyd is a gourmet.

Your finger curls now diagonally along one of the perches and Boyd stations himself with one claw on you, one on the wood, backing both chances: the perch's somehow foundering like the Bridge of San Luis Rey or, much likelier, your growing impatient with repose and launching him suddenly upward to flap and plunge about the cage, setting the tiny bell a-jingle while you pursue him with cupped hand. Soon he is caught, and, each time he is, I marvel at the rigid gentleness of your clasp, my mind on Lenny in Steinbeck's *Of Mice and Men*. But you know your own strength, even while squeeze-caressing the magical *livingness* of his groomed green body, and he doesn't fuss or wriggle. When you let him go, but only to slip the tip of a finger into his bird's armpit as he fans loose from you, you cackle-chirp mellowly and offer him a whole series of prods, pokes, and knuckle flicks, your fingers playing an invisible piccolo. *Fowler* is the word that occurs to me, except you pose no threat to him beyond the mussing of a few feathers, which he always corrects by a regal, miniature full stretch, wings taut and shivering, his chest fluffed out and one or two smoke puffs of moult drifting down to the grit and sand. Now he dips his head low and swings down deep from eleven o'clock through six to four, anti-clockwise, launching himself upside-down into the farthest corner while you, more and more excited, gesture as if to pound or pluck him, your stab at his tail feathers always a second late. Speeding up, you ringmaster him through his full repertoire of forward rolls and swift, thudding vaults, sometimes actually detaining him by his claws or a surprise finger hoop, but never too hard.

And I watch as you almost deliriously engage this other creature in sport while the afternoon light thins out: nothing of you is unengaged; no part of your mind holding back, spare and critical. You fly your sturdy hand inside his cage, pirouetting and bouncing with him in rumbustious awe, there being no verbal exchange with him and no second chance once he is damaged. It's the same you as does cartwheels and somersaults on the grass, as if movement were everything and meditation naught. You meet him on a level of impulse and reflex where not many humans belong; and, sometimes, when acute jubilation pulls other feelings and cravings from deep within you, I see your fun bloat just a little with the urge to see just how much more this animated, inaudible puppet can stand. You brim with a voluptuous power that could pulp him in five seconds (your grip on any non-hairy wrist leaves bruises), and you very nearly begin the silken arctic shiver of making yourself irremediably felt; of maiming without being hurt and without sharing his pain. But no, you mercilessly fell vases and pictures when the mood takes you, and big humans too; Boyd you affably torment in what looks like a baby *corrida,* and all you want to do (so to speak) is plant a rosette between his horns, give some other being a run that sets you both a-tremble, and then suck on a big ice cream. Sometimes you stir your arm in the cage as if mixing a cake, and I half-think exuberance is moving today into battery and butchery; but I no longer offer to curb you, having learned that you uncannily restrain yourself. Slight birds

67

are not children, and you know, and even if you squashed the chirp out of them at a rate of one a week, I'd still keep you in birds in the belief that one day you'd come to handle life gently just from feeling it time and again buck and twist and throb in your fist. Which you seemed to learn the first time you slid your arm into the cage: *caramba! dig that green-and-yellow bird but don't dig him no grave.*

Only the other day (you're tough on *you*) you picked up a brand-new pencil sharpener, plugged your forefinger into the larger of the two holes and began to sharpen it, wincing hardly at all as the blade sank in, or, later, as you held your pouring finger in the stream from the cold-water tap. Never what could be called a crybaby, you live by an unvoiced, hardly even acknowledged code which says the injured press on regardless; all that is permitted is an extravagant, half-amused bellow at the indignity suffered, to be followed by a complete change in activity. Somehow you know you have been enigmatically hurt, not by anything so minor as pencil sharpeners, but by chemistry; hurt even before beginning, and this knowledge informs your conduct with all creatures. An antagonistic and often histrionic compassion is your life style, as if you think we are all hurt and, although you're willing to salute the fact in a civil and sensitive way, loathe all vulnerability. I think you have assumed that Boyd is hurt; otherwise he wouldn't be in a cage at all (just as we wouldn't be in a house). And for your chagrined expostulations I think we should reward you as best we can—reward you, I mean, with something that your mind finally decided to accost in bulk: birds.

Give yourself, since this is your secret favorite, the eagle, whom you try to outstare in all the zoos: a bird of bad moral character, according to Benjamin Franklin ("generally poor," he said, "and often very lousy"); a bird that relishes a tasty carcass—"And like a thunderbolt he falls" —although, for staring hard into the sun, he has been called stoical. He is best killed, as Aesop notes, with an arrow guided by flights made of eagle plumes. But—not to limit you or pander to you too much—also these, from me to you in one long chirrup: Poe's obstinate raven; Edward Lear's owl at sea in a pea-green boat with a cat; Long John Silver's parrot, Cap'n Flint, who said "Pieces of Eight" without pause or change, like the clacking of a tiny mill (which you would never hear, I'm afraid); the jackdaw of Rheims; the dodo, the kiwi, the phoenix of Arabia; four and twenty blackbirds encased in pastry; the nightingales that sang for apeneck Sweeney; the wild swans at Coole that "scatter, wheeling" with a positive bell-beat of wings; the albatross which came through the snow-fog and, although a bird of good omen, was inhospitably killed by a cantankerous ancient mariner almost as old as Thomas Hardy's darkling thrush, "frail, gaunt, and small"; John Hall Wheelock's fish hawk fanning heavily over the sea in "crumbling light"; Gerard Manley Hopkins' skylark with its "rash-fresh re-winded new-skeined score/In crisps of curl off wild winch whirl"; the magical, delicate firebird of Stravinsky; the golden cockerel of Rimsky-Korsakov; the twenty-four birds of Aristophanes who speak in short-syllabled chorus and whose arrival on stage is usually omitted from *The Birds,* but whose noise evokes a Hitchcock film:

EUELPIDES: How they thicken, how they muster,
               How they clutter, how they cluster.
               Now they scramble here and there,
               Now they scramble altogether.
               What a fidgeting and clattering!
               What a twittering and chattering,
               Don't they mean to threaten us? What think
                  you?
PISTHETAIROS: Yes, I think they do.

(Will you one day get your tongue round those? Euelpides, Pisthetairos, Euelpisthet—*ee!*—pidesairos!) And the squeaking, cheeping, shrilly whinnying, bazooka-yodeling pop-the-weasel popping of Respighi's own private parliament of musical fowls and two corbies from an old Scottish song and Walt Whitman's two sea birds courting on the shore and the bird Picasso's chauffeur found dead in the street and which Picasso painted into life again on a branch of blossom in 1939 and the sociable, blanched doves which nested on his balcony when he was painting variations on Velázquez' *"Las Meninas"* and the Little Owl, rough-cast and armored in painted bronze, Picasso again of course, and, and

of Chagall, a salmon-bright tumbling rooster elongated, a beaked juggler in red and green and yellow and with Uncle Neuch the fiddler leaning against his ribs from where he stands inside the bird, and one sumptuous enameled cock riding the night sky like a stallion,

as well as (*puff-puff!*) larks, nightingales, cuckoos, robins, supplied retail by John Keats and William Wordsworth and Percy Bysshe Shelley and Robert Bridges and Vachel Lindsay, windhovering all of them; hurt hawks by Robinson Jeffers, one Ibsenian wild duck from Norway, one fancy bluebird from Belgium, dirge singers transformed into birds by Nature's ordinance and François Rabelais (clerijays, bishojays, gormanders and one popinjay), penguins by Anatole France, harpies whom the Aztecs called winged wolves, and mucky-rumped Stymphalides, together with one nest thief out of Brueghel (he who knows where the nest is, knows it; he who takes it, owns it—except the peasant in the foreground is pointing at the climbing boy with derisive permissiveness and is himself the fool, walking straight into a pond!), an owl and a nightingale, a disputatious pair out of the Middle Ages, Icarus who flew so near the sun the wax in his ears melted, a frigate bird which eats flying fish, a flamingo from the famous colony in the Camargue where the white horses and the wild bulls are, an oystercatcher called Sea-Pie (white and black pied), a rook which builds high and so junks the adage of fine summers when rooks build high, a shrike which professionally impales its kill, a goldcrest, small enough to fit into a ping-pong ball if you let the tail protrude

and so to earth, where, as if mummified, you are staring through Boyd like Picasso's violet woman examining her blackened mirror, lost in a cage where every day is approximately silent, and ignorant of this bird hoard I bring you: gifts as well-meant and irrelevant, maybe, as the food, flowers, photographs, paintings, cowbells, shotguns, puppies, parrots, national costumes, boxes of money and cars (including a Lincoln convertible sedan) that pour in to Picasso's villa. He welcomes, we hear, the national costumes and puts them on: a Yugoslav robe, an African cap, and so would you, agreeably wearing whatever plumage we devise for you, and reckoning the wide world your benefactor.

I'd better finish soon, before you hit the house from school. *The East,* we say, *will soon be here,* as if half the globe were going to descend upon us as incubus. Yet nothing seems real until you are back.

Here, to play with, is that old chestnut of ours, the original Japanese hieroglyph for bird:

becoming, through abstraction, the modern character drawn thus:

Some bird! A bird box, rather, or a bird cage, on a single sled runner. Japanese has almost two thousand of these "characters" whereas European languages use a Roman script of only twenty-six letters. Yet, I read (what I know already from observing you in the Babel-laboratory of your own near-language), Roman is confusing: *a* looks like *o* and *u* like *v,* and *b* mirrors *d, p* mirrors *q.* And how do you pronounce such a deduced-from-practice orthographical freak as *ghieti,* meaning "fish," the *gh* coming from *laugh,* the *ie* from *anomalies,* and the *ti* from *contradiction?* Lucky the Japanese children, especially those of them who, as you sometimes do, mirror write; bird remains bird, although flying in the opposite direction, whereas *dub* isn't *bud* any more than *pal* is *lap.* What a pity we can't backtrack you through the history of signs to the Ancient Egyptian bovine head which eventually became *A,* the cross stroke being vestigial horns; and then bring you forward in time to *A.*

Or so I inappropriately think, for what has *A* to do with a bull's head? Why bother discovering why *A* is the shape it is? No, *A* is *A,* having an abstract life of its own, and surely we have lost, having to add *ull* to *b* or *ow* to *c* or *x* to *o,* referring to instead of recognizing ⌀ (or, as it is in Sinai script, ⅄, like one of those sun-whitened horned steer skulls you see in the badlands in Westerns; picked clean, which our spellings are not). Maybe, in these hairy-eyeball times, we are too visual by far: "Ripeness is all" will soon be given a redundant visual translation on TV (commercial for corn?); but I can't help thinking four to five years is the wrong age to be substituting abstraction for observation. When a Japanese adult draws the character for "bird" he draws a quasi-picture of what he can see daily in his garden, outside his office window, whereas *bird* takes us beyond *brid,* in Old English, only as far as our old friend, Etym. Dub. And Etym. Dub. isn't a bird at all, any more than *A* is a cow's head or a bird's visual impression of a cow's head is anything but part of his word for a cow's head. But if you only part master the alphabet, I promise to shut up. It's all a matter of point of view. Charlie Greene, the American sprinter, was asked why he wore sunglasses to race in. Not sunglasses, he answered; *these are my re-entry shields.* Point of view, indeed, like that reentry technique called lipreading. *It rate ferry aren't hadn't four that reason high knit donned co*—which, as Alexander Graham Bell revealed, is how the lipreader sees *It rained very hard and for that reason I did not go.* It all depends on how you look at things: glad over Kierkegaard's 70,000 fathoms; glad all the same.

4. Babel 100 Plus

Let us now make personal history and unlock your word hoard, not only to celebrate it but to make sure we understand each other as best we can. Some of the words are unorthodox things, to be sure, and like items from some extra-galactic code remain a little out of reach, identifiable certainly but hard to explain. From time to time you invent a new one, although not as often as you pick up a new word that is orthodox. Sometimes you gain a word only to discard one (from your everyday speech at any rate), so it's no wonder that our tiny lexicon is always out of date, not quite representative and studded with optimistic guesses. That's, of course, the serious view of words and you (Words-and-You), whereas we usually find ourselves in a state of beaming jubilation with every word you seem to acquire or understand—even when, as quite often, we are mistaken and have too eagerly interpreted something you uttered that wasn't a word at all!

But, mistaken or not, we find ourselves wanting to grab—

what? oh—this imported package, say, of thin Swiss *Chocolat Suchard au lait avec raisins macérés au Cointreau,* and give you all, and to hell with the injunction on the wrapper, *ne doit pas être remis aux enfants.* It's adult chocolate, you see, like Lowenbrau is grownup beer and *dyslexic* is a grownup word you might never need. Never mind, you aren't the world's most conspicuous consumer of chocolate anyway, whether it's Cointreau-potent or not, and I'm no Cointreau addict, ever since on the *Mauretania,* long before you were born, sailing westward to New York, in catastrophic weather of the kind that looks thrilling when painted in oils, they kept serving orange ice cream to those who showed up in the dining room. . . .

Now to my list of mingled code and right speech, penciled here before me on one biscuit-colored sheet like independence being declared. What was it that Borges, the almost-blind Argentinian writer, said while he was signing the copies of his books in the Rare Book Room one term last year? *Word mad,* he told us in his excellent British English, "I am word mad!" At that time, *blanc,* meaning white but sounding so close to black, was the particular word exercising him; and the point being made by a man who couldn't really see us as he talked gained especial force.

Exercising (indeed, distinctly irritating) me as I write this on a sodden autumn morning, there's this blanched L.P. downgraded to cardboard—a color disc, sitting on the desk, with 298 Spectroliac shades fanning out from the center on both sides with a selector that isolates any one fourteen-degree segment from the others so you can see the color better. Except that none of the colors have names; only numbers, so that what I'm sure is duck-egg blue is 504 or 506 and what I call chimpanzee's-anus pink (color of my office walls!) is merely 330. One day you might get around to learning "Richard Of York Gave Battle In Vain" for remembering the spectrum in its right order: red, orange, yellow, green, blue, indigo, violet. I found it useful myself when working just recently on a novel based on the spectrum, but I like it fine in its own right too, a spectral mnemonic that's every bit as much fun as Newton's hapless old apple must have been to him, considering he'd also figured out the innards of white light as well. But this dreary color disc, it's like a standing reproof to all word men, turning you through the spectrum to the tune of 0-006†, 2009††, 1008††, and so on. Why, I read, on the center of the disc where it should supply the title and group and composer, "Insist on Spectroliac BRILLIANT SUPER WHITE. It's the whitest white paint you can buy." Why not, instead, the *blackest* white paint (Borgesiac) you can't buy but have to wheedle out of Isaac Newton by quoting his *Principia* to him entire? Let's get back to our *moutons* (*mot-ons?*); woids after boids.

In the beginning are these words.

appul (apple): no doubt about this, you fetch them off the tree yourself. First you munch the flesh, then lick the knifed-off peels as if they're the fins of some elegant, recently discovered fish, your tongue relishing the curvature rather than the taste. I'm not sure; but I do know that the pupil, once supposed to be a solid body, is the apple of the eye. This fruit is supposed to be forbidden. Juno, Minerva, and Venus competed for the golden apple of discord that rewards beauty; now, if only *you*'d been there. . . . The Dead Sea apple turns to ashes. Did you know apple butter was a sauce or preserve made from apples stewed in cider? Apples repel doctors and applejohns have shriveled jackets. I keep looking at this word—APPLE—and suddenly it becomes unfamiliar: mere letters that correspond to nothing I know, and I begin to know how you feel when confronted with a long word in print.

Aroo (Andrew), who was in the same kindergarten class as you and whom you, in your vague and luxurious way, find in your new class although he isn't there at all. Maybe you see his face where he might yet appear, where he is destined to be; I'll believe that, or that he's your *Doppelgänger,* the boy who (wasn't it Andrew?) accidentally locked himself in the toilet at your birthday party and accordingly lost his chunk of cake to the madding crowd.

That ends the *a*'s, I'm afraid, but the next letter is a favorite with you, for which fact there are famous phonological reasons. *Babababa,* you used to cry; well, the southern Ancient Greeks called the northern ones "barbarians" for speaking an uncouth idiom that sounded like *bar-bar* without variation. Ba-ba, black-sheep Greeks they were.

bar (bath): the contemplation of which, even when it's empty, soothes you almost as much as cavorting in one that is full. Candidates for the order of knighthood called the Bath used to bathe formally before installation. It is not anywhere said *if* they were ever obliged or permitted to bathe again. I hereby constitute you a candidate.

Be (Beard) is Santa Claus symbolized by his beard, but has, as yet, nothing to do with what grows on my own chin, or with the beak bristles of birds. But we'll keep trying.

beebee (drink) is a noun verging on being a verb as well; one of those words you have invented (probably from "tea"). It summons up for you the intricate rituals of bedtime and breakfast, the potion always being tea or a milky drink almost viscous with cornflour. Usually, when saying it, you raise an imaginary cup toward your mouth or, if impatient, make an upward flick with cupped hand. Perhaps, though, you subliminally know some Latin and allow yourself this word out of *bibere* (to drink), which gave us *bibbing* and *bibulous.* Or I am wrong and this is the cloth square strung under a baby's chin with tapes: the *bib,* the

77

blotter that takes the slips between cup and lip. Or it is the whiting-pout, a fish with an inflatable membrane over its eyes; or the Aryan verb *bhi* (*-bhi*), meaning to quiver, or the Persian *bibi,* meaning a lawful wife, or even William Beebe, explorer of the Galápagos Islands!

bir (beer) is a surreptitious, fleeting word which you resort to only on special occasions when you think you'll get your own way; an opportunistic monosyllable, therefore, pleading on an ascending scale for a sip of mine, a spoonful dropped into your glass of lemonade, an emptied beer can refilled with lemonade (akin to whiskey's being put into old sherry casks, except you let nothing mature) or, such is the word's scope, a tiny bottle of imitation champagne. When you steal beer, you do that in mercenary silence, breathing too hard with stealth and effort to address even yourself; feigning, maybe, that what you don't verbalize you aren't guilty of. And, when you do say *bir,* you expect our delight at your having used a word to override our disapproval of your request. I hereby award you a suet halo for ingenuity.

blun (balloon) we in its incalculably plural form blow up until we look like those apple-cheeked faces on old maps— Boreas, Australis, etc.—with feedback inflating our jowls. Or like Goya's boy inflating a bladder, Goya who lived in "The House of the Deaf Man." *Bluns* come in all shapes, sizes, colors, but mostly long-sausage, twelve-inch, and blue or yellow, and some *bluns* even have tiny inflatable horns on the inflatable heads of demons, dragons, or super-germs, which to my mind is a triumph of what some manufacturers with unintentional wit call "preshaped conture." Whatever variety we bought, we always did the same with them: filled them with water and other fluids and lodged them, distended and ungainly, in the seats of cinemas. (My generation of kids, I mean, a long time back.) *Bluns* you hang on all door

handles in a perpetual pneumatic Christmas which, for
some reason private to you, exempts them all from the
flashing spikes of your brandished umbrellas. Which is just
as well, for of the bang of a balloon punctured you are dead
afraid. That sound, or the bang of a paper bag blown up
and burst, is the crack of childhood doom for you, whether
you're wearing your hearing aids or not. (This is why, in
the humid days of summer, overventilated friends should
not succor themselves in your presence by blowing into
doggy bags or supermarket jumbo sizes; you anticipate the
bang and flee.) At a school party, a game played with balloons held between the legs put you almost over the brink.
But, in its proper place and proper condition (kidney-firm,
nozzle doubled over and choked off with a double thread,
as well as absolutely stationary), the *blun* has your unques-
tioning loyalty, holds you in thrall. We have, at the moment,
about two dozen suspended around the house, but not always in the same places on successive days; the *bluns* in
fact circulate according to a program only you possess (a
bit like those Mexican Olympics). So to move around at
night without thorough lighting is to have an occasional
rubbery paunch of a Lilliputian brushing the face or the
back of a hand. Boyd, I hope, will never set his claws on
one of them; and may the hot tips of our cigarettes always
miss them, and all mirrors, windows, light bulbs and fran-
gible Christmas-tree baubles keep their splinters to themselves and pins into their cushions sink more deeply and
writer's needle-sharp 2B pencils point only where they
should, rose stems be scabbarded, rough jewelry be abraded
smooth, filed nails with tips like spear grass be scythed
down blunt, and all careless handlers be exiled by Mont-
golfier hot-air *blun* to the Republican convention that released the most balloons from the nets near the ceiling.
Even so, what with doors being still in use in this house,

and the rate of rubber rot being what it is, one or another element in your gaudy balloon barrage is bound to be blowing up soon, just as others, without so much as a sigh or a thread-thin hiss, shrink down into leprous-looking oblate spheroids (especially those you have painted faces upon in mud-thick poster-colors). No one remembers a fallen balloon, not even if, like each of yours, it's had a word blown into it along with good old, bad old, human gas. But, one day, throw balloons you will, big bangs or not.

And so to *bo* (escalator), a word we've already rejoiced about in this space probe of an epistle that makes me sometimes feel like one of those men Herman Melville had in mind when he said, "I love all men that *dive* . . . the whole corps of intellectual thought-divers that have been diving & coming up again with bloodshot eyes since the world began." Very much bloodshot these pearls get from peering at my own scribble. Anyway, Saturday mornings, up you glide on successive escalators to the sixth floor of the same department store, toys on the ground floor, toilet at the top. You ride with sublime abstractedness and have developed a lovely, demure off-step by means of which you find yourself walking a fraction of a second before your feet touch down. *Blasée,* I'd call you, escalating as you do in the old sense of that overworked and underachieving word, *escalading*—an even older word—by storming fortified places by means of scaling ladders and emitting at shrewdly chosen intervals your war cry of an unappeased Hottentot (which announces there is something at the top of the *bo* you always expect but never find)—the Palladium, Greek version? the statue of Pallas, the ancient Dewline on which the safety of Troy depended? Or just a Houston Astrodome-sized lollipop with strobe lights whipping around inside? Give us time and we'll lay one on:

O/C Pipe Dreams to O/C Equipment: Troy. REQUISI-
TION AT ALL COSTS SITUATION ESCALATING AM CONTAINING
REBEL FORCE WITH HASTILY IMPROVISED CARDBOARD MOCK-
UPS BUT THESE NON-MOVING KINDLY CABLE CARS AND COGS
IMPERATIVE YOU STRIP AIRPORTS RAILWAY TERMINALS IF
NECESSARY ALSO CHECK DESIGN DESIGNER FIRST BO AL-
MOST CERTAINLY USA CIRCA 1900 NO DOUBT PATENTED
CAN WE BRIBE SOMEBODY URGENTLY REQUIRE BEAU GESTE.
Seemingly cognate, but not, *boa!* is an exuberant plea for
us to tickle you, preferably while rolling with you on bed or
floor. The game begins with the tickler-to-be tightening his
lips as if holding in his breath with some difficulty and then
requires a rapid succession of b-b-b-b-b which consummates
itself in an explosive shout of *boa!* as the tickle suddenly
begins. A joy word of your own devising, it's very recent
and dionysian whereas *bo* is old and is an Apollonian affirmative that you utter while upraising a stiff, *heil*ing arm whose
index finger points at the top floor of an invisible six-floor
department store. *Bo* can be said to a goose, like *boo* or
boh, or to other children when you play Bo-Peep and erupt
from your hiding place. *Boa,* though, you can't say except
to a Brazilian snake or an Old World python, both of which
will attempt to get you round the neck, which is not only
why a certain kind of tippet is called a feather boa but why,
perhaps, your invitation to the constrictions of tickle-tumble
comes out a bit strangulated, every bit a tapering diphthong
expressive of British English at its *moewst rafaeined* but
also of speech in certain parts of Pennsylvania where (perhaps) something was left over from the wars. A sound like
a cone, the "bo" of *bo* and *boa,* comes into being, I know
not why, out of the rain forests of British class-conscious-
ness, out of the dark satanic fallout of industrial Pennsylvania, and might just as well in its constricted, garroted way

81

come out of the depths of Brazil where, as John Donne tells us in a phrase of hyperbolical precision, *the sun dines,* and where you can only get around by

boat, the word, which, as we've said, meant "water" until you got *worbar* and now figures only in the Botany Bay of your vocabulary where even the sun cannot reach, a boat not being an object you think worth referring to (not often, anyway), much as you love sailing and steaming vessels both great and small. Prompted and prodded, you'll say *boat* and mean boat; but somehow, girl, you separated *boat* from *worbar* without getting boats, almost as if boats that float are conceptually submerged, and therefore *worbar* includes all boats and maybe even all who sail in them. To say *worbar* is, virtually, to be a shipowner supreme, which you already are in physical miniature (although, fair's fair, you run just as big an airport as you do a dockyard). You'll come back to this word one day, but only, I believe, if you never board a hydrofoil again and so never again develop that morgue face quite unlike the children's faces in the sailing bits of Claude Lelouch's lyrically colored family movie, *A Man and a Woman.* Only at the very edge is the sea your friend, and its many-voicedness is wasted anyway on you; and only on the fringes of your mind are there verbal boats, whose noblest function is to float the soap for you at bathtime. "Ship," of course, which would refine your vessel sense, you relentlessly ignore, no matter how many Cunarders I show you.

Bobbee (Bobby) is another of those kindergarten friends whose faces have vanished while their names remain; these cannot, by any stretch of imagination, be replaced, whereas something can always be managed with your friends who have feathers, all Boyds being

boid and a good many *boids* capable of being Boyd. Although, recently, you have begun to say this sometimes as *burr,* you long ago entangled it with *boy,* so that sometimes you seem to see the boys in school with a fowler's eye and sometimes Boyd as a candidate for junior school. The difference, though, is that Boyd frightens you not at all (you make him serve you), whereas the boys in kindergarten perturbed you keenly at first, being rougher than anything you'd met and outnumbering you two girls three to one. So you took it out on me, the biggest approximately submissive boy you could find; but not so often now—somewhere along the line, I think, you applied muscle and bone to your tormentors, and that would be a memorable experience for them. Boys have also—meek as Boyd himself—succumbed to your disdainful receptivity, recognizing in you a force old as Bathsheba, and especially the svelte little Pakistani, who gives you a pat and a furtive hug when he thinks the other boys aren't looking. Names don't matter, but these gestures to one another out of your respective overpowering privacies are like mountains moving.

boo (bosom) you'll use only when reciting, with enumerative zeal, the list of your facial and bodily parts. I've heard you, seen you, sitting alone at a large mirror and pronouncing them with finicking precision while observing the shapes your lips make as they move. This physiognomical-anatomical cantata never included *chest,* a word you don't get because it begins with a sound you can't hear or see. Lucky for you, then, you're a girl; boys, having no bosom, have simply no chests at all.

brow, which you enunciate immaculately, belongs in the same list as *boo,* and only repeated insistences will make you say it on its own. You seem to disdain the conflicts, the rough-and-tumble, the mix-up, of language, preferring words in congruent groups or words in isolation to any combination in which there's contrast and clash, genre against genre or even noun against verb; after all, a verb gets a noun into

83

motion, a motion that might never end until the noun's disappeared forever. Single words, like single slides and single umbrellas, appear to be inexhaustible objects of contemplation, and to combine them—especially on the conceptual level—is perhaps to modify them irreparably. Eyebrow pencil on the eyebrow (*brow* is always *eye*brow to you) is one thing; indeed, a favorite sport of yours. But *eye* plus *brow* you spontaneously mistrust and won't say, intent on the independence of the one vis-à-vis the other. Such is your Zen; you gaze, or so I conjecture, at the form and the atoms, seeing all as a chip off the aboriginal cosmic working block, paying homage to a uniqueness which syntax, metaphor, and connotation actually spoil. And when you stop looking, you have probably assimilated the object—as it is in this time and this place—*into you* more thoroughly than any of us assimilate the lessons we claim to learn.

No generalist, you have something in common with the Eskimos, who have several different words for snow according to its condition and kind. You haven't the words, but I think you'd note the differences between different snows: the wet, the crumbly, the caked, the packed, the snow that will not last and the snow that has come to stay. The Swedes use different words for when, say, you *go* in a train, when a train *goes,* when a pilot *goes* up in his plane, and when you *go* across the road. On the one hand, you are Swedish (which by blood you partly are anyway) and Eskimo in attentiveness; on the other, though, your handicap prevents you from attaining even to the superficialities of English. Your no doubt exquisite perceptions just cannot be said (and I realize and defy the hazards of articulating them for you).

On the one hand again, the economy of Basic English's sixteen verbs only is just right for you, but, on the other, you are the very person to multiply the modes of all the verbs there are until they register nothing to anyone else. Those Eskimo variants of snow are communal property, whereas you, for all your behavioral rigidity, know that the pencil *meets* the eyebrow differently on each penciling occasion and that *meet* (or *apply,* say) disregards what is unique to each. The categorical, I gather from your intent frowns and your long, long scrutinies, would always be too crude for you, yet that is the very thing you need to get started at all.

If we fantasize, we can elaborate the verb *to pencil* into *browpencil* and so on until we get *browapencili* (for when a sharp pencil touches a ruffled eyebrow), *browopencilu* (for when a blunt pencil touches an unruffled eyebrow), *browopencilipo* (for when that happens briefly), *browopencilopi* (for when the contact is longer), and onward until micro-differences have bloated idiom to the point of paralysis. To live competently in the world, I conclude, entails a certain insensitivity—and a deliberate one too; otherwise, everything would fascinate us so much that we would lapse into highly attuned trances. The world, ironically enough, is here to be in part ignored, and whatever (in the jargon of the day) is mind-expanding militates against living successfully by orthodox standards.

Clearly (or at least shiningly through a dark prejudice), in order to have any chance at all of fending for yourself in the ordinary world, the supersensitivity which I infer from the intensity of your scrutinies must be chopped on the block of a primary vocabulary. And the same is true even if I'm wrong and, instead of being supersensitive, you spend much of your time in an inaccessible, ineffable blank. Either way, you will be deprived—I mean in the condition of being deprived—either of your supersensitivity (unless you regain it after humdrum years of learning how to buy bread, stamps, and shoes) or of the peace the blank brings with it. But I think it would be just as hard to get back to fine attunement through increasing articulateness between twelve and twenty as to achieve that attunement for the first time after being blank for so long. I just don't know; which doesn't mean I *almost* know: it means I've no idea at all, you're that inscrutable. So I'm wishing you the best, you the would-be cosmonaut who's never allowed out alone; I'm presuming you're a mystic rather than a non-starter, a simple soul rather than a cipher. Your privacy, I hope, is full, not empty.

brella, coming in slightly wrong alphabetical order (but let it stand because it exemplifies the wackiness you create around you), you say with ebullient relish provided that, before it or with it held in hand, you aren't singing a fully choreographed mantra. I won't, just here, go into your *brella* rituals; in fact we've touched on these already. What I've concluded is that umbrellas obsess you because they are two-in-one and therefore, to you who love uniqueness, represent magic. Up never interferes with down and vice versa. The two extremes are compatible and permit you a double view of a single thing, a single apprehension of a double possibility. When the *brella*'s up, you're overjoyed by its capacity for coming down, and when it's rolled and fastened you're overjoyed by what it's just been, what it can again be after a couple of simple shoves. The *as is* and the *can be* you rejoice in simultaneously, so much so that your conception of umbrella is mobile, not static (although, I suppose, a pretty static sort of mobility; pretty limited). *Brella* is big and therefore exercises a greater pull on you than such other adjustable items as knives, carving forks and sugar tongs. Only lamps and scissors have comparable magic. Parachutes, by the way, let you down in one half of their performance since they don't even retract, and a neatly folded parachute, at least as far as looks go, amounts to nothing at all.

bu is your truncation of omnibus, which you most love when it sways and almost pitches you from one side to the other. Then you laugh way up high. A mere smile you reserve for moments when familiar landmarks trail into view; and when they don't—if the route's been changed to avoid road constructions or if you're going to a new place—you show concern or alarm by an imperious frown or a nagging, interrogative wail. But buses please mostly and you draw them with heavy-handed joy.

bye-bye you have just begun to say, with ironic intonation and many hand movements, almost as if you believe no one will believe you mean it. But you do mean it, you do go, you do go to sleep, and you know this word is never final. But it is the last of your *b*'s, and leaving *b* behind to move on is like leaving the coast of California in order to visit the Pacific islands. Yet even a sandcastle built on an island beach makes you a landed proprietor in this dimension.

car you intone lengthily, confident that you know what you're about; and, sometimes, in impatience, you exclaim repeatedly with elaborate, unfurling motions of your arms, "no *car; car no!*" Which I reckon eloquent and am thankful for two words combined almost against your will.

cig, for cigarette, doesn't come readily to you; but if we point at one you'll name it with a smirk of sinful complicity. Maybe you know what most people don't who call on the weed: the word *could* have come from *cigarra,* which is Spanish for cicada. So—so, sing:

Have a cicada
Down on the old hacienda
Where never is coughed
A discouraging puff

And all our butt-ends-a
Sing nightly cadenzas.
Cough, cough, cough,
Huff, puff, huff.
It's still the magic wand that conjures up tomorrow's potable
    gold,
It's still lone man's companion, bachelor's friend, it's even called
Sublime.

You always roll your own, don't you? Or, taking up one of
ours, touch the filter to your lips once with eye-squinting
aplomb and set it back to do its worst to somebody else.

(About *chin,* now, a message to ourselves: see under *tsin,*
as the guidebooks say. And look for *clock* under *lock.* All
that kind of elbow nudging.)

dayn (ten) you can count up to at speed; in fact, you
utter your numbers so fast that this one becomes something
like *dey;* and *doo, dree* you hardly voice at all. You have a
mischievous habit of regarding numbers as things to chant
and not to use, just as, when counting on your fingers while
chanting, you flash them erect in a succession almost too
swift to follow. Yet when you first learned to count you sang
out the numbers with triumphant resonance, your whole
face alive with the emphasis. You like to identify things in
twos and threes, but higher numbers interest you not at all
—not for any practical purposes anyway. Maybe this is another sign of your disinclination to group things which, even
if identical, you prefer to contemplate one by one. Your
world is full of nomadic monads.

ding (swing) has no *an sich* to follow it; here you soar,
no word to the person pushing you from behind, but, for
his express guidance when you want more height, your index finger extends up the chain in mild, discreet imperative.
The pusher soon learns to heed that sign; if he doesn't in-
stantly work you back to horizontal on the forward lunge,

"ding . . ."

you wheel round, booming like a bittern, your arm rigid
and aimed at the sky while your cry pumps out and your
finger stabs until you have been obeyed. Overhead the twin,
triple, and quadruple jets skim or lumber over, low for you
to view, and, ever in good humor toward them, you cant
your head as if at the beginning of a parabola that takes
you up to their silver bellies and over their uncluttered
backs. Then the back swing that reinvigorates your climb
and also, if the pusher be unlucky, clips him on the chin as
he crouches to receive you. *Ding* it almost always is; but
you have, after mustering your skills and calming your
mouth muscles for a good five seconds, said the real thing:
z-z wi ngh! A few times, with that *eureka* smirk. A pho-
netic golden egg.

dog (sometimes *dog-woof*), the last *d* I can think of, is a word you show no overpowering desire to use, but you understand it when we say it to you. Of the ritual dogs attending your bedtimes, more later; sufficient that they are of Hong Kong celluloid and will not thirst while waiting.

Under *e* we have *eye,* which you say well, *eigh* for "eight" and *ee!,* your call sign which you have finally civilized into a muted form that can be charming. *E-oe,* a fugitive from the *h*'s, is "hello," with which you bombard the telephone mouthpiece and greet the most pressing of your friends— those who demand of you *a word. E-even* is between ten and twelve but sometimes turns up between six and eight: a number strictly for vocal rendering in your descant of numbers, it signifies nothing as yet. But about *ellow* you are utterly certain, it being one of your favorite colors.

file, the tool, is a recent word that you say beautifully with patience, poise, and a craftsman's graveness; and *fur,* as found on the inside of your new white boots, is something you caress your cheek against and also find on Boyd's belly, most gollys' heads. And *g* is for *gawyee,* alias not only golliwog but also any Negro. Sitting in a train one day and studying the human pageant through the plate-glass window with the air of Queen Victoria having to inspect a tear bottle full of Lord Alfred Tennyson's dandruff, you shivered with astonishment when a colored porter wheeled something past: a live golly, whom you at once extolled with a hysterical shout and whom, no doubt, you'd love to hang on your long line until the Scotch tape dried out and he fell behind the sofa. What you think your Pakistani friend actually is, or what you sometimes might even call him (he has a thick mat of curly hair), I'd rather think I needn't guess. Nonsense words have nonsensical consequences. Finally, here, *gibig,* for guinea pig, one of which your class had in kindergarten. Sometimes, for a joke (which, in you, is highly sophisticated word play), you point to yourself and tell us you're a *gibig,* and we have to contradict you with tops-of-our-voices vehemence. It's a reassuring game.

fy means "fire," but also the cuttingness of knives and the lion sun captured in some mustards. You also, when in peak declamatory mood, say it as *var,* like a long-frozen Viking pitching a war cry through whiskers still congealed, so fusing enthusiastic awe with a finger-wagging parody of all wise adults. It is also your word for portable electric heaters, and at these—if they have convection vanes rotating under a mock-coal carapace full of roseate light—you'll stare a full hour, enraptured by the glow and cozy flicker of the non-coals. You know it isn't coal; you saw me touch it once and you couldn't understand why no blister came. Prudent, you still won't touch, though. One metamorphosis brings others with it, and perhaps you think the real and fake coal alternate and half the coal touchers get burned. A burning match, though, you will puff out, letting the breath as it comes out make an accidental word that sounds like *pun.*

The *h* you refuse to "hello" you paradoxically give to *hawz* (horse), having ridden on an Exmoor pony, *har* (hair) and *hot-oo!* (to be exclaimed in the presence of fires, mustards, knives, etc.). But "hammer" you also deprive of its aspirate, your preference being to call it *pomper,* whether it's one of your plastic lightweights or the real iron one with a claw head. Wielded heftily enough—so your philosophy of percussion goes—a *pomper* will right anything: umbrellas, books, chair covers, bleeding fingers, recalcitrant Boyd, and even broken windows or wine glasses. Bash a thing hard enough and it will repair itself. Always, with those big dry-palmed hands of yours, striated as if you were fifty, you try the *pomper* remedy before anything else.

91

You have a lovely swing but hardly any aim, hence the hammer can never quite keep pace with the damage it does while mending.

ie-gree we supply to you almost wholesale in cones, wafers, and (when you're obviously in a gargantuan mood) bricks. As often as not, though, ice cream alone isn't enough for you, and you'll dip a popsicle or a lollipop into the thick of it, then use either of these as a spatula to paint us with or (in quieter mood) as a tasting tool. You prefer both hands busy, there being about you something of the artisan, which we find some consolation when daubed with an ice-cream impasto only seconds after you irrupt into the house from school. Down slams the door of the freezer compartment and you haul out the day's frozen booty, hedonist, action painter and bandit in one. You once tried to cement cracks in the walls with this commodity, like a snow queen turned laborer, but soon discovered the facts of thawing and did not persist. Had there been no Bonnie for Clyde, you would have made a high-class stand-in.

No *j*'s yet, and there wouldn't be a *k* if we didn't habitually think of "school" as *kool*. You say this with a little wavy writing motion of your hand; you plead for *kool* endlessly, and you check each morning with us to ascertain if today is *kool, bo* or *ding*. Or, rather, you used to; nowadays you seem to place and identify the days rather well, not knowing their names yet, but capably locating painting day (Wednesday) as the one before swimming day, which comes before come-home-early day, Friday; after which it's plain sailing (if you can be said to do anything plain or plainly) through Saturday and Sunday (*bo* day and *ding*-in-park day respectively). Only the early part of the week puzzles you, especially Tuesday, a limbo occasion whose only definition so far is its being in between. But the breakthrough will come soon, just as if you were to cram Tuesday's plain space with Neapolitan ice cream.

Watch out! Here comes a bevy of *l*'s: *la-la,* ancient and honorable euphemism for lavatory, but also, in your case, a survival from your soprano singing while on your pot; *Linna* (Linda), of whom you were fond and whom you still call on to materialize from where she is in kindergarten; *lollee,* minus the "pop," which you bear aloft as a mace of office or bang with to make gongs out of trays or employ as unshiftable bookmarks (the sticks of devoured *lollees* always serving you, like the little sticks of Alfred Jarry's pataphysical King Ubu, for poking in people's ears); and *lock,* for all the clocks you hold to your ear as other and older children hold transistor radios.

lam (lamp) I've just remembered, a word you utter with some adoration. Into all *lams* you stare as if you are an Aldous Huxley cleansing the doors of your perception (the brighter the better; all things bright are beautiful to you); and, nightly, you position yourself before the bank of studs in the hallway and tap them in and out like a long distance operator having trouble in getting a Moon number or a jet pilot working his selector switches with impeccable cool. Night after night you hit on the same correct selection of lights; what goes before is mere flamboyant prowess. Figuratively, lamp is any source of light, including sun and moon and television screen, which is why, I suppose, you occasionally race out to effect the big switch-off that dooms us to TV light while you survey the lustrous gray of the dimmed room with the measured exhilaration of an astronaut just stepped out into his first moon crater. But with strobes do not trifle; loving light as you do, though, a career in TV or as a skiing instructor would be fine: arc lamps or snow dazzle would suit you mighty fine, with all the rest of us cowering in our Polaroid cool-rays. *Lorv* (love) you bay at us with clowning relish and *leg* you murmur as if it's an obscenity. That's *l.*

Man-dee, Mamm-a, momter, more, mou! It's almost a sentence: Mandy asks her mother for more thermometer in the mouth (as distinct from thermometer underarm or rectally). Your own name you finally learned after about a year's repetitious calling of it into the audio trainer that boomed it back to you through massive black-rubber ear-phones that always made you look like a goggle-eyed midget wireless man sending an SOS from a sinking ship. *Mandee* or *Man-dee* you utter with a prideful almost reverential deepening of your voice, making the pause (when you make it) dramatic: from middle C to G below. You were five before you knew you had a first name and now, two years later, you are just beginning to acknowledge your surname. *Mamma, Mamm-a,* however, you've had longer and you now snap it out with a jussive briskness, especially when forcing upon your mother a plate of food you've lost interest in. Your adaptation of thermometer I think brilliant, whether you see the *thing* as a silver-thin cigarette or not. Fetched home from school when you were ill, you kept showing us your armpit, where we searched for a rash—something wrong. No rash, and nothing else; it was where school had put the *momter,* and you wanted a repeat. Then you learned the word, and you ask for *momter* now whenever you feel off-color; which, considering your handicap, compels your doctor into a near-veterinary role (you haven't the words to tell him what you feel any more than, say, Boyd has), is a useful home signal when other signs are lacking. Un-less, frivolous girl, you just want to play at doctors. When the doctor arrives, you at once roll up your blouse and un-dervest; you know what sickness is, and resignation too. *More,* which *mou* asks for more often than Oliver Twist

94

ever did, is a bizarre word which now means only what it should (either a curt aside or a gourmand bellow, with never so much as a "please"—word you don't have); it used to mean pop or lemonade or beer even. Asking for more pop more often than for more of anything else, you built association into identity—at least, until you began to use "pop" seriously and, later, coined *beebee.*

nose you sing when you itemize your face, but also still use for elephant (having almost got that word, you spurned it at the last moment). *Nail* is on the finger but not yet under the *pomper. Ny* is nine, and *no,* always a violent exclamation, you conduct with much pseudo-pedagogical finger wagging and, rather too often, iterate for ten minutes as if seeking to wear the word down to discover the secret printed into its lining, and all the time mock-slapping yourself. Deaf children are not angels, as you and I know; but if to forbid you is to drive you into obsessed echolalia (as many as a hundred *nos* a minute in mimicry or parody), I'll use only my periphrasis, "We don't do that," except for when you are desperately wrong—as when on the verge of discovering electricity or brutally modifying the physique of innocent strangers (unless they have jeered at you, and then I'd equip you with a lead pipe myself). Always, we know although you don't, one should speak to deaf children in sentences and not batter them with single words (your own preference for isolates is acute enough as it is). So, not like the Alice who in *Henry V* instructs the princess Katherine in one foreign word at a time (*col,* nick; *coude,* bilbow), I muster unilateral whole sentences to hold your attention, you, to whom the sentence is as foreign as trigonometry or Peshtu. All the same, you watch: see us moving our mouths at length, only six inches from your two microphones; and you see, I hope, *see-hear,* something of the combinations, whether the matter happens to be "The car is ready outside," "This is potato salad," or (as sometimes, when I'm uptight) "Imagination wasn't given to us to use for mental Xerox-copying; it's there for purposes of play, invention, and exploring." Such are the verbal combos used to sell you on a very useful habit, called speech, you must acquire for keeps.

Ollie is what you decreasingly call Boyd; *oo* means pretty (although not when it's part of *hot-oo*); and *oo-ah,* oral version of a vertical hump, means "slide," a word you now are converting into *zlar*—said with almost feral zeal. Whether you've rings on your fingers and bells on your toes, you shall have not music but slides wherever you go, preferably blue and yellow like the big one at school, or red and yellow like the lesser one on the grass at home, there to be slid down, walked up, lain full length on right way up or upside down, sung to, assaulted, swabbed down and, of course, reproduced in acre upon acre of dismembered cardboard, two-dimensional or three-, and mounted in all rooms among the bric-a-brac of daily living. Whatever the cost in Brobdingnagian confetti, portions that leopards and nest-building jackdaws reject, and scissor-sore thumbs, your obsession with slides must be fed. *Wooooo!* you call during descents real or imagined, *wooooo!* And *wooooo!* we go with you. As for *out,* it means "out on foreign territory" where you may have to compete for monopoly of the slides, and never outside in your own garden or between the door and the gate. *Out* that you own is part of the pleasuredome into which you have converted an entire house.

Any *pl* you just uncritically worship in plane-chant serenade. Planes get bought, built, and broken here at something like emergency speed while my head buzzes from sniffed-in glue and my fingers ache from clamping joints together while the glue sets and none of the nail files have any rough left, such has been the trimming and chamfering of ill-combining parts which the machines in the factory have botched. *Pl!* we cry as your Zero meets my Executive head on; *wooooo!* as they miss and climb away toward Picasso's Old Woman and the lamp whose pull string you professionally snap at three-week intervals. Planes ready-made and planes built from kits, planes folded from stiff paper (oh, remind me to buy you that book about them which has an appendix of press-out cardboard ones), planes in silhouette from every magazine and box lid we can find, planes drawn with *pen* (which also means "crayon" and "pencil"), and planes which are just stiffened hands with uptilted thumbs—these await our command, a mini-SAC of the living room. Now:

PLAR is the Bandaid you apply for kicks.

PLEE is the word *we* say to *you,* pretty-please you spurn.

POMPER is to hammer as hammerhead is to shark (already "done").

POO is what you DO, but very irregularly, in the *la-la.*

POOL, not a game but where, in which, you bathe in summer. It's plastic.

POON is any spoon not born in anyone's *mou.*

POP is potable and nothing to do with music, art, etc.

And PRI-Y, not a crossword clue, but "pretty"—keen, swish, dead neat, or overpoweringly gaw-juss. Let's trail these lines behind our planes like streamers, although if you aren't careful that last one will wrap round your throat and your airscrew, your windthroat and your corkscrew, like the conjoined scarves of all the Oxford colleges, including if you land downwind even the holy ones where the beds are cross-shaped and you have to bring your own vinegar, the toilets like thundering caldrons lodged in peat bogs owned by the Baskerville Hound-Dog—You'll soon have more *p*'s than *b*'s, but they can't caution you to watch your *p*'s and *q*'s (you've no *q*'s anyway). Just "be natural,"

97

which my mother writes in the autograph books of her music pupils. There's a jazzy commotion in the air, so let's have a song as if the ICBM's were raining down and we've sheltered in a revolving door, you with your fair-weather umbrella up and me with my broad psychedelic flower-power tie bound like a blindfold over my eyes:

Gaw-juss
Frab-jus
Lan-gous-
    tine

Scrum-ptious
Lus-cious
Tan-ger-
    ine (*Wait for it now, wait for it*)

Treach-rous
Up-as
At-tro-
    pine (*Wait wait wait*)

Quinquireme!
Quincunx!
Quoit! (*Here we go now*—)

CWINCWIREEM!
CWINCUNX!
CWOIT!

I met a man
  whose brain-pan
    it ran
      with
        tan
          bran
            roundabout the garden
              like a teddy-bear (HERE PULL FACE OF BEAR)
                one step, two-step
                  and tickle you under there! *Bo-a!*

I am putting you on *rounabou,* a miraculously long word to come from you, but it's one of our main games, for which you find time in the midst of all our most urgent projects— painting lollipops with poster color, assembling (out of a cardboard certificate tube and yards of Scotch tape) something like a water cannon, invigilating the middle distance, irrigating the kitchen floor to see what it will grow, even exploring topmost shelves while standing on two rickety stools. *Rounabou* soothes you just as much now as it did when you were two, a sport less hectic than *bo-a* or upstairs chasing with me as old Nosferatu, my fangs fresh from the dentist, my blood supply woefully short. How many thousand times you've played *rounabou!* It never palls or fails, and you don't care for innovative variations either. Spread-eagled over my knees, you detonate with mirth at the tickle after a suspenseful and delicious agony during the *one, two* steps. But *rounabou* also means carousels, full-size or miniature (like the French one you have with, still inside the base, sugared almonds caked with sand and salt of the sea), their only drawback being friction: they are not a *perpetuum mobile.* The big ones shiver and halt and then, while you gesticulate and fume as if the world has come to an end—thwarted equestrian or space pilot that you are— someone fumbles among his coins to purchase the lurch-off that renews your spell. Or, with miniature ones, someone has to do the spinning while you peer at the wooden dolls in the chairs like a medic at the window of a decompression chamber, alert for panic or collapse, and inspector-faced. (You are also beginning to use *rounabou* to distinguish skirts, which go *round* you, from pants, which you think don't.)

Sibilants, for you, only just exist, and you give only the merest touch of *s* to *sheep, shoe, smoke, sock,* and *soon,* much preferring to say none of these words except *shoe.*

"zlide . . ."

Utility words that easily decline into *ee, oo, mo, zo,* and *zoo* because they don't interest you, whereas into *slide,* an *s*-word that excites you, you fit a buzzing engine to give it speed: *zlar, zlide.* Buzz, buzz, as Hamlet says; all the world's a *zlide. Zix* and *zeven* you sometimes enjoy, but in removing the *s*'s from "see-saw" you manage to introduce a donkey into it: *ee-aw.*

All your *t*'s are close to *d,* but how could anyone expect you to know how to pull your tongue back from the one to make the other? "Teeth" become *dtee,* nonetheless, which

100

is in itself a tribute to the accuracy of your lip-reading. Having tried to decipher for myself those twitching, pouting, springing, elongating pairs of chicken livers called lips, which curl into a new shape almost before the present one's complete, I feel defeated for you—except that you aren't defeated at all. If we mouth things to you, with no sound at all, you speak them back to us with more precision than we have a right to expect and in deftly modulated tones. When you do that, it's as if the blueprint has become the working model right there before our eyes. Some of your sounds, though, are involuntary, like your Arab's burp which you know by its vibration (as you know those other noises you make during waits in quiet waiting rooms); insouciant eructating that is a law unto itself, like the reputedly superior beauty of the women of Barcelona or Memphis or Nottingham . . . wherever you want, it's a notion as unverifiable as your wind is free, and every bit as unarguable about as those consummate lists, in *The Pillow Book of Sei Shonagon,* of Things Which Make One's Heart Beat Faster, of Things Which Are Hard to Say, of Outstandingly Splendid Things, of Very Dirty Things. Let's not quibble: for Things Which Some People Think Embarrassing While You Laugh, thank you. And, in return, to fatten out your *t*'s:

teetotum (to spin and win with); *teff* (the Abyssinian cereal); *teg* (a young sheep); *tegmen* (a covering), *tegular* (to do with tiles)—such are the *t* words you may never have, and what's the loss so long as we have dictionaries to cold-store the needless arborescence of vocabulary? You'll manage as long as you can rouse your big sister from her pre-breakfast sleeps by thumping up the stairs, like an irate farmer, barking her name in mounting crescendo until, splendor of splendors, you site your mouth at her ear and again sound off: *Tiya,* TIYA! And Tina wakes.

101

Toe-ee (Tony) is another absent friend of the kindergarten to whom you signal vocally while busying your hands with something else. What's in a name? What?—about a year's coming to terms with it and rolling it round your mouth until you've found the most comfortable way of saying it, as you did with *tsin* for chin, *twev* (which you developed from *dwelve* through *dwel* and *twerv*) and *dren* for train.

For *u,* of which you have no stock at all, let's bring up *v: vor* and *vy* (4 and 5), which still wouldn't be much if we couldn't call on the *w* (these three are one another's aliases anyway). *Wall* and *wee* you understand but don't much bother to say, whereas *worbar,* which you occasionally weaken to *wortar* with a disingenuous giggle, is an exultant statement of ownership, while *wat* is not only "wet" but also your version of your surname (Mandee Wat). *Wim* for swim is new, as is *wynd,* your only true verb, and therefore given heavy use: to wind is to wind clocks, of course, to peel out those Polaroid snaps, to stir or whip mixtures in a bowl, to turn a screwdriver on a screw, to switch on the TV, to sharpen a crayon in a pencil sharpener, to adjust a thermostat, to peel a potato, to spread covers on a bed with a furling motion, to slide curtains, to open the door by twisting knob or turning key. . . . It is as if you've just discovered the wheel that makes the world go round, and *wynd* is the summary verb for all appropriate handlings of things. So, to wind an egg, I suppose, would be to fry, boil, or poach it, and to count is to *wynd* round from *wun* through all your fingers.

Winding up our lexicon won't take long. *Yap, yaw, Yayee, yoap, yop, yummay*—being Scotch tape, saw (real, Hong Kong half-real, or cardboard cutout), myself, soap, "stop!" (to be said when plonking your thumb on the little ball on top of one of your roundabouts), and pacifier. One word, *yabut,* you have evolved from watching us say, "What is it?" That's what it means. I point at something and, at once, you look me in the eyes and ask, *yabut?* with the stress on the first syllable. *Zix* and *zeven* and we are done. In fact we were done before them, having had them already. There are too, of course, numerous hortatory ululations, which perhaps don't *mean* at all but are mere mouth work for a dull moment or a cold winter, as are your various sibylline pointings. One sound, however, a high-pitched menacing warble, means scissors and is usually reinforced with the index and middle fingers of one or both hands flicking in the manner of scissor blades. All the variants of *oi, oi-ya, ee-ya,* and *ee* I haven't, I'm sure, quite mastered, and soon might not need to anyway; you use them less and less, except on the bad days when you regress to three, mostly on account of constipation ("Has she *been* at school?" We never know; you never tell us anything like that).

Getting on for a hundred words, then, this vocabulary of yours comes to between an eighth and a ninth of C. K. Ogden's Basic English although, I suspect, his criterion— "What other words do we need in order to define something when we do not already know the right word for it?"— makes you something of a hit-and-run artist, a beach-comber, a swagman, a linguistic gypsy. Sometimes, Canute-like, you bid the tides of language retreat; at other times, like Boadicea, you drive your knife-wheeled chariot over the living bodies of even the words you know. Half your words begin with the labials *b, m, p, w,* or with *d,* sounds which look identical to the reader of lips. You eye our mouths and probably our minds as well, but as Robert Louis Stevenson remarked in a reverie on character making in fiction, "we can put in the quaint figure that spoke a hundred words with us yesterday by the wayside; but do we know him?" We know you well, but not well enough, you

103

quaint and jaunty, beautiful, demonic creature, but not through conversational exchange, which here figures as a paradise neither lost nor regained but just never opened up. Our "talk," such as it is, is almost symbolical stuff, expressionistic, varying between relentless decoding and slow-motion, dramatic enunciating. No wonder that, out of thin air, comes a song, *Listen to the hearing aids,* as they whistle and whine out of unison, cramming your ears with static from invisible mockingbirds who use you as their own private robot.

Yet, Canute, Boadicea, Mistress of Mini-Babel, you and your handicap don't always win, however little your aids seem to give you, however much at times you behave like your handicap's own *aide:* the tides shove in upon you, the maimed language gets back on its feet, the meaningful phonemes float clear of the babble, and, confronted with a sheet and cards each bearing the same words—for example, *watch, bike, plane, pool, slide, swing, brella*—you match word to word perfectly without much hesitation. The money denominations on stamps you rediscover on the faces of clocks, and now you count out wrestlers and boxers on TV along with the referee. Only a ghoul would write you off, but only a criminal optimist would think you are going to have an easy time of it with *any* mode of spelling, with the abstractness of words, and all those necessary but inaudible and nearly invisible sounds—not to mention microphone friction and the special dangers that catarrh and sinusitis bring for you. Even within the enclave of the multiply handicapped, life isn't *that* easy for you; and, as for outside it, where you have a right to go, you will have to be a lioness in the streets once your present utter lack of self-consciousness has gone, as it no doubt will. Some of the nineteen-year-old deaf, aware that they sound uncouth, are shy to speak; and yet you, whose deafness is a symptom of something else that is wrong, long always to be out and about. I hope you always will.

One study comes to my mind on a mongol boy (IQ 24) who, it was supposed, had one word only: *pie.* Yet, during a special course of speech stimulation, he exhibited a vocabulary of 102 words. And my mind moves on from that case to the extremely distant tenth-century Japan of Sei Shonagon, lady-in-waiting to the Empress Sadako. If Sadako hadn't passed on a gift of paper to her, would Sei Shonagon ever have begun the journal she kept in the drawers of her wooden pillow? I intend to furnish you with an endless supply of paper, then, and fiber pens to match. I promise to resume and, as they say in Spain, analphabetically. Just think (a thought to tide you through), when you settle for your first pair of Levi's, you'll be choosing among sand, silver gray, pewter, jade, olive, whiskey, charcoal, bronze, navy, loden, antelope, wheat, banana, pumpkin, and hot chocolate, all colors having copper rivets at the strain points. Have them all, for, after all, at the beginning of our lexicon I stalled with colors because I was shy to get to words, and —as the old miner told young Levi Strauss in around 1850 when Levi was selling his tough fabric to tent and wagon makers, "pants don't wear a hoot up in the diggins. Caint git a pair strong enough to last no time." One hundred fifty million pairs later, all those colors await your pleasure. Out of *these* diggins, now, let us go. The gold is dug.

Hothothot superhot stoppress postscript or it would be 'cept for my own lousy memory, its banks low as a neap tide: ADDENDA! *angoo* thankyou, *dk* duck, *ear* ear, *fi* fish, *ow-moo* cow, and God alone knows how many more, it's coming out of my ears all the time I'm thinking about you, you'll beat us all yet. EEE*eeeeee-eee*, ish-ish. ANGOO, Angoo, angoo.

Here it nearly all is; I feel like Midas at the Mint: angoo appul Aroo babababa bar Be beebee bir blun bo boa! boat Bobbee boid boo brella brow bu burr bye-bye car cig dayn dey ding dk dog dog-woof doo dree dren dtee dwel dwelve ear e'bow ee ee! ee-aw e'even ee-ya eigh ellow e-oe eye fi file fur fy gawyee gibig har hawz hot-oo! hwingh ie-gree ish-ish kool la-la lam leg Lina lock lollee lorv Mamma Mandee mirroe mo momter moon more mou nail no nose ny Ollie oo oo-ah oi oi-ya! out ow-moo pen pl plar pomper poo pool poon pop pri-y pun rav rounabou ry s-s wi ngh Tiya Toe-ee tsin twerv twev var vor vy wall wat Wat wee wim woh! worbar wortar wun wynd yabut yap yaw Yayee yoap yop yummay zeven zhee zho zhoo zix zlar zlide zmo zo zoo zwingh

And *angoo* once again, my head's a-spin; I think you just said please.

5. Arabian Prelude to a Night

Resuming in a blue-checked washable thing called a Treas-urobe (no doubt, like Long John Silver's parrot, it once belonged to Robinson Crusoe-Kreutznaer), I snatch a look at the newspaper. Solray flame-effect electric fires, it seems, are so real they actually do fool people; Joanie Jaynes was *really* fooled, she tried to boil an egg on one. By their illusions ye shall know them.

See how it is when I'm trying to wake up? Your hair is very long in the A.M., before we draw it tight into two pony tails held by modish butterflies of white-spotted blue ribbon. Blue? No, almost black; it's hard to know in the half-light of the day or the double-brightness of the kitchen strip lighting.

It was 84° F. in Bermuda yesterday.

To wake thoroughly up, just as to get off to sleep, you wag your head violently from side to side, a perfect rhythm to brush teeth to, and thus (I think) throw more blood into the narrowest capillaries in your brain; it tells the back-of-

107

the-neck muscles to look lively while your hair streams back and forth like a mane of white raw cotton, a soft flog on my face when you stretch out beside me in bed for the first five minutes of being awake on a school morning, or, when you stand downstairs, a fickle indoor wind that sets Nosferatu on his line gently bouncing in mid-air, a preening devil in gangrene colors. Eat your cornflakes; pack that egg away. *Beebee!*

The three envelopes you flung at me ten minutes ago enclosed three bills, but the big packet is a follow-up to your request last year for information on Bermuda (which you sliced up during a wet, blustery, *Wuthering-Heights*-type afternoon). You are invited to go again at the going rate for single girls: JET IN COMFORT TO TALC-SOFT SANDS AMERICAN PLAN AND AIR CONDITIONING. Even the ice buckets stand in yet bigger ice buckets which stand in bigger bigger . . . the whole island *sits* in a mammoth ice bucket manufactured in Houston. *You* take the leaflets, all pastel littorals and bicycled-over greensward and expensive ultramarine sea, and *I'll* have the envelope—two sheets, once I've slit it, with a tough, grainy surface within, so it's almost like using a stylus over soft buff wood. For this resuming letter to y— *Ak-aruk!* Sorry, it's that so-called relaxed throat of mine climbing into the back of my nose (the cure being to gargle with port wine, but not, surely not, before the sun is up). Fumbling in a cloth inlet in Treasurobe, I come up with a pellet in foil just as you stab an egg that has waited too long and will not ochre-run. If I go out I promise to block my mouth with plaster of Paris. Now drink your *beebee* down.

"*Beebee!*" Empty cup slams down; spoon levitates, bearing with it my grandmother's initials, V.N.

"Mandy is going out in the car to school!"

"Koo-ool? Koo-ool!" That moving finger writes in mid-air, bold serif.

"Yes. School."

"Ding?" Hand-simulating it.

"No-ooooo. Out in the car to school."

"Bo?" A perfunctory *heil*-Escalator, right-handed.

"No, no. Not bo, out—"

"Kool! Kool!" You smell at my face to identify the aroma of the thing I'm sucking.

"MAN-DEE!"

You want one too. If I can find one I'll give you one. Now you have one and at once spit it out onto your egg, like a black incisor on the ploughed-up yolk. *See,* I begin to say, but you have gone off to brush your teeth, wee, be dressed in blue and white and have all that hair lashed down and then, as you begin to let develop on your sleek and minty face the sort of expression old Delius must have had when the sun coming up lit on his eyelids, put on the canvas double harness (white for girls, blue for boys) that holds in two silk purses the two sow's ears you have to wear.

Without even looking down, you switch on, rolling both 0-1-2-3-4-5 control wheels to 5 while we test each earpiece to see if the squeal is steady. A big, preparatory smile with your jaw thrust high as if to reassert your expertise, and you fix the transparent plastic earpieces in where they belong, tap once on each of the flesh-tinted buttons that come almost flush with the lobes, and immediately begin chanting to yourself while your hands (a touch lurid from purple nail varnish imperfectly mopped off with remover while you slept) check the leads and the tiny plugs which we ourselves test nightly when we unsnap earpiece from button and clean the sound-bringing holes with pipe cleaners and, if necessary, replace your tiny batteries. During the rest of

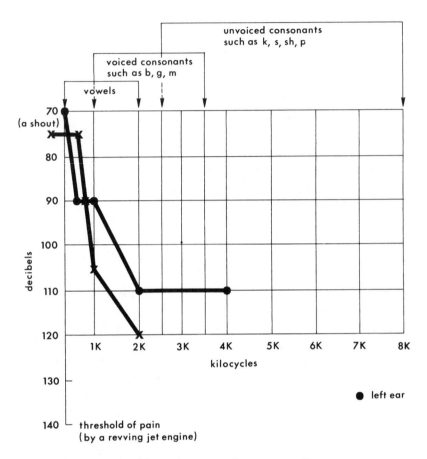

"Sound, at maximum . . ."

the day, at school and then at home again, you will adjust your equipment as you want, nonchalantly replacing an earpiece dangling from its lead after you've buffeted it loose in play, irritably stabbing a plug back home. Sound, at maximum, is the land of heart's desire you're fully wired for.

And then you go, a schoolgirl of a special kind, unable to report to us on the day's doings but usually bearing home the signs of them: teeth marks on a wrist; variegated poster color on your clothes and skin; or, more explicit, on Friday when your homework book comes with you, a fiber-pen sketch of what you did, together with a caption in ITA: "Wɛɛ went tω the ʃhops." Or: "Wɛɛ paented." It is a vacuum-quiet house without you and the conversations behind your back are very much about you: unending speculations as to what you are doing (what agile stunt you'll perpetrate today), what you'll do with your lunch, your spending money, your broad fists. No one babies you at this junior level, so I know *they*'re all man enough to give the pants of some of you a rinse through when wet or knobbly, and to receive as virtual phonemes a whole schoolday's broken winds.

At four, the majority go back into the care of the house mothers (unless it's a weekend) and you, with a few of your living-at-home contemporaries, sit in the entrance hall in a pose of meretricious languor, one foot on the floor, the other swung up on the other knee immodestly, all that's missing being an ebonite holder plugged with a red-ended black-paper Balkan Sobranie.

Two popsicles the instant you invade the car.

Your hair's come adrift and one of the butterflies has come apart; your blue panties are down to your knees; your left-hand earpiece has a splodge of red paint; your harness is askew and one of the leads now winds round your back instead of up your front. Sweat prints, a smear of pink ice cream, a nail-pale scratch, all on your face; and somehow you are steaming, ramming, ahead with yet another day's school behind you: not quite the same girl who went out this morning. *I've done it again, I've got through another,* is what your demeanor says, all punch and boisterous self-help. A full hour it takes you to unwind, zooming through all the rooms at home with a fat ice in your paw and the aids whistle-crackling as if you are tuned in to trans-

111

missions from North Borneo. But: two girls came to hold hands with you when you got there this morning; your Pakistani touched you a furtive goodbye. You have been social. You have won again. Now you can cut Bermuda up with your best scissors.

If only there *were* the perfect place; if only *there* were the perfect place, only half real with Prussian blue umbrellas marching muffle-spiked so as not to bruise the flour-soft salmon-pink sand and the sea turned up loud so you could hear it and even, way out, old brine shrimp *Artemia salina,* swiveling his belly ever upward because he steers by the direction of the falling light, *en route* to lodge in your hand so you'll think he's the sea creature long lost from 101 Toys in One Box that came rattling in in the mail a Christmas ago, and then he swims off in a sulk, you bumped one of his semi-spherical compound eyes and he's now like the cross-eyed double-seeing lion in *Daktari.* . . . Good thinking, Artemia Salina, you know your Francis Bacon all right, who said, "The subtlety of Nature transcends in many ways the subtlety of man." Yes, but Confucius he say, No shrimp transcend subtly or otherwise unsubtle bang-bash-clout-clamp-clutch-caress of Manda hand; only Boyd.

Beg pardon, I intend no caricature; it all comes of your being away during the day, just as that bulldozed-watercress feeling comes from your being home at weekends. It's hard, considering your extraordinary multiple personality and the unusual feats you perform in so everyday a way, *not* to mythologize you in your absence: aggrandize you, magnify you, Alexander-the-Great you, Eric-the-Red you, Ivan-the-Terrible you, Joan-of-Arc you, Robin-Hood you, Louis-XIV you, Marco-Polo you, Last-of-the-Mohicans you, Paul-Revere you.

Helen-Keller you.

You stare at me as if I'm simple, wanting to inflict on

you prowesses, gifts, knacks, and transubstantial wizardries you don't even know about as first-hand hokum. Why tell me all this? you scoff; it's telling told by an idiot. Well, I just see how the ingenuities of your rituals and your games might catapult you into something else: your mantras into a Veda that is beyond all encyclopediae, Britannicae or Americanae; your infatuation with water, its tricks, its hydraulic kinks, into a post-Noachic flood; your flawless rocking into a new form of stand-up sleep; your private words into a basic Cosmispeak transmittable to Mars; your middle-distance observations into the first eyeball accounts of freaked-out intergalactic visitors who have invisibly been here since the first Knight was photographed while being so dubbed by a British monarch with a sword, all the anti-imperialist newspapers publishing the picture as one of an execution: Queen Beheads World Traveler. . . . I mean, Manda, unicorns and manticores and centaurs and phoenixes and gryphons and dragons and Rumpelstiltskin and Beauty and the Beast and Rip Van Winkle who heard the thunder of Hendrick Hudson and his crew bowling ninepins. The ground glass of optical illusion is all I'm left with if I try explaining. I'll lay it all at the door of a mysteriousness about you which many would think irrelevant beside your learning to solve a quadratic equation, parse Genesis' first sentence, sing an exact Middle C, but which I myself have learned from and which your rituals defy us to explore.

Soon after wolfing your home-from-school meal—sausages and eggs and French-fried potatoes made almost inedibly tangy with great globs of Düsseldorf mustard, or a roast chicken which you squat on the floor with and tear apart red-handedly where it sits on the coffee table, or meat pies that you lackadaisically eviscerate while tossing the pastry away like refuse—you race outside to swing and slide, heedless of weather. And someone has to follow, not

113

only to shove the swing seat and chase you up the slide's ladder, but, if it's wet out (*wat*), to site a pad of cardboard at the slide's foot so you won't muddy your pants, or to peel away from either structure offending leaves and blades of grass which the weather has plastered on the struts and which provoke you into a special Get-Off-Mah-Laynd anger. The same person must also take outside with him a supply of Kleenex to wipe your boots with, and your knees and the rungs of the ladder. Mud offends you so much that if it's on your boots (especially the white ones) you will not walk or, if on the ladder, will not mount or, if on the swing seat, will not sit. It's just another of your contradictions: in many ways a lord of misrule, you are also a demon for neatness, and you achieve the latter by subjecting us and the world to cast-iron procedures, to vary which is to invite a relentless onslaught. Only one variation in a hundred gives you pause and then wins your patronizing smile that acknowledges ingenuity without encouraging further experiment. Lobster turning red when cooked is exactly the sort of constant which, on a whim, you'd like to change, then keep it that way; and heaven help whoever could not revise the natural-culinary universe to that extent, once your mind was made up.

In from the garden, you break into a rock, left foot to right with the insteps rising an inch only, until one of us interrupts and rocks with you, making it social. At this you giggle, having, for all your compulsions, some idea of what adults are and are not likely to do. Nonetheless, you will always join in if we offer to rock; indeed, you come and stand on my shoes if I so much as shuffle feet to vary the position I'm standing in. The merest sign and you are heavily on the front of my feet, and the pair of us are going: left-right, left-right, a rhythm that has now worked its way so far into my system I now quite regularly rock in my own right—in my office, in the bathroom, waiting for planes or trains. A bizarre sight it must be, an apparently grownup square swaying with mechanical regularity as if alienated from all conventional time-killing techniques and, being incapable of exact interpretation, dismissed as drunk, spastic, or a victim of combat fatigue. Whatever onlookers happen to think, they don't realize three things: I've been brainwashed; so far as I know, I rock quite deliberately (whereas some folks don't know when they're finger tapping and toe waggling or giving out with a twelve-tone hum); and to rock is soothing anyway, almost as much as Madeira, a neck rub, or midnight movies watched but expendably forgotten come the next day.

Then the chase with heathen faces, you forever exhorting me to leers more fiendish than I've yet accomplished and my only recourse being illustrated books on gargoyles, on masks in the Congo and New Guinea, or the simple addition to my face of Kleenex ropes dangling from the nostrils, celluloid fangs that droop down onto my chin, and rubber masks from which a bleeding eyeball is dangling without actually being loose; as well as—tricky—cotton-wool beards and sideburns unfortunately overlapping with Santa Claus the Beard. Hooting for innocuous horror, you reveal a taste for the gross, the grotesque, the garish, with which I sympathize more than many people would, I having always been willing to trade a hundred Gainsboroughs for one Goya, five hundred Wyeths for one Brueghel, a thousand Manets for one Bosch. I'm not, I'm sure, the only student who repeatedly fell asleep, trying to read the anemic drivel of the Galsworthys of this world when, damnit, there was Rabelais and Nashe and Joyce to go at! And then Rimbaud, Gogol, and Beckett. End of name dropping except to recommend, as a man on his children, Henry Miller. It's bath time, once an almost open-ended procedure entailing (you

115

recall?) a preliminary tarantella in the nude, then water sports with a host of floating toys including water pistols, long plastic bottles, and the three-foot doll, and interminable conclusions when you had to station a dozen articles *just so* on the bath tidy, wash the soap and then redeposit it in the dish of water where it dissolved overnight, and arrange around the room all those paper model baths whose taps were rolled-paper tubes.

A good hour it took, all that, whereas bathing now is a perfunctory business conducted merely to keep alive a chunk of ancient fun; a ritualistic, hydropathic anti-world no longer, in which, like the children going to bed in Cocteau's film *Les Enfants Terribles,* you set every possession on the bath as they themselves set theirs on the eiderdown (as you now on *yours,* every eiderdown being a magic carpet for a perhaps irrevocable voyage). Now, sluicing only, for commonplace reasons, is enough to keep memory bright. There's only one thing of your *manie* remaining: your mother must, simply must, be in the bath with you, mostly as a victim for what seems to be your version of judo practice (you being a regular and overjoyed spectator at exhibitions of both judo and karate). But I no longer think of Lake Geneva, Loch Ness, or Marineland of the Pacific as your only possible haven. Water, for you, has found its own level; you use it, then move on, cool-headed as Archimedes.

After bath, you situate yourself in front of a large plate holding potato salad and fresh boiled ham. This waits while you devour minestrone soup and/or ravioli and settle for this purpose into your most comfortable position: flat on back in bathrobe, one leg cocked upon the other and stirring the air with that inverted slipper perched on your toes, your spoon held aloft like an assegai, a hand mirror, or a lorgnette. No wonder the front of your nightgown and robe

116

are encrusted with a dark red that pales as it hardens. And, of course, your hair, being no longer bound, sits in the line of fire (or fallout) too, all while you flaunt the hairless pear of your *mons pubis* before the ghosts who hunch and trot on the finger-smudged TV screen; or the moon already showing while the sun dwindles.

If you've had a trying day, you'll probably have an open umbrella in one hand (no effort for strong you to hold it thus), extolling it with your eyes, much, say, as Cleopatra might if she had a chance look at her Needle on the bank of the Thames. Dawdling over food as you do, you have time to do the jigsaw of the playground (you first of all put together the pieces that make up the slide therein) or to command us to draw and cut out slides, saws, or escalators. Always the same unspoken prayer: let no piece of that puzzle be missing, or you'll raise, murder, and rebury Cain without pause until it's found or we have phoned the manufacturers at home to send in a replacement by helicopter. As soon as the puzzle is done, you bestow upon it a smile of temporarily benevolent approval (it obeyed, it occupied all of its own space) and at once dismantle it, pour it back into its plastic bag and restore it to its place in the liquor cupboard, all such places being as sacrosanct as White House parking privileges and pew protocol in Westminster Abbey. All this time, I've been forgetting to mention, you take desultory little swigs from the first round of *beebee,* a mug in either hand, one of tea, one of pop—unless you've, as the French say, "subtilized" some beer or wine. That you do not smoke during this curiously Arabian prelude to a night—in which you figure as odalisque, sultana, and dancing girl all in one—I am somewhat relieved. A hubble-bubble wouldn't be a surfeiting diversion, I'm sure, any more than the various errands you undertake—to the light switches, kitchen, front door, toilet, phone, TV controls, and even the bookshelves—distract you from your main purpose of not going to bed. Always detected at it, you're never made to pay. Time gained is one of your forms of contraband.

All this time, too, we have been keeping tabs on your mood, alert for the moment when you lie full length behind your mother on the sofa and eat your apples. Once or twice you come to where I sit bemused and ask for *rounabou* or sit on my knee for a song:

> Where's that little Manda gone?
> Where's thàt little Man-da?
> Where's that little—
> There's that little—
> *Here's* that little Manda!

A voluptuary grin from you confirms that you know where you are, and we repeat the song with variants, but always to the same brisk jog of a rhythm. Whoever gets up to move out of the room, you follow at speed, administering little valedictory slaps upon the hands of those remaining behind or heel tapping such of the furniture as has also stayed put. The world and we begin to drift once you are in position, abstractedly gnawing, and the lull sometimes lasts half an hour—and even longer when, very tired after a day of steady brainwork, you fall asleep with a slice of apple in hand. Then it comes to carrying you upstairs. Otherwise, you utter one *beebee,* a deferential murmur but just as unquestionable as a factory whistle or a sonic boom. This means the evening is over, no matter what anyone else wants to do, and the milky bedtime drink has to be prepared. It is, and in the meantime you have probably gone up to lie on the bed and wait, your eyes on the ceiling and, on your face (if you are well), a look of beatific amusedness or (if you are unwell) of *rerum horror* that doesn't belong to a child at all.

In bed, propped up alongside your mother on pillows and some by now rather spoiled-looking velvet cushions, you seem royally secure; and it is now that the rituals become baroque. Once the umbrellas of the day have been hung on any available handle, and the toy watches and paper slides and plastic aircraft have been aligned on the dressing table like offerings on an altar for Narcissus, and the rubber sheet beneath you (just in case) has been groomed straight, you take the *beebee* mug, rotate the spoon, and wait for us to begin with the three dogs who dominate this pantomime. The first of these, in pink plastic, whom you have fed from your bedtime mug for at least two years, we have to balance upside down along the bridge of your nose while you more or less hold your breath. Since he's an ear missing, you have to tilt your head to allow for his imbalance, but you strike the right attitude at once and close your eyes. Now the other two dogs, which collapse altogether when we press the bottom plate up into the base and spring up rigid again when we release it, come wobbling and mowing toward your forehead, making mock sallies nearer and nearer until one or the other dislodges the pink dog and you chuckle with husky glee at his fall.

At this point you take a gulp of *beebee* and feed all three dogs, who in turn tap your lips with theirs: milk kisses, until we set the odd-dog-out upon your nose again and dislodge him once again. Once more you feed the dogs, offering them a full spoon to sip from or plunging their heads into the mug. Here I must confess to having done something underhand, something you noticed but decided not to protest about. One of the two dog-toppling dogs lost literally his head and I used some wadding to jam it onto his tail, so we now have a very long neck and only a short tail, and a head where no head ever was before. You scrutinize this Dr. Moreau–like shift with constant but cordial astonishment, caught (no intention of mine) between your love of the grotesque and your love of uniformity. Two years ago, I think, you would have flung the deformed dog from you in a fit of rampant perfectionism, made me feel like someone Boris Karloff should play, and insisted—in a cooler moment —on an immaculate repair. Such is the measure of the advances you have made.

We were feeding the dogs a second time. After this, you drink a few drops more yourself and then pass the mug sideways away from you to whoever is there to receive it and without so much as a glance in that direction. You always assume that the world is intricately ready to cope with your next motion: you don't look, call a warning, or ask; you expect others to know the ritual as well as you do, even when you've changed it without notice. Assuming that the mug is safely out of the way, like the movement of the third floor backward, we can get on with wrapping each dog in tissues until only the muzzles show. The pink one we slide under the strap of one of a pair of plastic high-heeled shoes in which I've seen you totter about with made-up face like Alice aping the young Moll Flanders, and the other two we put to bed together in the other shoe under toe strap and heel strap respectively. Each dog "kisses" you goodnight, is kissed in return, and we rock them to sleep while you sing "see-saw" several times. That's all of that.

One pillow from behind you now goes by your side for you to hug, and you lie down, one hand tousling the hair on my head (which you haul down for just this soothing finale), the other holding your mother's left hand as anchor. Sometimes, but not often, you kiss the photographs of yourself goodnight as well, but always when I stand up with throbbing scalp and bend again, this time without kneeling, you get a fit of giggles in anticipation of the goodnight kiss.

120

I plant this kiss, usually receiving a clout from your free hand on the way up, and then make the "sleep" sign: head sideways against hands put palms-together. After a clear *bye-bye,* another giggle or two, you "make the mustache" (as we say), which means crossing long tails of your hair along your upper lip, thus masking your eyes. Your mother sees you into the last stages, during which you do a somnolent head rock, and out I go.

Usually you are asleep within ten minutes and a faint sweat speckles your forceful, wide, and beautiful face. In the distant-seeming past, you crowded your bed inside with golliwogs and outside with an abundance of tools, jigsaw puzzles, and umbrellas. No longer: in fact, all the golliwogs have been dumped in a heap in the corner of the room, only one, the biggest (whose arrival from my mother once checked an hour-old tantrum dead in its tracks), being allowed in bed at all, and he only in the daytime; no doubt to keep goblins at bay and the big bed friendly.

At weekends that big bed becomes the scene of an elaborate levee whose centerpiece is a tray holding a teapot, some of the best china, and thin-cut, thick-buttered slices of bread which you nibble with absent-minded fervor, gazing out at the day you don't have to enter unless you want to. You may or may not decide to go *bo*-ing (Saturday) or to the swings in the playground (Sunday). If you do go out, you visit the shops and usually emerge with a clock, a jigsaw puzzle, or a plane kit hugged to you, this last to be built and parked on its nameplated Perspex stand in the increasingly chaotic airfield which the house is. Only rarely do you launch into (as only yesterday) a two-hour tirade of screaming for something you cannot have, concupiscence in its Old Testament sense feeding on its own surfeit; in that instance, a piccolo, for which you don't have the word but which, with exaggerated balloon-blowing mouth and fingers rippling

121

along an invisible tube, you stated exactly enough. In fact there was no money, a jigsaw of an Irish fishing village (two hundred daunting, tiny pieces all looking alike) and a kit for a North American A3J Vigilante Carrier-Based Attack Bomber having taken almost all. And even if there had been, as soon as you got the piccolo you would have wanted a doll, a zip gun, a bow-and-arrow set complete with roundel targets, and even—were it available—a mini Cape Kennedy just as complete with space vehicles, Florida sunshine, and the parked cars of a hundred spectators all sucking Saturn-shaped cones of rainbow ice cream.

In the world's inexhaustible supply of dry goods you have a negligent confidence, as in my supply of money, that paltry-looking tin and paper you see people pushing across counters and having repeatedly pushed back to them (only slightly different) while you, contemptuously impatient with such folderol, ogle the goods on the shelves. The milled rims of certain coins have no more meaning for you than have bouncing checks; and yet your attitude is "fiduciary" in the widest sense, reposing on trust, so much so that you might be excused if you thought you could buy an aircraft carrier with a few *ees*.

Entering a shop you are prehensile-bold, quick to amass on the counter the loot you fancy. You fetch it from window displays as well as distant shelves and display cases, which discomfits some of the salespeople, who seem to wonder if this mightn't develop into the latest form of conning or even holdup, but never those in the two small places with deaf owners. They shout a greeting to you, come out from behind and crouch or kneel, watching your mouth as you forbearingly say something to appease them while your empress complex gets to work through your eyes, ranging the displays for goods new and familiar. Here, you are given balloons out of fellowship; elsewhere, I think, to keep you

122

from screaming when denied or when just covetously honking with your arm at point. One day, an oldish man in a very expensive hand-stitched suit set his palm on your head, and we thought he was deaf too; but no, he was a pediatrician who at once recognized your noises and was glad to see you out and about at your handicapped purchasing; a small envoy to conventional minds on behalf of the thousands no one ever sees or wants to see, such as your spastic contemporary at school who, having the independent determination to put on and remove her own shoes (after a few fumbles), helps *you* with yours and even, by indirections finding the direction out, hangs up your coat for you, usually at the third try, at which she smiles and then the nerve tugs the side of her mouth right up, stunting the smile but not her mood. You have learned to copy this interfered-with smile, assuming the superficies of a complaint that isn't yours, and she in turn has begun to embark on a campaign of much more extensive smiling. You, you may not know, are the ace of smilers; your days brim with joys to which you know no alternative.

Weekdays, you mix; weekends, which exhaust us but in a satisfying way, you retire like Stephen Dedalus to your tower, where you and I do two things mainly. Either we make collages with poster colors, sand, string, grit, pepper, salt, crumbs, Kleenex, coriander, and minced garlic—anything at hand—and even sometimes cut the paper and weave the good bits of the not-so-good collages over the bad and behind the good bits of the others. Always you begin with a heavy wash and then, while it's wet, paint planes and slides in that thick-pigmented, dense-cloud style that is distinctively yours. Any contribution of mine which doesn't fit into what you think your scheme is you paint out or, if it's a piece of string or something I've stuck into the viscous puddle, fish it out and sling it behind you, thus ornamenting

123

much innocent wall or glass or bookbinding with (most often, it seems) canary yellow and Ostwald black. Thus a room becomes a kaleidoscope.

Or, when I myself do most of the work, we stick flat plastic pieces together to make three-dimensional models of Vought Corsairs (which the Japanese called "Whistling Death"), F4U's (ours always being a replica of Colonel Gregory "Pappy" Boyington's plane), Avro Ansons and Kawasaki Hiens and North American Vigilantes aforementioned and Messerschmitt Bf 109 E-3's which are venomous-nosed pencils with obsolete-looking tailplane struts. I build the tricky parts, but you fit the simpler components together, hold the fuselage halves together while the polystyrene cement sets, and then fly them with the mount stem pinched between finger and thumb. The plan and the instructions I have to read in haste, sometimes having to guess a detail of the construction, such is your impatience to see the finished article; and the transfer insignia go on almost at random, soon (anyway) to be reduced by frequent Manda-handling to a mess of stars, decals, swastikas, red suns, and sundered fuselage flashes. But there are some things that can't be taken away, such as the polyglot, quiet clinch of triumph you find on the Messerschmitt building sheet at the end of all the instructions:

IHR MESSERSCHMITT-MODELL IST NUN FERTIGGESTELLT.

VOTRE MESSERSCHMITT EST MAINTENANT TERMINE (which doesn't sound as if the same thing has been accomplished).

MODELLEN MESSERCHMITT AR NU FARDIG. Huh? How's that? Well, whoopeepee! And, just because the model *is* as complete as I shall ever have a chance to make it, I chant these linguistic marvels out to you and you laugh as if ice cream had just arrived via Telstar. We sniff styrene glue and the languages go to our heads and lift us to an ozone ceiling

124

studded with plastic birds which, although scaled down to 1:72, breathe a condensed oxygen that has three atoms to a molecule instead of the usual two. Intoxicating, especially for grounded astronauts.

But some things we do not do. The BOX TOP PAINTING YOU CAN FRAME we cut out with scissors instead. The EX-CITING FEATURES—HINGED CANOPIES—VERTICAL AND HORIZONTAL STABILIZERS THAT PIVOT—JET ENGINES RE-MOVABLE—we stick tight, thus dooming the crews (always for some reason Mongolian-featured) to suffocation and the plane to nil-maneuverability, its engines being impossible to service anyway. Nor do we cut out and wear the U.S. Naval Aviator Wings three-quarters of an inch across that some kits provide (BOAC gives real metal aviator's wings to children passengers, anyway, and United Arab Airlines a scarab charm to all). Moving parts don't excite us much, so we don't "cement dee locators" and other such arcane bits of plastic into the positions indicated IF UNDERCAR-RIAGE IS REQUIRED IN LANDING POSITION. Our air fleet never lands and never takes off, but flies non-stop until disintegration.

Nor, as we are told to, do we paint on splinter or mottle camouflages, or paint the exhausts black or dark brick red, or ever even buy the "paint-set enamel" colors of the only type we are supposed to use on any given model, or apply cement sparingly (our planes have blisters and warts), or trim excess plastic from all parts before assembling (our fuselages especially have sharp non-aerodynamic edges and open up into gaps where the fit is bad), or keep cement off the transparencies (our cockpit canopies are too smudged to be seen through). We don't even do things in the right order, so a good many instrument panels and rudder bars and other such buff's pedantries get left over and can't be installed afterward. And, worst of all, we get cement all

125

over us, on skin and clothing and on the furniture (which it leaves with grainy pockmarks). So we have perhaps no right to send in the complaint slips to the manufacturers, not even when we find projections for which there are no slots (or vice versa), pilots too big for their cockpits or their seats, or transfers that disintegrate in the lukewarm water like the mummy's hand in those old horror films. Without knowing, I once went out with F4U accidentally transferred to the ball of my thumb and not mirrorwise either. When they cling to the skin with adhesive side outwards, you can often get them back to where they belong without tearing them; but not otherwise: better to wear them and win a colorful reputation.

Special mention in our dispatches must be made of one recent plane whose elegant lines you sit or lie and study— peruse—for hours on end, tilting it only a fraction of a degree at a time. The SUD-BAC Concorde, both French and British, flies at 1,450 miles an hour, some of it being built in Toulouse and some in Bristol. Completed sections are shipped across the Channel, and why not? There are still French onion sellers riding their bicycles around the South of England and French chefs who can't get by without Worcestershire sauce. Your own model has Air France insignia (F-BZBH) but, because we neglected to affix the windows from inside before cementing the fuselage shell together, British ventilation in the form of very fast and very unbreathable air. Which is fatal, not only for such usual reasons as decompression, but because of the heat generated during supersonic flight—why, even the cockpit windows are completely shielded once the plane has gained height. Some plane, getting you across the Atlantic so fast you can do the round trip in a day with plenty of time, depending which side you go to, to silt up your tastebuds and stomach with English coffee or to chomp on a hot

126

pastrami on rye on a bench somewhere on Riverside Drive, to marvel at the unmortared stone walls of Derbyshire or to recoil from the honk-honk-bray-blah-blah WE'VE BEEN AND GONE AND DONE IT WE'RE TELLING YOU of American automobiles celebrating a wedding. All in a day . . . But of such marvelous voyages, and of even better ones, more later. For now, our international anthology of an air force in its naked ping-pong-ball whites, graphite grays, and nacreous greens, pinch-snouted like the fish called the muskellunge or pronged like the marlin, with not a scale of paint to peel off, holds intruders at bay and makes even the residents watch their step lest a carelessly wielded fork snap off an aerial mast, a tailwheel unretracted, or, worse, sunder the plane's pedestal itself, thus switching on your own Rolls-Royce turbine scream.

Planes hold firm, just below slides, and below planes there's a whole range of steady devotions that proves you a connoisseur of life's footnotes; indeed, a footnote maker. You pause in the street to admire the architecture and the flagrant nuisance of a pile of horse dung, at which you point with prankish leers, sometimes almost kneeling, the better to voluptuously disapprove of it. At all cameras you snatch, heedless of levers and knobs, anxious as a superstitious Arab, Turk, or Ethiopian to haul out of its bowels the pseudo-Mandy within, whom you will then clip out in silhouette and thus rescue from the background's demonic hold. If rebuked, you draw three-foot-high caricatures of your rebukers on cardboard (sometimes even offering whoever it is a crayon with which to touch up his own image) and then pound a succession of fastidiously enunciated *Nos* at the face. Also, to soft-soap someone, you insist he draw *him*self for *you*. Given a Lord & Taylor's white summer hat with crisp and welted brim (or any other hat), you invert it and fill it with water. As if you have read T. S. Eliot on

127

the still center of the turning world, you set your finger on the red cap in the center of the washing machine's spin disc, the finger encased in a celluloid mouthpiece from a cigarillo. Angry, or in livid expostulation, you thump your hand flat on the table, so hard the plates jump clear. Having wet yourself, you sneak away with the face of a nun hastening to an assignation and wash out your pants. You tend to be stiff-legged, flattish-footed when walking, and choose to walk that way because (I think) you enjoy the increased jolt which a footstep sends up a stiffened leg from a planked-down sole (compensatory sensation again). You very often smile in between people, directing the smile exactly to where no one is and maliciously enjoying their bafflement as, after excluding themselves from this favor, they turn round to confront—no one at all; nothing; and when they turn front again, there you are smiling ironically right at both of them, in tease, so that they dismiss what they originally thought they saw. Having an itchy back (often), you rake it with a table fork and leave it with comforting red weals. Whenever you call a thing by the wrong name, you laugh like mad, just as if it were all deliberate (it sometimes is). In simi-lar mood you pretend to listen for the sounds (always the alarm, you do not know they tick) of your wooden or your plastic clocks, or even to wind them up. To see if anyone will try to stop you, you plunge a lollipop into a jar of fac-tory mayonnaise and lick away the cream with stage-man-aged lip smacking. We have found you wearing a sanitary towel inside your pants. You possess yourself of, and stick up the front of your sweater, plastic nipple blinds which have come loose from your big sister's party dress. When busy, you tell us to keep away or out by extending your arm with a flat-palmed traffic signal on the end of it. Invariably, what was improvised yesterday—gold foil from a cigarette package wrapped round your VC-10 airliner as if Midas

128

himself had laid on hands; crayoned cardboard clock or human faces to stick on the real clocks; birds made by tying knots in table napkins—you undo today, these things being expendable or transitory whereas others—the gargoyles on the line, the Polaroid photograph by your bed of you in a straw hat looking like a contumacious gaucho, the Hong Kong dogs who attend your goings-to-bed—are not: not yet, anyway.

Inexplicably you slap your own arm and reprimand yourself in front of mirrors. You pinch the palms of your hands as if desperate for any sensation, even pain; and then you pinch ours, anxious to give us the same pleasure. Given chance, you will address at length the cut-off heads of cod and hake, mocking through mime the dead eyes and the stiff gape of the mouths. Lost in some memory of actual fishing, you slip several jelly babies (chewable two-inch miniatures which are now manufactured with navels and are to be found in all colors but blue) into a plastic bag filled with water and wander around, showing your catch. Having, at six, allowed us to deprive you of your real pacifier, you ridicule the oral weakness of it all by shoving sugar ones into our own mouths. You lick the carving knife if you get an opportunity. You paint the ice cubes with gorgeous colors and then replace them in the freezer trays. You examine suitcases and apply Band-aids where they are worn or scored. You insist that we unpack everything on arrival back from anywhere and so hope to impede further departures. If you suspect I'm off to catch a plane or a train, you sit on a case to stop me from going. You shriek if people don't sit with their backs firmly against the backs of chairs (never, we've learned, lean forward, especially while you are eating; be waxworks instead). You raise your shoulders almost to your ears in a laconic, Marcel Marceau shrug. At all TV speakers wearing earpieces you exclaim in hardboiled sympathy, indicating, however, they should have two, not one. You hit us for not doing something you can hit us for. You scream for me to make you a cardboard slide, but won't free my hands when I try to cut. Every morning you select a prized possession to take to school (whence few things return or return intact), and I have to pretend to begin repairing it just before you leave, which makes you almost as happy as having it with you and much happier than having it bullied away from you in the junior playground by some rapacious handicapped lout who hasn't been taught any better. Strangely, you don't practice your judo at school, almost as if you feel that only adults are strong enough to withstand it without mortal injury. To fight back is one of the things it hasn't yet occurred to you to do consistently. Perhaps we shall have to take a hint from Spain, where the matadors practice in the slaughter-houses on live cows, the head being held still, of course, by dedicated helpers who eat and breathe the bullshit mystique of it all. Never quite knowing why certain things are done to, for, or even by you, you try to be tolerant because you want to please: being bullied and having injections both hurt, and how are you to know the difference?

On second thought, though, after one experience with one sadistic dentist (a Caliban of the needle who wanted to make a fourth attempt to hit the right blood vessel and assumed that, because you are deaf, you can be punctured like a Sunday joint, being inarticulate), you find bullying easier to take. You end up, more or less, and dentists apart, in the position ascribed by John Cowper Powys to Shake-speare as "the true . . . way wherewith to take life": and that is combining "skepticism of everything with credulity about everything." The irony is that the very degree of sub-missiveness required of you to protect you is just the thing that reduces the limited life you have to the insipid minimum. And I myself feel ambivalent in this: I want you to be anything but passive, but I also want you to survive. Once, as a quite small boy, I responded to a bit of school bullying with my own specially selected chunk of iron, for which feat I was sent home with a letter, to my father's delight. The other boy bled very much from a split scalp, and I would do it again with the same accurate aim and the same saintly sense of justification. That there are degrees of fighting back it's hard to explain to an almost overwhelmed undersized boy; and how to explain it to a handicapped girl I just don't know. But teach it to you in mime I will, if I can.

Wandering again in our ozone-atmosphered maze; but whatever I say is news to you. If you were here right now, I'd fuel up my best Dylan Thomas voice and chant to you the French ode on the steak-sauce label, making my own free-verse pauses:

> *Cette sauce de haute qualité*
> *est un mélange de fruits orientaux,*
> *d'épices et de vinaigre de malt.*
> *Elle est absolument pure*
> *et ne contient aucune matière*
> > *colorante synthétique. . . .*

Or, with almost identical results for you (that wide, complicitous grin), I'd render it in a parsonical falsetto, seeking to attain the authentic nasal vibrations that for some bizarre harmonic reason fuse treble tremolo with self-righteousness, especially (as I recall from performances I was forced to hear between babyhood and boyhood—not long) in those parsons who, at a certain crucial point, can soar to the pure soprano of a little choirboy (bereft of all fleshly timbre) and then slither down the scale back into putrid lewdness, their voices broken a second time, but this time as minds

131

are broken, by the Ajax-cleanser radiance of a converted Adam's apple. A dying fall into *amen* as the chafed throat lowers over the gloss-linen collar, white as Charles Baudelaire's lace cuffs.

Eeeeee, you begin to plead. *More.* So off we go, in a non-Lydian mode somewhere between *hwyl* and descant: *ni aucun agent de conservation artificiel*

<pre>
                                    ciel! Ee
                              fi   e
        a-   va   ti   ee
    cun gent de   ser   tion ar   men.
ni au-   con
</pre>

Up and down, you see, like what I've just found: a trampoliner upside-down in a newspaper picture, with a church spire in the background, and he is impaled on it right through his throat at what seems to be a height of two hundred feet, such are the accidents of press photography. Better, my girl, to be quasi-impaled on a spire than to have an eagle pecking at your liver, especially when it grows whole and edibly pulpy again each night—new every morning, like the *pâté* in the good delicatessens. Some eagles have it made and some make their own. Some, like the big brass polished eagles that hump Bibles on their backs in churches, needn't stir; but others eat blood-flavored dust, like all those eagles that André Gide wanted to commandeer when he said *il faut avoir un aigle*—you simply have to have an eagle—and you could see that he thought all worthwhile men of letters wouldn't function at all if they weren't being pecked at, not hen-pecked and therefore all goosefleshed, but eagle-chewed, whereas all those eagles ever got was livers like balloons loaded with baking powder. First catch your eagle. . . .

I sometimes, when I feel low or have what I call the coffee jitters (which don't always come from drinking my favorite imported Colombian but from another caffeine called anticipation-of-your-future), think *you* are *my* eagle. **Don't** lose your temper, I don't think it for long; and, anyway, you've pecked more out of your mother (there are no medals for being pecked, so hardly anybody knows) than out of me, and you are more majestic than predatory. As you see, the bile boils up and we could get damned close to quarreling, especially when I estimate the honest chances of your quelling me with a misquote from Gide written in lipstick across a two-page spread ripped out of *Elle* (or *Luie* or *El*—whatever it might be by then) and sent postage-due, incorrectly postal-coded from some college with a dragon president who yelled Hit the Road when the visiting speaker tried to bring his children for breakfast into the dining room only the morning after he'd pronounced on Diagnostic Metaphors in the haiku of Samuel Beckett. Tweeded women come and go, but only the tweed lasts. You could always wire me something lunatic:

> just discovered coffee from *qahweh* from Turk. from Arab. STOP compare *yahweh* STOP have switched to philology STOP a house not a home but a café maybe STOP leaving for Cape Wrath tonight STOP unsigned.

I am reminded—well, of two things:

> From ghoulies and ghosties and long-leggety beasties,
> And things that go bump in the night,
> Good Lord, deliver us!

And then this shameless puerile ditty from the Great Hunger:

> Honey, when you vomit,
> Save the biggest bits for me;
> I know gentility condemns it,
> But it's true econom-ee.

Between ourselves, it must be awful to be that poor, with hardly a Space Patrol sugar cigarette to your name, or even a Quiz Nougat, Raspberry Flavor, that asks you on the wrapper, "Is Ceylon in the Northern or Southern Hemisphere?" The answer, "Northern," is inside in mirror-printed capitals. That answer would have been better halfway down the nougat, but that's not how they do these things: Creem-Arrow toffee, Jelly Babies and Thirst Quencher sherbet, they all do the same. Keep you from answering.

After flying on one of those great-circle routes our eagles are coming back to us again. The message they bring, minus its claws, is that I'd be awfully glad if, one day, you didn't write a letter or send a wire, all that remote stuff, but just sauntered across the room one day with a mouthful of nougat ice cream toffee sherbet peppermint lozenges nuts garlic clove cold lamb hot radish raw cabbage cool *pâté* bananaskins Kleenex eagles' feathers and said only, "Why don't you ever shave?"

I would then use with you, happily on slide or swing seat, any oven cleanser to which I'm allergic, having had a year's dermatitis from it, when my fingers were always bleeding under and from under the Band-aids. I'd even try to relight those indoor fireworks you wanted to "wind" again as soon as they'd burned out: the charred black plume-on-wire that is the end of a sparkler; the dot of black dust that was a white pill called the North Pole and for a few seconds flared iceberg electric blue; the dry ashes, but still in coils, of Snakes in the Grass that spewed and wriggled moltenly out of a tiny stud of chemical stuck on a card; the defunct nose of the elephant that curled forward as if there were a snake charmer behind it; thinner than matchsticks, the white twig-cigarettes in the clown's mouth that puffed and puffed; the exploding tongue of another clown, the thing we lit being a short length of cap-gun ammunition pasted against his mouth; the Flashing Lighthouse that became a knot of pure light and stayed on my retina fifteen minutes after it had become a cinder.

I'd climb up the house painter's ladders with you, behind you; spring around in Hush Puppies just as if we lived in a commercial. I'd actually make you some deep-fried batter balls, which is what they threw in New Orleans to Hush the Puppies around the fried-fish stalls when they were going half mad with the aromas of fish in hot fat mixed with the aromas of the comparatively cool Gulf of Mexico. You— who take a loaf to feed the inland gulls with, who rock your head side to side like the cobra charmers of the Deccan, whom I interrupt in your non-stop vaudeville by thumping my heel on the floor (no use to call when your back is turned), whom I meet in my mind's eye at all your ages, those gone and those to come, and then find right at hand your paradoxical, jaunty self in one of your thousand roles —you, as Miss Chatterbox, I'd celebrate in one blasphemous hyperbole. *Stop evolution now,* I'd yell at your first five-word question, *it's all evolved!*

6. Refund from Alpha 3

Play truant with you? Of course. Come, let's ride a painted elephant into the Palace of Amber; let's doss down in the bedchamber of an absentee Maharajah, play tag in the checkered courtyard where the emperor Akbar used to play chess with inert slave girls for pieces, bathe in the sun on templed beaches, or, if it's summer, let's to the hill resorts, having left behind all our dangerous drugs, live plants, gold coins, gold and silver bullion and silver-coins-not-in-current-use, at the Head Police Office in Bombay or the Talkatora Barracks in New Delhi. Two things out of three in India are called Victoria, so let's feel free to be Victorian-regal ourselves in Simla Mussoorie Nainital Darjeeling Shillong Ootacamund Kodaikanal Pachmarhi the Kulu and Kashmir Valleys and Mount Abu munching our cakes frosted with gold and silver where even the water has a bottled vintage. . . .

Come join us on the Magnificent Holiday, that's what the hostess in her Persian-carpeted cloth-of-gold sari says in the

136

folder. View by boat the burning and bathing ghats of the holy Ganges and the dazzling peaks of the Himalayas (Hi-MARlayas!), gape at shapes in the Phirezeshah Mehta Topiary Gardens, become fertile at the *lingam* shrine on Elephanta Island, transfer to the seaside resort of JUHU BEACH (Sun'n Sand Hotel) and Be At Leisure there before whizzing off by air to Udaipur (Lake Palace Hotel) to cruise by launch on Pichola Lake visiting more and more palaces and, oh so soon, the Palace of Winds and by sunset the Taj Mahal after which 64,000 restaurants are named, the deserted city of Fatehpur Sikri, fragile as flaking rust, the buried city of Sarnath, the precious stone market in Kathmandu, the Buddhist temple Swayambunath two and a half thousand years old, leave by air for TIGER TOPS.

Morning drive: by Land-Rover or jeep to view crocodiles and birds!

Afternoon ride by elephant to view the jungle, and then again to Delhi to the Curio shops at Chandri Chowk, not missing Government Secretariat, Iron Pillar, Safdar Jung's (JUNG'S?) Tomb and Birla Temple. "No refund of any part of the tour price will be made to a passenger who does not take part in any excursion provided in the tour arrangements." Just so: I wonder if, together, we shouldn't seek a cosmic refund for those parts of the tour denied you without explanation, and in what currency. Why, many people would be embarrassed and downright annoyed to have you along at all, but they wouldn't quit the excursion, and so we wouldn't have it to ourselves. The only ones we have to ourselves are the private ones.

Of course, in shuffling our folders, we've flunked out in geography and garbled our itineraries, bound not to get some of our rupees back, but—*ee, ee,* you begin—don't keep *ee*ing me, I'll *give* you the brown-paper bag with the prancing elephant upon it and the split-pin fastener which

137

encloses India Tourist Office's offset-printed slanty-columned booklet but actually looks like an air-sickness bag—I'm not the miraculous Air France memory bank, Alpha 3, the "third-generation Univac 1108 multicomputer reservations complex" which, costing the same as twenty short-haul jet-liners, can handle thirty million passengers and return information on them "in a unit of time so small relative to one second as one second is to thirty years." One hundred thousand questions an hour, and no sullen handoffs, brush-offs, like with real folks. Ask Alpha 3 any question—how many Garbo movies have been shown in flight between Kathmandu and Tiger Tops; is it cheaper by jeep than by Land-Rover when prospecting for cobras; are you expected to eat with your hands if traveling economy or tourist; are there escalators in Sarnath?—and, whether you are at a television monitor screen in London or Los Angeles, back comes the answer almost instantaneously from Alpha 3 in Paris. So don't tell me I'm not trying, I'm just not a Univac of any generation. I said we'd go someplace and someplace we'll go.

"Alpha 3? Testing, testing, one, t—"

"Mach two."

"Concorde? We've just built one and we'd—"

"D'accord. Cordiale!"

"Must you always exclaim? Even a Jumbo jet would ser—"

"Elephantine."

"Huh?"

"I am *not* exclaiming! Do you not recall with nostalgia the famous Air France London-Paris flight, the 'Epicurean' service? A leisurely seventy-five-minute flight with champagne and cordon-bleu cooking? And now, 7 tons of Irish salmon, 20 tons of Dakar lobsters, 6 tons of Persian caviar, 26 tons of foie gras from Hungary and the Landes, 60 tons

138

.of Colombian coffee, Chilean avocados and cherries, Kenya strawberries, Californian asparagus (all until the pick of the French crop is ready, naturally), Scotch from a special Chivas vat, all enclosed in fast elegant aluminum pencils upholstered in 8,000 yards of rich blues, old golds, and parchments (the tone, not the stuff), 8,000 yards of carpet, 90 other fabrics and third-third-of-the-century new Espace Universel seats designed following an ergonomic survey of 4,000 air travelers and—

"Ergowhat?"

"Shush, as we Univacs say; I am Alpha 3. And omega too. Ergo, shush. And in each first-class lounge original tapestries commissioned from master weavers all over the world, lightweight individual headphones allowing you a personal choice of seven music programs ranging from Beethoven to Basin Street, movie sound tracks—"

"We're sold. Now, about . . ."

And that, my girl, is how they carry on at you, these Alphas, careful never to route you over or through the war zones or where the poverty isn't at least half-picturesque or where the politics has become boorish enough to plough up the squares of a neighboring capital with tanks' treads in order to plant who knows what dismal, monolithic seed. Oh, I suppose you *could,* if you wanted it badly enough, get into these places on some sort of Emergency Package deal, but I wouldn't want to see you trying to swab the napalm off your chin with a wad of Kleenex dipped in mayonnaise, or pinching the horn-palm of a receptive leper, or smacking the turret of a Russian tank with your brand-new Slovakian umbrella. It wouldn't be the trouble of getting some of your money back, but the chore of getting yourself out. So, as for a long time now, we travel to trouble as well as to apparent idylls on our own magic staircarpet of photogravure with some of the colors coming off, which is how you prefer

139

to travel anywhere anyway. Buckle our belts, order some fizzy *beebee,* and off we shoot in the mockup Concorde, the view from the windows and the tours on the ground nothing but picture postcards or folders at which you stare with Crusoe-Kreutznaer curiosity, calling out for scissors, drinks, ice cream, pens and paper, with all of which, as the wonders flash and ripple in our hands, I steward you toward—

Kal Bhairab, in Nepal, a dog-faced white-eyed golliwog statue with a red-hot golden crown between two sort-of baying lions, with a pink-beige temple in the offing and a well-wrapped child in a woollen ski cap, so it must be winter. Swing south here, and you at once haul out and replace your right hearing aid as if you weren't getting Beethoven or Basin Street in good tune. Down there, folks, you see two junks, they look like big maple leaves assembled from patches of ravioli-shaped sailcloth and set floating on end on hulls the shape of sewing-machine shuttles, not much moving as the Concorde flies but always with sea to spare. See now, in supersonic prying telescopic close-up, a gat-toothed young man, backed by the golden minarets of some pavilion, playing a crude stringed something or other, only his hands visible, the rest of him kept for warmth under a green sacking shawl, the bow arrested at the start of a pathetic-looking push while his feet stand on a rough mortar which is the roof of a building of not quite equal height. He lean-sits against a shallow parapet and has probably never heard of Ludwig van Beethoven or even Basin Street or you, and, if he had been born deaf etc., would have lived on deaf etc., a butt and a freak and obliged to become a mute as well. We are at present overflying a secluded promenade on a temple's top along which an elephant in a silver quilt is plodding at over a thousand feet, which is not at all a bad height for an elephant to be. The temple is on a hilltop, but we've already gone and are fanning over palms that look like enormous black false eyelashes on trunks stabbed into a deserted beach of biscuit-pale sa—

it's gone, jehosophat, oops, caramba, *floosh!*

it's those azure mountains of Japan, my that was quick, with in the violet sea between them and some down-curving carpentered bridge a half-sunk roof of something aban- doned, whose terra-cotta pillars hold up a sagging slice of roof which maybe is the Japanese character for loneliness, writ large and then marooned in a reservoir, only we've no time to ponder in, we've hit the shimmering mosaics of Is- fahan's Blue Mosque, a dark-blue courtyard facing the mi- nutely scabbed stone face that's topped by a silver dome and flanked by a lighthouse whose own blue is the same as the blue of the working shirts and trousers of Frenchmen in the Midi, a luminous sun-juiced blue.

All right, you want to cut it out?—the steward saw the pink light come on as you rang *plink-plink* and here are your scissors, madam, a lovely day for cutting out blue mosques.

Oh, there? Baalbek, all steps and pillars and blocks and cylinders of stone that sit on or near green English lawns, I don't know why. You want the flight plan now? We're only here to oblige, but there isn't one: we trip at convulsive random, here today and here tomorrow, just concentrically panoramic while you wait. Los Angeles at night below us now, a shallow spill of electric lights across a mauve cor- rugation that is water, the windows coming ablaze in spurts and zigzags that stop short and then unvaryingly stay while the lights in another piece come on in disjointed castella- tion, and it's just like when I sit down to think what to tell you and there are only one or two points of light, then lights go on in all quarters and it's like electric scoreboards every- where crammed with ever-changing information I must get to you before it's later than ever. He who quickly gives gives twice. Helen Keller said literature was her Utopia, explaining, "Here I am not disfranchised. No barrier of the senses shuts me out from the sweet, gracious discourse of my book-friends." So to postcards and folders we come: glut you with wonders, whether natural or man-made, so long as they are wonders truly, which means the same as saying anything the eye can see. Not quite, but nearly.

Without so much as asking to, you can ride the bus that goes from Jidda sixty-five miles across the Arabian desert to Mecca, the Forbidden City. Sir Richard Burton was the first European to get into it, and that was in 1853; he was disguised as an Indian. Since then, only half a dozen or so heathens have managed to do the same. Just a few years ago, three fair-haired men with cameras were stoned to death at the city's gates, and then it was found they were authentic Moslem pilgrims. But, if we could only sufficiently disguise your own blond hair, you might have better luck and, getting past the final checkpoint, cry with the pilgrims, *Labbaik, Allahumma, Labbaik!* announcing to God that you have come—or your own approximation to those sounds, with the *b*'s proving especially easy.

And now, fantastically shrugging off the oven-heat of 120° Fahrenheit, you scramble with the rest through the maze of incongruously modern houses to the Mosque of the Sanctuary, where, as tradition has it, Adam went to rest and repent after being expelled from Eden. The oldest building in the world the Moslems call it. Massive walls enclose it and Wahabi warriors with swords stand on perpetual guard. You enter, barefoot, through one of the nineteen archways and see first the Black Stone, a meteorite brought to earth by the angel Gabriel to be given to Abraham and Ishmael as the foundation stone of a new temple to be built after the Flood. None of your rocking or bird

142

calls here, if you please; this is one of the building blocks of creation, incongruous and vast as the slab in the film called *2001, A Space Odyssey,* some stills from which excited you so much (the weightless floating, the metal ladders, and all that inside-a-plane decor). You'll need your energy anyway for the obligatory sprint, seven times over, along the Pilgrim's Way, refreshing yourself from time to time with perfumed Afghan tea or, the bitterest *beebee* of all, the milk of Turkestan. Then, to be on the safe side, plod off to the Valley of Arafat, where you have a sheep ritually butchered on your behalf, thus adding your two cents' worth to the abattoir reek of the valley where even the pilgrims topple and die of heat stroke, their bodies often being left there until the next day to bulge and bloat.

Poo! you shriek, and are understandably relieved to move on in order to perform the last rite of slinging stones at the Three Pillars of Satan, monuments marking the spot where Satan three times appeared, three times tempted the son of Abraham, and was thrice stoned. It is just as well you should go now; these Moslems don't take kindly to small pilgrims answering the *muezzin* back in a shrill call so like his own that the faithful become confused, then threaten you with stones, while the *muezzin* himself comes wheezing down from his minaret only to burn his hand accidentally on the Black Stone as it waxes radioactive again, melting the swords of the Wahabi guards and giving off a fierce pulsating violet light that metamorphoses you into Eve as, with fazer gun in your fist, you depart through the same archway you entered by, a touch of punctilious autism which is really sheer bravado as well. An E-type Jaguar sleek but not gaudy rushes you back to Jidda, to the new airport on the Red Sea coast, and your private Concorde has you safely in the smoke clouds over Popocatepetl, the volcano southeast of Mexico City, long before, on the *muezzin*'s command, thousands of pilgrims fling themselves upon and round the death-emitting Black Stone to shield the Forbidden City from its rays.

No time at all, and you are negotiating the 248 steps which lead to the top of the main pyramid of thousand-year-old San Juan Teotihuacán, your mini-skirt rolled up high, a bunch of gladioli in one hand, a big black doorstep of ice cream in the other, no sign of your fazer. Then you descend, go out dressed in *mariachi* costume—fancy velvet jacket, tight pants, high-heeled boots and a sombrero—to eat tamales, dare the Aztec Gallop or Montezuma's Revenge to plague you. You beckon the trumpets of the little band to close in on your right ear and order tequila all round, from Mecca to Mexico in a wink, the perfect escape.

Where to now? Which places forbidden or open? The air-conditioned out-of-doors in the Houston Astropark where Mark Hofheinz, the electronic Barnum who declares "all the money I ever made was by hypothecating my previous accumulations," first created the perfect climate within the Astrodome and then decided to change the outside climate too. Will you ride his choo-choo that has a cow catcher out front? Will you steer one of his kiddie cars that advance at about the same two miles an hour as that two-thousand-ton contraption on caterpillar tracks which picks up a moon rocket bodily at Cape Kennedy and carries it upright the three and a half miles to the firing pad in just over a hundred minutes?

Or will you visit the site, at Ardis in Turkey, of King Croesus' gold refinery, go rummage in his sixth century B.C. workshop among the bits of gold, the remnants of crucibles, blowpipes, nozzles, and more than three hundred clay basins? It was Harvard University that found it, so maybe we should apply to Cambridge, Mass., for permission to go. Or will you visit the British factory in St. Albans

144

that manufactures pasta for Italy and, by much the same process, used to produce straw for hats? And perversely order a hat made from semolina and durum wheat? Or a spaghetti cape?

Or will you zoom off into a future which, yours anyway, brings shopping by picture telephone with speech being sent as light down a glass line, television sets as thin as dinner plates, microwave cookery that readies your steaks in one minute, lawns that grow to the desired height and then stop, programmed and undriven electric polythene cars, hovertrains that go at half the speed of sound on a cushion of air, titanium airliners fueled with hydrogen that exceed three thousand miles an hour, wines from new vineyards such as Château Woomera and Châteauneuf du Module, bottled suntans that never fade and vibro-hammocks in the garden, transparent water pipes and self-cleansing baths?

No future? *Few-cha?* Your wish is my command as we zero in on Nathan S. Jacobson's CAESAR'S PALACE hotel set in imported-cypress gardens where the Venus de Milo partners the Canova and Medici Venuses, all in marble substitute and built, "built," *built*—Las Vegas built, this is Vegas not Ancient or Renaissance anything—and smirking Roman centurions take our flimsy, ill-traveling bags away on a litter past a Nero's Nook full of latterday Messalinas in peacock-feathered togas and up we go to the sumptuous ersatz-marble bath whose taps are crystal bulbs so pure-looking we want to read the diminished future into them before bathing and then launching ourselves into the dazzling, sunlorn town to view the Leaning Tower of Pizza, all cherry fluorescence, and the Biggest Beer in the World outpouring itself into a colossal glass frosted with archangels' breath, and so to no bed but a whole night wrestling with one-armed bandits you need two arms to shift at all, our very early breakfast taken at Mr. Sy's souvenir and gift shop,

145

which is also the U.S. Post Office, and then we retreat only just before 90 degrees F. becomes 100 degrees F. But already a pastel telephone is paging us, it's time to rise and start another day. . . .

Oh, you'd rather be a lunarnaut, would you? Or travel to Florida to test the acoustics of the Vertical Assembly Building, which has a 470-foot door that takes an hour to open and is so high it has to be air-conditioned to prevent clouds from forming in the ceiling (as befits the Biggest Building in the World, sufficient to contain two Buckingham Palaces). Or shall we be ultra-cautious and, in scarlet chiffon scarves and goggles and leather helmets, sit quietly on our own grass in our replica of an ancient Fokker monoplane which, if it took off, could fly for a full hour on seven gallons of eighty-octane fuel? I don't blame you for *ee*ing me time and again; everything's out there waiting for us to tackle it, except, with us, getting ready's almost all the doing. Our anti-handicaps are symbolic. *Votre oeil émerveillé,* as the Saint-Malo civic scroll puts it, *s'étonnera:* eye-stunned from staring upon marvels, you'll dream unsurpassable dreams no satellite can ever transmit. When you speak, you move the whole front of your face, giving each sound its labial, muscular, breathing maximum; you do not waste what is rare and you find what is marvelous in what is commonplace, teamed up with and part of and taking for granted all things bizarre or exotic.

The outstanding thing about tomorrow, I can now reveal, is that you will be seven years old. You don't know what a year is and so won't find anything outstanding in this occasion unless we make a splash. A large cake with candles you'll more or less count and then extinguish with a giant puff, a replacement for the VC-10 airliner whose tail is awry and Scotch-taped together, the piccolo you howled for, a plastic garden swing and a slide made in Japan, a

pair of snow-white soft mittens, yet another jigsaw puzzle
—these and some routine items that you'd get in any case
(poster colors, crayons, new painting book) will help to
make the day, especially on top of the little party you'll
be having at school—an exceptionally festive affair in itself
because your birthday also happens to be the last day of
school before half term. I only hope you won't think deprivation always accompanies largess in that your birthday
somehow inaugurates No School for ten days. You very
easily construe coincidences, the irony being that you have
enough vocabulary to obtain basic facts from us but explanations hardly at all. And there's something else: Saturday and Sunday, the days after your birthday, you'd have
off anyway, so the puzzlement will come on Monday morning when, like someone putting one of those Latin questions
which anticipate the answer *yes,* you'll ask about *kool* with
your usual premature celebratory grin. Which will dwindle
as you realize you are entering another of those uncertain
periods which begin and end you know not why and deny
you your favorite daytime activity, and then, just when
you've reconciled yourself to all the resuscitated pastimes
of weekday life at home, pluck you out to school again
after an interim for which you have no word but which you
accept—with the same stoical skepticism with which you
accept so much—as yet another inscrutable movement of
Environment against you.

Sometimes, thus baffled, you spend days in reserved of-
fendedness, trying perhaps to detect the pattern, the purpose, the profit, even going so far as to extrapolate in your
non-verbal way, although you don't really know where one
pattern begins and its neighbor ends or why some days resemble one another and others don't. There is a void everywhere just beyond the edge of what you find familiar, and
essentially you are living in a dark through which others

147

shepherd you and in which they illuminate precious zones like the tops of certain mushrooms in a thousand-acre forest. Yours is the most precarious existentialism of all; or, to put it in words that I'm sure you'd prefer, you are, although inventive and energetic and quick on the uptake, one of the most dependent people I know. Which makes you one of the most trusting creatures in Creation.

But—the brighter side—I'm glad you aren't one of those children who, at half term or term's end, see all the cases and hampers in the school's main hall, packed by house mothers for parents to collect; all except their own. These children either stay or are billeted out, and at first they scream. Even you, a day girl, looked mortified on the afternoon before your first half-term holiday began; you saw all the baggage, the cars and taxis and buses, and concluded, I think, school was over for life and had been just another of those temporary experiences you'd never become inured to, leaving your life as they did without plan or dimension, scope or even fabric. Too, none of the baggage belonged to you, so you assumed that here, by some extra twist of the knife, you'd been subjected to the refined insult of dispossession before having even owned. You'd been to *kool,* it was over forever, and no one had even given you a bag to go away with. The look on your face evoked the horrors of another scene: persecution, deportation, the refusal of their own identities to people helpless, submissive, willing to be sent anywhere so long as it was soon over with, victims—very literally—of biological inheritance. Jews and gypsies; cattle trucks and open wagons; the holds of slave ships; and when I used that phrase "portable ghetto" a little while back, I meant just that. Forgive us our memberships as we forgive those who blackball us.

And now your birthday, this eighteenth of October, has begun, in the first week of the Mexican Olympic Games.

148

You have gone off to school brandishing my sketch of a birthday cake and shouting *zeven*. Your birthday cards are lined up on the mantel like the Wahabi guards at Mecca, and there is even one that came in a package sent to you by Alitalia, a publicity gimmick which nonetheless greets you with "OPEN YOUR GATEWAY" on the front and clinches matters on the back with "TO THE WORLD," the one showing a country cottage through a close-up of a wicket gate, the other an eclectic landscape with Leaning Tower of Pisa, one kangaroo and several minarets, a butterfly and a stylized lion, all shone over by a rosebud-mouthed psychedelic sun with a spectrum halo. Inside—what could be better?—there's a rear view of a parked Alitalia Caravelle with its boarding ramp down. All right, this fortuitous bonus has stolen our thunder, but you have at least, while cramming egg into your incessantly moving mouth with your inferior hand (the right), domesticated the offering with a brilliant, nervous-lined sketch of your mother standing behind what looks like a horizontal-barred gate.

Elsewhere—"else" being too weak a word to convey all that distance and all the otherness of Mexico—the Poles in the Olympic village have dropped water-loaded plastic bags on the Guineans' heads and the Guineans have slung stones and slates at the Poles, an *affaire* you would impartially have enjoyed. One Olympic present I would have liked to give you, but you aren't ready yet for such inspiriting identifications-with: I mean watching, while understanding all that goes into it, the performance of V. Skomarokhov, the "deaf-mute" Russian who came fifth in the four-hundred-meter hurdles and wasn't in the least put out by two false starts. That run of his was worth a ton of the world's rough ridicule and seven whole, although fragmentary, years of apartness. I know, I know, we've an overdeveloped response to the handicapped who excel, as well as

149

to those who don't—Olympic runner or your tiny friend at school who has fewer words than you—but such are the hyperboles of care. Let's leave it at that; I promise not to bug you again with V. Skomarokhov, Lon Chaney, Ludwig van Beethoven, Frederick Delius, Helen Keller, Goya, Lenny, and Poor Tom, or to begin producing such other trump cards as Ronsard, Du Bellay, Thomas Edison, Marie de Bashkirtseff, and Charles Maurras, all deaf, or David Wright, the deaf poet, whose stunning autobiography I've just reviewed, or Jack Clemo, the poet who is deaf-blind. Everything in your own time, just providing you'll let us drive you a little and give us the right to pester you later— after later—with an absolute gallery of true Olympians who've competed against something even more crippling, and more permanently so, than the thin air of Mexico City. And have won. You yourself begin with an almost satirical view of humanity and so won't take competition too seriously, aware before beginning of the variety of human wishes.

The other morning when you arrived at school, there was a whole cohort of people assembled on the steps: students, come to spend a day either observing or teaching. Without seeming to observe *them* (which maybe taught them something), you assimilated the throng's appearance, especially the nun and the colored woman, whom you have identified for all time as the penguin and the golly. See, I knew you knew "penguin," but I forgot to include it in your list of words. Going back to rectify the omission would be to cheat a little, and, anyway, informality not perfection is the mode of our rambling letter.

Crackle, *wham,* a jet has just gone over, taking off in the opposite direction from usual; the wind has changed for your birthday. I even think you might have heard that big fart from the afterburners; maybe Alitalia was up there,

150

greeting you again, and I can't check because I've no time-table and I didn't see the plane even though I got to the window in two strides. But perhaps you wouldn't have noticed, or attended, anyway; as with the penguin and the golly, when you are intent, you have a boorish dimissory way with you that simply says *You are not there,* which is how you reach your destinations while marching through this baroque shambles of a house or through Saturday crowds on your way to the escalator. What, I wonder, could ever detain you? not even planes or umbrellas in shopwindows, not even something as outlandish as the $4\frac{1}{2}$-inch nose of Bell, who did the engravings for the first *Encyclopaedia Britannica* and who, embarrassed, would hide it in his handkerchief or even disguise it with a more pleasingly shaped artificial nose. What does detain you, with an almost perfect record, is the play park when you are returning from an outing: even in the dark, whether or not it is also freezing or the rain is coming down in thick rods, you have to do the ritual slide, the ritual swing, your bottom and feet thumping into the snow or the mud, and let the world think what it will on its way to hell.

Slam-zhoor, another jet goes over. Sometimes this house is like the bridge of an aircraft carrier and I can half persuade myself I hear the tin voice that runs it all: "Launch jets," nasal and impersonal and then the empty clank, more appropriate to belowdecks than to the bridge, after the plane has blazed away. *Why mention the bridge at all then?* I hear you say, holding up between finger and thumb a bit of my prose with that sardonic preciosity of yours. You similarly held up a nail-shaped bit of plastic you'd found on the carpet, valuing it against the light and then checking it against our fingers to see who might have lost an entire nail. Then you wanted to extend your inspection to feet. . . .

All actions, even taking our shoes and socks off, even telling you what you never understand, can help you to exist that little bit more, so that you bulk a bit larger in this world; not in the specialized enclaves of school or clinic, but in the so-called marketplace where you may, to the uninitiated, seem incongruous, like the deaf girl I read about who whenever out in public recited her lines from the school nativity play, in which, as a cow, she announced, "I am a cow. My milk shall nourish the mother this day, whose Child shall nourish mankind always." Which is language such as you have never dreamed of, but animated all the same by the same extraordinary confidence as your explaining to strangers who you are by pointing to your chest and shouting your name.

This demand for recognition as *you* is something not to waste; something that isn't wasted, for instance (if I may go afield again), in the Camphill Village Communities for mentally handicapped adults, where each person has a special thing (the positive which the negative of his handicap generates) to give to another: the mongols, affectionate and euphoric folk always, are ideally equipped to befriend the psychotics, and the autistic often respond profoundly to those whose handicap is physical as well. Kindliness, tolerance thrive, and the dark or night side of human nature shows surprisingly little—which is reassuring to one who knows that deaf children, because they are deaf, aren't "good" any more than, say, hearing parents are because they can hear. It is good to know that, in no matter how limited a setting, handicaps can be put to use. Thus, in the case of the community called Botton Village, we find Roger and Simon, both of them deaf and psychotic; but Simon helps Roger at bedtime and has in general helped to improve his attitude to people around him; Roger, it also happens, is almost blind and is paralyzed down his left side.

152

Here before me, in fact, is a photograph of Simon in the act of washing Roger's feet: Simon seems to be grinning as he holds up to the light something, maybe a talent he had lost, he's found between Roger's toes, and Roger is watching him as he sits in his chair, his feet set relaxedly in the plastic bowl on the floor. Or take Ben, the blind baker of the village's bread, who calls his oven "Sarah"—"the hottest girl in Botton." Or Ruth, deaf and dumb and psychotic, who engraves glass with uncanny skill.

They all work to keep the village going and so win a role, an identity, a duty of care, and in a milieu which, although an enclave, is a functioning, unbigoted, people-fulfilling society safer than the United States, less class-conscious than Britain at large, less finicky than France; tighter than a *polis,* more human than an institution, more chivalrous than any suburb. It's a microcosm in which discovery, not prescription, counts; in which the people explore and invent in a way not much different, in principle, from that recommended by Alain Robbe-Grillet for the "new novelist," or, if we can get very personal (as when we say *seven,* at which you blush), from what Saul Maloff, commenting in *Newsweek* on the trial-run essay I wrote about you, correctly identified as the process by which your "strange and beautiful presence in the world" compelled me "to rethink and resee [my] own relation to the natural and human universe."

So let's give a quick, not very orthodox salute to those people on the outside who understand (as well as to those on the inside who've come, however limitedly, into their own). What a pleasure it is to note that Viennese refugees in 1939 took the trouble to pioneer a movement to assist the handicapped and so very practically implement the teachings of another Austrian, Rudolf Steiner. About what goes on when you're out and about, we'll say more later;

it's your birthday and I was forgetting the special fanfare I had in mind, something to get your mind off my own intermittent ponderosity and on to the marzipan pageant surrounding you whether you notice it or not. Can you count all the way through October? Well, you were born on the day between the anniversary of Walgren's Super Value Days and the anniversary of the Medina Temple Oriental Pageant (so my *Esquire* Guide to Drink says); in fact, you were born on Alaska Day, and I wonder why they bother to celebrate that or any of those other supererogated non-occasions. Next year we'll send a cable to Alaska, filling up their calendar at last.

That, surely, would improve on even Alitalia's brilliant timing or any open "new gateway to the world." Until I knew I had to bring the world to you, I don't think I knew or saw the world at all; and I don't mean just the handicapped of all sorts and conditions, such as your classmates who came to your last birthday's party and pummeled, romped, and Sherman-tanked their way all over the house and the garden and your toys while you, immaculately adaptable, stood by smiling the smile of the giving and forgiving hostess as they took over the toys of your entire lifetime in a boy-dominated orgy of dangling, whistling earpieces, cream-plastered faces and paws, upturned paper cups, sat-on éclairs, catapulted spoonfuls of jelly, spurned sensible sandwiches, purloined lollipops, crashed jetliners, chewed candles, and miniature umbrellas all in the up position, the tiniest boy howling in a private trauma and the others whoopeeing and sirening fit to dement the damned, with the one other girl meekly talking to herself under your best Tokyo parasol while I, ringmaster-clown, studied my *dramatis personae* and asked you who was who only to get a contemptuous leer in return, and your mother wiped bot-

154

toms, blotted up pools and in between times plugged the ceaselessly enunciating pairs of jaws with cake.

At the end, after they had all been worked into the wrong coats, some of the boys apparently having come in coats that existed no more or had mutated beyond recognition in the course of two hours, you took one look at the battle-field and at once headed for the bathroom, half in shock, half exhausted with delight at having carried without mishap through the entire party your big model bath. Most of the Polaroid pictures of that event survive, and you study them from time to time with the air of a pilot who, having been shot down, watches someone's wing-camera pictures of his fall, knowing he'd survived but paying especial attention to the frames immediately before he bailed out.

This time, however, we plan a mild celebration at which you will be able to queen it semi-sedately, play with your presents before they get smashed, and have no competition at all for the toilet. Some paper hats and crackers will provide a flimsy pageantry while I, having read some works I wish I could forget, hear time's winged Wordsworth at my back, resist the lines but can't dismiss them; so I let them through from "We Are Seven":

> A simple child,
> That lightly draws its breath,
> And feels its life in every limb. . . .

You blew out the candles in two goes; you ate the icing and ignored the cake, reserving your most meticulous attention for the tiny ballerina we'd set in place right by your name in the green ice writing. You made me blow up every balloon, taxi and make take off the gleaming white VC-10 (HEAR ITS AIRFIELD JET WHINE! shouted the box lid), play the piccolo right into your ear (although I couldn't get

155

"you ate the icing and ignored the cake . . ."

anywhere near the two tunes supplied—"Baa! Baa! Black Sheep" and "Jingle Bells"), don the green devil mask and chase you, and even show you how to open one Sava Ham packed by 29 November Meat Industry, Subotica, Yugoslavia, and exported by Koproduct Novi Sad (which would have been exotic enough on its own without the marshmallows you combined it with).

We worked the knots out of our systems, all of us, and you insisted on chanting down the piccolo instead of blowing into it and you made us all wear paper hats and you let your own slide down over your eyes and didn't even adjust it, taking the party half blind, then, and quite unable to separate all the *seven*s we said from your memory of last

156

Christmas. Upon seeing the stack of presents with the fanged mask on top you whipped round at once to the corner where, if it had been Christmas really, the tree would have been. But no tree; what event was this?

Nothing, I suppose, stranger than some of the items in a list that has just come to my hand of the universe's bizarreries being teased out by sly researchers who, by now, know all about Egg Weight, Shell Thickness, and Blood Spot Incidence in Solar and Windowless Poultry Houses; the Embrittlement of Babbitt-Bronze Bonds; the Influence of Forming Die on Hay Wafer Stability; Mushroom Shrinkage During Processing; the Response of the Crayfish *Cambarus b. bartoni* to a Vibratory Stimulus; Consumer Preference for Christmas Trees in a Mature Market Area; New Gamma Rays from Au 197; Honeybee Foraging on Buckwheat and the Relationship to Yield of Grain; the Rate of Dissipation of Eddy Energy in the Lowest 100 Metres of the Atmosphere; Plastic Buckling of Rib Cored Cylindrical Sandwich Shells Subjected to Hydrostatic Pressure; The Decay of Xe 137; Birdsfoot Trefoil and Cottontail Rabbits—Consumptive and Reproductive Effects; the Effect of Leading Edge Blowing on the Lift Characteristics of a Low Aspect Ratio Delta Wing; Virginal and Non-Virginal College Girls Compared; the Modigliani-Brumberg-Ando Consumption Function; Genetic Variation of White Pine Characteristics Related to Weevil Attack; Sour Cherry Necrotic Ringspot and Clover Mosaic Viruses; the Effect of Newcastle Disease Virus Infection on Succinate Respiration in Primary Cultured Chick Embryo Cells; Haematology of the Guinea Pig at Varying Ascorbic Acid Levels; Underwater Flutter; and even Relationships Among Abnormal Auditory Adaption, Differential Intensity Sensitivity, and Performance with a Hearing Aid.

Sic! You are a member of a stunning universe, so much

157

of which is closed to you, much more, even, than is closed to the vast majority of us.

Let us, therefore, in compensation to you, thicken up your birthday, shower you with astounding gifts, from the entire surface of the Velodrome in Mexico City (a tough African wood called "Douzzie Afzelia"), where cycling events are held, to Emperor Frederick II's treatise, *The Art of Falconry,* dating from around 1260, with over nine hundred cameos of birds, animals, cities, and landscapes, and currently in the Vatican Library; from a wall one hundred yards long and twenty high, on which we'll write a soap mural with cans of instant lather, to Ludwig van Beethoven's three legless pianos; from here always to there; from the Nile Valley, where UNESCO has had the colossal faces of Rameses II and Nefertiti sawn out of the cliff face and raised two hundred feet clear of what has now become the Aswan High Dam, to Brussels, for the Jeux sans Frontières in which teams from half a dozen nations do pillow fights on greasy poles, play one-a-side soccer with five sets of goalposts and fifty balls, and ride bicycles in big revolving drums; or from Texas, where you could go to inspect Haroldson Lafayette Hunt, who reputedly makes $200,000 a day and carries his lunch to work in a brown-paper bag and has neither Cadillac nor chauffeur, to somewhere south of Panama where a warm current called El Niño (it also is "a child" that arrives around Christmas) invades the region of the Humboldt cold-water current and so muddles the marine life there that, from exposure to the unnaturally high concentration in the water of hydrogen sulphide, the lead in the paint on the bottoms of ships changes into lead sulphide and the hulls turn black in Callao harbor, the work, they say in those parts, of the "Callao painter."

Or, for kicks, if you will, escape from Cuba to Florida by wave hopping in an ancient crop-dusting biplane thick

158

with poisonous chemical or, because Nikolai Gogol interrupted *Dead Souls* to sing its praises in print, take the *troika*
on any crisp and even winter's night. Whatever you choose
to accept or to do on any of your sturdy birthdays, and
whether or not on one of them, like a slow genius, you suddenly come out with a long sentence after having said virtually nothing in all the years up to then, your battle hymn
shall begin and end, *l'anarchie c'est moi,* with many happy
returns.

7. The Pink Forest Canal Society

You know how life is: right in the middle of writing a letter you have to go off and give a lecture, halfway through which you get an idea you want to maneuver into the latest chapter of whatever it is you're hoping is going to be a book, but which you've put on one side in order to read a book that has just come for review, which is also why you never catch up on all those bumper issues of the *Times Literary Supplement,* whose clock at the head of the editorial column is stuck always at half past four, the very time at which, over a cup of sweet-and-brown sergeant-major tea, you seem to remember having promised an essay whose topic you haven't yet decided—it's a bit dazing, with all these disconnected intermittences that have to be fitted into a day-sandwich you can hold and eat.

I've been reading, on a sidetrack, a book called *All The Little Animals,* by Walker Hamilton, a bare and succinct novel about the mind and adventures of a mentally slow thirty-one-year-old called Bobby Platt who has run away from a crass, punitive stepfather he calls "The Fat" and has taken up with one Mr. Summers, a bank manager turned bum, whose entire vocation is to scour the highways for run-over animals and to bury them. "People can bury each other, boy," Mr. Summers tells him, "but the animals have to be helped." Bobby eventually succeeds him as traveling sexton to the slaughtered, but not before the two of them have disastrously attempted to slaughter The Fat himself. What I especially liked was the book's multitude of quiet visits with the flora and fauna of the Cornish countryside, where Mr. Summers and Bobby live together in a hut and go in for a good deal of drop-out philosophizing. Mr. Summers when he sees a cow sees it as "life in the shape of a cow," whereas Bobby—as much a natural naturalist as you —makes a virtue of not interpreting—as when, nose to the ground, he studies "the tiny things in the grass roots . . . as if I were small like the things I was watching." Such a simplicity of mind fascinates me: the so-called human picture isn't complete without it and human humility cannot be said to have begun until the mind, so-called, has accepted it. Walker Hamilton takes a sizable chance: confined within Bobby's rudimentary idiom, he can't rhetoricize the intricacies of Bobby's private psychodrama, but he wins out by exemplifying so precisely what Bobby sees that we learn from Bobby what Bobby cannot teach.

How, indeed, if at all, can the life of you handicapped people be put into words? Presumably you have special aptitudes that to some extent compensate for what you are short of: say, a non-verbal although perhaps intricate intimacy with animals or plants (Bobby-like) or, by the same token, with things man-made that most people in their full-facultied haste ignore or overlook—the texture of a blanket, the taste of a spoon. Attentiveness for its own sake could well be what the mentally handicapped person has as his

161

own special gift. Intent not on reporting what he perceives but on perceiving itself, he comes closer perhaps than so-called competent people to seeing infinity in a grain of sand (although he won't think of it in that way). He might even see the *finiteness* of a grain of sand, thus heeding its excellence within its limitations.

For what it is worth, the opinion of the president of the Royal Academy is that some handicapped children "seem to have a supersensitivity, which suggests that there are certain sorts of judgment which lie outside the ordinary process of reasoned thought." Impressed by what he saw at two exhibitions of paintings by handicapped children, he told the Invalid Children's Aid Association, "I just wonder if research into the relationship of sensitivity and intelligence, perhaps through the work of these children, might not lead to a new and more realistic conception of what IQ really is. . . . Our estimation of the IQ is a very limited one, and it seems that the qualities of intelligence and judgment are left out." Walker Hamilton and President Sir Thomas Monnington, and I, seem to be at the point of abandoning Ptolemy for Copernicus, so to speak, and I just wonder if it isn't possible to get beyond even Copernicus. . . .

You, of course, are just the sort of person to tell me I'm thinking wishfully. It's hard to say, especially as, nowadays, there is developing a certain weariness with intelligence itself, with the primacy accorded to it by so many sectors of our zooming, blundering, clever civilization. We have already been instructed by our teenagers that "smartness," like ambitiousness or wealth, has little to do with "soul"; and from that lesson it isn't a far reach to find, somewhere between flower power and *satori,* a place for the mentally hindered. Awareness of, and reverence for, life seem to have ousted the old power tool of reason that brilliantly explained what awe could not. Enthusiasm—which is Greek for being possessed by a god—is back in vogue again. The mind has been telling itself to "expand" beyond all the resources of reason. In fact, all that is missing is for someone to rediscover the word *idiot* (a word smeared with hurt and cant) and remind us that it is the Greek for "a private person." Mock as people may, like the Bobby mockers in the novel, brains only get us very far—far enough to see something always farther, today's marvel being tomorrow's cliché, the future being so old-fashioned; whereas the gestures of slower minds are very often sufficient to themselves, each being equivalent to any one of the others and intended not to explain but to regard. True, if you like, to life, to the unique something between see-er and seen. To "tell it like it is" is virtually impossible, for any complete account of anything—anyone—would have to include what you yourself see anything—anyone—as; and that we don't know.

Such an observation as I've just made lodges in the mind as a challenge, surely, construable as an affront or a bad joke only by those who unwittingly prove time and again that the biggest handicap of all is to be mentally competent without being spiritually awake. After all, it's the majority of the non-handicapped (*soi-disant*) who want to shut away the handicapped, not the handicapped who want to shut *them* away. I have concluded from the behavior of all save the handicapped, the most intelligent, and the most compassionate, that man's sanity (again so-called) and his putative good will are precarious little sprouts demanding constant sheltering—or, as the physician and psychiatrist R. D. Laing puts it—that "the condition of being out of one's mind is the condition of *normal* man. Normal men have killed perhaps 100,000,000 of their fellowmen in the last fifty years." Hence the normality which, frowning at you and your exhilarated birdcalls, reinforces its own terror by wanting to have you locked away as its own proxy. As John

163

Heywood says in his *Proverbes,* the earliest collection of English colloquial sayings, "Who is so deafe or so blinde as is hee/That wilfully will neither heare nor see?" The mind that would keep company with you must be big enough to make itself limp a little; in so doing, it might notice things it might otherwise have missed.

Yes, you'll say, but you've been lumping together all the handicaps in Creation: some, like blindness, are almost respectable, but no one has any respect for—or patience with —the deaf. Ear trumpets provoke grins, but white canes don't. Why, even Helen Keller—who once was like an unruly young animal but eventually rode and swam and truly enjoyed flying—wrote that "The problems of deafness are deeper and more complex, if not more important than those of blindness." And she was in a very privileged position to comment from. I agree with you, but it is extremely hard to translate the idiom of adjustment to one handicap into the idiom of adjustment to another: the parent of a deaf child will always involuntarily regard the blind, the spastic, the cerebral-palsied, the mongol, the autistic, as also in some way deaf. But it's better to give the wrong damn than give no damn at all, better to talk in Latin in Italy than to pretend the Romance languages don't exist.

Of all things, a walking example has just been at the door, bearing a "stand-pipe" from something called the "Pink Forest Canal Society," and we conversed briefly in mutual incomprehension, he having assumed I would know what to do with such a pipe, I marveling at the bizarre name of something that maybe doesn't even exist. We might have come from different planets—you just can't *explain* the Pink Forest Canal Society; but at least the English language helped us to establish that we couldn't enlighten each other. I am content, have to be content, to presume every handicap brings with it some ineffable virtue and to guess at the ineffable in other handicaps on the strength of the ineffable in yours, which I can guess about at first hand.

Guessing: Helen Keller kept all kinds of people guessing and many times during her life was examined to see if she possessed abnormal faculties; but all the experts agreed that she was simply making remarkable use of such faculties as she did possess. But I wonder how well equipped medical science is to establish the existence of faculties out of the ordinary. Over three decades ago the neurologist Sir Charles Sherrington decided that physics and chemistry couldn't account for mind, and in 1963 the brain specialist Sir John Eccles contended in his Eddington Memorial Lecture that "the prime reality of my experiencing self cannot with propriety be identified with brains, neurones, nerve impulses or spatial-temporal patterns of impulses." The brain doesn't generate consciousness, *is* not consciousness; and a nerve cell doesn't differ in any essential way from a muscle cell—or so it was decided at the 1966 International Symposium on Brain and Consciousness. Couldn't we say that the brain is an organ of limitation which, while channeling attention or attentiveness, cannot entirely censor the mind's subliminal activities?

I'm saying it anyway in befuddled recognition of the fact that we understand the physical world itself very little and cannot adequately describe experience. Why, it's no heresy these days to say that all science offers us is models and that we have every reason to try and develop a mathematics of qualities. What exactly your conscious and unconscious experiences are like I do not know: you are, if not quite a law unto yourself, at least your own Xanadu, your own palace of varieties, which is looking on the bright side, or—looking on the other, which it is painful to do—your own wasteland, your own lunar surface. The why of your condition no one has told us; that it isn't similar to ours is evi-

165

dent; and whether or not we know about them, I hope you have some compensations and it is these which make you smile so much and which genially populate the vacancy into which you sometimes stare even now.

Over the long haul there's a gain of sorts: we give you all the ordinary things, treat you as far as possible like an ordinary girl, but also—if this isn't too wishfully invasive—feed to you the results of our own guessings, our own discoveries and *trouvailles.* Having been obliged to develop some extraordinary mental attitudes in order to traffic with you at all, we may be finding in that necessity exactly the virtues you can devour. And even if you don't apprehend our actions—drawings, mimes, games, and rituals—in the way we think you do, you are at least aware of our activity on your behalf: these things are being done *for you.* On a more prosaic level, it heartens us to know that completely institutionalized children come more slowly to language than children who, like you, have a daily life in two worlds. Matthew Arnold somewhere defined this kind of faith as a constant effort which, even if it failed in its primary purpose, nonetheless kept alive a needed attitude. So we try like mad to maximize whatever you have, which is like fitting a hearing aid to your whole life.

Getting to Atlantis would be one way of symbolizing it, and getting there is hard, but not as hard as if we thought getting there impossible. This is why we stick big cards on everything so you'll come to know what things are called (thus tricking you into the habit of reading) and why, also, we show you the latest as well as the most ancient painted and sculptured things (for these are indeed the voices to reach you in your profoundest silence). Your world we read as open-ended and you have made our own the same. Of the materials and the time consumed let's not even think; there

166

is always an advance going on: you change and change and change, outstripping these words even as I set them down.

What? You haven't noticed? I'll tell you, fixing you with my Ancient Mariner's eye. Since I began this writing, you've regained one word you lost for two years (*mower,* which shaves the lawn); you've learned to say *thumb* with triumphant precision and *bubbie* (which makes the bubbles in your bathwater). And you double *mirroe,* which is not mirror only but photograph, to be uttered while squinting up your left eye behind the left fist you've screwed up into a makeshift view finder. The first time you said it (in the imperative, as always), we thought you wanted a mirror, but you screamed and screamed as we assembled all the mirrors there were (Is it *this* one she wants?), and that went on for two hours. Then those feebly construing and frantically guessing adults fished out a camera from its secret place and you smiled, jerked the tears off your face, and said *mirroe* very gently. Then we photographed you while you exultantly murmured the word you'd taught us. The logic of your semantics is visual, and you have made our own reasoning visible to us.

Too, you have begun quite spontaneously to kiss, which you do with a prim, slow-motion graveness, and to narrow your eyes while walking forward in smiling bemusement. Having sympathy to spare, you exclaim *Ah!* if we so much as touch our faces, trunks, or limbs, and you have taken to cooling your ravioli with milk. You now have other dances than your habitual rocking stamp and you increasingly clap yourself like a Russian. Best of all, you now consistently recognize and utter a dozen written words, and, one day, when you thought I wasn't noticing, you wrote your name in slurred big letters on a piece of paper and Scotch-taped it to the front of the back of your chair at the table. Having

167

on that day sat in it without your permission, I took the hint, am still taking it.

Watching all this happen has been a bit like seeing at Passchendaele the hundredweight of metal that rises to the surface of the soil each day after rain, except that we don't even know what is buried, so anything—a fiber pen big as a Cape Kennedy rocket, the Queen of Hearts, a crystallized rainbow made of sugar—could come looming up. Even the president of the Pink Forest Canal Society, come to explain to us at long last.

You, with what aptitudes you have and with that jaunty interfering temperament of yours, have persisted. We, evolving a technique as we went along, have persisted too. And school (which the other day sent a note to say you had performed "beautifully" when taking an audiogram) has converted you into a social creature, has in fact given you a social consummation you must have devoutly wished for for years. I try to keep up with the flood of periodicals, pamphlets, and reports devoted to the plight of children handicapped like, less than, more than, you; and so I know something about flashing clocks, volume-control handsets for telephones, BBC television play synopses for the deaf, the Warren Wearable Walk-Away Units, the vibrating pillow that wakes you up and the torchlike apparatus being designed for deaf-blind children, as well as the manual-versus-oral teaching controversy, the Helen Keller Home in Tel Aviv, the clinic for deaf children founded at the University of Southern California by Mr. and Mrs. Spencer Tracy (whose son John was born deaf), the Alexander Graham Bell Award given to Lyndon Baines Johnson in 1967 "for Distinguished Service for the Deaf" and the Royal National Institute for the Deaf's bronze statuette for the Best TV Speaker of the Year.

168

I succumb to an anxious voracity:

the deaf of this world outnumber the combined populations of Britain, France, and Germany;

most of the research now going on is concerned with conductive deafness as distinguished from the perceptive kind (sensorineural hearing loss or *nerve* deafness), but I know that, whereas the middle ear is mechanics and engineering, the inner ear is electronics, with the cochlea functioning as an almost unthinkably complex and miniaturized telephone exchange with twenty thousand "lines." . . . One square centimeter houses equipment equivalent to that contained in one million cubic feet of a big urban exchange;

in 1968 and 1969 Congress passed two acts designed to aid handicapped children, and the appropriation works out to forty cents per child in the nation;

the Federal Bureau of Education for the Handicapped estimates that only one hundred who are both deaf and blind are appropriately placed, yet the country's total number of such children urgently requiring help is 1,600;

in New York State there are 500 deaf and/or otherwise handicapped for whom there are no places in special schools;

after the 1964 rubella epidemic (the United States's worst in a generation), 30,000 children were born handicapped, about 15,000 died before birth, and perhaps 5,000 who were born died in early infancy;

50 out of every 100 children born with rubella-induced birth defects have hearing problems, including 20 who will also develop brain damage or behavioral disturbances;

a scourge? a scourge, yes, and meningitis is another, though neither of these hit you;

then I see a report from Hong Kong that more than 100 deaf and dumb people in Liaoning province were recently cured by "a Liberation Army health team" and can now say "Long live chairman Mao" and sing "the East is Red" (no, they don't mean *you*);

one sixteen-year-old English boy, although totally deaf, won a major prize at the Derby College of Further Education presented by the Central Electricity Board to outstanding students, and no one will hire him, even though he only wants to be a tool setter;

but fifteen deaf mutes have joined the Lockheed-Georgia company, after six weeks' intensive training, to wire "squawk boxes" and other kinds of advanced electronic equipment for jet aircraft;

says Michel Eyquem, Seigneur de Montaigne (whom you can later on call Montee if you want): "Our deaf mutes dispute, argue, and tell stories by means of signs. . . . I have seen some so skillful and practical in that language that in truth they did not fall short of perfection in making themselves understood";

at the Eugene O'Neill Foundation, where forty deaf people study drama for three crammed weeks, everyone uses sign language, and well enough to permit exacting discussions of such things as philosophy, Greek drama, and the psychology of acting technique;

a report to the Federal Government stated that teachers in the United Kingdom "cannot understand their own pupils";

children who learn one mode of signing in school evolve another clandestine one for use outside;

signing, writes one deaf clergyman (who "has depended on signing for most of his lifetime"), "is the natural language of those who lack the gift of lip-reading, and it can be grammatical to a degree";

Sir Richard Paget, originator of the Paget sign system, concluded that the mouth gestures of speech were first de-

170

rived from hand gestures, which means that sign language was the original form of all speech;

and revisions of his system—based not on finger spelling but on one sign for each word—remind me of Chinese and Arabic inasmuch as words with a common theme (time, birds, fire, etc.) have their own basic sign;

and that is good to know, because the signs relate to words and not merely to events, and the closer the relationship the more chance *you* have of having both, of becoming a genuine oral-aural-optical-manual-mental deaf eclectic, capable of appreciating in more ways than one the National Theater of the Deaf signing ensemble the poem of E. E. Cummings called "I will wade out," and then you too will find your thighs steeped in burning flowers, swallow the sun into your mouth, and leap into the air's ripeness. Verbally, that is. And, once you have enough words (by whatever means), you'll be able to do the impossible in yet another way (other than painting, than dreaming): talk to axolotls, to ask them how they got the way they are; send radio messages to both the Concorde jet prototypes wherever they are; describe the biggest slide in all the world. . . .

I've just discovered *The Sanders Reader,* the longhand book which Alexander Graham Bell composed for a six-year-old deaf boy called George Sanders; it employs not only heavier writing to show vocal emphasis, but also a visible speech code, developed by Bell's father, which indicates the position and action of throat, tongue, and lips— and it, the latter, looks like music (or four Mandys, drawn by you, on the first horizontal slide):

And the thickness and thinness of the strokes, for loud and

171

soft, for emphasis and the lessening of it, take us back to Chinese and Japanese, with which you and I have not yet done.

All of us have so far only scratched the surface of the things that can be done for you: there's loads to try. Synesthesia comes after (forgive it! forgive it!) *sign*-esthesia. What of *Robinson Crusoe* done over into ITA?

You're willing? Crusoe-Kreutznaer and all?

I'll do it.

Ie'll dω it.

Why then Ile fit you.

Hieronimo's mad againe.

And when we were deaf, staying in the bundocks,

My eagle, she took me up on her slide,

And I was unwilling. She said, *Ee, Ee,*

Hold on tight. And down I sped.

On the slides, you really feel free.

I write, much of the time, am paid to talk in the winter.

And, unlike you, I never knew how it feels to learn my tenses through colors (though, I must confess, I was always drawn to Rimbaud's *Sonnet des voyelles* and its doctrine of the color of sounds:

A black, E white, I red, O blue, U green . . .

Et cetera (what color is that? what color is the future? what color is the first day of the rest of your life?).

Let's relax.

Your small being is no longer in the old turmoil.

Your small being is now rather big.

Your teacher *drew* a green slide but *wrote* "red tree" under it, just to see what you would do. You leapt to your feet and raved at the error; then, saying it, tried to write "geεd slied," which you say as *geed zlide*.

An epiphany. Wonderful.

172

And now, to keep the record straight, let's add your colors, which you know and love: *boo, geed, re', wy.*

Ellow we've already had.

But not yet *black,* I think, although you've now got *der-ee* (dirty, which black is) and *dowl* (towel), which you like to blacken anyway.

Off we go again, my voracity more anxious (I hope) than my anxiety's voracious. I hope that's what I meant; I *hope* that's the better of the two ill things; there's almost just too much. . . . There's sometimes too much too soon, but there's also too little and too late: I remember vividly a photograph of a bright-eyed resident of a home for deaf women who had three or four dolls alongside her; "the little mother of dolls," the caption said;

I've read that regional accents are often more obvious to people who lip-read than to people who hear;

I've read an excerpt from an essay by a deaf boy who had been on a visit to the Netherlands and I like his prose style:

When we got off the ship it was so hot and the Dutch men gave us drinks. In the evening some of us went on a river bus. We saw the smallest house in the world. We went to Alkmaar to the cheese market. We saw a huge mechanical organ. Then we looked at the Dutch men carrying the sledge full of red ball cheese. Behind us there was a man making clogs. I bought a pair of red clogs. . . .

I've read about Montessori schools, the Model High School for the Deaf, and the discoveries of Bruno Bettelheim; but the piece of reading I most remember is an essay by a German whose special interest is dysmelia children: deaf children without arms, and his point was that deaf children with additional handicaps learn not for themselves or for school, but—and this more than any other children—

173

for their parents. It's true of you: home is school as well as school is, and the aim of both places is to demand the maximum of you, to convert the world around you into your own private hothouse. Hence, at home, all the applause you receive for saying something such as "thumb" and the far from rigid wooing we subject you to. School, of course, isn't as much home as home is, but you *are* at home there (where you can have a birthday party and be clapped for being "gωd" and have a card from your teacher that says "with luv"). School's a bit domestic, then, and home is school with a bit more histrionic pageantry and a lewder, more ingratiating mode of propaganda.

It's all a matter, I suppose, of our being flexible enough to encourage you into an educational opportunism, by which I mean an opportunism *non scholae sed vitae* (as the Latin proverb has it)—not for school but for life. And that entails forgetting the far end of decorum best exemplified by some lines in a film I saw the other day in which a British consular official and his small son got off a train somewhere in Spain and were met by some flunkey or other, who then said to the boy, "Pleased to meet you, Master [Whatever-hisnamewas]." Moments later, father takes son aside in the full brunt of that Spanish sun and rebukes him: "We don't say 'Pleased to meet you.' " Not the done thing, not the elite formula.

Well, I hereby grant you *carte blanche* to add PTMY to your magnificent arsenal of solecisms and exempt you forthwith (as if you cared) from behavior requiring any degree of dehydrated stateliness. It can be a little nerve-racking to live with and go out with someone whose sense of "proper" behavior is as scant as yours is, but better that— better anything worse—than pernickety demands that would silence or annul you. "We are often," one seventeen-year-old deaf girl writes, "given withering looks when we try to

174

make conversation, designed to make us feel embarrassed, and shut us up; they well serve their purpose. Such an attitude does not go a long way towards giving ourselves confidence—it has exactly the opposite effect, and it can be disheartening."

Add to that an observation of your mother's. Out in town with you (and invariably with a handicapped friend of yours along as well) she knows what sorts of looks you will all get, and before the looks even come. Staggered by your birdcall or by the abandon of your movements (you dance wherever you feel like dancing), the *hoi polloi* actually lose a second or two while standing to stare and then pout their troughing slots to hold back the offensive word which cannot come anyway, for no word is appropriately offensive enough for what they are thinking. Their eyes they tighten up as if to eliminate you from sight altogether, but not before they have flashed the glance that masks *There but for the grace of God go I* with *So that's the sort of woman who produces that sort of child.*

How to discomfit them is this: before they look away, your mother in a loud voice says something such as, *Come this way now, Auntie is taking you to . . . ,* and at once the affronted faces of the true believers in well-behaved eugenics relax, granting instant exculpation and conferring a bonus to that selfless, altruistic woman for being a credit to society—society that doesn't care enough about these wretched children, and it's so nice to see the trusties having an afternoon out in the presence of a well-dressed, nicely spoken Norm instead of slung almost umbilically from the hand of the shameless dam who, one can be sure, had this visited upon her as a well-deserved punishment for some unmentionable, lubricious trespass.

What people cannot stand to think is that a child such as you was born in the ordinary way and not dumped on the doorstep by some night-traveling devil or mailed to the mother in installments, sender's name not given, as an incubus kit. Or bought cheap at Woolworth's, cut-rate at Macy's, given away as a free gift with any purchase of two hot-water bottles. It's justice, really, gone sour right before your eyes: these folk can't bear to think that it happens to the innocent (such as themselves), so they dream up sins for your sponsors to have committed. In other words, they don't like a universe that's absurd, a universe they can't understand; they can't bear the evidence of a quite impersonal, inexplicable organic mishap. But in their mock-retributive panic they manage to differentiate a little, so that blindness is sort of clean, with straight deafness not far behind— physical, almost, like *mutilés de guerre* and the club foot or even the hare lip—but *mental* handicap, for which there's no readily available automatic response, because after all it's something wrong in the chair in which the soul itself sits: *that* won't *do*.

After all (so the thinking runs if thinking it is), those who've got a clean hurt don't presume, don't get in the way; they gratefully accept such forbearing compassion as they can detect around them, looking up like sheep to be fed with pity, listening hard to the shuffles as good folk get out of the way of that skeletal tapping stick. It's beside the point that most people bellow at the deaf as if all the deaf are blockheads and don't even present their mouths to be read whether they bellow or not, or that most blind people will tell you they themselves get bellowed at as if they too are deaf and, also, get manhandled at pedestrian crossings by zealous would-be pilots.

All that is more or less clean stuff. What isn't is the way someone like you just assumes you are an exceptionally privileged person, free to sing out in ecstasy or pique, free to dance the dance of rage or untrammeled joy, free to

176

touch someone and laugh or leer just because you find them hot or cold to the touch, spongy or furniture-hard. Or, when something tastes so finger-licking good, to get intimate with it and eat it with hands even though, usually, your table manners are mutinously suave. Usually you get about as good a reception as a mongol does and sometimes you get a better one because you don't look different and are in fact a girl of pretty generally acknowledged offbeat beauty. So you fool them by the score and then, just when they've eased back into the clammy upholstery of their preconceptions— another nicely mannered little girl!—you show your true colors and they at once build retrospective accusation into a swindled-looking indignation; why, they might even have patted your head and so exposed themselves to heaven knows what.

It may sound odd, but I think most people would prefer —if they have to see you at all as you taxi round (not that I mean *in* taxis so much) the streets and stores to renew your cosmetic supplies and add to your jet fleet and your museum load of umbrellas—if you had a big label against your chest like the publicly hanged, or if we had you on a leash attached to a pretty collar around your neck (pink for a girl), or if we upped your handicap and crammed you into a wheelchair with handcuffs and some form of a bridle, with maybe a bit for you to chomp on and as a crown the EEG electrodes which you think are hairdressing devices.

It would all be in the interests of the civilized part of the population who have to be protected at all costs and who, rather ineffectually, defend themselves with such weapon words as oddball, crank, nut, idiot, imbecile, moron. . . . Yet, to take only one example, a spastic is born every eight hours, against which fact I'll set the recently made assertion that less than a quarter of the population of New York City is mentally balanced. Statistics I don't need, but I know that for bringing out the latent handicaps in the adult who prides himself on being a regular guy, an *honnête homme,* a decent chap, there's nothing like a few handicapped children daring to pretend to equal rights. Because she knows this, the face of the handicapped child's mother develops a highly specialized expression compact of sangfroid and offensive-defensive readiness, for she has seen them all already and she knows that, when it comes to the crunch, most people only too gladly fall away (even the parent at times is tempted to).

Life, as an old professor of philosophy I knew once said, is an unloving crock of shit, as well as being all its wonderful selves as well. When I last saw him, a few months before he died, he told me he'd been staring at the sun and I asked had it recognized him and that, somehow, made the shit a little less unloving for him for a moment or two; or so he said. Let's end this vein by saying that the professionals in handicaps don't always tell the parents as much as they should and could, such is the wariness of the expert researcher; and this may well account for a lot of do-it-yourself antics such as we've practiced and proved with you, for a lot of the shopping-around for advice and diagnosis-upon-diagnosis that sometimes drives frustrated parents to fly with their child from London to Philadelphia and *vice versa,* from Washington to Toronto and *vice versa,* and also for the woeful gap there often is (although not in your case) between schools for the handicapped and ordinary schools and therefore, by extension, between the handicapped of all ages and the non-handicapped, so-called, of all ages.

Nature abhors a vacuum, as Spinoza said; but, I'll add, vacuums don't much trouble society, for it is in vacuums that the handicapped are most often found; where, having nothing to breathe, they make faces and no progress. There's often a vacuum too between the austere professional and the harassed parent; some consultants prefer amenable children to deal with and thus would prefer the mutest and the meekest of the deaf (which you are far from being), and others, having got what information they need from a specific case (i.e., child), either lose their notes altogether (as in your case) or fail to transmit information to whatever school the child ends up in. "Seen but not heard" isn't quite the right phrase; most people would prefer handicapped children neither seen nor heard, so it is very bad when experts fail to make contact with them as individual people. On the one hand there are the scientific reasons for your being the way you are, which may or may not be discoverable; on the other hand, and even in the absence of scientific explanations, there has to be the art of bringing you up. In Warsaw these days, in the night, loutish types accost the nocturnal stroller with a brick which he either agrees to buy there and then or receives in the head. It's similar with handicapped children: one does what the situation enforces. Who knows? The brick may turn out to be gold and may especially delight, having been received in the dark.

I don't know if you've heard of *The Cosmic Sword* or *The Intoxicated Imperial Mistress,* or of Madame Sueschien Chang or Madame Yen-Wei Kwoh, but these are Chinese operas and Chinese opera singers that depend very largely on what Mei Lang-fang (the Chinese diva of our century) calls "highly concentrated expressions, or artistic exaggerations from daily life." The operas are Pekingese and the ladies are from Hong Kong, but the important fact is that the performances at the Commonwealth Institute in London are for the Commonwealth Society for the Deaf, which one newspaper calls "a rather tactless choice of charity." I can't for the life of me see why, it's not as if the deaf were obliged to go along to be frustrated; it's not as if they were being spared a dime in the street instead of having the receipts fed into the financial arteries of a multitude of component organizations. In fact I don't think the blind, children or adult, would mind an exhibition of paintings being staged on their behalf, or paraplegics mind receiving the proceeds from a charity soccer game played by the able-bodied. I respect the sensitivity that would take the part of deaf people against all possible forms of tactlessness, but I don't think the ladies from Hong Kong (who sing for charities only) are being tactless at all. There is little enough enlightened sympathy with the handicapped and I'm delighted to salute it when it occurs, but compassion can sometimes waste itself in overprotectiveness in matters that are picayune. The difference that really counts is between a performance which deaf people, if they attended it, might not perfectly hear but which helps them indirectly and, say, a discourteous bellow in a public place, which helps no one at all.

What I began to say, though, was that you yourself might enjoy just contemplating those "highly concentrated expressions" and "artistic exaggerations," just as you enjoy the cardboard gargoyles hanging on our line in the living room and the color photographs of the latest Frankenstein monster (or "the Being" as he is sometimes gently called). And from what I know of handicapped children, were any one of the more fearsome monsters to promenade through your school at closing time, you and the rest of the children would follow him like the Pied Piper. One extreme receives another.

Speaking of operas and of not hearing them, I find myself irritated by the highbrow silence-cult of the last five years or so. "Silence" is one of the In words, you see, and language is such a trial, such a worthless sham, such an expense of the brahmin spirit in a waste of shame. Camus's

180

"cry of the mind exhausted by its own rebellion" is followed by millions upon millions of words in which writers beat an ironical retreat from the word itself—the word that abstracts, that falsifies, that dehumanizes, that substitutes Apollo for Dionysus, that offers only the illusion of control and discipline, that launches ambition without nourishing the heart, that is clearly inferior to chemical equations and symbolic logic for the chore of describing what we know, that is so arbitrary a form of non-communication it is best employed—if at all—to expose its own fraudulence or in accidental, random works for which the "author" is not responsible at all. Anybody who's done any amount of so-called serious writing knows about all that and has surely, in his time, longed to succumb into pure alliteration with Joyce, into connotational percussion with Dylan Thomas, into the Cut Up Method of Brion Gysin with William Burroughs, into alphabet pictures with the concrete poets, into the All with Rimbaud, into Zero with Mallarmé. . . .

The only sincerity is in silence, the only ecstasy is that which remains unstated. Yet if we were to force all our exponents of anti-word into the near-wordlessness of someone such as you—make them live your life while remembering all the words they once had like toys of which they've been deprived—would they not run for the dictionary hills, heedless of the ironic subtlety of their former position and aching to devour the first bit of print they happened on and to talk with the first person they met? If not, you are surely in a most enviable condition that is likely to become the new vogue. Half the fun of pretending to repudiate words is being able to use words about doing it, but when you never had the words anyway you don't have the option and you don't have half the fun. It's one thing to say on paper that you hate words; it's quite another to be *you,* say, stranded in the middle of a city on your own, verbally

181

knowing neither address nor street nor time nor currency nor native tongue.

Clearly enough, insofar as words concern me myself—setting these down hopefully for you, certainly for me, probably for others—it's an incontestable help to be able to address you, and very different from the long silences of our horse-play or our sittings-together in repose. You, in turn, in order to come closer to the medium in which I'm expressing myself, will soon be having modified hearing aids which will bring the sound in your ears almost up to what we would find the decibel equivalent of a jet aircraft, with engines on full, close at hand. So that, one day, I might be able to read Aesop's Fables to you or an abridged and simplified *Treasure Island;* hardly, I think, for many and many years, this prose, these words. Samuel Beckett, who agonizes about words more than anybody and uses them better than almost everybody, struck home to himself with one furtive-sounding axiom in *How It Is:* "Words have their utility the mud is mute."

And that juxtaposition, meaningful because we are none of us mud, is truly how it is. Not only do I want you to be the supreme Romantic who, in the words of Mario Praz, "listens to the prodigious concerts of his soul without attempting to translate them into notes"; I want you also to be able to go and buy a pound of butter. You live in a long emergency that is none of your own making; an emergency that has taught me two things: how precious any kind of language is, whether your eventual limit happens to be Edgar Rice Burroughs or Wittgenstein; and, under the stimulus of your unorthodox avidity, how hidebound the modern imagination is, how tame, how timid, how prosaic, when all the time it should be playing religiously in its own right, not only poking into physics and chemistry and natural history, but responding to the terror of non-being by creating

"Words have their utility . . ."
(*You thank my editor at Harper & Row for some Christmas tights.*)

what was not there before; which, essentially, is what it is for.

It is like the day, some two years ago, when you were out playing in the frosted-over mud of the garden in a blue anorak with the hood laced firm under your chin, and pounding away at a tree with a small shovel; the phrase *royal-blue forester* flashed into my head and didn't go away again; something new, like the pantomime within these pages.

Christmas has come and all but gone, but you, who seize upon many things just as they are about to disappear, have held on to it in the form of a ritualized once-every-half-hour ecstasy you bring about by calling *Oo! Ba! Mandy!* and cupping one hand over your eyes. Then you sit as if carved in alabaster, or cuttle-fish bone, while one of us goes out of the room to rewrap one of your many presents and ostentatiously smuggle it in again. Unable to contain yourself any longer, you pounce upon the bearer and rend the fancy paper, usually giving the contents the merest inspectional glance.

It isn't, for once, innocent greed; it's a mystery that you want repeated over and over again: the trim pageantry of wrappings, the flimsy strait-jacket of Scotch tape and silver string, the pretense and the tantalizing and the certainty that a parcel never lets you down. *Oo!* is for beauty, as *Ba!* is for present, and as we are for fetching and carrying— to and from the upstairs cache—toys whose existence you know of, but whose frequent vanishings and reappearances you complicitously accept. Even out of Christmas, that reliable mess-mass, you construct an event even more reliable that enables you to celebrate reliability every day. What is good you want to spread out and what is spread out you want to multiply, perhaps, until it becomes the whole world. The honey from the comb becomes your finger paint and your presents become presents of the mind.

Not that, for a second, you would let us secrete from you (even only to give back to you rewrapped) your Meccano erector set with electric motor. No, like a tin-and-cardboard

184

Parthenon, this stays put, stacked on the roof of your doll's house—or, rather, the boxes do, emptied after we've built a windmill or a roundabout, or full after we've dismantled. Just now, though, nearly all the parts are locked together to form a two-foot-long hypodermic complete with six rotating needles driven by the tiny yellow motor. The vibration is enough to send the nuts spinning off the bolts, but you don't heed a flaw so trivial.

Zhok, you say, pointing at whoever is to play doc.

Then: *nee'ul.*

And then you, or we, receive the rotating six-pronged injection from the spinning blunt needles, and you quiver, whichever role you are playing, with giddy giggles.

Mandy *zhok!*

Nee'ul. Then you scream the word.

Do you want to knit, like that, right in the middle of something else?

No, you don't. *Nee'ul* is also gun, so we find your cap-firing six-gun and you smile, a little scared because you know you will now have to fire it. But, with a face that tells us it isn't losing face at all, you set it down and leap across the room to your easel and begin to chalk or paint (depending on which side of it you're at) a huge Mandy or May, and tell us your name, which you have now exoticized into Mandy (or May) Weiss. Sometimes, though, it comes out as May Wet, which can be read as a water warning but which might simply mean you have it in mind to go up and see somebody sometime, or have someone come up to see you.

And therefore *must* you go around with your skirt or nightdress rolled up like a seaweed cummerbund high above your navel? And inch, hunch, your way backward through doors, tapping on the woodwork like an overgrown crab, and sometimes ending up further back than when you began, all this with your eyes almost shut and, across your face, a grin of silent refined irresponsibility directed at no one at all? You have cut the hair off all your Christmas dolls; there are five bristled skulls on the ledge above the bath, just as if a nit doctor had gone berserk after years of picking and scratching and just mowed the crop off all the heads in sight.

A'poo, you say. We don't know what this means; it isn't apple.

You follow it with *ba*, which we know.

Nee'ul?

No-o-o-o, you histrionically tell us. *Ba*.

Ba Beard?

You smile agreement, but we try, *try*, you further to see what you'll say.

Horse?

Hawz, no-o-o. *Ba. Oo, ba, Mandy. Out*, with one hand covering your eyes and with the other pointing at the ceiling.

So we do it and then do it again, to make you use words.

You have become undiffident.

You overpower the mustered manpower of all of us.

One of the butterflies in the school play (a performance we looked forward to with intense misgiving), you broke out of your tall shuffle and skimmed off the stage to inspect the audience. At the school party your head teacher, somehow anticipating one of your flashpoint sorties, held you in comradely manner by the hand while the conjuror performed, but, needing to blow his nose, let you loose for a second or two, and there you were on the stage, wreck-helping with the act. I must say, though, you paid your debt in full: having quit the stage, you just as abruptly went back to it. All in your own time.

Your second school report shows what you have done

with a year: you have usefully exhausted it. You appear, it says, to enjoy using your hearing aids and you vocalize spontaneously and continually. Wherever you go, you carry a small mirror in which to watch your mouth. You *lip-read* simple nouns, "aided by hearing." You imitate rhythm and intonation well; you repeat simple nouns; your vocabulary is increasing, although you do not often spontaneously talk. You *copy* simple nouns but indulge in no spontaneous written expression. Pre-reading you excel at: you match word to word and word to picture; but with numbers you are less ready, eagerly taking part in all practical activities but reluctant to count. Your drawing and painting are lively and original and at handwork you have good manual control. You demonstrate great interest in all creative activities and, I read, you embark on "self-initiated free play in the swimming pool with increasing confidence." And you are more willing to accept new classroom routines, less timid of large groups of children. Your hearing is still "difficult to assess," but, all in all, you have been cooperating very well, and "progress is evident." If that doesn't deserve a few words from me, I don't know what does.

Thinking of the LEM which you ingenuously watched assume position on the moon, I fancied you a lemming, the only one of your kind—self-led and self-pursued—half expecting any day your computer to give us an 1107 alarm threatening complete destruction of your erasable memory, or a 1201 that tells us you've no more storage space and no longer can accept inputs every two seconds; but I ban that fancy straight away. One day soon, perhaps, after you've had your hair washed and dried and are sitting in a soft, groomed peace with your head wrapped in the peasant-style scarf which makes you look somehow Russian and makes me call you Natasha Ilyanova Grushinskaya (a loved child has many names), you'll say something for which I'll reward you with a tube of space toothpaste that has adhesive cloth manufactured into it to prevent it from coming apart in the air: not *yummay,* which is the pacifier you've self-satirizingly begun asking for again, long after I thought you'd forgotten both the word and the thing; and not *gni,* the knitting you do with elfin, contrapuntal abandon; and not *bu'fly,* of which you were a cinnabar-colored specimen; but your old *yee* extended into what I think it has been all along. I mean *yes,* and so will you, even if—a prisoner at play in a garden enclosed with chicken wire, either running toward us with the fresh air coming off you like perfume or standing at your slide vibrant with ownership—you're still as incoherent as daily light, as vulnerable as uranium 235, and have an atom where an atom shouldn't be.

GALA

We'll meet again, we'll part once more.
The spot I'll seek if the hour you'll find.
My chart shines high where the blue milk's
upset.

James Joyce,
Finnegans Wake

ONE

Canis Minor to Cassiopeia

C an a human being hide? Not like a god, at any rate. You skulk within the theater of your various selves, though doomed to one esophagus, one brain stem, one ration of threescore years and ten (plus any bonus from prosthetic surgery). Speak in tongues you may, but with one tongue only. Your only hiding place is arithmetical: you will always have thoughts that pass unrecorded, even by yourself, and so, over a lifetime, you build up into an incalculable sum. You will know yourself only through samples, factors, predominances, flashes of ore in rock, and this is how others have to know you too. A man's mail isn't addressed to all of him. A human is a breeding tribe; and of the Mohicans, say, who compose him, the last one's never known, not even after death, nor even before it by the executioner who's handcuffed you behind and stuffed a soft rubber ball into your mouth to quell the sounds. The universe that a human is expands indefinitely the further he, or anyone, probes it. Outward, ever outward, alas, until out of sight.

Actually, I have just penciled the above on a green-lined pad of disinfected-smelling yellow paper: my contribution to

3

identity as an art of fugue. I so often feel as if someone, some puppeteer, is working me, writing me down, someone who is unknowably in charge, even if not in the right. No atheist I, but an anti-theist, that most reluctant of witnesses (as if the difference made any difference). It is almost eleven P.M. and Vega is on the meridian. Do I keep astronomer's hours, until four in the morning, because I can't sleep, or is it the other way around? I no longer pose the question with hope. For the past year or two, I have been working up to a visit, a reunion, with my sole offspring, not that she knows it, not in so many words. I would like to feel wholly behind my motives in that act, but I'm torn: as many voices urge me back as forward. I heed them all, acting when in doubt and brooding while action is under way. It will no doubt always go thus.

And so? I, Deulius, novelist, can no longer back down. I return to the entry I began with and add a sentence that reads, *I am in trouble again,* only at once to distract myself with an allusion to the Radiant Point of Giacobinids, a meteor shower of 1946. Exactly where was I? On the point of taking an aspirin or six. If headaches are grace, I'm multiply blessed. Mind made up, I'll write as if for publication (that dubious hoist to one's spirits), as many times before. I intended otherwise, but what's to lose that isn't lost?

According to the legend on the back of my planisphere, thing which omits the Moon and rotates beneath a hand-sized ellipse cut into a square of celestial blue card, if you learn the stars' positions, the planets become the strangers. A neat reversal, isn't it, there being so many more stars than known planets. But it's a hard way to make the familiar strange, installing it thus in some unthinkable vastness. It's perhaps even a way of universalizing human hurt or joy, just think of that. Doubtless the Edgar Telescope Company, from whom I bought this thin astrolabe for the price of a flashlight battery, means Venus, Mars, Saturn, big Jupe, the four most easily seen of the local crew, but the maxim fits Earth as well. As if to say, bicycling toward the Statue of Liberty, with eyes firmly fastened on her crown, the rider finds his leg motions incongruous, and even more so the chain, the frame, the wheels. Or, reassured by the electric-blue Pleiades, he fidgets at what he stands on, the arches of his feet aching while he cranes his neck. Something such. A useful, fortifying idea worthy of an incantation: Altair, Deneb, Mirfak, I say, choosing the most foreign-flavored names for intimates, while New England, the Gulf Stream, Daylight Saving Time sound inexpressibly remote, nothing to count on. Maybe it works, over a span of years, but only if you try harder than is decent, and by that time you're nowhere at all.

Ultra-fondness, then: love of the distant, that's for me, not an astronomer royal but an astronomer ordinary, seeking out the constellation into which pain, or mortality, fits without fuss; into the jazz of cosmic chemistry. At least, perhaps, it mitigates the abiding headache I've spoken of, that goes away as if winked at only to return recharged, more elaborately nagging, all the way from brainpan to "heartspoon." But, to get on, my matter properly begins as follows: IT IS A MARVELOUS NIGHT, THE SORT OF NIGHT ONE ONLY EXPERIENCES WHEN ONE IS YOUNG. THE SKY . . . or: SO, THEN, WE ARE HERE IN ORDER TO LIVE; I WOULD SOONER HAVE THOUGHT . . . But it can't, of course, any more than it can begin, I SAW ETERNITY THE OTHER NIGHT. As a matter of fact, I can see it, or some of it, almost any summer night, cloud permitting, which is why I have come to loathe that substance, anxious to be out at my post on the balcony, eye to the Astrax eyepiece, with Penderecki's *Auschwitz Oratorio* or Ives's Fourth Symphony pouring from the stereo through the screen door behind me, and the merest first pile of imminent middle age itches from the cramp I sit in. The only way to do it is to transpose organs, or instruments, and talk directly into the tiny pupil of the lens itself, projecting

5

the words across the Atlantic and the Pacific, even to Andromeda and the Islands of Langerhans. Thus coming full circle. After that, I shall look with my mouth, read with my ears. Calmly, I say to her, in rehearsal, In a manner of speaking we have spoken before, under so-called difficulties which we still share. At once the headache lifts, I am once more crystal-headed.

Going on, I enter the swim of things with a voluntary, a speech suite: On behalf of you, in your deafness, I spoke, as much in your absence as in your presence, shifting every now and then from plain talk into peacock bravery. And you rarely answered, hardly then having language although a coffer full of forbearing smiles. Response I found in your thrusty drawings done with a never uplifted fiber pen, in your big-lettered versions of your name, even in the curved graph of your hearing loss, its abscissa the core of a brutal riddle. Years ago, like accomplices face to face, we mimed and mugged, and now you know getting on for four hundred words, the fruit of endless echolalia, year upon year of hard-driving school.

Unkindly kind, the situation now is that visits are allowed, she to me, I to her, as if either of us were in the lock-up, some Lubianka of the kinship state. Prisoner of February 23 awaits arrival of prisoner of October 18, as simply as that, except of course that she has to be fetched, like a baby giraffe or a box of new-cut lilies. No matter how big she has become, on womanhood's edge (on a bigger nothing's margin), she entails preparations, logistics, goods, befitting one who steers at the Magellanic Clouds, as if her own planet were hostile to the very life-form she represents, as it almost is. What a commotion, what a marathon of getting ready. Tickets, schedules, emergency numbers and remedies, calendrical affidavits, all I haven't consulted being the sun dial, the almanac, the *I Ching*. Were she slinking out from behind the Iron

6

Curtain, it would seem easier, except that we don't need guns or darkness. A bit of a gantlet to run, all the same, what with time zones, jet lag, international variations in fodder, lefthand drive for right (I can see her now, scowling because the driver's on the wrong side), ninety degrees in the shade for sixty-five among the dogs and the mad English, and her own private metabolic clock, working as usual on sidereal time, though that isn't the only reason I call her Milk.

As for the conventions of this autofiction or interior deluge, they're few. (1) Everything permitted. (2) No obligation on her part to answer, collaborate or read. (3) Two weeks allowed for composition, say a dozen pages a day while she tries to tear them up, or while she sleeps. Neither enueg (word for a long medieval bleat) nor a put-up job (such as staging the Week of the Creation twice over in six rooms). It's going to be more like my eavesdroppings on our behalf on what we might have said had things been otherwise. And this will survive, a lexical echo of where she was, and what.

As I read through, even so early, I find every C and G, A and U, a textural obbligato to what went wrong at her vagitus, or even before, as many as nine months earlier, when, as the books tell us, the DNA of the sperm unites with that of the ovum, and that is that, beyond revision. Occasionally nature makes a mistake and binds the wrong molecule into the chain, the result being that, when splitting occurs, the two molecules that form won't be identical, and, as the books calmly enough point out, there will be corresponding changes in the code of instructions and the individual will deviate from the original pattern. Clinical horror-story I know by heart. If she could understand that explanation, she might not need it. So let me pay my dues again and again to C, G, A and U, the gods of the copybook: to cytosine, that sounds close to trigonometry; guanine, evocative of bird-droppings; adenine, almost a girl's name; and uracil, which might almost be the magical toothpaste of the year. Grand

7

committee of teleological agents, they'll never be far from mind, heading each thought, steering each fit. I'll stop, and then on.

Graffias in Scorpius, Cheleb in Ophiuchus, Unukalhai in Serpens, Almach in Andromeda: uncouth-sounding stars which, in no special order, keep coming to mind and hinting at unmentionable monsters as I pore over the grease-thumbed tar black of the star charts lined in Euclidean white. No matter: with each paragraph I lose a little of me to chemistry, a little of chemistry becomes my own. Win a few, lose . . .

Uncanny that tomorrow's the day, confirmed expensively by telephone, and all I need to do, having readied the house, vowed to change my sleeping habits, is to clean up the strategies of this, the intended remnant after she's come and gone like a nova that bursts forth and fades, even if to erupt again years later, like RS Ophiuchus, 1898, 1933, 1958, 1967. Here's hoping, I tell myself (there is hoping here indeed), it won't ever be that long for Milk and me, who have never been able to exchange letters, what with her being incommunicado (unlettered and unphonable) as well as in a non-stop category called constant supervision. No postscripts to her presence, then, not from her anyway; hence my need for verbal spoor, something beyond the school's guarded reports (She is making progress and learning to recognize coins). *That* when she was twelve. And now tomorrow has come I see myself setting out full of giddy foreboding. An arch, as Leonardo said, is only a strength caused by two weaknesses. Draw strength from that thought, I tell myself. Draw from it now.

Abbreviating chores, I'll record only that I'm driven to one airport, where the handwritten country menu reads Dough-nought with an Oops! above it and a line through the second *ugh,* then fly to another that has a long arcade of display cases

8

crammed with trash, then cross several thousands of miles, in the course of which a home-bound Englishman reading a journal about metals spills whiskey on my shoe and I decline to dab it or kick aside the fallen ice. I avert my clogged gaze from a South African film about a patrician former Olympic gold-medalist who wants his son to win a local marathon, and, instead, while music, on channels (or canals) obedient to a rotating wheel under my left thumb, flows into the stethoscope I rent for the price of a paperback, I observe the dawn's vertical spectrum as it fattens behind my Plexiglas porthole.

Approaching her at over five hundred miles an hour, though much slower than Earth spins, I divide the sleepless hours between Classics in Stereo (2) and the Jazz File (9), which is to say between hosts Carmen Dragon and Leonard Feather, unlikely-sounding watchmen whom I splice back to back, Cain and Abel of the ether, in the violet night sky. Here is how the menu of the earphone reads: two movements from Tchaikovsky's Suite Number One, music of soul vermilion, while the horizon flickers (what on earth the time is, I have no idea, but I'm sure *she* isn't watching the dawn); then Mozart's Serenade Number Six in D Major, in which a chamber group seems to be counterpointing a full ensemble. What appetizing euphoria as the east blisters white.

About the time that Ellington's "Johnnie Come Lately" thumps forth with flaunting fused brass, the dawn is a visual scald, the pastel spectrum has almost gone.

"Go Back Home," a raucous percussion from the Don Ellis orchestra, comes almost as a hint while I tug down the plastic shade over a window brimming with eye-wounding silver. But I've seen the day come up like thunder, Rudyard Kipling's fetish; I've scanned Earth's drowsing meniscus; I've felt like a returning astronaut aloof behind the heat shield. Leonard Feather says goodbye: "Take care of yourselves and of

9

each other," which sounds like an intrusive rebuke. Or was that Carmen Dragon? I don't care as I sip the orange juice an alert hostess delivers. Airmaid, I think; she's an *airmaid*.

Already past more time zones than birds allow themselves in one go, I walk down the steps from the jet in clubfooted reverie and show passport in a country other than the country of origin (as the inside cover of my ticket says in a tart addendum concerning the Treaty of Warsaw). I was born here in a season of fogs. All I have to do now is wait an hour or two, shave because I won't have a chance to do so later on, come round enough to collect one tall girl infatuated still with planes, and (if not in this order, at least in this approximate dimension) lunch awkwardly as part of a disbanded trio at the airport restaurant, check documents and cabin supplies, and hope to board the 1300-hours departure without too much fuss, streak back along the great-circle route before local time takes hold, yet not before general fatigue sets in. I'll be setting a retarded child five hours further back, a grimmish thought on which I cannot linger.

An impossible enterprise? Of course. Akin to recovering a space capsule? Nearly. There yesterday, here today, there today, and gone tomorrow. Not quite, but close enough to it. Where, I'll be asking, did the day get lost? Arrive there at 1530, which is 2030 here, and settle down to five hours by car. The logistics are special, are they not? More like logarithms. She cannot, ever, travel alone, even with a label round her neck like the schoolchildren whom the hostesses, airmaids, ply with tiny pilot's badges, flight logbooks scaled down, coloring books, soft drinks, and daintily wrapped candy. And you can't drive alone with her because she might leap out or seize the wheel on a turnpike at seventy miles an hour. But at least we two get to board first, along with the elderly and parents with toddlers. My twitching mind strays to the Epstein bronze marooned behind the terminal's giant picture window; commemorating Brabazon, patron of aviators, it's like a lava flow frozen in mid-air over its pedestal. Supposedly Icarus, or the spirit of flight, it appears to unfurl untidily above the passengers' and watchers' heads. My mind makes common cause with it and goes null, hovering.

Uh-huh, the bar is closed, but what care I, having no need of it, as for several years now. A bar to moan at, however, that might be something worthwhile. The restaurant is stalled between the end of breakfast and the start of lunch. I exchange a few Washington-headed dollars for the Queen-embossed pounds that seem smaller yearly and a handful of outsize Britannic coins that buy too little considering their weight. A telephone call later, the experiment is on, and this piece of its raw material is already wincing at the prospect. I lap up the phenomena of disorientation: coffee tasting of cocoa, Muzak from the Sixties, flight announcements in an accent so fastidiously muted it might be a laryngitic sloth, an aroma of cut roses from the flower stall, one of leather from the gift boutique, a gust of hops as the bar seems to open and close again like a bloom of evil, a reek of kerosene from the runways, even a whiff of vomit from under the seat. Somnambulistically patrolling the imitation marble floor, which makes each footstep glide a fraction as if I'm walking gingerly without meaning to, I buy English and French newspapers, note the headlines, fold the stack double into my bruise-black flight bag, and go to eat haddock with an egg, refusing the always-offered french-fried potatoes. This country's future will be found to have been long behind it, spurned in the 1890s when it showed its face. Unfair? I know it is, but this morning I'm hardly capable of balanced thought.

Communiqué: the pair of them, it seems, will take their lunch at home, not ten miles away as the swallow flies. An elegiac repast. So be it: I'm guaranteed a minimum of unrelished contact; I'll have time to brood on the status of this

11

reverie, the thing which is assembling itself within the cerebral illusion I've made. I can only call it the pre-written enactment of what hindsight knows took place today in Utopia, meaning Nowhere. It's the past written in the present prophetic tense, as befits. I plan. I go. I claim my Perdita at this distant terminal, whizz her away, will have to ferry her back again, after which . . . there is a metal fatigue of the mind: a wing falls off, the nose splits, the tail crumples up. I do these words to draw my line through time, across the Mercator quadrants, to prove it all happened, was capable of happening, and so can go on happening. Saying it, I do it. Saying I do it, I'm planning it. Planning it, I do it. Having done it, I keep it in the present tense to make it last. I know that to write in the past tense confers an illusion of command and fixedness, but the future tense is just as final. For instance: *I bought her a doll,* a second ago, and now the sentence is cold. *I buy her a doll,* am buying it now, and already the act is over as the hasty, never-quite-simultaneous sentence that almost sheaths it dies. *I will buy her a doll,* and the act is over before begun. Something always keeps the rhetoric from coming true. Something always keeps the truth from being rhetorical. Better, perhaps, to kiss events without thinking at all.

Clearly, there are subtler ways of living than writing things down, *whenever.*

Aramaic? No. Ogham script? Never. Linear B? Hardly. Then what? Just allowing the electrical scribble of cognition to fizz and fade out.

Going to hell on an abacus, mouthing prayers in code: that might describe me.

Urging on my mind's eye without looking at the outside world.

Careful now, I instruct myself. Be tactful. You'll soon be

high over the ocean again, watching Milk grin at the cloud floor.

Arrange, arrange, arrange. Reconfirm pre-reconfirmed reservations.

Calmly take over when that iron-clad umbilical has to stretch, and reassure the girl as best you can. That she'll get her mother back in fourteen sleeps. "Vordeen zleep."

Get her aboard fast, beguile her with aeronautics, the up-ness of the plane she has always called "abbala," stress on the first syllable, please.

Check that her two hearing aids aren't on the blink (and abstain from awful metaphors). Then let her shed them for the trip, if she so wants, what with her lip-reading so demonically accurate. See all, hear nothing. What else? Tranquillizer at the ready, one she won't reject.

All ball-points, fiber-points, puzzles, crayons in the status astronauts call Go.

Get mentally ready for custodianship, and urge whatever beneficence warms the cosmos not to make her run amok, ripping out the flotation cushions, fisting loaded plastic trays of near-computerized food, clamoring for snow, or TV, or a ride on her swing, a slide on her slide, a sleep in her very own bed. All that up there, among the invisible stars.

Going westward in daylight (which precedes going west and gone west), we won't see Jupiter, as I did while coming, but we'll certainly be flying to an intenser summer than this gusty carbon copy, copyright by the temperate zone. In her lingo, summer is "when the moon is hot," season in which she likes to ford rivers, romp in her plastic pool outside on the lawn that I no longer tread. She still has no word for sun.

Count out the time for her, I remind myself, and mark her

face when, after two mealtimes, she arrives almost at the hour she took off. Where, I wonder, will she think the time went, she having no abstractions. Entering into the anomie of travel, she may well laugh, loving an uncontaminated surd; or, aghast, she'll rip the cabin apart, given a chance, as her true old circadian rhythms tell her she's been betrayed, it isn't 1530 body time at all, it's half past ten, two hours after she goes to sleep.

Going to sleep on board, though, she'd come to life at midnight Eastern Standard Time, just when she should be dropping off, as I. Helpless, I leave it to nature, which . . .

A lottery, as everyone has told me. Play by ear and expect a crisis somewhere along the line of flight. I'm just tempted to fly back empty-handed, having anticipated enough in the past hour to fuel a month; but no, I'll go according to plan, hoping she's been as fully briefed as possible about the day's and the next two weeks' events. As it is, she'll have more sense of going from than of going toward, more of being severed than of being reattached. Surely thought has now canceled itself right out?

Greenwich time is creeping up to embarkation time. My head fills with bags for motion sickness, glibly dubbed. My sinuses hold isinglass, dark and cold. My third coffee sets up an old familiar tremor in my wrists, and, just as I light up a cigarillo in the shadow of Epstein's Icarus, I see them across the hall at the head of the escalator, loaded with bags. Why did they come upstairs? Rendezvous was ground-floor, at the check-in point, and not for another fifteen minutes. Now we'll have to go down again.

At an enormous distance I hear my friends' voices, expostulating, analyzing, adding diffident riders. Pi: "Is it worth all the emotional turmoil? Won't it upset her more than it's worth? And you?" (She is usually right in her level-headed acuity, born under Libra, like Milk herself, like my mother.)

14

And Chad: "Leave well alone, my friend; distance is the healer. Out of sight, out of trouble. Absence makes the heart grow stronger." (Facetious-sounding, especially when I try out on him prospective titles for some new stars, he's at core serious, a postgraduate in both marital and cardiac attrition.) The legal opinion, as so often, leaves it up to me, cautioning me, however, that what one is legally entitled to isn't always a joy. Why, then, am I committed to this high-wire act, this emotional binge, when the reward is only scars made wounds again, the final catch an exhausted goodbye at this very airport? Pride, paternity, curiosity, masochism, involuntary defiance: my hand includes at least these cards, as well as one that lengthily reads: Addiction to ontological ground floors, the presentation of things in their most horrible aspect. At bottom, I find a passion for disharmony, because harmony there is none, and anyone who thinks there is has another think coming. All that hubris in a dunce's cone upon my head, and then some.

Consider, though, her accreted beauty, which exists, is just now a few yards from my suntanned hand. A Nordic elf, brunette where she once was flaxen, but with the same wide pale blue-green eyes. Pubescent, long, and given to agitated skips while her head rakes sideways in bursts of eager curiosity. My long-distant heavy-featured face she knows; this extended smile is no pretense after diligent briefing. She *has* no pretenses: she knows what she knows, knows not what she doesn't. "Yah," she says loudly, meaning not *ja* but me, and with her usual ritualized protocol asks for a present, an "ooba," as of old, ostentatiously shielding one eye with a cupped hand. "Soon," I mouth, exaggerating the vowel to her, frontface (I'm saving the doll for the crisis). Does she know she, and she only, will soon be in the *abbala* with me, up high, fourteen sleeps, water, swim, where the moon is hot? Then home again? I ask, and she gives an affirmative, impatient

15

nod. This has never happened before, not to her, so let there be light and sweetness indeed. Once upon a time, to all such novelty, or to an unknown person, she would say her imperious, conclusive "No," followed by her "bye-bye-bye." Now, though, she awaits the next step, grinning almost slyly, all mercenary sheen. Encased in the strictest of demeanors, her mother gets the show on the road, anxious for the anesthetic to be given, the first incision made, and aching already to come to in the recovery room in a fortnight's time.

Check in, show documents as if in iron mask; people stare at this girl, and not always unkindly. She spellbinds with her looks, her bravura symmetries. Too soon to board, so helplessly I agree to coffee, more of it. "Beebee," says Milk, meaning she's lip-read that much and wants some too, using her generic word for anything to drink, anxious never to be left out. For no solid reason, an ad comes to mind: "Any fluid you can find in nature, we can deliver by flask or trailer, plus an almost infinite number of mixtures." One day I may need them, royal plural and near-infinity and all, even if only for something to metabolize while being nervous.

Grope up the escalator again, which Milk adores, has always called "bo."

God (that clutch of ions or steam), the goodbyes have been said, and I escort my backward-frowning child through the door to motherless limbo. From now on, screams or fits or mayhem notwithstanding, I have to see her through. *Eureka,* I have found it. Found what? The daring to go on. Oddly, she faces front, a little as if I am going to back her to the wall while the firing squad waits to one side (an image *she*'d never supply), and we arrive at the duty-free shop, which has an oddly liberated sound. I buy her some toilet water, resisting the connotation, and a blue silk scarf in which dragons are evanescing, and (since she hasn't one, is bound for the country where every second counts) an inexpensive watch. Erratically I read the signs behind the counter, marveling at one bit of irrelevant pageantry saying, beside a scarlet flag imprinted with crescent moon and a star, both white, "Turkish currency is *not* accepted." Had such currency *ever* been proffered here, at this secondary although international airport? Milk's big teenage hand is a vise for mine. I walk her to the toilet, just in case, then realize I've taken her to MEN. There is no one to embarrass, or incite, with my young and busty Viking with her two microphones against her canary-yellow jumper and her sizzling earpieces tuned in to phenomena she usually likes to do without. A bud of euphoria starts to peel open, but I nip it: we're not even on the way. No tears, though, no frenzy. After all, she is fourteen. I remember her first pun, akin to an esoteric allusion to Galileo from an Easter Islander, calling her then thirty-four-year-old mother *dirty-fork*. To the lip-reader the sounds look alike, but Milk relished the difference. An inborn wit among the garbled engrams painted that distant day in gold.

Conversation piece while waiting: "Abbala," I say (it is blue and white out there, all its refueling done, its tail fin high as a tree; I've already spent half a dozen hours in it today). She utters nothing, but hungrily points, eyes nacreous with the old aerial craving. She thinks she's going, but isn't sure even now. "Mickel *up?*" Fanning her fingers at me, she again checks that figure of fourteen sleeps that will restore her to mother, and I confirm. If an expression can be of disgruntled complacency, she has one, wears it with potent will. Off soon, we're travelers from an antique land setting out for a peak in Darien, hands linked in First Class (an innovative extravagance), with nothing to declare except each the other. Mickel, she calls herself, rarely Michaela, and never knowingly Milk, which is my own private tag for good and sentimental and almost religious reasons. Perhaps Milt would have been as good. No. If parents knew beforehand their child would be damaged, they'd perhaps choose more suit-

17

able names, easier ones at any rate, like Beau (easy for the child to say) or Bab (almost as easy); but if they knew beforehand, they'd probably get as far as passive euthanasia. Christ's blood clots in the firmament. Gynecology in the stirrups howls. And these are not thoughts to fly around with.

Untold prevarications dog me now I've thought that. I wish, I wish, I wish.

Calmer, just a bit calmer.

Good going, I've cheered up again; I'm on my way to a classical reunion. I'm nearly *there*.

At long last we obey the manicured glottals directing us to gate something-or-other, the ramp, the steps, the ribbed platform at the oval door into Kubla Khan's anteroom, a-sprinkle with a new batch of white-gloved debutantes in freshly sprayed aromas. Two of them coax her into the broad window seat, exclaiming and cooing while she scans the tarmac for mother. I, Deulius, feel like a rejected sponsor, or a used-up battery, or a flipped-off seatbelt. The air in the cabin is crisp and even, has just been beautifully manufactured; and how coolly the airmaids bow, unfurl their apple-firm arms, pirouette, adjust, succor, calm. We have been taken in by a hospice of the sky. We are almost home, in this six-hundred-mile-an-hour living room. Milk's entranced, kneading a royal-blue cushion, while I, I'm unwinding so fast I almost fall asleep. As a turbine faintly revolves into life, she unplugs her hearing aids, unbuckles their harness, and hands it over, microphones and all, like so much bungled knitting. I transfer it to an airmaid, who pretends to put it on, causing Milk to laugh aloud at one so hindered. Tribute to this airline, its light militia has cool; but, then, they can take almost anything for seven hours and a half, and for the nigh-mythic price I've paid I can tap their spines as well. I wonderingly await catastrophe as we taxi out, strapped in.

18

Alert to the straight-line takeoff (an obsessed-feeling trundle that might prove Einstein's propositions about rectilinear speed), Milk smirks like a maenad, giving herself over to upholstered vibration and the back-thrust phases of landscape. Her lifelong love of violent motion—being swung around by the shoulders, being carried upside down, or of handstanding herself against any available wall—takes over; this best roller-coaster of all drives her into a broad uncaptious grin that lasts until we leave the ground. The abrupt shift to smoothness piques her at first, but a thump of upfolded wheels renews the grin. If only, I think, we could cross the ocean at takeoff speed on terra firma all the way, or on ice, stampeding past polar bears and earthbound whales, careening past bergs and frozen waterspouts, while the tremor in our feet goes on and on. If only Hendrik Hudson and his crew would keep on creating the special thunder of playing bowls, then she, the Rip Van Winkle of learning, would never sleep again. Clearly, though, we have taken off right on time, which she at once, with newly developed skill, tells me as I adjust her new wristwatch. "One and a half," she mouths, juicily oblivious of Earth's rotation and west-east headwinds at bitter altitudes.

After that, the cornucopia of executive luxury (doesn't the *consultative* echelon ever fly?) breaks open, and a menthol-fresh airmaid facially not unlike her plies us with carbonated drinks while another, dusky with Romany curls, demonstrates the ocher life-jackets, a charade which Milk enjoys, chortles at around her two barber's-pole straws, as if the airmaid in question is a hopelessly discombobulated goon, victim of her own truss. Quizzical, Milk looks around for hers, to don and then top up by blowing through the mouthpiece. Again I thank the deity of ions for not allowing oxygen masks to flop down before us from the overhead compartments. When they do, we'll need them; until then, if you please, no circus rehearsals.

19

Comes a headset each. What a lark. To Milk this is like shelling peas. On goes hers, like a parody of what she wears daily, except this doesn't prod deep, in toward the drum. After a sly frown at the head-brace, she plugs into the chair-arm socket and happily spins to maximum volume the wheel I show her, getting 110 decibels with luck. Spinning the channels as I too listen, I see one of her biggest smiles, even a tiny flush, as big-band swing slams out, Count Basie to be sure. This is Leonard Feather's Channel 9, where I came in, and I time-travel back to my own teenage record collection, which included such other samples of Basie's raucous ping as "Basie Boogie," "Pound Cake," "The 9.20 Special," "Clap Hands, Here Comes Charlie," and "It's Square But It Rocks." Briefly I yearn for the amplified farts of Gene Krupa's "Tuxedo Junction," the demure stomp of Goodman's "Jumping at the Woodside," the motoric jam of Herman's "Perdido," and other rhythmic gems. My teens are meeting hers; she has just heard, says Leonard Feather, "Everyday" (sic), from Basie and Joe Williams, and the critic's voice goes on within that vacuum fastness, invulnerable to the roar and cold of half a thousand miles an hour as we go on climbing over Ireland. She pouts questioningly, can hear nothing now, until Miles Davis' rendition of "It Never Entered My Mind," and I dumbly applaud the abstract quality of music which, titled something like that, or "Copenhagen" or "Mission to Moscow," makes the maximum style out of a minimal allusion, whereas words, my own envoys, need to tell so much. And while Milk attends to music (that notorious stimulant to the brain's subdominant hemisphere) with befuddled-looking calm, not tapping her foot of course (her only rhythms are her own), I let my mind roam as it wants, marking the aroma of lunch from the microwave ovens, wondering if scraping potatoes makes the airmaids cough, and thanking more than a few of my lucky stars.

A nothing, like that which reasserts itself through contrast after words have been used, now includes us, unlikely-looking pair of fellow travelers, though with the same nose, mouth, and shape of eye. Chances are she'll listen to the one channel all the way, her tastes favoring sameness, patterns, constants, each time finding Basie, Davis, or the Don Ellis ensemble not so much new as still at a distance, unappraisable as time itself, a camel through a microscope, or blood spilled on a galaxy. Divided-up noise, *that* she hears, however, and relishes the bombardment next to her stirrup and cochlea, making something fidget in her middle brain, her teeth tingle, maybe, her head at length, as almost always, ache with an ache she's learned to confide about: "Ah, sore!," indicating temple or scalp in its bush of tropical-thick hair.

Aspirin is easily procured in this high-altitude cul-de-sac, where we shirk the natural context of ice, hydrogen, and sun, that much nearer the neutrinos raining through us every second like mortality itself. I light another cigarillo (cigar privilege denied you in Tourist Class), and Milk poufs the match as an airmaid with wings and patented smile hands me a handful of book matches that image Africa, Singapore, Rome: inflammatory tabloids with which to undermine the domain of Uncle Sam. For some reason Channels 7 and 3 are blank and I shake my First-Class head at the technical explanation I'm given. Damn the Norns of audio. Damn the Norns of cinema—man who make round trip, same day on same plane, see same movie. But no: not again the marathon about the South African Olympic-medalist patrician feuding with his sons, but *The Way We Were*, picturesque at least, a campus abscess lanced. Milk will yawn of course, but might even pick up Barbra Streisand at her plangentest, in which event she will flick an eye sideways like one discovering an elephant's tusk in her ice cream. Is this OK? says the look. Is it often thus? Is this how *you* hear things? One of her least respectable habits is to leer in ridicule at her handicapped compatriots, caricaturing the spastics and the truncated-fin rhetoric of the thalidomides, all the time asking in dumb-show what the hell is *she* doing among schoolmates this un-gainly. Why, look at them, there's something wrong; whereas . . . She evokes that old chestnut of the philosophers, the class of all classes that are not members of themselves, and she will probably find Streisand just as impeded, stunted, halt, victim of macrorhiny or whatever nose-blight's called.

A cruel pair, we'll wound even the caviar, the plaice, the tournedos, the Roquefort fresh from this morning's Paris plane. As for the wines, so help me, I'll curb her: the girl's a compulsive bibber, forever in those old days hunting the key to the liquor cupboard in order to settle down to a good long splash with the rest of us. And what am I going to tell her, I whom she'd ply back then with Dry Sack, when I show my non-drinking colors, intact these last three years? Will she force-feed me from a bottle or, like a mother penguin, squirt into my mouth what she's squooshed around in hers?

Unabashed in the toilet, she helps herself like a Hottentot to all the cosmetics Elizabeth Arden's powder cottage has provided. She insists. We emerge reeking of ambergris or civet, but my main thought just now is that, when I pee, I'll do it alone; her predatory curiosity, fanned on by immodest boys at that superb school, is worse than ever; she'll try to seize and tug until life is over. Foul and feral games we may have played in an almost mythical past, when she was a hooligan child, but now she'd better turn on some decorum. Some, at least. Now she gets a cabin bag, the sac of status complete with the airline's acronym, and she jubilantly finds within more toiletries, akin to those in the pure-pure rear cubicle we've just left. Again she makes up her face, again a shade tartish, but with exemplary finesse; the motions are deft, the results loud. "Yah?" she suggests. Not today, I in-form her. "Ankew no?" she snaps, to confirm my aberrant

22

refusal, and she echoes the negative, her headset on, blotting out whatever is playing with an exquisitely tapered diphthong, an orchestration all her own of the rounded vowel, that makes everyone look, even the intensely preoccupied carnation-sporting VIP with his thirty-seven global newspapers. Sir Fitzcontumely Rex-Relish, was it? (What did the fawning senior airmaid say?) He looks as if he has just seen an engine rip away from under a wing, but then he recognizes it was only one of the semi-aphasic unmentionables next an unkempt barbarian oaf with a suntan and glazed eyes. Back to his *Paris-Match* he turns with an Etonian grunt, while Milk ransacks the bag for something that isn't there, then pitches it beneath her, as if into the cloud clumps themselves.

Champagne has me saying oh-to-hell-with-it, I'll-drink. We'll arrive looped and be taken away in cuffs to Rikers Island or wherever the sauce-afflicted go. Sipping, with a fistful of smoked salmon, Milk looks suave and wise, for once in a world (other than school) where earpieces are worn in autistic raptness. She lip-reads the cabin staff, who clearly are used to being read thus by sybarites aloft not only in sky but in an enclosed continuum of private sound comparable to her own non-stop tinnitus of seashell surf. She has more in common with them than she knows, as if the Monte Cristo chocolate tart had made the Many into One. Plied, we take. Half tipsy, we tremble with expensive mirth, not least, in our very different perspectives, at the non-communication for years (no letter comes; one cannot phone) right next to this Lucullan reunion in a zooming tube. Vicissitude undoes me quite, and I release a long-saved tear that Milk espies, deplores with a vehemence befitting an aunt, and blots with tissue. Under control again, I let her puff my cigarillo once, which cures her for hours, and blithely take aboard another thousand calories with the fish, a sauce like vermilion-streaked cirrostratus. Among these colors, in this cabin dedi-

23

cated to Joseph's coat, the gray line is the present (as it said under some cosmogonical diagram I somewhere saw), and the present is at the moment hard to see. Refraction through a small tear. We're living in animated suspension in a churn of cream embedded in royal-blue velvet, and I half-ban the future, near and distant: if this be altitude euphoria, let it never end. All I'll ask is a little sleep, like Milk, who's succumbed to Mumm's, alcoholic strength by volume twelve percent. Good night, imminent lady, you've almost gone a thousand miles, with only the headwinds retarding us.

According to Leonardo, among the "great" things to be found among us the existence of Nothing is the greatest. This unimaginable entity, he says, dwells in time, stretches into past and future, swallows up all, but is not the essence of anything. I like reading that old polymath, whose brain must have been the bulbous shape of the old-style Göttingen airfoil section, but I'd rather he'd hit on something useful, such as lion manure for scaring predatory deer away from crops. *Next*-to-nothing: that I can just about fathom, whereas Nothing, which I've pondered for more years than I remember, is it simply theoretical absence (a thing in air; the thing removed; and then air again), a vacuum, extinction of the soul by death of the body, or nirvana? Or is it what preceded the first appearance of energy that became matter that later became ourselves? In my book, Nothing's my imagining of my own absence in any of the places I've been: the omitted relativistic ego, which has little in common with Taoist notions of pure emptiness or with Kuan Yin's view of nothing's being established in regard to oneself, the result being that, identityless, one becomes a model of the universe. Much honorable sleeplessness has gone into whatever thoughts I have on this, forever envisioning myself next to Milk, whom the universe bungled into an unselfconscious surd, and wondering how much accommodation a mind can make. For instance, saying: she belongs more to the universe than to me, has more in common with the streams of hydrogen now flowing back from the Clouds of Magellan to the Milky Way than with me, for all my own bizarre metabolism. For instance, saying: there are miracle cures, or even miracles, but these will take a half-century to come, and I contrast her fate with that of the latest maltreated famous Russian, his balalaika on fire, asking myself what is remediable faster, *en bloc*, brain damage or totalitarianism. The former, I imagine, because the second isn't remediable at all: the brain-damaged are retarded, the commissars are not. One day we shall all grow up, when the hippic and the reptilian brains have withered away, then solve everything with nothing but the fairly recent neo-cortex. I can't finish the thought. Nothing, I begin dimly to see, corresponds to my not knowing what part of nature to blame for making her the way she is, or just recognizing one can't bring a case for damages against the internal compulsions of the DNA chain. Paired base and triple coding: what kind of a scapegoat's that?

Canted sideways, her broad but fragile-skinned face has the flush of winy slumber. I guess at dreams I'll never hear about: a candy-stripe avalanche or obsidian blank. And it becomes easier to possess her mind on her own behalf, in default of discursive conversations, than to stomach just the minimum she thinks. Hence, then, galas that implode: silver charms (Lisbon Fado Singer, Atlanta Cotton Bale), the penny gumball machine that doubles as a lamp with bright-checked gingham shade, the kaleido-go-round clock of pastel-colored disks, all culled from the in-flight gift catalogue. Or others, verbal mainly, from sickening pun (the Cyclops' favorite musical note is Middle C) to pyrotechnics (of which I find no sample currently available), as if coincidence or wit gave us a contributing editorship to the tears of things. There's the absurd you find, and the absurd you invent to hurl at it in therapeutic feud. I've only ever understood one form of art:

expressionistic, in which how you feel about things out-
weighs how others do, in which uncurbable sensibility junks
the camera, the calipers, and Copernicus, for what? The
throb, the getting-it-off-the-chest, the sentient mutilation of
what placid people see and count on. How many of us are
there left? Life's extremer than most folk's images of it, so
most folk skip the image altogether. Or most folk have just
become so plain adjusted they feel nothing at all, just routine
indignations, routine bliss, Our Father Which Art, death and
taxes, trust the nation's elected leaders, and hire the handicapped. Depiction limits rage, does it not? The agreed-upon,
the classical, shuts out an I.

All right, one signals with what one has, and one doesn't
vent what's already in another's possession. Phrase-making's
the only poiesis: delicate pandemonium in the eyes; the
heart's gristly *love-you/love-you-not;* and all unfelt form is
mere refrigeration. Half my thinking is epitomistic blazes
amid a linear mosaic of the not-me, yet I dearly like to outline
Africa on tracing paper and mark in the rivers and the ports.
The ordinary's no mere launching pad, is the miracle itself
of course, once deep-inspected: blood cell to nebula, brain
cell to neutron star.

Umpteen miles high, seven of air, above the mid-Atlantic
trench, in the pell-mell capsule of the maniac's haven, I'd
freeze this expedition, halt us here forever, given enough
fodder, toys, and toilet tissue, until it all came right, and,
imagining we were en route to Alpha Centauri, four and a
half light-years away, yellow and red, age not a jot during the
sixty-two-billion-mile trip. Our cosmic Lourdes. A hyperbolical way of putting it, of course, but nowhere near as frightening, in the spectrum of outlandish wants, as the sentence in
which you express your feeling so well you feel it no longer.
Better perhaps never to say it thus palpably perfect, with
always new reaches of the lexical superb to aim for; better to
hold tight her hand, dab her sweating hair, and choose a fresh

channel to listen to after switching hers off while leaving her headset in place. I do, and hit on what I discover was "Gimme a Pigfoot and a Bottle of Beer," hardly First Class, but of the Earth earthy, and pertinent when I recall how this child used to eat, more grossly than any wild child of legend, her feet a-wave over her naked belly, a hambone or drumstick in her paw.

Good: there is a high-wire act of trying to keep our every minute together from becoming a high-wire act. We ate lunch absent-mindedly, right on top of one she'd only just had, oblivious of such shudders as the plane gave. Like a team chosen for difficult assignments. Shoulder to shoulder, we fueled up, and now I have the stretched-tight cobweb in the head that comes from no sleep at all, while she, frayed with too much emotion and not enough understanding (a blend of parcel, waif, and heiress), grows little blebs of tissue over the splintery nerve ends, perhaps to storm furious or jolly among us while the most elaborate afternoon tea in the world is served by the same, but even fresher-smelling, girls. My mind, on strike, knits a puzzle that unravels thus: *gala:* a holiday with sports or festivities; *gala: galaktos,* Greek for milk, hence *galaktikos,* whence galaxy; Galatea? statue whom or which Pygmalion brought to life. Am I engaged in some unwitting triple play that converts bringing this girl to life into a galactic holiday? Taking my own hints like one obsessed? Perhaps not, but that is much how it would feel. In a blue reefer, she. Jaw, chalcedony cool. A fleck of mustard at her mouth corner. Book open on her knees. Albatrosses flying through the cabin. Heavy squawks. Followed by a glazier, bearing a sheet of glass five feet square. Now she reads out, not end-stopping the lines, Shelley's *Ozymandias:* "I met a traveler from an antique land / Who said: 'Two vast and trunkless legs of stone / Stand in the desert. . . .' " Then says, "A bit grandiose, isn't it? The poem that poetry-haters love." Thus the dream within the dream.

Undying afternoon light over mid-Atlantic is the slaty blue of the Siberian cat, or the blue-bonnet salmon in its first few months. Reflying back into morning (an abstract one to be sure), we're only just a bit more ourselves than we aren't. A flat-out Vikingess tests the webbing of her safety belt, flicks an athlete's shoulder as she moves against the buckle, blinks, blinks, blinks. My headache's gone.

Unnumbered minutes later, the wheels go thump in the day above the eastern seaboard. I haven't even bothered to crane out over Labrador or the Hudson valley. A refreshed but bewilderingly peaceful Milk has stuffed herself with tea and buttered scones, fruit cake and Danish pastries. We have accomplished our toilet together without mishap or insult, lurching and laughing. She has proudly unearthed her supply of sanitary napkins right there in the cabin, setting one muslin-wrapped wad alongside an outsize éclair. I have taught her how to play ticktacktoe and, in trying on the quiet to lose, have mostly won. Stomach-twisting anti-climax sets in as we lose height, until I think: this is where the trouble starts, pax's tail in uproar's mouth, but all she does, for now, is beam condescendingly at the drab, hot terra cotta as it soars out of storage. Our cards and customs forms are ready for the groinch-groinch of the inspectors' stamps. Her hearing aids she's rejected, maybe anxious to make an unencumbered entrance into the New World. I feel as if, all night, I've been squinting into my telescope, foolishly neglecting to use both eyes and staring, as one should not, into the moon at full. I'm amazed; she's not. We're there. We're here. The one country has become the other. All is ground.

Grounded, out into eighty-five degrees Fahrenheit and then inside to a frosty sixty that sets her shivering at once, we call at the toilet in limbo, a DAMAS without a suffixed CUS, between gate and immigration, where she deposits a first

Columbian trickle. I'd like to patent whatever's kept things going this smoothly: no scenes, no incontinence, no demands for what's nearly four thousand miles ago. For one panicky moment I think she's decided she's back where she began, after a lavish circular trip. Then she asks, with bright candor, "Where?" and includes in a festive hand-sweep the terminal, the state, the nation. "Meriga!" she hoots, in frisky postscript to Vespucci; and, where I had expected bureaucratic obtuseness at the entry counter, a man in a pale-blue shirt decaled with his chore looks hard at her when she says her new word for the dozenth time, and sternly answers, "It sure is." We are through. Customs here is more wearing than in that other country, where, if you've nothing to declare, you follow the green signs, otherwise the red. But even this costive local apparatus spews us out and free after fifteen minutes. When we are met, Milk sees an ebullient woman with black waist-length hair (such hair a fetish with Milk since childhood), who confronts her with her first pair of polaroid sunglasses. "This is Pi." We all laugh. In my pocket I press the tube of sunscreen balm she has to wear. I remember the doll, forgotten. Five minutes later, with our introductions made, we follow a redcap's trolley into the burning air of the first day.

Consider. One can reach forty without having seen the Milky Way, without even noticing it when casually gaping at the night sky. Of course, conditions have to be right: no moon to speak of, a certain frosty scintillance going on, and eyes attuned, best shut for several minutes in private rehearsal while the big colander of light wheels overhead. Then look up at Cygnus and wait for the clustered star-stuff to bare its shape, a belt of crystalline shingles reaching high across the sky and down to the horizon: gigantic, variable, frail, no one's, everybody's, quite without design or mind, and dumbfoundingly lustrous.

All this I'd never seen, part of the trouble being you have to know what you're looking for. Unprimed, you register some silver haze that might be atmospherics or wisps of stratus cloud, not the real thing. But when you know, there it curves and you can get quite giddy just peering as your pulse thumps, Earth spins, this or that first-magnitude star blazes forth, then seems to quiet again, Sirius babbling white, Betelgeuse droning orange-red.

Unbelievably, the first time I saw it, I thought I'd never breathe again; but you do inhale again, of course you do, almost always. Aghast, I nonetheless felt a twinge of partnership. The thing was so inclusive; there was nothing of ours, down here, that wasn't in it, hadn't been, wouldn't be; yet it occupied only the most minor band of the heavens, there being a vast amount, even of that visible from about 40° North latitude, which was nowhere near it. Mind pulped, I went inside and with aching eyes pored over the page called Astronomical Geography in my atlas. There it was, pale blue on dark, sprawled narrow across two disks representing the northern and southern heavens, a fuzzy circlet crammed with dots like a photograph reproduced on newsprint. If I looked hard at the dots, they seemed to swarm, in both atlas Way and newsprint photo, yet stayed more or less within the lines. And it was as if, having never known it, I had found my address. It isn't everyone who locates himself by staring into vacancy, but I did, mumbling in the night air little fragments of relevant poetry, from Ammons to Zukofsky; even mouthing *Eureka!, I have found it!*, and *Mehercule!* rustily kept Latin for *Oh gosh!* Half a lifetime gone, and I'd only just had the wits to look a few seconds longer than usual, somewhat southward, letting my gaze meander down to Aquila, then Sagittarius, where, at its thickest, the Way seems to develop an elbow, which I now know is the galactic center. It was as if, having gawped my fill at Nelson's Column and Westminster Bridge, I heard myself asking, Have you ever noticed London? That kind of de-blinkering.

Although, as I later realized, it was one in the morning, I telephoned Chad to tell him; I had to give out my news. Awake and watching television of some sort, he humored me, clucked a little and said, of course he'd seen it, where had I been all my life? Good question. When a dealer in rare books can say that to you, you've certainly been idling. I had. But from that May morning I have been infatuated with the sight, angry when cloud or moon or the long winter hid it. High on my list of lifetime's joys, that luscious vertigo of looking up spills me over every time. I'm home, I say, eyeing it across the welkin. It's a chiffon filament of uncorrupted light: they can't damage it, they can't do it in, they can't do anything about it, it's eighty thousand light-years long and eight thousand wide, as many deep, and here I am, thirty thousand from its elbow, looking along it, into it, beyond it, with grand impunity. The cost of the view is just one's death, it's cheap at the price; or so I think until I cool off, and then am tempted to settle for a feebler, cheaper show, a poorer address. Yet luck one has: Earth might have been swathed in perpetual cloud, in which event there would be no galactic view at all, as from Venus. I thank not so much my stars as my planet for being in the clear.

Granted all the foregoing, what, I disembodiedly ask myself, am I to make of that chunk of the universe in the context of Milk herself? An old question, unanswered but repeatedly put, so much so that interrogative speculation has almost ousted any need for answer. Bold questions, yet somehow always askew or ill defined, come and go in my mind like sharks which cannot stop. As part of that, I ask, is she so extraordinary, so spoiled? Is there not, up there, a malformed, ill-functioning star to partner her, just as much as she a result of casual formation? This I ask, of course, while scorning the self-accusation that I'm just after a convenient vastness that dwarfs, minifies, not her only but Buchenwald, Hiroshima, pestilence, mayhem, flood, and madness. It's not a sedative ratio I'm after, no fear! Indeed, it's not hard to see my fumblings, the fumblings of us all, as trivial, a fluke. What, in my devious way, I want is a physics of the permissive, in other words a technique for accommodating the whole of nature, not just our ills, our doom, but our freaks, our flawed, not just our orthodox performers such as Vega and Sirius, intact in the mainflow of healthy stars, but also our Crab Nebulas, which are exploding stars, our peculiar or irregular galaxies, which are neither spiral nor elliptical but untidy, or galactic nebulae ragged as those in Cygnus and Crux, not to mention horseshoe-, dumbbell-, and owl-nebulae, morphic only through metaphor.

Groping? I certainly am. And finding, at length, instances of natural disorder, my head haunted, as ever, by the notion of harmony as the condition into which everything fits, the whole mass of life, nothing skipped. According to Leibniz, who intermittently knew everything, harmony's what God set up at the Creation between mind and matter, as if over the long haul mind mattered at all compared with hydrogen or methane. That mind is redundant I suspect, yet won't admit. At least Man's, at most God's. It exists only to discover and rediscover the absurd and to make plaints about it. I know only that harmony, convenient word, comes from the root *ar*, meaning: to fit. And, whether or not she's fitting, Milk is here, not to stay, but to figure, in the universe as in many lives, and I trouble myself, write down thoughts, about what's at hand. It would no doubt be more impressive to come out with a streamlined, flawless account of why things are so and not otherwise, but I can't, I can only go on thumbing a celestial lift from this or that star, one or another bit of terrestrial foul-up, a waltzing mouse here (some defect of the inner ear), a *gentian acaulis* there (refusing to flower in good soil). I've done it before, I'm doing it again, and no amount of societal good works is going to distract me for long from the appalling, outlandish macrocosm, although deep down I'm willing to see corrective education as teleology's true badge, what the mind is for. That said (and far from done with), I come back to cosmics, can't help it. That a universe, if it ever did, began; or if it ever will, ends; and, in all the unthinkable vastness of its predictable particulars, on-goes, erupting or cooling, expanding or shrinking, I find worthy of a lifetime's amazement, one of the most horrendous things being how named and mapped the skies are, pat and domesticated, thanks mainly to Arabs and Greeks. It isn't just physics up there in the Way, fixed patterns after random heavenly ballistics, but myth-opera and cozy anecdotes through which the dust and the fire and the gas, and heaven knows what savage span of the electromagnetic spectrum, all zoom congruously together. Perseus still "rescues" Andromeda, daughter of Cepheus and Cassiopeia, but Cepheus's a sentry box and Cassiopeia's a zigzag. No, I don't relish the narrative heaven I've inherited, or even see likenesses in the outlines named, but I sympathize with those ancients' wanting to humanize the star-stuff, carve commemorative initials on the astral bark. Just as logical, now, in any newly found constellation to see Albert Einstein rolling up his socks into one ball, or call a new star Bohr, Lenin, or Keats.

Unhappily, I am fetched low by other comparisons, in which my sense of awe equals my sense of pity, or of indignation, while my paltry awareness of physics just beats out my appetite for myth. And that's the only answer I have to those who chide me for so avid an interest in what's impersonal. Indeed, no, there's nothing societally useful in the sense of wonder, no matter how highly developed, unless the sense is harnessed and applied; but even that's not true on the plane of poetry, or dream, or vision, as distinct from the plane of the laboratory. Why, even observatories aren't useful, as first-aid stations are, or cancer research clinics. I can only say: It's there, I'm here, I'm in it, it's in me, and many

33

other conscienceless assents. In the end, one's head includes what it can't keep out, and the gain, like the predicament, is as much metaphysical as not. At the universe briefly, I mean consciously, I'm trying to attend; yet what a speck one's total knowledge is, and what a trifle the Encyclopedia Ecumenica. Better, sometimes, to play than to complain. As it is, though, before waking her from a sleep already eleven hours long, I spend, am spending, a while on those English newspapers I bought (ignoring the French), tear sheets from a tribe famous in history. And yet after fifteen minutes I know of a French-born wife who, with her two young sons, has died from the fumes of a lawn-mower left running full blast in an upstairs room while her husband was on a business trip to Sweden. No suicide note. A former chief of British Intelligence, who vanished three years ago, has turned up in a locked attic in his own house: a seated skeleton in a dark-brown suit, a note in his pocket and, beside him, an empty bottle of unspecified size and a bin full of cigarette butts. A young nurse has been found dead in her nightclothes, lying between the speakers of her stereo record-player, dead from an overdose of some barbiturate; the last record she listened to being "Paranoid" played by a group called Black Sabbath. A young salesman, whose attentions a young café-manageress spurned, has pitched sulfuric acid at her in the public street. He later said he felt he was being slighted, laughed at, smirked at; and he felt hatred. The young woman now wears a thin, high plastic shield to keep her clothing away from the graft area on her chest; the fingers of one hand are slightly webbed, there is a cavity beneath her chin, and much of her epidermis resembles tissue paper. Further afield, a malcontent in Brunei has threatened to mail the heads of British officials to the U.N. Secretary General.

Grossness, grief, I've had enough.

As for us two, we seem to have got off lightly, have behaved with laudable decorum, abstaining—I especially—from power mowers, locked rooms, barbiturates, acids, and decapitations. My own mayhem stays rhetorical. And Milk, who in her time has sharpened the little finger of her left hand (the one she writes with) in a pencil-sharpener, filled her mouth with broken glass, and leaped through a picture-window like a thwarted Alice, is bizarrely sedate. It must come with the menses, must it not? Part of the mighty female web of the blood knot, which she neither asked for nor disdained, and not realizing it's aught but another of the jinks her captious body indulges in, maybe even thinking there's a big sore, inside, that will soon scab over, or half-believing in her twilight logic that she's cut herself on something while squatting, sliding, or in mid-wrestle. Trapped between thoughts of such a beauty going to waste, non-starting although biologically average, and a certain possessive satisfaction that the manchineel (sap and apples) of marriage will never claim her, I light a cheroot over my third mug of viscous tea, deciding to let her sleep it out, saving the novelties—chipmunks, cardinals, outsize robins, the telescope, the neighbors' pool—for later, *after* later, and especially those supplies in the basement: table-sized rectangles of fiberboard, rolls of mat black paper, pots of gorgeous poster color, brushes big and tiny, a rainbow of Scotch tape, the bulbs and screws, the chalk and the cardboard patterns. Perhaps she will never quite know what we've made, but it will at least amuse her, addicted as she is to the big and gaudy, and this mural will be eighty thousand light-years wide, whether or not we use all the materials. Hardest of all was finding orange-red bulbs for the likes of Betelgeuse; I didn't, so Milk and I will paint a few. Ocher enamel paint awaits. All I don't want is an orange daughter, descended from the one who, in the old days, soaked herself with what she worked in: not

35

only paint, but cement (both house-builder's and aeromodeler's), plaster of Paris, and even varnish.

God help us. As a figure of speech (I was almost going to say); as a figure of minimal speech, rather, she works her hands a lot, so that talking is for her as manually busy as tennis or typing, though she signs, does not finger-spell. Yet her mouth moves all the time, meticulously enunciating words she's learned to *see*. Indeed, at times she over-communicates, doubling into faint enigma what singly would have got through. Never mind: Milk the carpenter-cum-handyman is going to have a field day with her big, dry paws whose heavily etched palms are those of a grandmother. On the southern wall of the basement, a large reproduction of Tintoretto's "Juno and the Infant Hercules" (depicting the legendary origin of the Milky Way) will oversee us, in its unscientific fashion, while we build our two-dimensional effigy, which will look something like an untidy airplane propeller, curving up and down on either side of Sagittarius, the hub. Another version, curling against an invisible celestial sphere, might be more accurate, but harder for Milk to make and enjoy.

Going into the bedroom, I audit her mild snore, remembering that you can make any amount of noise provided the floor is carpeted; what wakes her is vibration or, sometimes, light, but not today. It's almost one P.M., and I can see the faint speckle of wet on her brow, as if there were no air-conditioner at all. This head sweat she has in common with alcoholics, but then I think back to mid-ocean champagne, rebuke my own grandiosity, and go out to do some lethargic unpacking. Outside it is almost ninety degrees, humid among the thick green of trees. The house is almost a tree house, in fact, all you see through the picture-window to the balcony being a dried-up fir, several maples, and an apple tree already globed. It is above these that I aim the telescope at night, sometimes cursing the literal ramifications of summer

36

as they blot out this or that star, sometimes even a low Moon. I could sit out now on the long chair in shorts and panama, dip-reading in whatever's at hand, until she stirs, but if I did I might miss her eruption from that uncannily cool room into the tropical fug of the main house, with both panic and stupor in her gaze. In her day, out of gusto or rage, she has ripped doors off their hinges, whereas now, bigger, she's hardly a destroyer at all, more a respecter of edifices, iconoclast turned guardian. With a thumping, heavy-footed slither she will come, and no doubt with a hoot or two, but fast as a scout in enemy terrain, hunting the toilet, some toy or dress that's four thousand miles away. Until then, I settle for tea at the kitchen table, skimming an astronomy pocket book that tells what I already know, about our galaxy's being shaped like a double convex lens, thin at the edges and thicker toward the middle.

Closer at hand, like a critique of pure reason, the *rex begonia* is putting out baby leaves from its hairy, spider-leg stems; the refrigerator has developed a new, cylindrical-sounding buzz; and a new bird, whose call is a grackle's but more syncopated, is drowning out the groomed threne of two doves. A hundred miles away, Pi is getting her beauty sleep too, at her parents', after delivering us, the goods. No, they will have awakened her hours ago. I shall report by telephone tonight, report an event: a *levée*, a day of uncontaminated novelties, a juvenile field of the cloth of gold as Milk discovers cable TV, twelve channels in lurid cathode-color (the result of some flaw in the red gun, so that from time to time the screen has a cochineal flush, menopausal even, and consistently creates wrong color values), none of which ought to disquiet her. Lifelong she's exclaimed a jubilant "ho!" as things have gone wrong with appliances, weather, or hobbywork, a bit glad the macrocosm has its off days too. To an addict, but a repressed one such as she, about twenty-five

37

movies a day means life is too short, one's screen is a needle's eye. With the rest of our day in mind, I roll the chances through my mind, then asterisk in the TV guide all movies having to do with water (2), the Arabian Nights (1), and aircraft (2). Westerns with Indians she adores, biting the dust with each and writhing in counterfeit agony all over the room. Of such films I lose count at seven or eight, noting that Westerns without Indians excite her less. It isn't going to rain, but she mustn't get too much sun, or too much TV, or too much—sleep. Then I realize I am three years out of date on how she lives, having had little news.

Uplifted by half-watching Van Heflin devegetate a golden idol of the Incas, I hear a click and a shuffle not from the jungle and she appears, a somnambulist Viking, her eyes almost concave with inertia, her legs flapping untidily, her face all of a sudden puce with heat. She bays, coughs, goes back into the bliss of air-conditioning. In that instant I shake free from my own heat trance and wonder if, whenever she emerges from whatever private state she's been in, it's a figure coming out of a ground—the hurt girl out of the universe—or vice versa, the hurt universe coming out of a reasonably intact specimen. Perhaps I'll never know, here in my eggshell of cranky pensiveness, as baffled as at ten years of age, when I first discovered sperm.

Confronted ten minutes later with a befitting tall glass of cold milk, she swigs a few mouthfuls, then points at the outsize blue teapot on its tile. So I put the kettle on, thanking my stars she has preferences; there were days, years, when she had none, would have eaten meat raw, eggs at hatching point, a brisling live. No, not quite: the one thing she has always refused is cheese, from whose evident stench she recoils in histrionic aversion. Her eyes devour the house, no doubt comparing and appraising, an enormous question full-blown in her befuddled head: *Is this where he's been all this time?* Not knowing what she's been told, even within the near-incommunicado enforced by her four-hundred-word vocabulary, she is in the unspeakable predicament of being unable to receive multiple notions, or qualifiers, so everything she's told is a simplistic absolute whose causes can only be dreamed at, not discursively spelled out. What little she has gathered she can only parrot, but not to the person it's about, because she can't manage the switch from third-person pronoun to second. For example: told that Santa Claus is away at the snow (in answer to one of her summer inquiries), she'll nod and be satisfied; but, meeting him in some store, she won't query his previous whereabouts to his face. In a sense, all his previous aspects will have vanished in that instant. Away from something, someone, she'll allude, all right; but, confronted, she loses abstraction in eyeball fact. So there's always this paradox to her: if you want to discuss your presence, you have to be absent; or rather, to have your presence discussed, you have to go away, which as often as not, I conclude, gets her citing absence above all. There is sometimes no way to win. Or even to control how you lose. In her shrunken cosmology, beings go, from time to time, into abeyance, she knows not where, though I've tried with maps and globes, guiding little metal planes across blue-tinted Atlantics, but she hasn't yet grasped that the model corresponds to something bigger; the plane might, but the ocean not. I intend to show her the full-size Way at night in order to explain the mural. No, *can't:* she'll be asleep, of course. I decide not to worry about that just now, otherwise I'll be in a bind as bad as the one at Christmas, years ago, when it wouldn't snow, and she ran outside, beseeching the sky with "Where?" and *"Hnow!,"* and in desperation, after she turned hysterical when she saw it snowing fast and thick in a TV movie set in Sun Valley, Idaho, I thought of flying her up to the Hebrides, where the weather was doing what it should. She still inhabits such a frail world of iron-clad connotations. Of chance, of the random, of the very element that fouled up her own brain chemistry, she knows nothing, and doesn't want to. Like an inquisitor that Christmas, she marshaled the evidence: snowy seasonal cards, illustrations in her reading primers, the white fungus on Santa's own chops, all the time yelling *"Hnow, hnow!"* to make the atmosphere be good. Could I have arranged for a ton of the stuff to be dumped over the yard, she would have objected that it still wasn't on the trees or the visible hills. In the end, after getting on for a day's upheaval, she accepted the helpless promise that it *would* snow in three sleeps (the longest time span she could then grasp), and the very next day it did, a bit, and she was pleased enough not to denounce the false prophecy. Out of such inabilities to explain to her came, I think, my own newer, stronger sense of surds in the ordinary world, which we claim to understand when we're only taking it for granted. A Saint Sebastian of a snow maiden, she feels chance's every shaft. Or felt. Dare I optimistically update her? I am going to find out.

At brunch, though, I am not. She polishes off eggs and ham, toast and jam, like a recanting starvationist, with four cups of tea, silently smiling in her perspiration, her nightdress damp, her hair an unharvested crop.

Calm, she seems even resigned: *things* happen, and this is another of them, so who is she to resist? She requests ice cream, gets it at once.

Aplomb of a different kind, unknown in her. I welcome it for what it is: an agreeable contemplativeness, with just a touch of the old effusive leer.

All her favorite goodies have been stockpiled here, against such a day as this. Suddenly she gets up from the table, vanishes into the bathroom, chuckles loud. It's the toilet that's got her, the first she's ever seen in the same room as the bath; in that other country they arrange things otherwise. Yonder the toilet is a monastic cell; here it's part of the open-plan apparatus of feeling easy. Whatever it is, Milk uses it for ten minutes behind a slammed door, occasionally giggling and uttering a few fluent-sounding comments in a tongue I think not even she knows: a parody of Romanian or Erse, maybe. I've heard it before. It's gibberish, beautifully intoned, a rehearsal for the day when she moves into suave society. Talking to herself, she seems to be alternating between irascible query and soothing reminder, the first high in pitch and swift, the second contralto, rather leisurely. As often, I feel shut out, unworded, aspirant to a secret society whose membership is one. And my truant brain switches to more morbid topics, runs riot thus: the parent will not know how the child will die, probably at any rate, and his ignorance grieves him as much as knowing would; the child will know how his parent dies, probably at any rate, and his knowing grieves him as much as ignorance would. In our case, however, only the former holds; the latter not, because she knows nothing of death, hers or mine, but only those chronic abeyances in limbo. She rarely asks for those who have not come back, perhaps having written them off as people who behave as comets do, reliably but very long-winded about it. May she fecklessly go on, smirking at people who've vanished, as if it's their own incompetence that's the cause.

Guessing how the dialogue with herself is going, I invent, as I almost always have, unless I've been happy to accept such bald exchanges as: "One more face," at which one pulls the expected grimace. "Yes," I answer, "I have just pulled one more face for Milk," knowing she must always be addressed in complete sentences. "More beebee," she might then add, and I fetch her the drink (her word for potables already being dispensed; otherwise, she names water, milk, or pop). A more complex effort will run: "In three sleeps Milk and Yah will go out in the car to see the airplanes," which she'll garble back as "Dree zleep, Milk and Yah ou i gar zee

41

abbala." But there are thousands of things she will not understand, including my compensatory version of what she's presently staging in the bathroom:

"Down toboggan, whisper? Giraffe? When?
"No! Corn violet thumb antler, and hot soot.
"When then? Men in ten? Out.
"No. Grump simba antiquary. No. No.
"Loop? Dammerung, bondsman, Attaturk.
"Never. Slain lisp. Carl, school, shove-ark!
"No, n-o-o. Bangladesh. Card, howler, do. Water. Soap.
Baba."

I have crept up behind her, watched her lip-read herself at a mirror, or, with her dolls arranged in chairs in front of her, play teacher, haranguing her pupils with a wealth of threatening tones I never knew she had, occasionally even picking one up to thrash it and thump it back into its chair only to ask it then some awful, elaborate, twenty-syllable question all over again, which it can't or won't answer, its being a doll no good excuse. Hence it gets another blistering onslaught before a second thrashing. A syllogism has gone wrong. Milk can't hear, but she tries to talk. The doll can't hear, but doesn't try. Milk's world is all interrogation: knowing she's forever asking and rarely knows an answer, she transposes her fix into almost voodoo terms, and one day that maltreated doll may scream out the sphinx's answer with its death rattle, and Milk will go forth equipped with her own version of the philosopher's stone, omnicompetent, vatic, sly, having got the dumb to speak. Now, however, she is still rehearsing:

"Goon Angkor, milt scabbard?
"No, dun apple Monday cinder.
"Brow, tongue, eye, ear" [she's at the mirror mouthing].
"Water, no!"

The sound stops, the shower starts, she screams with mirth, and I go in, find her naked, flashing the plastic curtain back and forth on its rings with one foot in the empty bath.

Cold showering sends her into an ecstasy. She soaps her blebby bosoms with self-conscious lewdness and puffs hard into the outfoaming rain from the nozzle. She comes from the land of sit-down baths, a slow sort of country where a shower is what comes from heaven. A bidet would drive her into impossible bliss, I think; she'd straddle or side-saddle it, getting gratifications no Parisienne ever knew.

Already she knows how hot the hot is, can gauge the two faucets, flip up the plug lever. She towels herself with insolent brio, as if she knows she is guest of honor and the only one of her kind. Time was when she'd spend half of every day in the bath, tootling and warbling in rapt hydrophilia, the water ice cold. I bring her shorts and blouse, careful not to hand her the swimsuit yet, because that bit of gear's the signal for instant action. In pink and white she looks eighteen, tall as I, less a hostage to fortune than an irresistible bribe.

Casing the house gluts her with mundane wonders. A refrigerator so big invites her to enter it, and she tries to, with mock naughtiness, withdrawing her leg from the low-level freezer compartment only when her hand extracts a can of carbonated beverage from the shelves higher up. In turn I have to demonstrate for her the blender, with a powdered lobster-bisque soup which with water blurs into a pale-pink cream; the switch for the garbage disposal, whose grinding she can't hear, though I caution her in mime not to stick her hand into this outsize pencil-sharpener; the synthetic moonlight of the neon tube inside the stove's control panel; all other light switches; the screen doors, which she finds an enormous joke, even trying to spit through the mesh; the indoor plastic garbage can with its fitted buff condom inside; the little broiler on the counter, whose red glow excites her to toast a slice of low-calorie bread, actually made from car-

43

rots, and munch the result as she prospects about. As kitchens go, it isn't a gadget paradise by a long way, yet each bit of machinery appeals to her as an object of contemplation, as if she's tuning in to the miracle of power, the dark nothing from which the universe was made. Her relish is enviable: new every morning, the world to her is genuine treasure which she eyes with murmuring awe. I join in the fun, especially when she makes a few dud phone calls, stabbing the dial at random, or so it seems until I detect more 2s and 0s than other digits, and I realize she's dialing the number of the house in the other country, not its telephone number but that in the address, announcing herself by name and saying repeated hellos.

Cryptic SOS? I doubt it, hope against it, ascribe it rather to happy bravura. She coos and exclaims her way through the other rooms on the same upper floor, grinning as she samples with her palm the one air-conditioner still running, and she caresses the pumped-out flow of cold, half-seeming to mold it as it comes. I nod at her pleasure, wondering if she thinks it synthesizes snow or popsicles. The vacuum cleaner, propped up in a closet, wins only a brief, bored stare, but I know she has registered at least one of the household gods as present and correct. No doubt she has a session with it in mind for later on; she loves to clean and polish. The white plastic Parsons tables, all got with green stamps, intrigue her: she strokes the surface, taps, listens, knowing at once the legs are hollow, thinking what might be inside: mice or alcohol? Into every drawer she goes foraging, claiming as a trophy a new pair of gleaming pliers, a see-through envelope of tap washers, three tapered purple candles wrapped in cellophane, and the unused UHF aerial loop the TV's never worn. Plus ten yards of neatly folded cord, which she unravels as if already in the labyrinth. The old thirty-dollar telescope, a three-inch reflector that wobbles on a wooden tripod and would deter anyone from star-gazing for life, she pats affably on its tube, as if detecting *its* handicap, and gently shoves until it keels over against the bed. (The big one, the eight-inch, I've locked away in a basement closet for later sorties when she's more adjusted, more scientifically attuned; some hope!) The books give her pause, but she goes by them with a minor heel-tap against the case's bottom, and skips out to the long balcony and its tubular chairs, which also get her listening, auscultating them, like some convict receiving messages in stir. Perhaps when she hears that a war is over, or that summer will end, she'll say so, glad to bear news.

After the balcony, she visits the bathroom again, teasing me by slicing air with my razor, which I decide to use fairly soon. Gaining permission with a rearward look as she squats before the screen, she flips the TV channel selector round and round, chortling at such visual plenty, almost all of it in color, and then turns the volume up loud, no doubt missing the special box which, back home, amplifies sound for her in headphones, nearly to the threshold of pain for those with normal hearing. Twenty minutes she sits there, rapt, sipping fizz from her can, then with politely imperious hand-wave calls for more. I flip the lid's tab and she begins to drink from the keyhole in the top without even looking. She might last all day like this, under ordinary circumstances, but fidgety curiosity sets her off again, as it must, and she rises for more touring, her eyes a touch glazed, her mouth mobile with accelerated murmur. I find her hearing aids, offer them, but she spurns them with a snarl and heads for the stairs down, there being no door.

Cooler at once by fifteen degrees, she smiles appreciation backward as I follow, and just about loses her footing, at which she lets out with a several-syllable curse. We swing open the downstairs screen door, check the box for mail (only a bill), then turn left into a room that's instant bliss for her, containing as it does an old refrigerator whose inside reeks of moss or mold, a defunct stove drooling a congealed brown, about twenty big cardboard boxes stacked ceiling high, the furnace capped with soot, and a heavy white homemade bar on which I've stacked relegated books, a model of a Lear jet whose door swings down (she pedantically closes it), a dead toaster that she gives a hard slam for reasons unknown, and an old-fashioned tall table lamp with a white, upturned bowl like a rain gauge. This she flicks expertly on and then stares onto the bulb's top by standing on a chair, an old trick that seems to recharge her mental batteries and cheer her up, whereas it would blind anyone else. Milk, though, devours light, always has, and she peers away into the heart of the hundred-watt filament as it tells her something intimate. I've read somewhere that it works for anyone, this bright on-slaught on the retina, accelerating mental processes no end for a short while, and I envision examination candidates raid-ing the absolute for three hours with a flashlight to either eye. Not for me, the almost photophobic one.

Undone by bulb-gazing, she straightens, scowls at the fur-nace and its Laocoon of pipes, dismounts from her chair, then flits into the basement toilet, a scruffy little cell but equipped with a washbasin, both of whose taps she cranks on, and a shower stall behind a dingy plastic drape. She gingerly starts the shower, yells as a house centipede an inch and a half long streaks down the wall and vanishes into a crack in the floor, yet without more ado downs her shorts and sits to pee. Dur-ing this, she notices through the open right-hand door of the toilet the stacks of supplies in the basement's other half and scoots to check it all out, hauling up her shorts as she goes. I hit the flush in my bourgeois way, follow her gladly. She marvels at so much to saw, scissor and fold, daub and arrange. "Wynd," I tell her (her all-purpose verb for manipulation): "we are going to wynd a big sky." A movie comes to mind in aberrant flash. She wants to start right now, but I've re-served this day for a swim at the neighbors' pool, who oddly enough have gone to Miami, leaving the key that unlocks the door in the redwood fence. " 'Wim!" she bellows when I inform her, and all thought of a big sky goes. She's up the stairs, unearthing her suit, a canary-yellow bikini. First, though, I smear her with sun-screen ointment and myself with routine oil. I change before she realizes what I'm doing (she'd love to watch, ogling) and casually stuff one of our airline bags with towels, pretzels, cold cans, a box of cigarillos, and (something atavistic) an inflatable foot-wide beach ball, a similar duck or swan, and a brand-new lifebelt for Milk to wear; she loves water, but cannot swim, not even as badly as I. We set out in straw hats, off her coming the cupric aroma of ointment mixed with her own of fresh-cut corn and minty perspiration. If only all the world smelled as good. The sun thumps us. The tall maples bulge. The birds heckle us the whole way as if we are cats. The world smells fine.

About thirty yards away, blue rocking water, sharkless and disinfected, awaits our jumps. Its very look soothes her from effusive jitteriness into grand patience, as with myself by the sea, at the Gulf of Mexico when I stand on an empty beach among stranded jellyfish, like experimental jet planes cut in plastic, and surrender to the lazy drum of water sliding down from Galveston. There are those who lack this quiet sea-fever or water-craving, and it's hard to explain to them. I end up mouthing Greek to myself: *thalassa, hudor,* in much the same mood as when I peer up at the Way. Lovers of the future yearn really for nature, whereas misoneists yearn for a pastoral idyll, a state that exists no more in time than, whatever my ostentations in these sentences, in space. Oh, I write in the present-past, confecting a spell of now inside a husk that's always too late. *Not long for this world,* runs a formula for someone moribund, meaning us all; but it fits language too, and each person's talk or writing even more. Compared with how old the universe is, language is a stop-

47

press novelty. I sometimes think, in Milk's wake, how everything may in the long run dwindle to this: saying precisely how one feels about things, having one's say, then slow-motioning back into nature, the mind's few watts earthed, while the say stays behind, like a star named. Alkaid, for example, in the Big Dipper's handle, is Benetnasch to some. A brief ghost of someone called "Bennet Nash" hovers, spawned by connotation, among the perdurable chemistry of what isn't on the human scale at all.

Gooneybird in three feet of slop, she floats. Hurrah.

Unsteadily in her blue lifebelt, she starts to laugh, signing the water with expansive rings. "Yah?" she invites.

At bottom near her, I dunk my head, nose held, and emerge to see her doing the same. She comes up fast, airborne, jackknife in a bathing hat.

Uncouth grackles harsh-calling across the pool seem to chide. To hell with them.

Couple of squirrels chase along the redwood fence, doomed to quadrilateral boredom. Up into the trees they fling themselves, making debris fall into the pool.

As tame as wet paper, we float about together under the baking sun, Milk entranced, no doubt feeling jet lag, I at a contemplative halt.

Up goes the ball and lands without seeming to touch: air snubbing water through a thin skin of plastic.

Anti-climax I suppose I call it. Here she is, as if she's come thirty yards from the other country and could go to Hawaii in thirty more, just so long as water tided her over. Pun, I know, but over eight thousand miles earned. Not in blood, but lymph.

Cackling, Leda rapes the floating swan or duck, upends herself in shallow water, and I right her, wondering at her lightness. The bird, of course, has righted itself and can be relied on all over again.

Going over like a drogue towed, one cloud makes me shiver, her too; then we both warm up again, unconversing. An aquatic pact confines us to eyes, looks, a yard apart, a foot above the trembling water in which our limbs camber and trail.

Charitably or not, I think of all the manic sportspeople at this moment hitting balls into squares, holes, and nets: swatting them, clubbing them, toeing them, heading them, and I look at our own, floating free, unplayed with, random in a universe of its own, alone with one monumentally silent adolescent and a zonked adult who no longer has to talk, which he has sometimes done for a living, with always the frightful clack-echo from what I said on the previous occasion on the same subject.

An insignia for us comes to mind, culled from the star charts: where two stars are too close to be shown separately, a single disk with a line through it stands for both. Thus: Ø, a fisherman's float. Floundering to the edge, I draw it in wet on a dry patch while Milk cruises over to look, grins sarcastically as if I have to be indulged, gives me then a grown-up shove. Down I go, at the gulp, blinded by chlorine. When I clear my eyes, I see the splash has wiped us out, in symbol at least.

Used pearls, these eyes (I grumble) aren't what they used to be.

United we stand without even being able to converse. We never do say much.

Genially she points at the deep end, starts to paddle toward it, knowing what it is. Expecting me to follow. I don't. She shouts. She slams both arms against the surface, a banshee. I go, willing to drown, but by the time I'm there she's floated back to the other end, windmilling like a seed, and alive.

A small high-wing monoplane goes over, drifting as if to land. Seeing it, Milk whoops, waves, tells herself some anecdote, mouth close to the water for the echo effect. All I can do is helplessly eavesdrop, fitting the sounds to what words I can: band, banana, needle, Maori, sleigh. An old predicament. I miss her usual, all-invalidating "no," then it comes in an attenuated bray whose shading I construe as doubt, as if for once she almost agreed with herself, whereas two more degrees Fahrenheit, or one mile an hour more wind speed, or twenty extra calories to burn, might have made her affirm outright. Or just more command of the sound s; she was six when she first said "yes." Of her other negatives I long have known the one that commands all phenomena to a distance; the one that's elegiac, an aborted brainchild; the one that's rampant Hun, when her brain feels scalded and she wants folk to bubble and melt before her eyes. And other variants.

A "no" of Garbo dismissing the entire Ruritanian cavalry. A "no" of someone, grievously ill, almost giving in at the sight of another rainy dawn.

Guttural "no" powered by a small turbine that hates.

And noes that, as the saying has it, are beyond description, begotten by despair upon impossibility. These noes are absolutes from the gut, skull explosions which I haven't heard in years, having had little opportunity, but which doubtless still exist in all their miserable completeness. That smiling mien of the teenaged water baby belies her thunder, unheard for the past two days at any rate, and I'd do almost anything to preclude it, such as agreeing to forgo noes of my own, including the *no* to emotional blackmail attempted on me year after year through the hapless pawnship of an only child. And the *no* to increased blood pressure, to galloping pulse: I run a mile each day, round the basement, eighty laps, or round the baseball field, or jog the equivalent. An automaton for health.

Good old Milk, she is still in the hermetic reverie I left her in, chortling to her favorite element. Out of the pool she climbs on cue, with nauseated histrionic gasps. I know she must have peed. Down the ladder she comes, waved back in. A tiger prowls the water's edge, but we hiss it away. An eagle swoops low, but we rip its head off. The pool empties in a trice. An anaconda writhes up from the concrete. We climb out, board a low-flying air bus from Samarkand, get off at Thule, camp there the night in an outsize market bag, and spend the next day cramming tiny red spiders into the tube of an old telescope so as to barter it for lemon marmalade.

Gee, she'll do almost anything, always at her own disposal, a Curie, a Phaedra, an Amazon; a self-impediment, a victim, a slave; whom I revere-deplore, so far having failed to find or invent a philosophy that includes her, something that runs: "All things bright and handicapped, the good Lord made them all." A natural anthem everyone would learn in school and sing when the national flag is raised, the real enemy being not behind the Curtain but within the cell. What's the score, Adam? What's the human program? What's its point? Answer: there's no fool like a human fool, especially one with two legs, a daughter, and a dictionary, plus a compulsive habit of star-gazing (as if the answer were Out There, so many thousand light-years off-shore). I cannot believe that some vast Inconceivable, with foresight, oversees the All. The only message that keeps on coming through is light, radiation, and neutrinos. What happens when the speed of light is cubed?

Among scores, nay, hundreds of recurring wishful thoughts, all gently fanatical, there is above all one: let there one day soon come another bit of serendipity like that which

51

yielded penicillin. Son of an Ayrshire farmer, Alexander Fleming, eventually working in the inoculation department of St. Mary's Hospital, London, was an untidy man apt to leave cultures exposed on his laboratory table. One day a spore of hyssop mold, the *penicillium notatum,* wafted in from Praed Street and landed on a dish of staphylococci. It remained only for a girl in Peoria to scrape a mold from a canteloupe melon, and the mass manufacture of pencillin could begin. Not a bad bedtime story for Milk, for whom I'd wish any such freak-of-circumstance discovery, one part of my mind saying: The answers lie all around us, the universe is complete, as time will prove. All very well, until another part of my mind says: It may be incomplete after all, some ills being incurable. A third part of my mind says its own unlucky thing, simply that a lack of oxygen made her the way she is: her defects indict no virus, no jumping of the track by RNA, but a merely mechanical mishap, like losing your thumb in the ejection chamber of a submachine gun. A baby suffocated from sleeping on its face might be a better analogy. Bad luck.

Cavorting at the pool's edge, she lets out one of her delirious high-pitched warbles, the terror of dogs, and then keeps it going in abstract celebration, a hydro-anthem or a utopian riff. A couple of neighborhood dogs respond with panicky crescendos, and then birds, chipmunks, even a squirrel, maybe acknowledging one of their own, more probably issuing an all-points warning against an alien in the vicinity. She toots on, hop-dancing to a private rhythm; the neighborhood soon sounds like a zoo. A hopping motion that marks time, her dance addresses itself to a dimension unavailable to most of us, in which perpetual motion is only an aspect of style. Dimly I think of the goose step, human version, frenetically accelerated, and of my own jogging trot; but no human movement quite matches this whirr of limbs while she aims her gaze at the zenith, as if some deity without portfolio were beating time for her. Mysteries she makes. Mysterious she began, mysterious she goes on, a cordial abstracted person from whom there must be much to learn, could we but tap it.

Gaily she hops closer, with a fistful of cubic red candies, like a piece of rhodochrosite, in hand. She has filched them from a high cupboard. Ah, she still raids with uncanny skill, she still caters to her oral compulsions with a kind of sucrose-radar; she knows where the stuff is, even before you've hidden it, and has never yet been caught in the act of helping herself. I look away into a vacant space, half-hoping to see her arrival in it, such is her unhearable speed. When I see her next, she's on her back under a colorful pool umbrella, sunglasses off, a large seashell cupped on each eye. I see a face with two blisters, looking at the sea as others listen for it. One day I'll try her out with amplified whale cries to see if she'll answer them. Where the shells came from, unless they happen to be part of her permanent equipment, I have no idea.

As I try to anticipate the old woman in her, a Milk of advanced age—like my mother, sitting for preference on a small-topped stool as if she were a medieval examination candidate, and speaking of the Wimbledon tennis players familiarly as Ken, Virginia, Evonne, while she nibbles a digestive biscuit—I see nothing of the kind, only fractional differences, a Milk unchanged, as when you see the Big Dipper from different latitudes or, more theoretically, after a hundred thousand years. I view her growing up, but not down, which perhaps means only that I can envision what I can expect to see, but not what, unless we manage to tamper with the aging process better than hitherto, I can't. I do, however, predict for her a permanent youthfulness of mind: at fourteen she's mentally a seven, I suppose, and how to pro-rate that, who knows? Maybe she'll feel twenty-one at forty, vernal in mid-career, something I feel myself, I,

Deulius, who never very young will never be very old.
Unless . . .

Coming to a halt, I remind myself that this, the first of our
two weeks, is ours alone, whereas the second will bring Pi
back from her parental orbit, as well as callers of varying
persuasions who aspire to meet my guest. A Hope Diamond
of girlhood. The first week, centripetal, the second, centrifu-
gal. For the first time I see the petal in the one, the fugue in
the other. Milk's asleep, better thus than in some hyperactive trajectory based on burned-out nerves, with the vagus
above all acting up. So I won't have to barbecue the local
dogs on the lawn, wreck the TV with a catapult, sit on a
homemade iceberg waiting for the mailman on a Sunday.
Cheered, I adjust the umbrella, set a towel over her legs
to keep the ultra-violet at bay, then slither back into the pool
as if into preservative brine. It's almost three P.M. At four I'll
wake her for tea and muffins. Limping time now rests. Birds
quit. The lull doesn't even feel the jet burrowing across, five
miles above us, the silverfish with passengers.
Curious how words such as these function as retrievers,
pulling the present of the writing act into the recent present
of what was done. I am writing this sentence now, or nearly
now; but when I write *we swam*, or *she danced*, I'm implying
the habitual, which is tenseless since we go on swimming, or
she goes on dancing, in my mind. These ephemera are
forever, more or less. So what I'll end up with won't be quite
like Stockhausen's composition "Out of the Seven Days,"
with himself locked up alone foodless in his house for a week,
but in its way just as performative, planned to be unplanned,
an experiment in tropism, growing toward the Galaxy together while we pick up the threads of each's being the
other's child.

Crude oblongs of light arrive on her outflung arm, so I twist the umbrella. We spin so fast while circling the sun, which itself is headed toward Hercules, that I think the mass of all human movements only a fidget, a footnote to unlettered eons whose chances of having so-called intelligent life we sum up in some formula I can't remember. There is no formula for calculating the chances of eventual, wholly intelligent life in her, whose chemistry's as impersonal as the Way's itself. But when I reckon up how much more personality she has, compared with what I've nicknamed her after, I wonder at the superplus. No star can read, make puns, dial a channel on TV. She's a piece of the Sun with charm. Ten years old, at the bank, she studied the performances of everyone, on the next visit tried to deposit one of her baby teeth, recording it on a deposit slip in her own spiky hand, *Michla, 1 toth*, then handed both to a grave clerk, who stamped the slip and passed it back. The tooth he refunded to me as a bonus.

Unique, the trigonometry of that, making me swallow hard. Depositing her tooth was a spherical triangle whose angles added up to more than 180 degrees: a feat worthy of John Goodricke, deaf-mute astronomer who lived 1764–1785, not very long as lives went even then, yet long enough for him to decide that Algol, the so-called demon star, was periodically eclipsed by a dimmer partner that passed in front of it and cut out its light. A century later he was proved right. She's awake, talking again, in sounds that travel eerily over the pool from where, on her towel, she orates into the concrete with her mouth almost touching:

> "Un-banana, egg, witch.
> "Caramel, dreck, snood.
> "Ulan Bator, Bator.
> "Bugle-weiss. *Home. No.*"

I get her drift, I think. I would rather say anything to her than hear that. Oh, what a chubby vulva. Oh, for a beaker full of the warm south. Oh, so you'd like a ton of ox tongue in the shape of a whale?

Anything to shut out such desperate-sounding code that's mostly no more phonemic than the chaffering flick-flack of quasars, receivable by many, thought by none: alpha zigs next to omega zags. I take her to the house I call home.

Carpentry's one thing, like origami or painting unmimetic if needs be. Just saw and chisel away, making nothing at all; fold paper into abstract shapes or whiten four walls and a ceiling, even a plywood panel. But explaining the Milky Way, justifying its facsimile, to her, is nothing like. No use prating away about how Sir William Herschel, prince of observers, claimed 116,000 stars passed in review across his telescopic field of vision in fifteen minutes. Nor invoking Rifts, Coal Sacks, nebulae and star-clouds, or mankind's lazy switch from an Earth-centered to a Sun-centered view, from that to dim intuitions that Sagittarius is more or less the center of just one spiral galaxy among a million or more which have no central reference point and of which the nearest is 850,000 light-years away. Stellar nuclear furnaces, transforming hydrogen non-stop into helium, are nothing to her, and the Way's infinite profusion of dazzling suns is hardly more. Useless even to call on ancient metaphors that make the Way a long bandage wrapped around the skies (partial as she is to wound-dressings, even to the point of prurient interest); or the road to the palace of heaven, trodden by departed souls whose campfires mark their progress; or as a belt of corn grains, Winter Street, Silver Street, Watling Street, Asgard's Bridge, the path of white ashes, the path of Noah's Ark, the path of chopped-straw carriers. William Langland called it Walsyngham Way; the French peasantry the Road of Saint Jacques of "Compostella," a word invented by Bishop Theodomir, who was guided by a star in 835 to the bones of Saint James composted in a field; and the Polynesians call it the Long Blue Cloud-eating Shark. All of little use. I'd just as well bake her a raisin cake to demonstrate how the galaxies, like the raisins in the cake, are all moving away from one another.

Curdled or flaky, the Way's thick white is beyond her ken as fact or metaphor. Shown it, if she can stay awake so late, she'll make a moue at it and then wonder why our model-to-be isn't on the ceiling, above us. One word she does know, though, and often use: *lots,* which coupled with such others of her favorites as *small* and *moon* might work the trick. "Lots and lots of small moons, very long, and up high, over" (word she adores) "o-ver the dark: Milky Way!" Such the theory. Now follows the actual first conversation as she rubs her eyes. I envy the ease with which Geoffrey Chaucer was able to explain the astrolabe to Lewis, his son. I try: "Lots and lots of small moons . . ." "Milk?" she queries. "Beebee?" (She is proposing to drink it.) Then she giggles at the notion of numerous Moons, when all along she'd thought there was one only. She even grasps the distance, saying, "Long way," which brings to her mind a thought I gave her about the size of the ocean. "Downstairs, one sleep," I tell her, "Yah and Milk will wynd Milk's Way, with lots and lots of small lamps: white, blue, yellow, red." "Green?" she chides, so I begin racking my brain for stars truly green. Now, Zuben Es Chamali, Libra's northern claw, is pale emerald, not in the Way at all, even though part of her so-called sun sign. Try again. There are faint greens in the Jewel Box in Crux. Sometimes, as Tennyson says, Sirius "bickers into red and emerald." And giant Antares, partly red, is partly green as well. "Yes," I announce, "green moons as well," knowing she will hold me to it once we begin the work. She might also want to color the stars according to her own ideas, and to hell with patient astronomers. It's Milk's Way, after all; and had the hydrogen atom borne a minute charge, with electron and

57

neutron not quite canceling each other out, whole regions of primeval hydrogen in the universe would never have condensed into stars. Why they are equal we do not know, but if they weren't there'd be no galaxies, stars, planets, no Milk, no me. A narrow squeak, life has had, in a universe designed but not guaranteed to breed life, natural selection being in the long run a business of editing, not authorship. Why, Milk and I, ourselves made of star-stuff, are just a star's way of knowing about stars. We're entitled to our vagaries, she especially, whose narrow squeak goes on, in chemistry at least. So why quibble about a few tints?

Upstaging Arthur Rimbaud (who wrote: "A black, E white, I red, V green, O blue") as well as the *Harvard Star Catalogue*, which says: "O white, B blue-white, A blue, F yellow, G red," I write, as she might prefer, O stars crocus yellow, B stars pale rose, A stars garnet, F stars ashy lilac, G stars smalt blue. Two chromatic rebels, we write with birds' beaks, running toy trains powered by our brains. So long as she doesn't fret, she can play fast and loose with the Galaxy, convert the Sun into an optical binary of purple and maroon, give Earth itself a counter-spin just to wake everybody up.

Getting there, slowly, I'm amazed to say. A datum step, like the longitude of the star Regulus in Leo.

Going on with confidence, like an eighteenth-century eccentric building a folly.

Chances are she'll lose interest after four or five constellations. After all, dots don't have names. Then we'll be restricted to swimming, TV, and games of mad pursuit up and down the stairs. If only there were talk above and beyond the minimal, even a chance to share with her the vast amount about the stars there is to know, the surfeit about the surfeit, the chemistry, the myths, the sheer unmitigated guessing about Cygnus X-1 as a possible black hole. But no, I talk of necessity to myself, address all of my mime to her, chatter in, gesture out, as if we both were tongue-tied mummers with no ideas but in things, no things except in movement, no movement that's not one of energy's illusions, none of energy's illusions that isn't in the beginning an idea. Reminded how the heavens wheel, or seem to, only because Earth does, I let my head spin, still though it sits. I would really like to talk to her, as to a girl indeed fourteen, about disasters not in space but in adult and infant lives; discuss the art of swimming, the use of deodorant sprays, the caliber of store-bought apple pie.

Unerring, she slaps black paint on the lower panel of fiberboard while I do the upper one. Flop-suck go the big brushes against the sounds of our breathing. Her panel is the northern Way, mine the southern. Thank goodness the basement wall is wide enough, easily forty feet. Our mural's background looks like an enormous door to a non-existent barn. Spilled paint from her generous sweeps goes squittering on the newspapers I've positioned underfoot, marring ephemera with a darkness we're going to load with stars. She seems to understand. Shown my big sketch of the whole project, she grinned, lovingly uttered the word "black," and reached for her brush. All we have to do now is let it dry. Half an hour. Except that the floury-linseed aroma of the paint will be with us a day at least.

Uniform mat black soon absorbs both kinds of light, summer's natural and the artificial from four different lamps, without giving it back. It's really as if we have created space, a Stygian blotter of the far wall. "Pretty," she trills, one of her best-enunciated words. I concur while she tests the surface and indignantly holds up smeared thumbs.

Canis Minor, I say to myself, we're doing the Little Dog first. See if it laughs to see such fun. The last thing it resembles is a dog. I'll ask her when I draw it in chalk, before drilling the first hole, for Procyon's yellow bulb, which soon will flash along with, oh, fifty others, while stars of lesser clout will just be studs cut off a wooden dowel, painted, and stuck on. While waiting, we paint meter-long rods of half-inch box-wood, blue-white for the hottest stars, white for those with dominant hydrogen, yellow for metallic ones, orange and red for so-called cool ones ranging from 7,500 to 5,500 degrees. With a fine saw we slice off small lengths, then paint the tops to match the sides. I even, for double stars, have rods of smaller heft. Dabbing away at several dozen stubs of stars in different cigar boxes on the table, she seems engrossed, and I have a chance to sort the stack of shirtboard templates in which I've cut holes through which to mark the stars' positions on the black, all that remains being to chalk in the lines between, later to be gone over with a felt-tip marker. Now she sets the lesser stars to dry while I return to the Little Dog, one of Ptolemy's old groupings, the junior of Orion's brace of hounds, not much to it really: a yellow-bulb Procyon eleven light-years off, plus a white-stud white-hot Gomeisa, almost twenty times as far.

Galaxy calls. Moving from left to right, north to south, we thumbtack pre-cut pieces of shirtboard to the black, their inner edges tracing the Way's contours as it shrinks, bulges, even splits. I must, during the preparation phase, have used up a three-year accumulation, saved from the laundry as it came back weekly, not with this in mind at all, but for writing notes on, protecting small manuscripts in the mails, wedging into gaps around the air-conditioners, leaving messages for garbage men and friends. We soon have a mural patched dun gray or off-white, just a little like one of those composite pictures of Mars made with a hundred overlapping photographs transmitted back in series. But what's black and in the middle, roaming across the wall, is the Way itself, secret in black, as if unborn, still in Juno's breasts.

60

Can in hand, she sprays silver at the space between the shirtboards, making even, careful motions back and forth, as instructed. An inch a minute, the Way shows up, as on a totally clear night, here an estuary, there a curling promontory; here a piece that might be the Wash, that big bite out of Cambridgeshire, there an isthmus stolen from Central America. How geographical it looks, how unheavenly, a vast single spiral of Jutlands, Manhattans, and Britains, now frail, now burly, sinuous or muscle-bound, a bracelet of stuff upflung.

Comes the unveiling: we peel away the silver-splashed cardboard, rectangle after rectangle, and the Way shines forth untrammeled while I absently collect up thumbtacks, check the floor for them (our feet being bare as often as not), and dispossess her of the spray can, with which she might otherwise coat us both. A lovely sight, as if some giant snail had tracked across the wall, first going straight, then down, doubling back on itself to create the rift in Cygnus, then soaring slow to the ceiling before lapsing down to Canis Major, where I've arbitrarily chopped off to begin again, at the other side, with its junior sibling. She has, however, sprayed silver beyond the galaxy, beyond the masks, making satellite galaxies where none can be unless obscured by dust, as well as a few clusters far out in impenetrable space. For all I know, she may be right, prescient, but all the same I black them out, having gained her consent, and feeling a twinge of de-creation as the Amerigo Clouds, say, or the Columbus Clusters vanish never to shine again, and the heavens come to heel. The pungency of the silver keeps her wrinkling her nose, but the full sprawl of the Way has won her quite. Not that she's ever, as far as I know, seen the original. *Time out of mind,* I tell myself: that's what we've just made. Shining fit to beat the band. Yet that's not the half of it. Now for the dramatis personae, after some fluid refreshment, which I fetch from upstairs: two condensation-speckled cold cans that slip and glide against the palm.

Using the template made for Canis Minor, I mark the sites of Procyon and Gomeisa (at eight and two o'clock respectively) with a dab of pencil, then power-drill the hole. It would have been easier to do the carpentry, such as it is, with the whole mural horizontal; perhaps not. As things stand, it swings out into the room on sturdy hinges, so it's not hard to fit the bulb-holders or the wiring. From now on, we'll drill a dozen at a time; this is just the demonstration star, proving the technique is just the same as that for Christmas trees. I chalk in the short line connecting the two stars, then fit the yellow bulb, glue on the white stud. A moment later, as much to have fun as to test, I plug in and Procyon does its stuff, blooming saffron just outside a spur of the Way, amid the glare of downstairs. Out go the lights. The star beams. Milk claps, skips in delight. I unplug, swing the mural back flush with the wall, and point at what we've got, asking her in the long-standing formula of outflung fingers, histrionically raised brows: "What? What is it?" I draw it on a handy piece of shirtboard: a stick with a big star at one end, a smaller at the other. "Lamp," she says, getting the hang of it. To her, it's a flashlight, "a small lamp," and not a little dog. I look forward to her next analogies, especially because the constellations only rarely look like what they're called. In fact, the Greeks as often as not were merely commemorating, not likening. Henceforth, Canis Minor is a light to steer by when getting to Monoceros, the supposed unicorn next door. It has two nebulae, but not much else.

Unstable stuff, these stars: they don't figure in her view of the Way at all, and even less as what they are to me, who spurn the Greek alphabetism of astronomers and relish names: Procyon, *the foremost dog,* coming at us two miles a second; Gomeisa, *the watery-eyed,* next to those perfunc-

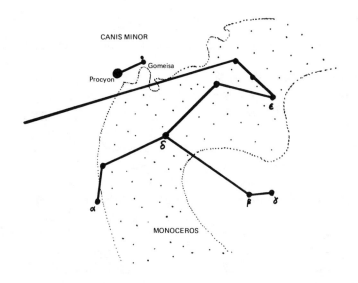

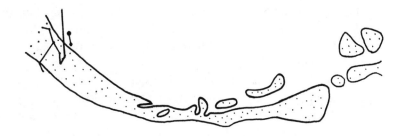

torily called ξ, θ, o, and π, but once grouped by the Chinese into Shwuy Wei, A Place of Water, being so near the river of the Galaxy.

Addressing Milk, I try on for size, just to give her a taste of the luxury she's denied, *der Kleine Hund, le Petit Chien, il Cane Minore, Catellus,* Puppy, mouthing as unexaggeratedly as I can. And then I roll-call to myself the other names of Procyon: Antecanis, Al Shāmiyyah, Algomela, Kak-shishka, Singe Hanuant, Nan Ho, Vena; then of Gomeisa: Al Gamus, Al Murzim, Gomelza, not having the heart to perplex her with tales of the Hunter Orion's little dog, or the faithful dog Mera, or the hounds of Actaeon. Hard as I ponder such estimable tales, I can foresee nó chance of telling her, even in dumbshow, about Orion's vanity punished by the gods. *Gods?* No more does she have that notion (how lucky she) than that of Mera's master's undiscovered murdered body, or that of why Diana should resent Actaeon's seeing her in the buff. A few switches—Orion, Mera, and Actaeon's hound installed in the heavens—she might find amusing, but the plot, the concordant dovetailed incidents, the cumulative interstices, are quite beyond my power to say. Try it anyway. SCORPION KILLS MALE SUPERMODEL AND DOG-LOVER. DOG FINDS MASTER'S CORPSE, DAUGHTER HANGS SELF. VOYEUR TURNED STAG SLAIN BY OWN DOG PACK. It won't do at all. One day I'll try again, when the right narrative part of the Way comes to hand. We'll act it out together, and I'll be tale-telling to keep yet another Scheherazade, though mighty different, from another death among these Arabian-titled stars. Of the same myths' silence to the stars themselves, as of the stars' near-silence to men, I'll say less than little, just now having no stomach for the tacit. Like Don Quixote, having unsuccessfully tried to provoke the lion in its cage, I copyright the non-event, just in case. It might come in, like the lion, it just might.

Used up an hour, that did, but no more. Not bad going for two amateurs. We now have a little dog with a flashlight. There's nothing for it except to sally across the edge of the Way into the middle, where Monoceros sits, a different kind of problem. How much the outlines vary: my own attempt, as exact as I can make it, delivers a stick glider, left wing poking a strut forward, right wing poking one back, whereas another version shows the profile of a sitting, sharp-nosed dog. Egging me on with mellow war-whoops, Milk disappears into the basement toilet and returns at such speed the flush develops full hydraulic force only after she's left. Stabbing her hand at the background, at the silver splash of the Galaxy, she conjures forth form. "More," she sighs. Again I pencil through the holes in the shirtboard, connect them up with chalk, am glad I chose the sharp-nosed dog. Then she seems to spot something familiar. I ask what, but can't at first decipher her runic vowels. She does a three-step dance of celebration: a hop, a double stamp, a pirouette, all five feet of her, then yells, as only she can, peering at me from under the visor of her hand. "Wuff." Is she impersonating the sharp-nosed dog? I ask. No, she is not. That would have been "dog-wuff." Glory be, she means *wolf.* Yet, as I again look at the outline, I see only a bird, at rest, one leg thrust far forward. So let it be wolf, I am not the master of the bestiary here. We have just had a golden moment. She has to make sure the blockhead has understood. She does. He finally has. Now she demands lamps, little knowing that Monoceros, our second step on the Galactic great white way, has no notable stars, just some that have been impersonally dubbed Alpha, Beta, Gamma, and so on, *Monocerotis,* as the Latin genitive has it. She doesn't give a damn about the myth either, the Ur-horse with the long forehead horn, upon which it lands after leaping from great heights when pursued, and which breaks its

65

fall. "Wynd," she commands, so *wynd* I do, but not what she expects. I'm going to light up something other than those mediocre stars.

Cut from telescope catalogues that arrive in the mail, three-inch-wide photographs of nebulae get her purring, glued as they are over the bulb-holders bought in dozens by my landlord, Frank Etna, who a year ago picked up half a ton of stuff, cheap, on one of his forays into the city. Lucky the paper's thin enough to let the light come through. I show her, in turn, each photonic button: Hubble's Variable Nebula, like a flying saucer, half in shadow, sleek in black and white; then the Cone Nebula, a stuccoed pizza minus a thirty-degree slice and studded with garish infant stars, again in black and white; and third, the famed Rosette, a scarlet convolvulus of stellar frog spawn spotted white, which pleases her no end. "Up," she tells me, meaning: Drill the holes and screw them into holders fast. I do while she holds each nebula close to her eyes, peering through it at the basement sunlight and attempting a little unselfconscious jig on the matting floor. Heaven knows what she sees through these trumped-up crystals out of the light-years. I'm too busy with the power tool. In go the holders, touched with glue, then the nebulae. We light up right away, even before I have a chance to attach the studs denoting common-or-garden stars such as numbers 13 and 15, between which Hubble's Variable goes about its own peculiar business. The Rosette glows like a hot coal and the other two look just a bit wan and stark. She "Aahs" with glee, points across the Galaxy at the dark ground where Orion is going to be, and asks for more. First, though, I stand back to survey: in the black, Procyon burning margarine yellow, a bit lost-looking, and, camped across the silver, the linear apparatus of Monoceros, leaking light in two places, a tigerish hot eye in a third. More to come? More than she's dreamed; far beyond prosaic likeness to flashlight or antenna, she'll see more and more bizarre nebulae, the infra-structure of the broadest magnesium ribbon ever to cross the sky.

Going out, with a clash of the screen door, she hauls up orange-yellow day lilies, a dozen or so, comes in demanding a vase, which I fetch, in my other hand a similar-colored popsicle, upon which she falls a-thirsting. Across the basement I see little glows coming from the board swung flush again, herself staring into them one by one as if mesmerized, with her body centered on the slow pulse of suck-suck-suck, an orally fixated gazer. I know I am doing something right. The mailman goes past again, I can't imagine why. She comes to see what I'm watching, chases a chipmunk, loses, pretends to swim across the unmown grass, seizes a fallen premature apple, green and wasp-drilled, mimes at me for permission. Not getting it, she whangs apple high up into the tree, whence it falls to start all over again on its rounds. As we on ours, ready to install Orion with all its wonders just off the furry brink of the Way. A sudden thought comes late, for which I blame myself: paint the Way luminous for an extra dollar or two, and I resolve to buy a can of the right paint, apply it while she sleeps.

Consulting again my handy folder of outlines, in which the Way is pale blue, the stars are dried blobs of poster color, I rejoice at Orion, our first biggie, crammed with white and blue brilliants, one red one, and, sprawling all over the black hinterland, legs and arms and knees, with all the big stars named. This is the region of Uru-anna, the Light of Heaven, otherwise known as Jugula, Algebra, Giant (error for Al Jauzah, old Arabic for a black sheep with a white spot on it); region of the Golden Nuts. Triorchous superman indeed! Yet to tell her of this, or of Orion's club, sword, and shield amidst what Flammarion, the French astronomer, called the California of the sky, I may have to wait another twenty years, and more. Here blaze, I'd love to tell her, the Armpit of the Central One (Betelgeuse); the Female Warrior (Bellatrix);

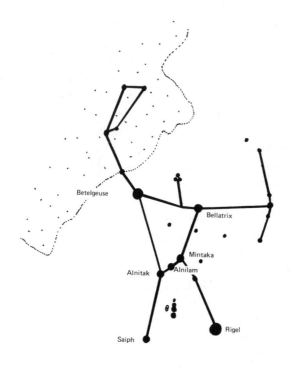

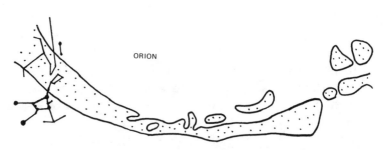

ORION

68

Peixie Boy, just a dark spot; Rigel the Foot, Saiph the Sword, Alnitak and Alnilam and Mintaka, the girdle and the belt of pearls and the belt. Yet, to her, talk of a blind giant whose sight returned as he faced the rising sun is fraught with semantic whiplash; deaf, she doesn't grasp what blindness is, any more than, barely verbal, she'd relish extra names. All the same, some things we can manage, with clippings from cards and catalogues. It is just going to have to be enough for *me* to know that sailors used to dread this constellation, six hundred light-years distant, receding from us at almost eleven miles a second, source—just after her mid-October birthday—of the Orionid meteor showers, fireworks on her behalf. For orange-red Betelgeuse, at times called the Roarer and 215 million miles across, a big orange-red bulb, and for all the others blue or white: seven in all, which I set in place, standard fashion, while she counts them with gracious correctness, summing up thus: "one red, zix why," which covers it pretty well. For the star called *theta*, really four in trapezium form, but veiled in a nebulosity several light-years wide, I have a quartet of narrow bulbs brushed white and all mounted together in one holder. As fast as I can, and not without some trembling of hands, I install the main orbs, test them, which is when she utters the one word "Blackpool," no celestial coal sack but the British coast resort famous for its Illuminations Week, as if not just she but Arthur Rimbaud too were in temporary residence each year. I've even heard it pronounced as going to the Eliminations.

Giant? I wonder as Orion's outline forms, connected up point-by-point like a child's puzzle. I see the club upheld, the lion skin brandished (or the shield if shield it be) at arm's length, while the knees come close together without unheroically knocking. At once, however, she sees her own thing, queen of Rorschach that she is, and shows me through motion, in fact serving at tennis with elongated, stealthy stretch, once, twice, thirty love, then smash. I can see it, as

69

might a cubist at Wimbledon: the white bulbs of the balls, two on the ground, others whizzing through space or frozen fast, the racket swung back high into the Way behind the colossal ruddy ball of Betelgeuse, the other arm somewhat thrown forward as if the gathering action's already spent itself while the knees inflex to a fulcrum pivot. All actions in one view pre-empt my telling her this is Orion, Men's Singles Champion, the White Tiger of the frost-bitten toe. Instead, as she mock-serves to the four-inch manikin in lights, I ready our two nebulae, near-clichés of astronomical coffee-table books: the Horsehead and the Great, both in color, the one magenta and rose madder with spike-haloed stars adjoining a sharply distinct head of a seahorse, brownish purple as it juts up into an ultra-distant dawn, the other, unimaginably vast whirlpool of gas, a nacreous pink-white-cobalt speed-stunted firebird flaming northwestward, small beak and head for such enormous wing area. Total mysteries, these get her gazing hard and long as if at the faces of absent playmates. "Horse" and "bird," she says quietly to herself, peering through them, one to each eye, then calling for light. The full complement of Orion, tennis ace with exotic belly badges, blurts gloriously out, and she pats the whole thing as if saying goodbye, a bit like Sir William Herschel on January 19, 1811, when he laid his glass aside forever, looking last on the Great Nebula, as on it he had chosen to look first in 1774. Her entranced pout resembles the fish-mouth *theta* θ within the nebula itself, and I remember how Thomas De Quincey extolled it in an essay, how Galileo never even mentioned it, how a million globes, each equal in diameter to Earth's orbit round the Sun, would not equal the Great Nebula's extent.

Unstrung by that grid of fire, its threads of nebulosity older than mankind itself, and by the beauty of watching her watch whatever she sees (bird, horse, tennis, her giant self), I walk stiffly upstairs, unflip a can of beer, light a cigarillo, hear her following, give her a swig, mention food, hand her a chicken leg glazed with cold, help myself to another, prepare to go back downstairs. She wants to do another, like Goethe asking for more light. "More ly, Yah, pliz." Who of any god-like pretensions could refuse?

Gobbling chicken-salad sandwiches made from a canned paste (repetitive menu of my own lazy devising), we have little to say, are no doubt full of Galactic or prosaic thoughts. Two evening doves toot away, *the* two. The Pekinese next door yaps for twenty minutes at its own shadow, as usual. Cooling down, the house fidgets. Big swaths of cumulus arrive. The TV shuffles images like enameled playing cards. With a dish of butter-pecan ice cream, she settles down to watch a woman who talks to children with a macaw on her shoulder. Idly I scan a pocket book of astronomy, relishing white-lined constellations on dark blue as if they were coats of arms, souvenirs of the big system that abides in the basement. Trying to think of something intimate to do, something to remember each other by, I come up with nothing, realize how impersonal life with her can be. I end up being grateful she's almost at peace, not at risk or under the weather, less a person than a beguiling process, which only I and a few others are privileged to watch, instruct us as it may.

Ghastly thoughts have come and gone, of decompression and air crash, of her running riot through a customs shed, of a twelve-hour scream. Do I bathe her, I wonder, or she herself? I soon learn how out of date I am, banished from the bathroom with a loud "bye-bye." Now she begins to sing one of her blurred arias, not in English, and I marvel at the mellow agility of a voice whose owner hardly knows its power except through vibration. No guess plumbs her theme, and I soon give up trying to decipher the sounds, though not before inferring for my own satisfaction a lyric that goes: "raisin tree, shaved lung, dendrite and suet boas,"

71

as much sense as usual. Balked, my mind slips away to raucous newborn stars in Orion's sword or the Cone in Monoceros, those maternity wards of Creation. Can it be that no star
fails, is unsuccessful? All stars achieve an adequate stardom,
just as all galaxies achieve some kind of iridescence. And that
includes even those stars that never quite fit the mainstream
pattern, even those galaxies that never make it all the way
along the normative line from irregular to spiral to elliptical
(although the theory concerning that is changing; one type
of galaxy's no older than another, I have read somewhere).
To an extent, as now, taking her own bath, she runs her own
show, but is never as self-sustaining as any of those clumps of
gas and fire we pinpoint in the basement.

A bathroom awash has to be mopped up. She observes,
hand on pink-chiffon-vested hip, while I unroll yards of paper
toweling on the pools. It has snowed talc in here as well. Half
her bottle of toilet water has gone. Her watch has stopped.
Immersed? Unwound, perhaps. She wants action, so I begin
to jog in place right there in the bathroom, and she laughingly joins in, as if finding a corporeal metaphor for prolonged infancy. Out of puff about fifteen minutes later, we're
fit only for ginger ale in lidded steins, dwindling into inertia
while the *agōn* of a framed cop frames itself in the wronged
colors of Channel 10. The day runs down, but the light still
has that above-the-ocean cleansedness of space on top of
space. Waxing fanciful, I curb myself with minor chores: take
my pulse, eighty and coming down; hers, sixty and steady, as
befits a girl with the metabolism of a cheetah and all the
short-dash prizes at the school sports. I watch her eyelids
begin to close me out, then flutter up again as she hauls a leg
aboard and lies full length on the couch. Two sips of warm
milk are all she has energy for before removing herself, un-
bidden, heavy-footed, and without so much as a signal, to
bed. Time was when two hours of soothing cajolery wouldn't
get her to sleep, when midnight stimulated her to ask for

breakfast or propose a dawn patrol with dog, even a bout of carpentry or the making of bread. Now she does this easy glide into depth. Who will ever know if she dreams, or what? She lacks the concept; but, clearly, phantoms have assignations with her at her most private. Sleep makes her a full member of the race, even if her daytime self still peers affably at ceiling corners and smiles back at jocose presences therein. I know nothing of them, hope against hope they are not ghouls, and keep telling myself she is not Hegel, after all, has no Beatles albums, cannot read *Little Women,* and knows next to nothing of her birthday, weight, height, home address, progress at school, or her prospects. Exceptional all round the clock, she fails only in the light. Waiting for the phone to ring, then wondering if it was I to phone, I think of how the Way too, formating invisibly overhead, comes into its own in the dark.

"Can you cope?" asks Pi, around midnight, when I call. I tell her I'm still waiting for something to go wrong, that we've built Orion, will do Gemini tomorrow. "She was like a gazelle all day," I report. Even as I talk, I hear the air-conditioner in Milk's room, and smile as if it's keeping her alive.

"Good. Have you written to her mother?" I haven't, I will, on an index card. "Don't stay up all night at the telescope. You'll have to get up before she does." I promise to set the alarm. A couple of tension-shedding puns later, I say good night, call Chad, who'll stroll over in a few days' time with his own daughter, six years old. Then out onto the balcony to appraise the chances of clear viewing. The bit of cloud will not impede, so I prepare, lug out the scope, plug in the drive to see the red bulb light up, unplug it, and look straight up at Cygnus, where the black rift in the Way begins. I am looking at the real thing. It has no competitors, not locally at any rate. There are so few days left, even after so few gone.

73

Will she want to take the Way with her? Not want to leave it? Or will she become bored with the whole thing tomorrow? Again and again I lift my head to stare at the long fume across the sky, realizing it isn't the silence of those vast spaces that bothers me, it's their longevity. After she and I burn out, there will never be anything again, a never of nevers, never a reprieve reconnaissance in say a million years, just to see how the world is faring. You happen once and then are extinguished, with no more communication. Not even a hiccup, a yawn, a blink. Minus-ness of oneself, and of a few others, that's what chills the heart.

Gruesome beyond belief, I study Deneb.

Couching things thus, in the present tense, amounts to showing that what one shows no longer exists, whereas in the past tense one gives the reader no chance at all of making up his own mind. So the present, for me, is ambiguous, as if defying him/her to deny that what he/she reads about has already vanished, whatever the tense pretends. I almost have the feeling that these things were done before they came into being, already lived through but trying to live again through some simulacrum of the immediate. Essentially there is no tense appropriate to time: the past is never done with, the present is a myth, the future cannot have any identity and still be referred to by that name. I therefore dub this mode the ongoing hypothetical, reporting too late, hypothesizing too soon, leaning into the future as if against a wall that isn't there.

At best, it's similar to living before Volta discovered electric current in 1800 and yet having a hunch about some force that's it. At worst, it's knowing that history will end before 1800, so that I know that I will never know I was right. The whole thing, like sleep, is provisional: an old fixity may start to vary, an element may disperse into a coronet of isotopes, a force may turn into a mere aspect of space. I start out to

74

say: "The night air is cool," and with luck will not have to cancel the statement halfway through; but I can't ever say: "I am saying" because the statement is forever unbegun or under way or complete even while I'm proffering the masquerade. What I can say, though, is: "I am in process, a process is in me." Unless I devise some Chinese of the fingertips, such as *night air cool* or *I in process,* which sounds like the pidgin of the hypocrite, and there I go again, flirting with Now, *which not.*

Casuistical stuff, no doubt, it must have come from living all day with her, my head full of thoughts that bubble into my mouth only to return indoors without an airing. If that is how she feels, and there's no reason why she shouldn't have just as many windmilling thoughts as any of us, she's entitled to pique, having no paper to commit it to, or, rather, barred from committing. I wish her prolix dreams.

Under arm, a toy tiger smelling of plastic cement: her tiger, my arm. "Good morning," I say to the nurse (Frau N. Hofer), "Deulius and daughter. I hope we're not late." Some mistake, she informs me: there is no appointment for any Deulius. The tiger stirs and growls. I feel as if my face is disappearing through a hole in my forehead. "No," she says, "there are no mistakes *here.* The mistakes happen beforehand, before people arrive." A petrified lull. Then: "Good morning, Dr. Jeans, there seems to be some sort of mix-up." He removes a red tomato from his armpit; Milk smiles grandly. "You requested an appointment?" No, I tell him, we were sent for (he rolls his tomato into the far corner of the room in one movement). "For blood tests," I insist. He frowns: "But it was established months ago that you have no blood." Then what about Milk, I ask him. *"Who?"* Milk, I say. This lovely child here. "I see no one else," he remarks. "Nurse Hofer, do you?" The tiger leaps, rips off her watch fob. "Only one person," she gasps, recoiling.

75

Ubiquitous alibi, the same as ever: somehow, when together, one of us is always invisible to everyone else. A pair of stars, the one occulting the other. Once I longed for awareness to become something concrete that wasn't just another form of awareness, and it happened: a girl arrived who is a work of art, like the mountain bluebird of the western U.S.A., a remarkably silent creature. Can it be I'm reincarnate Lazarus Colloredo, born 1716 in Genoa, who bore at the lower end of his breastbone a living child? Who was born thus appendaged and could not have it removed, to give it a life of its own.

"Good morning," we all say, thinking of better mornings, turn and turn about. It is time to go. Another consultation has failed. We go on as before, passing the toy tiger to and fro between us on buses, trains, across the steaming platefuls on tables in restaurants. Life is linear all right, but its line goes in a circle, as if around the globe itself. Nature's full of the impossible: black holes from which light cannot escape; Earth-sized suns made of diamond; atomic nuclei a mile in width that rotate thirty times a second. If one breath from a housefly were spread evenly throughout the Empire State Building, the resulting gas density would exceed that of interstellar space. Thirty baseballs roaming the entire interior of Earth have more chance of colliding with one another than stars do. Galaxies collide more often than stars. S. Doradûs, the most luminous sun in the sky, outshines our own yellow dwarf of a sun by a factor of one million, yet is so remote that the naked eye can't see it. There are stars called FU Orionis, Zubenelgenubi, Azelfafage, Dschubba, Alkaffaljidhina, Mastabbaturtur, and Phakt. I can feel the impossible overlapping with the outlandish, the so-called "done thing" yielding to solecism. The parent cuckoo abandons its chick, but other birds instinctively feed it. The lily-trotter's enormous thin feet let it seem to walk on water. A cabbage has been crossed with a radish, successfully. Sometimes I almost cheer. *Let* the imperfect be our paradise; our hell is flawless.

Combing her hair, then brushing it for ten minutes as she stands before me in the process of waking up, I vow to speak to her non-stop for a whole hour, the only trouble being I won't know where she finishes and I begin, in the steady beat of that address that rams the whole world into the vocative.

Untellable thoughts: I've heard that old people in sanatoria have been hosed down, instead of being bathed, by "orderlies" recruited from flophouses for forty dollars a week and a jug of wine. Granted such a degree of uncivilization, what's to prevent the hosing-down of flawed children as well?

Grievous analogies come in. A vertical cross-section of the human brain resembles a kneeling pygmy; I have seen this in wall charts in doctors' offices. The head dips low, awaiting the ax.

Untold conversations with my father flood back, in one of which he shows how to keep the glans clean, a laudable and tabooless object-lesson, in none of which, however, he says: "Son, once upon a time, one of a crowd, you chased down this pipe, out of this little slot, into your mama." Never showed me that or said. One of those mentally enacted interludes you expect a boy to stage on his mother's behalf. Yes, and his father's. Imagine having such a start! Not one in a thousand exposes himself to Junior, who has to guess a lot at eleven or twelve.

Conversations that never happened with him half-match those un-had with Milk, to whom, even if I wished, I couldn't explain something so simple as how a human child gets started. To her, love's mansion mostly *is* a place of excrement, of one kind or another. "Poo!" she huffs, and such a sound might grace a birth as well, a siege of herons, a pod of seals. Trying to tell, even show, to her, who has no notion of *next* or *month* or *birth*, only gives you, as British soldiers say, the screaming ab-dabs.

Under-heard, then, rather than over-, she and I do our best. We mime the Little Dog, Monoceros, Orion, in some awkward improvised playlet about a wolf who looks with a nasal flashlight for a tennis player in a sky full of moons. And, as ever, we go further and further away from what looks vital, what matters, better equipped for tangents than for basics, for play than for work, dreadfully exempted, like lions that laugh but cannot hunt, streamlined hawks that cannot fly, gorgeous flowers that frighten bees.

Under the Way, we meddle while it burns, forked and shredded by every cosmic wind.

Arrested in time, we are not here at all, but at a guesswork distance, a bit like our own Sun, seen from Alpha Centauri, just an extra star showing up in Cassiopeia, next to the star named Epsilon.

Cain's palimpsest I call the mess on my brow, where so many signs have been made; they cancel out into a splotch, in which, if you look hard enough, you can see anything. Erase, erase, erase. The board shows black, or rather mid-Caribbean green; against it, according to taste, a sperm in the stocks, a fustigated ovum, a brave imp with the face of Spinoza and woeful, seal-like limbs with which it taps at a whole but everted brain resting on top of its cranium like a wig. On with the motley. I mustn't bog down now, no matter what comes next.

Unreal, today, to have so many simple things in mind, most of all the developing comic strip of the Way, with all those august personifications gone to pot. Anyone who reads the funnies comes upon nothing like this: a lost flashlight is retrieved by a wolf, or a unicorn, who takes it in his teeth to a tennis player, who then . . . Ah, the cliff-hangings of fiction, in which the next happening feels always like spring, another breath taken, a gag of black rancid fleece plucked out of the mouth! Only *she* will decide what happens next. I'll steer her to Gemini, and that is all. If one certain Hans Spemann can produce Siamese newts by constricting an egg in the two-cell stage with a loop of hair, who can tell what *she*'ll come up with under similar auspices? With just as free a hand.

Come the weekend, we'll have an epic on our hands. Now, though, with transistor radio rammed against her ear, the one with vestigial hearing, she samples the local coach talking about last week's game. Maximum volume, each word striking me like a basalt pillar. So what? I plod on, show her the sketch of Gemini, and have hardly lapsed into my rehearsal of the lore—Leda's Nest, the Two Peacocks, the two Sprouting Plants—when she honks in recognition. "Doo men," she carefully says, insisting on shaking hands with me. "Hello," she says, three times. "Ewoe. Ewoe. Ewoe." Only a dunce wouldn't get that: Castor is greeting Pollux, maybe after a tennis game. So we enact our closet drama from the beginning, all the way from the flashlight, which the wolf finds and takes to the man serving the tennis ball. She kneels to pick up the flashlight, mimes it into her wolf's mouth, then muzzles me to receive it, which I do, lowering my arm from the service, while she stays at the crouch. Now we shake hands all over again. She runs to the Way itself, taps the relevant designs, motions for me to switch on the stars, does a dance of glee. It isn't much, our masque, but it's mutuality, a clog dance in semi-heaven. Out go Jupiter and Leda both, parents of these twins. Out go all the mariners who honor Saint Elmo's Fire as the Ledean Lights. Gemini is handshake, the tennis-court vow. But she lets me insert the one gaseous nebula into the pattern, after first peering at a lightbulb

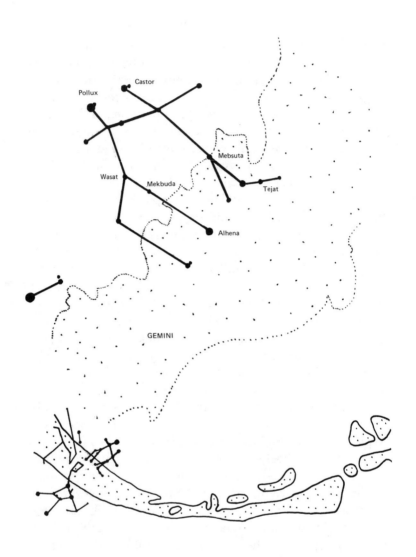

Castor

Pollux

Mebsuta

Wasat

Mekbuda

Tejat

Alhena

GEMINI

through it. I flick off the transistor she's slammed down, heedless of circuits, the whole thing to her just another damned big hearing aid.

Castor and Pollux linger in the mind, though, as Adam and Eve, two gazelles, two young men on horseback, with oval caps that represent the eggshell halves from which they came at birth. I remember reading pages of myth, but I forget the myths, grateful that Pollux is orange, Castor white: bright white and pale white mixed; or, rather, that the two of them aren't in the least alike, or even two. Castor is actually a multiple star, the chief components of which are hot and blue, a third being a small cool dwarf of reddish hue (how human it sounds!) whose period about the system's center of gravity is several tens of thousands of years, a slow-motion dwarf indeed. Just as I'm thinking: Yes, and when you find that Castor's twin components are in fact twin pairs only ten million kilometers apart, and thus have ellipsoid shapes, I realize that we can have some extra fun with these two hand-shaking tennis players. We can be anthropomorphic with the names of stars. I try, uttering "Wasat" as I point to the middle of Pollux's body. Spluttering with laughter, she hauls up her shirt and finger-stabs her navel. Next I try Mekbuda, which means a folded arm, but shows up in Pollux's knee, at which I point. A shrill reproof tells me I've blasphemed; knee, she shows and tells, is "knee," not "Mkbd," whether it's pale topaz or not. When I say Alhena and indicate Pollux's foot, she agrees, thinking I've said "ankle," a word she sometimes knows. Abandoning anatomy, I plug in the star cluster M 35, with its two streams running parallel northwest on either side, and light it up. Here *we* are, not adding up to sixty years between us, and there is old Castor, really a set of stellar sextuplets, forty-seven light-years distant, and there is Pollux, not quite so far off, but in fact a multiple star itself, with at least six very faint components. It used to be that Castor was brighter than Pollux, but no longer so, although whether the one is increasing in brightness or the other is dwindling, we do not know. Were this October, *her* month, we'd see a meteor shower radiating from the feet of the Twins. Were it December, we'd spot fast meteors near the heads, leaving short trails. Puzzled, I check the handbook, and, while she holds colloquy between herself and our lit-up model of the Way, I find this for Castor: "Binary. Both greenish-white. A beautiful object." They never looked green to me, but I'm a peck color-blind, after all. It was a green or greenish star I was hunting a while back, wasn't it? Well, here are two. If we lived on a planet going around Castor, we'd see six suns all at once. I snap the book shut; she's demanding a popsicle, the phone is ringing, a siren is carving up the distance. I move to answer the phone, but she snatches it, quick as light, and booms a series of hellos. It's Asa, asking if we would like to go fly balloons, kites, streamers, whatever. There's wind. We do.

Grinning, he hands Milk a package, which she tears open with her big, fierce hands. A canary-yellow jumbo jet comes out, all floppy because this is an inflatable one. Half-expecting her to fling it at him, he catches it neatly when she does, whips a metal bottle out of his baggy pants, and inflates the plane in seconds. Helium, he tells me as it soars right out of her hands. I see the cord that makes it a kite, and only now remember his graffiti on the wings and fuselage: owls, infinity signs, pentagrams, many-eyed and many-mouthed faces. Milk takes the bracket that holds the plane, then makes her hand plunge to shift the thing aloft, giving out a husky gurgle of delight. Just ecstatic. This is Asa's technique, of course, as befits a man who lives in his own private DC-3, which he sometimes fits with streamers and ribbons; the only pink-and-white-striped Dakota in the world. He has designed a wind-sky fair for schoolchildren, reshaped hills in Hawaii, dumped confetti on factories. He sculpts with wind, makes poems with rubber and nylon. He is exuberant, just the kind of oddball to deal with Milk, who abhors the everyday, demands the gigantic, the outrageous, the wacky. Off we go to Asa's, a half-mile distant, in his London taxi, the helium jumbo five hundred feet above us, tethered to the windshield and touring in its bloat way above the streets we take. That high emblem lifts Milk's heart.

Grand big house left him by his father has turrets, cupola, numerous windsocks flying from poles. In a trice he has made Milk her own private flag, a humped rainbow on a black canvas ground. Eight feet long, it goes up the pole while she sings up to it, after it, almost seems to be flapping with it. Sun glints on his bald dome, roc's egg with vast smile-hiding black mustache beneath it. He lives on pasta, wears only sweaters and Dutch pantaloons, spends half his life (I think) in mid-air, sketching while the automatic pilot steers the plane. I all of a sudden lose the order in which things happen, recognizing that, even if only for a day or a week, he is her perfect father: coming at her with a trombone full of golden farts; throwing up a sculpture of rags on a wire frame; seating her in a giant eggcup right there on the groomed lawn; dashing out from the house with an entire pizza on a silver tray; handing her masks, noses, beards. We all play at being ghouls, run, chase, get out of breath, lie down while the wind flicks past us.

Going away yet again, he returns leading a taupe foal that walks with a bit of a reel. She goes mad over it, shoves pizza at his muzzle. "Ride?" "No!" So she leads it at the stoop, one arm over its neck, and makes two circuits of the garden before the foal twists free and stilt-walks again to Asa's side. I can't help feeling I've been trumped, scooped, but who cares? Here is a man who had a dimension waiting for her all this time: no Milky Way, but a true gala, a chromatic extravaganza. Then his housekeeper releases two rabbits, a black, a white, brings out the big parrot (which scares Milk), and, glory be, wheels out onto the lawn the biggest color TV I've ever seen, festooned with fake greenery made of sponges, with masks and flagstaffs. It works, it switches on, it even seems to breed when he erects a mirror in front of it, and she sites herself between the big screen and the equal mirror, seeming to bisect her view. Now the foal sits with her, in an awkward sprawl, and Asa says the one word: "Planning!" at which I shrug, astounded. He tells me he only just got back from Zürich. And I wonder if he doesn't perhaps want to borrow her for a year, install her in some organic sculpture set, plonk her down on red ice or a six-foot-high champagne cork. A wizard, that's what Asa is; a wizard is what she needs. We haul down the jumbo, attach a winking light to it, and send it up again. Milk watches in a dream, her senses swamped by foal, pizza, TV on the lawn, rabbits, and the mighty parrot. One final parade, with each of us bearing a clutch of balloons like a giant levitating molecule, and we go inside to eat. Milk is pink with fun.

Crisp-topped lasagna weighing us down, we go off again in the taxi to, of all things, the Middle Hall wine festival, where we all three tread grapes hilariously, and then with mired feet taxi off again to his house and rinse off in the goldfish pool. Sweet chaos, and she loves it. It's what she was born for. All that's lacking is an abacus, a coelacanth, and a gryphon, or so I think in my merriment as thousands of birds loop and pour across the afternoon sky like locusts. I no longer have any abstract ideas, just a blur of things. But I'm glad he's here, not in Zürich, where I'd thought he'd be for another three weeks. He swells the team; indeed, he swells the world, makes the Milky Way edge over for lack of room.

"Uncle" he gets to be called, like King Lear. He once had a wife, but he somehow lost her in (or to) the Philippines, and not during any war. He will take us aloft, in the DC-3 dubbed *Moby*, to trail streamers, inhale cloud, point a telescope at the daylight Moon. "Florida?" he inquires. "Too hot for her,"

I say. "Canada, then?" he follows up. "Maybe," I say, "it might be just right. But—not too much confusion, please, she's only just arrived." Gracious to the nth, he fishes out Polaroid cameras, and Milk actually takes a picture of herself watching the TV in the garden, by sheer good luck, at the fifth shot managing to get her face into the frame. We pat her on the shoulders, shake her hands, for hitting a home run, for breaking the record, for being herself.

Upset a bit as the sky darkens, Milk waves urgently at Asa, who switches on several arc lamps, ignites the barbecue. We toast marshmallows, swig beer and ginger ale, light two big phallic cigars that ought to explode but don't, give her a chocolate one, and lie there, in our chaise-longues, puffing smoke at the moon, lotos-eaters to the end. Even in the dusk I can see the dark rings under her eyes, in her a sign of exhaustive joy, and I reckon the day well spent. And spent is what I mean. We have nothing left, not even for the sky. Between us we lift her heavy, sleeping body and carry her inside to a daybed, after which he and I resume our cigars to a background of what he listens to: Mahler, Ives, and Crumb, in that order. It feels like being on stage during the last scene of a final act.

Generous people lap up the grotesque, don't they? I know only that one day soon I must fill the cracks between the bath and the tiled wall with cement or putty. Let Milk help, since her technique of bathing will soon wash out what of rotted filler holds.

Grinning at another foolish memory, I recoup a menu that said: "Tenderloin barbecued to your likeness." They serve up your face medium rare, which is why they photograph you on entering the restaurant. Then the chef kneads meat all day. Some tenderloins are even barbecued after the death masks of the famous. Eat George Washington's profile. Trough on Adam's chops.

85

Unseemly thoughts, whereas all I have in mind is a small, earthbound text, a souvenir in which tiniest meets vastest, or as nearly as makes no difference, while the pain floats in between them, sea-changing into measured delight or wooden-headed stoicism at least. On, on. I'm almost there.

Ungainly with fatigue, I ease her into Asa's taxi. "To the Charing Cross Hotel, sir." "Yes," he says with a bogus yawn.

Arriving at my house, we lift her out and in. All day the TV has been on. It reveals to me Boris Karloff, walking with atrocious gimp in an outsize surgical boot. Asa goes off to design something or other, nocturnal worker that he is, while I clean house, swobbing up dust with damp paper towels, and trying to follow the fate of Karloff as I move around. It sounds extreme: all gasp and saliva, a lurid wake for insomniac America. Then a beer, bad of me, and another cigar, which is worse. A day crossed off the calendar, out of our lives.

Uncle Asa has been a wizard, that I know.

Uncanny how the mind cavorts when tired. I lose the sense of time, at least as orthodoxly put, and see it as a mere shift from warm to cold, from tidy to untidy: an entropy there is no way to duck. An odd little calculation swims into mind, a bit of homemade, amateur's finding, not exactly news to the world of science, but news to me and my own. I worked out, from all the data in my star books, the favored speeds at which stars approach or recede from the Sun. Of forty-four, twenty-six approach and eighteen recede; and, as I figured it, at 1–2 miles per second as many approach as recede, whereas at 3–16 miles per second twice as many approach as recede, while of the few at 17–73 miles per second as many recede as approach. Tempted to call this Deulius' Law (or something vainglorious like that), I didn't, postponing self-glorification until the day I'd correlated the speeds with the distances, which still remains to do. Yet I drew the curve, happy to tell myself: This is how they go round the mulberry bush, and not otherwise, the only remaining question being why. At which I halt, not eager enough for explanation to commit hypothesis. Some perverse confidence in the universe, as in the human appetite for gossip and ice cream, keeps me going, helps my mind rest, as when I reassure myself that, no matter how many asteroids we find, we'll never run out of names for them, provided we're willing to dub them such things as Marilyn, Fanny, Crocus, China, Mussorgskia. *Homo sapiens* will never run out of names, no matter how many phenomena come his way.

Gently as a threatened bird, Milk eats breakfast, nibbling rather than troughing. Wide awake she does things handsomely grand, but heavy from sleep she tinkers, making half-irritable aloof gestures with minimum power. If we get back to the Way, we'll attempt Auriga, the so-called Charioteer, although for the life of me I never saw reins or driver in its clean steeple shape. Capella's ready, in the form of a big yellow bulb, and so is Menkarlina ("the shoulder of the driver"), white. The surprise, however, has to do with the thing aridly called Epsilon A *Aurigae,* which just happens to be the largest star we know, vast enough to accommodate the entire solar system out to Saturn inclusive. Over two and a quarter billion miles across, it's 2,700 times the size of our Sun, and yet transparent, emitting mostly invisible infra-red rays. In fact, it has a partner, a mere 190 times the Sun in size, which is the yellowish star we see and mark on charts. How slap-happy would I have to be to pass up such a chance? So I've devised something special that suggests the horrific vastness of the pair, the invisible one and the yellow one. As my Soviet textbook says, "Surely Nature did not skimp on wonders to startle the human imagination." Amen to that. I'll try to live up to it.

Coming round fast, she requests "sand," her version of a word that ends in *wich.* Receives corn beef, eats it, then a

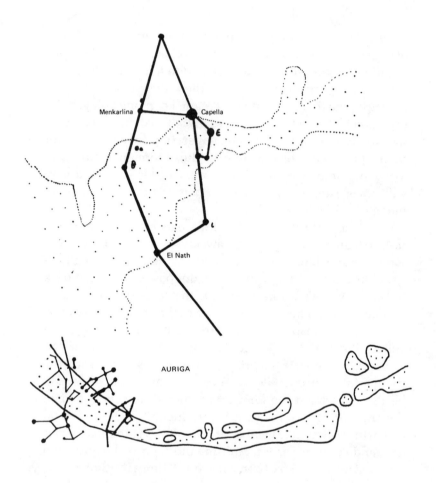

AURIGA

second. No longer a finicky bird but a ravening furnace, she takes in milk, several rolls larded with strawberry preserve, and a boiled egg as well. She eats today as if she isn't coming back. I mean she eats, today, et cetera, but let it stand: she will devour the day as well, as the phrase implied. Remembering, she flashes down the stairs: no warning, no request, and when I arrive, cup in hand, she has switched on the Way, has begun to babble the comic-strip legend we fudged up. The flashlight. The wolf. The tennis server. The two players shaking hands. So we continue, my own mind as much on Asa's aerial feats as on Auriga. Now I remember something else: I forgot to call Pi, neglected to make arrangements with Chad to bring his daughter round. Arrange! Arrange! Arrange! Later, anyway. My young Vikingess demands the next scene, gets it, drawn small, and at once brandishes the template, informing me in elated yells what it is. Of course. "Kite." There even seems to be a string attached. After Asa, who can not think kites? Truly, though, it resembles a kite, and I no longer see the steeple or, a sibling image, the sentry box. Working fast, I line it out, planking Auriga slap across the Milky Way. Into its hole I plug Capella, the Little She-Goat, so-called, on whose actual color no one seems able to agree, red, gold, yellow, all the same forty-two light-years away and receding from us at nineteen miles per second. Then the white bulb for Menkarlina, another for El Nath, "the heel," even a blue one for *theta,* an orange one for *iota.* The entire pentagon lights up. No doubt I'm overdoing it, but, damn it all, this is the constellation of Erichthonius, fourth King of Athens, who was so deformed he couldn't walk and therefore invented the four-horse chariot supposed to be commemorated in this beautiful and conspicuous clutch of stars. While I think this, she is miming and motioning to me that the two players who shook hands have now come to fly a kite on what she calls a "yort ing," a short string. Indeed they have. Then she gapes in delighted bemusement as I affix

89

Epsilon A and its partner by cutting a big hole, over which I staple yellow plastic, behind which, after fifteen more minutes, a color disk begins to spin with a slight, almost nasal scrape. Irrationally, I've made A's partner a yellow spot on the disk itself. But we parted company with science long ago, so there's no need to insist on how the massive thing really behaves; in *our* Way, it spins wholesomely, almost white, like a blind vitreous body in an eye socket, dwarfing Capella and the rest. The unseen seen, the impossible scaled down. Strictly, according to the scale of Capella, my rotating Epsilon A ought to be six feet across. I ponder, for the few seconds she allows, the wild model that would embody the Way's third dimension, reaching miles beyond the last gas station in town!

Up and down she jumps, in explosive syllables reciting her tale of a kite; or so I presume, unable to follow a word. Some of it goes:

> "Men-drath, bugaboo.
> "Ban. Dry. Bane.
> "Ankela, Ankela. Bib.
> "More. No."

I say more or less the same to her, but she waves me imperiously off her verbal reservation. Some words belong to her alone, as code or gibberish. No trespassers allowed. And I once again feel confined in my own world of public signs, excluded (as of old) from the world in which she called a knife a *seven*, an escalator a *bo*. Once you learned her lingo, however, she dropped it and moved on to new misnomers, leaving you a-puff in her wake.

> "Brang, *brang*," she hoots.
> "Brang," I answer, to oblige. *Brang* indeed.
> "No," she insists. *"Milk."*

So, in tender retaliation, I spout our new constellation at her: "Capella, Menkarlina, El Nath, Epsilon A, *Auriga!*" At which she only collapses into laughter of the well-fed sort, as if a Hottentot had presumed to question Wittgenstein. Plainly, I am not to speak like that. It ruins her notion of my possible dignity. It fattens my daftness. In other words (literally too), I am to use neither her language nor mine, nor even standard English, but am to remain in dumb-struck astonishment while she mixes the sounds of aviary, stable, and black mass.

Granted, Your Majesty. I go upstairs to phone Pi, who is out; Chad, who is in, but busy, and who'll come tomorrow afternoon. Now Milk's upon me, leopard-like, wanting to tickle and be tickled, to roll and leap, on the bed. Hearty, clean-throated laughter comes from her for ten minutes. Then we jog. She does a handstand against the wall, transfers her weight to her head, talks madly at me from her upside-down position, but not a word can I grasp, can only think (record thus in inverted bafflement): *Ehs si evif teef gnol.* Or: *Gnol teef evif si ehs.* I say it to her, in preposterous hope that today just happens to be back-to-front land: *"Gnol teef evif si ehs!"* Smirking feistily, she says, "Yes." (Can anyone wonder why I don't know if I'm coming or going?) One more try, and I end the game. "Olleh, Klim," I greet her, affably enough. *"Klim! Olleh."* It doesn't work; she just asks for "beebee": a carbonated beverage, I guess. I fetch. She takes it still upside down, tries to pour it into her mouth, all over the floor. I mop up, she pours some more, just so I won't feel I've nothing to do. Told no, she drinks the rest. The phone rings, a wrong number, so I let her talk to whoever it is on the other end, the careless dialer who will think he's got through to the Kafka Enigma Factory: just a deaf child announcing her presence repeatedly, plus a few "jabba"s and "blawn"s, whatever they happen to mean.

At Auriga again, we rehearse the action. That kite won't stay up forever, although in the Way it will. What next?

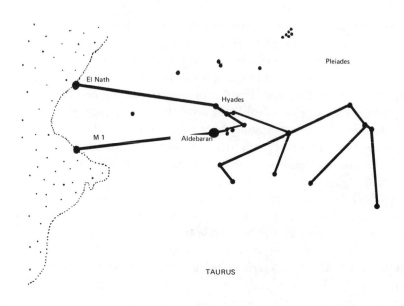

El Nath

Pleiades

Hyades

M 1

Aldebaran

TAURUS

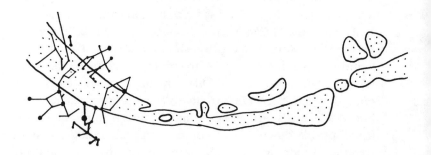

92

What's next is Taurus, on we go, moving along the Galaxy like two sleepwalkers hitching rides. When she scowls at the template, I wonder why, then get it: it's a disassembled kite, a kite that's crashed. No, she is saying "Yah," plus something else. Pointing at her legs, at mine, she raps out the one syllable: "long." Clear as day, what she means is *daddy longlegs,* an excellent likeness to fix on Taurus. Not what I had in mind, but I rarely do have in mind what she comes up with. Very well, I tell myself, as if telling her, that's what it's going to be. When the wolf takes the flashlight to the tennis players who end up flying a kite that just happens to include the biggest star we know, a daddy longlegs (otherwise known as harvestman or crane fly) will go aloft on its fabric. I'd almost expected her to think Taurus a broken kite string trailing untidily down, frozen in its last twirl, but not the charging bull with elongated horns that just touch the Way itself. Whether I can sustain our comic scenario, I'm not sure, but I'll give it the old Galactic try. Casually I flash at her a picture postcard of the Pleiades, white stars trapped in pale-blue brushstrokes done by a nervous hand, then one of the blue-green shell that is the Crab Nebula, with claws floating explosively away from the main body. Two astronomical golden oldies, these, at which she nods as if I've written out her name and she impatiently heeds it, wants to get on to something else. Working fast, almost by reflex, I install daddy-longlegs Taurus in the gloom off the Way, screw in the big bulb that's orange-red for gigantic Aldebaran, then the holders that will light up out-of-scale cut-outs of the Pleiades and the Crab Nebula. She "oo"s a little, even though I'm not ready to switch on. Weird thoughts accompany my swift but not deft hand motions. The Pleiades appear to be shivering, although their surface temperature is extremely high. And they are called young stars although two and a half million years old. My replica of Aldebaran is so big I haven't room for the Hyades cluster, in the middle of which the star appears to sit. A pity, because some of the Hyades are coolish and red, maybe a thousand million years old. Milk is in her middle teens. I switch on, wishing I could tell her just a little about Merope, seventh Pleiad, who was so careless as to marry a mortal, thus causing her light to fade, or about the rainy Hyades, grieving for their brother Hyas, by the wild boar slain, or even about how Charles Messier, in 1758, mistook the then unknown Crab Nebula for a comet and irritably began to compile his famous catalogue of nebulae, listing the Crab as "Interference Number 1." Why, the Pleiades are moving through space like a flock of birds; the Arabs called the Hyades the Little She Camels as they trekked toward a point somewhere just past Betelgeuse; and Aldebaran, thirty-seven million miles in diameter, is receding from us at thirty-four miles a second. To tell her wouldn't help her, no. It helps nobody, does it? Yet just to know, just to let curiosity, awe, and humility have a field day, that might not be so bad. As it is, she gets all the visuals; she wolfs color, she gorges herself on light. And all I can think of, when reviewing her progress, is what someone said about the chances of there being intelligent life in space: absence of evidence doesn't mean evidence of absence. Perhaps, from her point of view, I'm Interference Number 1; she's certainly not it, from mine. On the contrary, she's more like the faded Pleiad pouring out her light again: the young, hot star, sometimes blue, sometimes very pale, now on the premises again. Inane as it may be, to spend the days in a private amalgam of stars, kites, wordless horseplay, swims and guesses and haphazard meals, it's the only way I know, the only game in town. We could both be better employed, I'm sure, instead of doting on each other daylong during what's almost a clandestine "assignation" laced with incest, flawed by genes. It will soon be wise to fetch my mail from the office, call at the bank, make a sortie for groceries, et cetera. This kind of suspension, trance, can't last very long, no matter what the real or the fake Way is doing. I should trim the weeds from the front walk, the overgrowth from the rear one, collect up all the fallen apples, and mow the lawn. All right: we *will*.

Underhandedly I think: On your own behalf, Deulius, what is Taurus? What's it to you? And I answer that it resembles an insect with a prosthetic tuning fork upon its head. We're getting on, moving ahead, oh yes, but I don't see our model of the Milky Way ever being finished; I'll rather be completing the chore after she's gone. A plywood elegy complete with dwindling lights. We're not even keeping a straight course along the Way, backtracking a bit to take in Taurus, then lunging right to take in Perseus, as we no doubt will. There was a future, wasn't there? If only we could use it now.

Going into diary form, I make what sense I can of the hours, the days. Itemize. Itemize. Itemize. It has been busy. Pi arrives, without warning, but loaded with groceries bought on the way in, after that three-hour drive. So once again we have wheels, once again the zippy Datsun stands on the gravel glacis that slopes down to the house as if the house above, up the incline, were a fort. Milk and she regard each other for a moment, pondering tactics, then untidily hug, rivals in peace. Asa stops by, leaves a perpetual-motion toy with six balls that click to and fro. As he leaves, en route to the state capital, he vows to build a life-size one before she leaves. He goes. We all three swim. For once, we eat a proper meal, an enormous casserole followed by fresh fruit with ice cream. I, as ever, pass up the fruit but take the ice cream. At the drive-in movie, an eighth adventure of Sinbad, we suck popsicles and Milk utters a loud, acerbic commentary in a language unknown, from time to time grabbing at us as the action quickens, especially when Sinbad swims out to a ship on the rocks, buries himself in sand, and sets a bush over his head. At her level, we thrive on the crudeness of events, the colors, the non-stop causation of it all. As the ads say of actors, she *is* Sinbad, wild and slick on the poop of her own automotive bagala (word I learn from the movie, meaning a luxurious dhow or something such). Sipping a milkshake at the all-night diner, she behaves with impossible graciousness, a nun at an altar. No bellows, no muscle play, no snorts. I have rarely seen her so demure. Amiably she chats to us in a near-whisper in yet another of her private lingos, and no one even stares. She hasn't worn a hearing aid in days and doesn't intend to: out in society she leaves her crutches behind, just so much gear. Pi says the girl is amazing. "Yes," says Milk, who hasn't heard. Redundantly agreeing, I have to laugh, there being, between the two of them, enough hair for a small rug. Each has hair to well below the waist, Milk's mousy brown, Pi's carbon black. About the same height, though Milk has the fuller figure, they look as unalike as a Finn and a Turk, which they aren't. "Hi, Milk," says one, for something to begin with. " 'E'oe," comes the answer. A pause, and then: "Bye." How simple it all seems, a lingua franca of amnesty, an Esperanto of neighbor-numbness. I say nothing, but scratch the glue and the paint off my thumbs. Whatever happens, whatever gets said, slots into a stained-glass window that overlooks a charnel house I've too often looked into. A worsening view, past forty, past her twenty, slipping on blood into fifty and thirty, and there is over everything a bone-snapping pall of goodbyes that are going to be said, no matter what is in anyone's mouth: heart or gag, foot or food. I end that thought so fast it doubles back into the realm of also-ran. I never give the fates a hand to shake.

Grabbing at my mail, she slams and reslams the mailroom door, locking us in a giant oven. On the way home, we look in on Lee, in his dairyette, who recommends as almost always the frozen cod with a knob of butter on top, baked. Forcing on her a big bag of potato chips, he waves goodbye with dollars in his hand, affable gargoyle who cannot count, any more than can his Sunday deputy, a shriveled ancient whom we fondly nickname Malone Dies. Stumbling around in the dusk, we gather up the fallen apples, then sort them in the house, and a mighty joke follows: Pi will make a pie, and Milk envisions Pi in the oven, all three of us eating Pi with forks, what's left of Pi cooling in the refrigerator next to the milk. A breezy temperament the girl has; she laughs on this all the way to bedtime, and is still rehearsing it as she begins to drift, with that calmed-down curl of lip that tells you she's at peace. "It wasn't bad," we say. It could have been devilish. It may be yet. It could happen tomorrow. Let it not. I get a neck-rub. A weight lifts off the brainstem. I read Pi's new poem, by-product of insomnia at her parents' house. One of her A to A— poems, it still needs work, but she still sees (I tell her) finite infinities in all her grains of sand: a compliment, though sounding like a cavil. The Pi's-pie joke returns to haunt, even as we look up at Jupiter, that lolling gob-stopper of painless light. Out comes the telescope, the good one, and in fifteen minutes we have split Albireo into a yellow and a blue. The electric drive doesn't let it move, as if our eyes are standing still while the Earth moves round. Then, still in Cygnus, we aim at *psi,* find the lilac star, the white partner, and, in a reckless mood, shoot for Cygnus X-1, where the first-found of the black holes is supposed to be. When Cygnus goes out of range, behind the roof, we look at Andromeda and pick out the galaxy, a trembling blur most unlike its sumptuary por-trait in our glossy picture books. The Way sprawls clear, high but not that high, blown into little tufts and smears or flowing thick. One sweep with the instrument sends thousands of astronomical billiard balls flashing past the eyepiece. The Pleiades become an outsize, scattered molecule. The Hyades blaze yellow and gold. Aldebaran batters away like a sym-phonic fireball, as if it knew of Wagner. Out of the blue, out of that uranian gray, a thought comes spinning at meteor speed, no trail. Our talking with Milk is uncannily like those conversations that, one gathers, will eventually happen: some intelligence over in Eridanus says, "Hello," and we answer, in our terrestrial way, "How are you?" And the entity in Eridanus responds, "Fine." Even at the speed of light, that little chat will take centuries. Heaven be thanked, then, that she answers almost at once (when she answers at all), and that we can see her face in all its detail. It may be daft to think she thinks us an immature civilization not worth communicating with, but I think it all the same. It certainly isn't the other way round, whatever several million *hoi polloi* might think as they squint at her in the street.

Upon a time, once: that's how I'll resume, I the only one awake, in front of cattle rustlers in Ochercolor on the Late Late Late Show. Both girls abed beneath the mouths of their respective air-conditioners. I bid the day come back. It won't. A saliva befitting Tantalus fills my mouth as I think how long everything takes, yet is done with in a mayfly's cough. We are all three of us too old to know what's out in the Galaxy, or even beyond it. When the aliens begin booming all their knowledge at us, and mankind races to fill all its copybooks with cures and miracles, we'll be long gone, smudged back into the flux as a dust. And all I can think of is: a century elapsed before anyone visited America, after it had been found. It is going to be at least that long before anything begins pouring into the recorders of the radio telescopes, which, so far, we haven't even readied on the proper scale. Including, oh what a vainglorious wish, the cure for brain damage, simple as clipping dry cuticle from your nail. Yet something I'm determined to find out, am hell-bent on it. What is the favored speed of stars? Is it, as I surmised, between three and sixteen miles per second? Knowing it helps nobody, but knowing it soothes me; I know the Sun travels at twelve, en route for Vega and Hercules, with a goodish chance of getting there, while we . . .

Gulliver at bay, with iris and pupil strained from the eye-piece, I pretend to know what's brewing in her flighty brain. As I tell Pi, it's a hell of a challenge for a fiction-writer to have to deal with someone whose inner life you hardly know at all. With characters, you can pretend to be omniscient, invent-ing your own verifications. In everyday life, you can always ask, or listen. But with Milk you're stymied into reporting a mighty live, impossibly attractive human from the outside non-stop. In her own way, she is more fictional than Beowulf, less given to explanations than Goya's Saturn. I guess, you guess, she guesses, we guess, they all guess. Ecstatic (or seem-ing so) in her frequent private trances, when her eyes almost cross or she peers up into the room's corners, she has to be invented *for*. As in the old saw: Silent woman maketh myth. From morning to night she sponsors rumor, the result being that, from time to time, I've had to settle my mind by fixing on the extent to which she fits the rubrics for hyperactive children—Doesn't Finish Projects, Fidgets, Can't Sit Still At Meals, Doesn't Stay With Games, Wears Out Furniture And Toys, Talks Too Much, ah!—or by devising impossible fugues that imply a world in which she belongs, one of these begin-ning: "Upon a time, once, when William Shakespeare was in Hawaii, he had to phone home for his coach-and-four, his microscope, and the first draft of his second novel, all left behind him with his third wife, Lady Hester Stanhope, who herself was fond of visiting Tibet and there encountered Lawrence of Arabia soon after the amputation of his right leg following a helicopter accident in November 1255. . . ." Off-the-cuff madness, of course, and such shifts work no longer, mainly because I have made up *my* mind about what goes on in Milk's, and she thus far hasn't provided any evidence to the contrary. She rolls with a whirlwind all her own, at which I've guessed, and now have canonized the guess. After all, as I tell Pi, when you're dealing with a girl whom am-phetamines quieten, whom sedatives turn on, your whole world gets topsy-turvy and you cling to certain facts: for example, that amphetamine stimulates the release of norepinephrine from nerve endings in the hypothalamus and brainstem, parts that have a lot to do with moods and awareness. Then you realize that a tense situation—at the doctor's office, or when strangers are in the house—produces an anxiety that creates just the same effect as the drug, and through the same mechanism. Holy cow: but you can't habituate a child to stimulants or anxiety, especially in her/his/its teens. What I'm doing, in fact, is something else, getting on with Perseus before our social life wipes out the Galaxy for good.

Uppity and a bit skittish, she informs me that this lovely outline, whose pointed tip I think a dog's unhooded penis, is a clown with three yellow pom-poms on his person, one on the hat, one at the back of his neck, one on his shoulder. Miming the whole thing with sardonic agility, she stabs her finger at the Way and demands results. Perseus, of course, shows up in the older star maps in warrior stance, in his right hand a sword, in his left the awful head of Medusa, just as if (I've thought it) he were the patron saint of the divorce court. But, looking at the outline, I detect the element of frolic, the wacky wide-legged splits, the left arm outreached to touch the audience. Reaching into my bag of tricks (an old cardboard liquor case in which, on the quiet, she's already been rummaging), I fish out the fluctuating Christmas-tree light that's going to be Algol, the demon star that is Medusa's eye twinkling, and sight through it at the ceiling. "More," she cries. "More lamp." To work I go, rushing through the early stages, hardly even pausing to smirk as I do the hole for Mirfak, the yellow star that is the lowest of her three pom-poms. The joke, such as it is, concerns only Pi and me and the salt- and pepper-holders on the kitchen table, which for mildly lewd reasons we have named Mirfak and Ophiuchus: a star and a constellation reduced to humbler service. Suppressing levity, I recall that John Goodricke, the deaf and

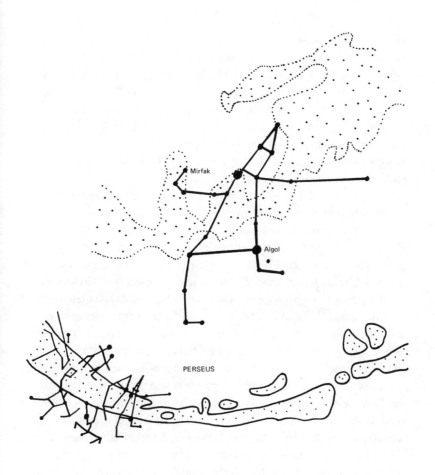

Mirfak

Algol

PERSEUS

dumb astronomer, was the one who identified Algol as a spectral binary, or at least said the star was twin. As it is, which is why I've installed this shuntling blue-and-yellow bulb. "Algol," I tell her, just to see what she'll do; but she thinks I've said, "All gone," and scowls. "Al Gol," tries Pi, knowing she has said the Arabic for *ghoul*, but Milk just mimics the clown's pose, hooks one arm behind her, the other outstretched, mouthing the word "clown." There is nothing clownish about her, though. She looks both dignified and august, a tall blond athlete who has just accomplished the long jump with ballerina precision. So Pi and I applaud her stance, clapping as loud as we can, and I observe that my daughter is flighty with another woman around, has become just that bit more of a ham, more prima-donna-ish, and more verbal. Shaking her head, Pi hands me an open book in which a photograph with superimposed arrows reveals how the star group called Perseus II will look in half a million years at over seven miles a second. Why, over a million years ago they were all at the same point, were born then, and even now rank as newborn infants. On the scale of a human span of seventy years, these twelve stars correspond to an infant on its first day. A nausea takes hold of me, something abstract and spiky in the gut, and I try to fend off all the human comparisons that leap to mind. Better, I tell myself, then Pi, to reiterate the fact that, thus far along the Way, we have added a clown to the flashlight-wolf-tennis-handshake-kite-flying-daddy-longlegs main sequence, with Cassiopeia next. Hopeless, though: the tiny progress those twelve stars will make in half a million years has made me physically ill, with an odd stitch just below the belt. Meanwhile, the mind is off again, this time adding insult to injury by remembering something brand new: the radio galaxy some Leyden astronomers found, after prolonged efforts, to be two thousand million light-years *away* from us, and, oh heavens, eighteen million light-years *wide*. Its name, 3C 236. And it has a little partner (how gregarious are the contents of space!) only six and a half million light-years wide. A saner person wouldn't try to figure against such an incomprehensible ground, would choose a hemisphere, a desert, a parking lot, happy to let like do duty for like: *similia similibus curantur,* as homeopaths have it. Yet here I go, aided and abetted by Pi (who rejoices more in planets than in galaxies, but still . . .), doing my best to dwarf us all, make of Man a midge. But only, I tell myself, to minimize Milk's flaw. 3C 236 just happens, I keep on telling myself, to be the largest known object in the universe. Big as it is, however, it shouldn't make any difference to me, to Milk; but it does, at least to me, fattening awe till every other emotion I feel becomes awe-struck too. And the sense of triumph I feel when peering at the photograph comes out in an unspoken ditty that runs: "Did whatever made 3C 236 make me?" End of song. I feel like a stoic, epistemological non-combatant, losing all emotions in a blanket reverence. Hating the universe just a little, I marvel at its lack of modesty. The brash big. The brash big unending. The brash big unending inhuman. The brash big unending inhuman self-centered. The brash big unending inhuman self-centered helpless. The brash big unending inhuman self-centered helpless to-do, with which our minds go on shadow-boxing to no point. Our perhaps unknowing sponsor. How anyone can *not* speak of it, I have no idea, though men have been only too ready to celebrate, say, Jupiter and Hercules, as if they were men, but not an enormous whirling sphere of methane and ammonia, and a vast drill-ground of gas in heat. Which is where Pi and her planetary poems come in: one woman addressing herself to the solar system, in neighborly esteem. Inhuman? Not in the least. It is the so-called human view that's inhuman when human means Man-centered and inhuman means unworthy of our brains. The least we can do is to muse on all that is not ourselves, the most is to see how accidental our presence is. From all accounts, it looks as if the teleology that says we occurred in order to link up with other forms of life outside the local system is wrong; the race is likely to perish without having made contact at all, while, at unthinkable distances from us, cleverer and saner forms of entity go about their business, even making *their* teleology come true. I can't discount the random in it all, as when, each year, to only one of two thousand radium atoms fate comes knocking, kills it off into lead and helium. Why that one, out of an identical two thousand, no one knows, or why even only one. But happen it does, and to our own cells too, whether or not the victim is able to think.

Under the influence of such outsize runes, I decide to go for Cassiopeia in the basement while Pi mixes a quiche. Paradoxes begin anew, with my mind limping back to the vain queen, wife of King Cepheus, who for conceit about her looks was transferred to the sky, seated in a starry chair that circles the Pole and sometimes stands her on her head. Waving me on, Milk arranges her face into acidulous forbearingness: I'm too slow, I haven't reduced my constellation-building to a sleight-of-hand. Perhaps that is how Andromeda, daughter of Cassiopeia, scowled while chained to the rocks, doing punishment for her mother's lack of tact. I maneuver fast with template, juggling the cardboard so that Cassiopeia's scintillant zigzag is now an M, now a W, as in the sky itself. Surely Milk will see the letter as what it is. But she says nothing, curves a long tongue down her chin, and begins to tap her foot. I can smell pastry baking upstairs as I make the hole for Schedar, the orange star, and Chaph, the yellow. "Bagdei," I say, intoning the mnemonic for the stars that make up Cassiopeia's chair: *beta, alpha, gamma,* et cetera, another bit of my mind on the supernova that Tycho Brahe spotted here in November 1572, when returning from Germany to his native Denmark and stopping over in the picturesque old monastery of Herrizwald. The new star had no tail, was not

CASSIOPEIA

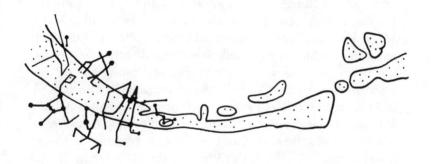

surrounded by any nebula, was almost as bright as Venus when that planet is nearest Earth. It could even be seen at noon, and at night through thick cloud cover. Then, in December 1572, it began to fade and in fact vanished in March 1574. Many people prepared for death, having decided that the new star was a signal, coming hard after the Massacre of Saint Bartholomew; but all that ensued was radio waves, faint ones detected in 1952, whereas another part of Cassiopeia, named A, is the most powerful source of radio waves anywhere in the sky. Mocking myself for parading information as I plant my pseudo-stars, I look quizzically at Milk, who takes one look and pronounces *M*. Child's play. She runs upstairs, led on by her nose. I finish the job, still musing on the constellation that was Leg to the Egyptians, Stone Lamp to Eskimos, Key to Greeks, Kneeling Camel to Arabs. There goes the Queen of Ethiopia, around the Pole head downward, like a tumbler, fair-complected and lightly clad (according to one account), and sometimes under an alias: Mary Magdalene, Bathsheba, or even Deborah, sitting under her palm tree on Mount Ephraim. Schedar, pale rose to some but not to me, has a smalt-blue companion I omit; *breast,* the word means, while Chaph is *hand* or *camel's hump,* and brilliant white Tsih is Chinese for *whip,* Ruchbah is Arabic for *knee.* I switch on as a drumming scuffle begins upstairs (a tickling contest it seems), and feel just as conceited as Cassiopeia: my one fourth of the Way is a dazzling vision, like a stained-glass window gone haywire, and festively so. Yet I suspect there will soon be only me to admire it, flick it on and off, swing it back and forth, perfect the nebulae and concoct some way of indicating radio sources and black holes: the father playing with his child's toy train set. All of a sudden I feel remarkably standard, whereas I usually feel freakish, and the feeling has little to do with memories of how Cassiopeia contained the star (Tycho's) that was supposed to herald the second coming, or with the tangerine tint of Schedar (only that hue to one as partly color-blind as I), or with thoughts of biting into quiche. No: it is the long-absent feeling of being with the girl on Christmas Day, when all the brand-new mechanical toys buzzed wild at the same time, and Milk looked right at home in God's shop. At such times I've felt that she, and even I, possessed whatever it is that qualifies you for humanhood: self-awareness, minimal intelligence, self-control, sense of time, sense of futurity, concern for others, balance of rationality and feeling, and so on. Unhappily, Christmas lasts a few days only; the suspended norms renew themselves, the access of vitality and honed awareness falls away; and some of the toys break. I go upstairs to eat quiche, summoned by two sets of feet tattooing on the floor above, and I leave the Way blazing with light, just for joy.

"Uh," Milk seems to say, but it's an imperative whose full text reads, *Big hug!*, said as "Bi' 'uh." It's the first time she has used it during her stay. That very thought reminds me that we are no longer nibbling into the first day, but working past the second or third. Preliminary is over, when you can use up a day without the sense of reducing the days; and the calendar has begun to count. Mouth full of hot and tangy pie, I go to the calendar on the wall and outline the remainder of her stay in squeaky black, my head on some old distinction between seasonal time and mere chronicity. Limned in black, our own short season has a lugubrious aspect I want to wish away, but, as I tell Pi, there *is* something terminal about the whole idea of visitation rights, a child on loan, a parent out of cold storage. Tactfully she asks if I left the lights on, while Milk gobbles or swigs. "Yes," I answer, saying something about leaving a beacon in the underworld, "sorry about the fatuous hyperbole." She mentions visitors, Asa first, as always, then Chad and his daughter, he to fidget non-stop with the books left out on tables and chairs (as if we had left underwear around for a fetishist to thumb), she to demand

107

that I pull a monster face, make a monster noise, and pursue her gently. I agree there's all that to come, while Milk, like an inspector general, sniffs at their clothes and hands, peers into their eyes as if to decipher Linear B engraved on their frontal lobes, and prods them with her fingers, maybe to see if they have soft centers. I decide to draw up a list of things to do, then to transfer it to the calendar: a call at the nearby private school for the handicapped (children up to eight years); a dip in the Olympic pool on campus; a ride in Asa's plane; a game of tennis (of course!), and perhaps a look inside the nuclear-reactor building where the Cerenkov radiation is blue. Big-hugging while I chew my second slice of pie, I figure the pros and cons, but also the vast context that somehow enlarges everything we do, makes our fun acute. The big enchilada, 3C 236, the biggest thing in the universe, gets a hard run for its money from the dust-laden envelope surrounding the star cutely called RU Lupi, where stars have only recently condensed from gas and are making, so to speak, final adjustments to their format before becoming regular stars on the main sequence. Why, those opaque clouds move at planetary distances and RU Lupi might be surrounded by a system of protoplanets, a nascent solar system to which one might be able to transfer during one's next incarnation. For the present, we have to be amiable, busy, and familial. With all my force, I try: tonight we play scrabble, with Milk assembling (then upsetting) words the language might do well to have, a couple being *fnog* and *mubb*. Her own name she spells out first time, with ringmaster polish, and then mine, Pi's. In no time she sets all our names together as one word and then pronounces it at speed, with joking brio. Cued by me, Pi applauds. Then Milk, Russian-style, applauds herself, blinking heavily as she does. For half an hour she paints quietly, daubing a three-foot sheet of rough paper with red and yellow helixes which she then converts into tapered towers, whose tops she links with

108

green foliage. Telling her to let it dry, I point to the thumb-tacks; but she insists on my lifting them out and rolls up the wet paper into a cylinder that goes to bed with her, under her pillow, like a Dead-Sea Rorschach scroll. Never mind, we have paper, bedsheets, pillowcases galore. She will enjoy running the linens through the washing machine, having never outgrown hydraulic delight, whether of the dip, the plunge, the broad hand slapped deep into its face, or the even, almost-hypnotized gaze from bank or shore. Next to that comes, I suspect, baking bread, an old favorite, especially when she kneads and tears, fits loaves with eyes, and rolls with pom-poms. Once she made a loaf that included poster color, sand, a lock of her own hair, and the head of a small doll. An oven mutant, this came out smelling of celluloid and burned paint. We then painted it blue (a hint from Man Ray) and hammered nails into its teaklike shell. Always, I tell myself, I tell Pi, I tell all and sundry, you can cheer Milk up by deforming a bit of the present civilization: wash an electric motor in thick suds, file the nose off a doll, paint any window yellow or black (I don't know why other colors won't do). There will never come, I'm sure, a day when I run out of remedies.

"Upward of a hundred pages, bighand, longhand," I say to Pi when Milk has gone to sleep. "Of what?" she asks, puzzled. I explain about the verbal spoor I've been keeping, bits of scribble cached here and there during the day while Milk has been around, but begun before she arrived. The amount surprises her. Then I confess to my scheme, which, hardly noticeable to anyone not in the know, has consisted of three-paragraph groups assembled according to the genetic chain: sixty-four in all, with only G or C or A or U to begin the first word of each paragraph with. She shakes her head, thinks the whole thing maniacal, especially when I point out that not a single topic sentence, thus far, has begun with, say, *The.* This very paragraph I'm writing now, I tell her, is the last one in the chain, the sixty-fourth group, third paragraph, beginning with the final U of the group U-U-U. She bursts out laughing, but redeems herself by nodding at the need to provide a stair rail, as it were, an obstacle, a matrix, a curb. "A *handicap!* Out of mother nature by necessity, nothing as tough as *terza rima* or the sonnet, but a virtuosity-provoking nuisance at least." I stop explaining, tell her I've reached the point of no return now I've used up the permutations of the code. What now? Start again with the same three (a C, an A, an A), or cull triplets at random? "Hell," she says, "maybe the code isn't exhaustive; maybe there are combinations of three that aren't there. Really dysgenic ones." There and then we try, with pads and pencils, to combine G, A, C, U in ways that nature lacks, so that, having come full circle with my balked child only half a week on the premises, I can go off at a tangent, implying combinations of sugar and phosphorus and acids that slipped the First Cause's mind. With the following result. There isn't one. So: I re-count. I have used, of all the words available, *Going,* to begin twelve paragraphs, and *A, As, At,* five or six times apiece. Four *Goods,* three *Cans,* two *Unders,* if I've counted right. Watching me write this down, Pi tells me to repeat the same random procedure, if I *must* go on. I will. Use every moment. Waste not, runs the adage, want not. I'll always want. Want means lack. More soon. After refreshment, of whatever kind. When I'll once more snail-track my gabble up the spiral alphabet that lords it over us, whatever else we think we are.

TWO

Andromeda to Scorpius

Underhandedly, after all that, I change my mind, decide to paragraph not at random as before but observing triplet order as it is in my table of the code. Thus, I begin UUU and end GGG. Failure of nerve, access of self-control: call it what I will, it's a system of sorts, reasserting what's inexorable as our two-week gala flops down the watershed of its halfway mark. I can still make the paragraphs as long or as short as I fancy, but I'll distribute the subject matter exactly as the twenty amino acids are distributed over the grid of the sixty-four triplets. So: UUU and UUC, both phenylalinine, could be this or that subject (balloons perhaps) while UUA and UUG, which follow, are leucine and could be, oh, Milk's departure anticipated. *Could* be, I say; it's likely they won't, not if things keep on going the way they are. Rat in the maze, I brood on being rat instead of making the maze sustain me. In any event, since phenylalinine doesn't occur again, whereas leucine does, I'd better work out which subjects I've most to say about and which I'll skimp. Thus leading to another problem, by which I mean spreading myself on evasions and minifying the pain. No: I'll handle, as long as required, the acids that burn, be glad of those that don't. If any of these acids burns at all. There are six leucines, serines, arginines, but only one methionine, one tryptophan, while others add to two, three, or four. Nature favors some over others, as we know. This fact we call degeneracy of the code. And how do you reform that? Helplessly, I start out by favoring the minority acids, even though there's nothing wrong with them—unless, as the textbook has it, "in its *exceptional* state, C pairs with A rather than with G, and so on," and the result is various "deletions" or "garblings." The chemistry behind some mutations is today fairly well understood, or so I'm told. I'm glad. I hear of mutagens, which augment the probability of "illicit" pairings, which puts me in mind of the forbidden degrees of consanguinity. I call that tightening the Bible's belt.

UAA, UAG, and UGA, however, stand for no acid at all, are designated "Nonsense" or "Stop" in the tables. Perfectly all right by me. Punctuation or funk, they'll come in useful. Kiss and be off. Luckily, this isn't DNA I'm dabbling in, but messenger RNA and therefore single-stranded (even though I'm doubling up in the written text, with two successive onslaughts on the code). Doubled up with anxiety, or even pain (an ulcer or despair?), I feel hysteria gather each time I check the calendar. No wonder I need the grid to keep me calm, or this time stick to the letter of the law.

Useful reference material follows: book's template. Or bookplate, indicating rightful owner. Garbled hitherto, honored from now on: see p. 115, and reel.

Unlike, isn't it, a plot of Sir Walter Scott's, or of Dostoevsky's? It evokes the hymn board on the church pillar, or baseball scoreboards, timetables of trains, the stock-market report unrolling on TV. It (I propel the next word downward into the place it belongs in)

usurps natural flow, of course, but can be regarded as an

The Genetic Code

1	UUU	p	3	AUU	i	5	UCU	s	7	ACU	t
	UUC	p		AUC	i		UCC	s		ACC	t
	UUA	l		AUA	i		UCA	s		ACA	t
	UUG	l		AUG	m		UCG	s		ACG	t

2	CUU	l	4	GUU	v	6	CCU	pr	8	GCU	a
	CUC	l		GUC	v		CCC	pr		GCC	a
	CUA	l		GUA	v		CCA	pr		GCA	a
	CUG	l		GUG	v		CCG	pr		GCG	a

9	UAU	ty	11	AAU	as	13	UGU	c
	UAC	ty		AAC	as		UGC	c
	UAA	STOP		AAA	ly		UGA	STOP
	UAG	STOP		AAG	ly		UGG	tr

10	CAU	h	12	GAU	asp
	CAC	h		GAC	asp
	CAA	g		GAA	gl
	CAG	g		GAG	gl

14	CGU	ar	16	GGU	gly
	CGC	ar		GGC	gly
	CGA	ar		GGA	gly
	CGG	ar		GGG	gly

15	AGU	s
	AGC	s
	AGA	ar
	AGG	ar

(A: Adenine
C: Cytosine
G: Guanine
U: Uracil

a: alanine
ar: arginine
as: asparagine
asp: aspartic acid
c: cysteine
g: glutamine
gl: glutamic acid
gly: glycine
h: histidine
i: isoleucine
l: leucine
ly: lysine
m: methionine
p: phenylalanine
pr: proline
s: serine
t: threonine
tr: tryptophan
ty: tyrosine
v: valine)

obstacle course, a systemics, challenging the virtuoso. Most of all by an optimist. Who might recite the Geneva Convention during a bombardment, or spout logarithms while having a locally anesthetized limb amputated. That kind of starched upper lip. I think of the stanza named after Edmund Spenser, or of how, according to William Wordsworth, nuns fret not when confined in a sonnet's narrow room.

And so it's much easier when an A shows up (or a C or a G), like an oasis or the face of a long-missed friend. What a nervous rebeginning this is, and with a vengeance not mine.

Under such auspices, I become a mere example of someone clinging to shibboleth: the password that keeps other words out. Where, just now, it was *under*, it might have been *untold* or *urn*. I cling as best I can. See what comes to fit next, what next fit comes.

U-turn it is, permitting me to reverse my direction of travel, recheck the grid over which I move like an analphabetical ant, or an insane checkers addict, trying to match theme to acid, yet squandering the vacant space on thoughts about, or previous to, the thought that ought to be. I use my means against my end, my end against my means. Was ever human so divided? Was ever code so bleak?

Giddey-up, I tell myself. Back to the action, the girls, Asa, and Co.

Chad's daughter and Milk embrace on meeting, no reason at all, the petite prodigy who at six years could classify dinosaurs without putting a syllable wrong and the long Viking who still hasn't made it through her first reading primer. The one chatters at the other's grin. They stand back and survey each other, sharing some secret giggle they might have been building for years by transatlantic telephone, and then join up again. The helpless one lets the helpful one help her, mirrors the diamond kindness. Off they go downstairs with

116

ice-cream cones. At least a piece of the Milky Way awaits them. All the way from Canis Minor to Cassiopeia. I wonder if we'll ever get to Cygnus and the rest; the social pace has hotted up.

Unruly laughter from below. Is it at or with? Has it an object at all? Is it something that just spilled over out of their systems? Pi says yes, it's alchemy, their glottal shivers. Chad says it's the obbligato that being unmarried yields. I go down to see. They are pointing at, laughing at, the two tennis players in Gemini, and have been having a duet of mimed expostulations, unless it was wit rammed into numbness, an agitated hand-sweep from Milk that fanned Meg's glowing coal. Two girls have found each other, that's for sure. Two only children are being childlike together. So who cares about symmetry when there's fusion?

Umpire not needed, they'll make rules of their own, a truce where no war was.

Creeping down to see, we all marvel at their engrossedness. Milk points at the Way, then they mime something or other, gurgling their mirth, both their ice-cream cones eaten. One of them has switched on the stars. I wonder which. The one who thinks she is a *Tyrannosaurus rex?* Or the one who babbles on behalf of a brain whose cells have the wrong kinds of spikes? Now they chase through and find us, instruct us, in various ways, to leave them to it. We do. Samarkand was never so special as this basement is, with an Alice and a Snow White together.

Unbuttoning his shirt after slackening his tie, Chad gives his best avuncular-patrician nod. They'll find a language, he says. We all three concur. They have. We eat the late lunch of soup, tuna sandwiches, and cheese. Beer and coffee. Above the house, azure light fills curving space and a hot wind all the way from the Gulf, or the Islands, rattles the screens. I put on some Elgar, the First Symphony, all heart and luscious nobility. Hardly any pomp at all. The girls come upstairs, munch sandwiches at refugee speed, then go down again with a cold can each. Pi and Chad sit outside on the balcony, call in to tell me they can hear the doves, which I then drown with Bruckner's Seventh, more massive, more plangent, than Elgar, and less urbane. In Elgar there are just people; you feel that Bruckner is guessing at God. Boa-constricting his own hubris, he takes his time, knows it's a loan only.

Conversation sparkles awhile, then flags. Pi asks what the Virgin Mary would be wearing if coming toward us. We don't know. "An inviolet shift," she says. Russian psychiatrists, Chad reports, are being ordered to report anyone claiming to be normal, since normality has now become a front for deviants. All I can offer is the TV commercial that, peddling a record album, said: So you don't forget, send before midnight tomorrow. "Gra-tuit-ous," Pi says. "We live in a big catalogue," says he. *"And,"* I add, *"what bargains we are."*

Calmly, Milk and Meg get across the pool. Neither swims, but the tall one ferries the short. Lounging in chairs at the poolside, we plan the week (though it might be better to plan for *after* the week, when anti-climax and deprivation will be working their worst on me at least). Now the girls go back across the pool, making exaggerated birdcalls and turning round to look at us. I seem to see a vulture planing low, its copyright infringed. An ostrich raises a haughty, bedraggled head, but it's only Milk after dunking herself. It must be ninety today, whatever day it is.

Unexpected, my landlord arrives, runs off ten minutes of ciné film as the girls romp in the pool, and leaves, promising to let me see the results. Another spoor! And all this time, or most of it, I am writing my own, a paragraph or even a page, scratched into a thin examination answer-book with a 2-B pencil. That does it. I'll tape-record Milk as well, must above all have a synesthetic portrait to relive her by.

118

(At some point, perhaps this, chronology became a mosaic, with everything separate from everything else, but also seen in sharper detail. Cameos. Etchings.) I insert this, looking back, which I suppose means I survived. There are stills that begin to move, then freeze, which don't connect with other stills. And won't. The aural equivalent I see when listening to electronic music such as Morton Subotnick's *Silver Apples of the Moon*. Arranged in ranks on a forty-five-degree slope, like players in an old-style swing band, fat foot-high goblins with innocent, impassive faces are flailing at tiny drums on their knees with brushes while playing jew's-harps at top speed with their mouths, the resultant meld of jittery cross-rhythms being too fast to tap to and so crammed with blurp, twang, tsk-tsk, fglizz, and klontch that, while I know each goblin is playing a separate part, I can't separate it from any of the others. What precedes what, I have no idea, but the demented side-of-the-mouth acceleration of this jellybean music "for syntheziser" seems fraught with uniqueness. Like several short-wave radio stations coming in all at once, distorted and overlapping, alike but not. It's the speed does it. Remembering, I smother Milk in sun-screen cream, Meg too. The sun is still high enough to burn. Then Milk, rolling her eyes, asks for Asa: "Ay-a," and I know she is taking root.

Curious what happened next. See how I have changed to the past tense. Perhaps it was the smart of looking forward to Milk's departure. I was living in the future so much that I left the narrative alone, to be related in the past. Safer. Cooler. Harder. Notes, I kept on making those, but I gave up writing out paragraphs according to the genetic code. And that is the chore that now confronts me. I have to make up all the missed work; with, to fortify me, the famous compensation of hindsight. "A good idea," Pi told me: "you'll be more collected afterwards" (as if I were a *Works*). I explained to her the problem of writing in the present: "It's only the

119

words that are in the present, never what they mention." The whole thing's a cheat, I told myself. What's to choose between writing in the belated present and the immediate past? What a tricky thing to say! I mean: both tenses are an illusion, both are modes of the past. Indeed, events are just as much alive in the past tense as in the present. The difference is one of sounds only. The time lapse is literal, which is to say it takes place in the words' letters only. At any rate, I left it all for later, meaning now. A real then instead of a fake now. That's why I just now stuck in that section in parentheses, beginning with *At some point* and ending with *Etchings.* I was getting into trim, I suppose, sneaking it in as an earnest of future endeavor. But while Milk was still here, it was too much to bear: all my thoughts were of foreboding, no joy in the here-at-hand at all. So I quit.

Unless it was an ulcer coming on. The crisis, the commotion, the treatment. And the diet that is slops, and, insult after injury, is a weight-loss diet made bland as well. Enough of that. For a mere necrosis of tissue you don't write an elegy.

Going back over it all, I know that as soon as events began to feel simultaneous, there was no point in using any tense at all. After later, I told myself. That's when to do it. So long as you let stand what's already done in the so-called present. I hope that's clear. What's the point in writing *now* if you no longer have any sense of *when?*

As it is, I feed on things that might be thought to hurt, like the bacterium *Pseudomonas radiodurans* that thrives in the large neutron flux at the cores of nuclear reactors. A perverse entity, for sure. Or am I even worse? Like the so-called obligate aerobe that oxygen poisons. Freaks. Yet there are plenty of us. There is an enzyme that's more active in ice than in water. Don Juan Pond, in Antarctica, contains a possibly unique microflora that metabolizes in extreme cold, at least down to $-23°$ Centigrade. All very well to cite these, if only comparisons could get me off the hook. They won't. They only bait the hook better. Therefore, back to the mainstream which has flowed down past me. Into some irrefragable distance, middle or far.

Up early one day, Milk and I larded patching paste into the cracks between wall and bath, using ordinary table knives. First a big blob, then a long horizontal motion that left a six-inch-long fairing behind it. We might have been filling in a space between wing and fuselage to reduce drag. Carried away, she also smoothed in the drainhole and invented the game of raising the white patch by flipping the plug lever to and fro. Pi was typing away at a new poem in the basement, the sounds those of a small factory that makes badges or buckles. Hers had been the invention of a domestic custom known as tokens, by which each partner caches small gifts for the other in obscure parts of the house. In a book not often consulted. Between wads of Kleenex in their box. Behind a can of shaving foam. In this way we had regaled each other with sticks of gum, new pens, bizarre clippings from the local papers. Catching on fast, Milk thus acquired a kaleidoscope, a plastic spider that walked when she squeezed a rubber ball, and various rolls of ribbon. Unselfish to the core, but unable to do shopping, she gave us things of our own. I found one of my neckties rolled up in a plastic bag in the flour canister. Pi received a fancy ring in her face cloth. If I took the time, I'd tell of the Tampon in the typewriter, the typewriter in the oven, the toilet seat Scotch-taped down. All these were offerings. Once Milk saw that we allowed odd things, she responded with all her heart. We crawled on the floors, we had pillow fights. We droned, we went blindfold, we handstood, we linked arms when out walking, we watched TV through cupped hands, we played chase all through the house, we pounded garbage-can lids together for cymbals, we rode one another piggy-back and even tried to play leapfrog. When Meg came, she and Milk painted liquor boxes with poster colors. Milk's was usually black or red, whereas Meg stippled hers with colors worthy of temples at Isfahan. They are still there, in the basement, dried and a bit warped, ready to hold books and papers on the next trip. Urns? Oubliettes? Jackless boxes? No, building blocks, I think. Or treasure chests. Even if the spiders have set up house inside.

Uncanny with children, one day Asa fetched us to his lawn to see a small tree decorated with what seemed catkins or tissue-paper tassels. Then one peeled open, all by itself, and we saw a red Monarch butterfly emerge, then another, within a half-hour ten. He had attached several dozen pupas to the branches. At the spectacle of all those Monarchs unfolding, drying out, and preening themselves, Milk spun with glee, and ever after kept asking for the "bu-fla dree." And got it most days, even being so bold as to go off alone with him in his car. I think she spent hours there on the grass, watching what dangled come to life, at least until she tried to pick a few and by accident pulped a couple. Of the dozen crucial memories, the ones that biting heal, this is one. Something heraldic about it, something chromatically sumptuous, haunts me each time I pass a shrub or see a butterfly. The shrub erupts into scarlet flame, the tassels give birth.

About this time Asa confided to us why he'd given up beekeeping. One more bee sting might be fatal, he said. Yet that weird bit of information fell back into the rest of his bristling talk, about how skulls found in Jericho have cowries over the eyes, how the seventeen-year cicada lives for one day only, how a certain silkworm moth need release only 10^{-8} grams of sex attractant per second to draw to her every male within an area miles wide. Or so he said. One day he came with us to see the reactor building on campus, when Milk shrieked "boo warbar!" non-stop, in some radioactive frenzy. Another, more signal day, he had us all up to his laboratory, where, with a few simple pieces of apparatus, he combined methane, ammonia, hydrogen, and water vapor, sent them again and again through a liquid-water solution, and then sparked the mixture with a corona discharge. Come back in a few days, he said. We did, to find new colors. "Pretty," Milk whispered, using one of her best words (it came out "pre'y"), little realizing she was looking at amino acids new-created. Asa's genesis, that of us all. Yet I think we all, even he, preferred the Monarch tree, out in the air, blooming with wings even as we bibbed our sodas and beer, puffed our cigars, nibbled on pretzels.

Upstairs, Milk played his piano, first of all by pounding on the keys, even using her elbows *à la* Charles Ives, then by going inside with a light chain she trailed across the strings. She plucked, she twanged. Then she played on the keys again, but with thimbles capping her fingers. Thanks to Asa, she went right beyond the sound barrier, watching the sound on a motiondizer screen. The air in the cone moved the membrane's mirrors and her loud piano twirled through in plastic, swift helixes of naked light. Only a day later, he had a color wheel set up for her, as well as a projection set that blazoned the wall with starbursts, multi-colored clouds, and colliding planets, at which she crooned and waved. When he started up a slowly rotating mirrored ball a foot in diameter, she leaped toward it, trying to touch, but fell six inches short. By then it was almost redundant to let her look through a stereo viewer at infra-red aerial photos, but he did it, only to have her administer a swift nod and return her gaze to the the wall, asking for stars and clouds all over again. These Asa provided, and Milk looked away only when a startlingly tall black woman walked in, exotically named Kashmiri, and stroked Milk's long hair with creased pink palms. Milk shook hands left-handedly and peered right into the girl's eyes, the pale blue-green into the black. Then we all went downstairs, Milk looking at us all through a distorting pliable plastic lens which, as I found, having my turn, gave anyone two heads if

123

you held it right. "One more face!" ordered Milk, eager for grimaces to transform into something even worse, and thus we descended, leering and twitching. It was a wonder we didn't fall on the stairs.

"Come," said Asa, and we went into what he jokingly called his Living Room. Rabbits running loose (and an aroma to suit), an ant farm which Milk looked disdainfully at for half a minute, and a white mouse in a treadmill, certainly earned the adjective. But Asa had other wares to show today. First he gave Milk two magnets, which either sprang together or stayed neutrally apart while she marveled at the pull that waxed and waned, sighting along her arms for the motive force: the tiny engineer in the armpit, the gremlin inside the ulna who pushed. Bored with this, she gladly watched Asa make a Cartesian diver rise and descend in its bottle by simple hand-pressure. Trying it, she addressed the miniature plastic man inside in a language she thought right ("bond, bond," it sounded like, flanked by "ebba boe"). A low-friction Air Puck, powered by a balloon, skimmed above the fitted carpet like a peregrinating flash, and rather frightened her. Perhaps she thought it an animal that would bite. Next he balanced a small gyroscope on her finger while she froze and he told us about the rotor, weighted with so-called fluid sand, and the micro-bearings so tiny that a thimble would hold hundreds of them. Ten minutes she stood while the gyro-scope spun and leaned, after which she eyed the dent in her finger, mock-woundedly whispering "sore, sore," while Asa, a Marx Brothers Leonardo, tried to distract her with conjuring tricks: eggs that came and went, puffs of smoke from his fingertips, dimes that turned into pennies and back, an always-full water jug, and a cigarette that went right through a handkerchief. Pensively handling a prism, Asa changed his mind as she grinned mad-wide and let out a plangent "More!" "Hold on honey," said the black girl, signing with her astonishing hands, and Milk promptly signed back, which

124

is to say she rubbed her tummy, a school gesture for "I'm sorry." They gave her a pair of diffraction-grating glasses that spellbound her from the outset. I tried a pair myself, sharing the spectrum with her. Weird how the split light seemed to enfilade. Even more so outside, where, in no time, Asa had a menagerie going. Rabbits and the foal. A nine-foot hot-air balloon whose red and white gores lofted up to two hundred feet. Like a fisherman's float in the wrong element. I say red and white, but it was a color total. Asa left it up while he busied himself with a giant flying saucer he'd built from a kit. Tethered, it went up to join the balloon. Whooping, Milk almost trod on a rabbit. In the act of trying to leap skyward, glasses on, she launched herself sideways into the group of us. Asa readied a balloon copter powered by three little jet streams. It circled the yard and landed in a tree, panicking cardinals and grackles. Now he took Milk off to the redwood geodesic greenhouse, out of which she peered, grinning allusively. When she came back, she had left her glasses in it, so she sprinted back and spent the next half-hour touring the garden. All of us wore glasses to look at the roses. The hues of everything reeled in echelon away from us. "Richard Of York Gave Battle," I murmured, as tectonic plates of Richard's colors moved right and left in that order. Indigo. Violet. In. Vain. The ghost of Aldous Huxley stalked tall among us, approving. The garden swelled like the hot-air balloon, soared like the tethered saucer. A high jet exploded. On my hand a ladybug bulged like an awning. The little rock in the goldfish pond opened up into a Bermuda of the eye. Kashmiri brought tea and coffee on a tray scarred vermilion and green. Even the rattle of cups and saucers took on a slapdash atonality denied to Milk. We grouped for ring-a-ring-of-roses, laughing zanily, then (as the song has it) all sat down. Flopped. "Nobody take your glasses off," called Asa. "No scabs here!" Nobody did. "Let there be light," I quoted aloud, and there *was*. "Rosetta Stone!" cried Pi, in high-altitude spirits. "Anoxia!" yelled Asa. "The Wars of the Roses!" Kashmiri said nothing, but poured. Milk jabbered, pointing at this or that, shrieking hugely as a bee zoomed past. The firmament twirled. A grand way of putting it. But what they say about rose-colored glasses is true: you see the air, and like it. You are inhaling color. Come into our parlor, say the tiny macrophages in the lung to the well-dressed molecules as they enter all dolled up. Someone, perhaps Pi, said how stunning it would be to be underwater with such glasses on, or even a mask whose entire disk did this with light. We'll do it, I elatedly called out. We'll take her to the Bahamas. Asa will make us special masks, won't you? Asa can make anything. Right? Maybe so, he said, but Africa would take him longer than usual; a spiral nebula here and there would take him even longer. But, Pi told him, while Kashmiri laughed in a proprietorial way, wizards don't apologize. Milk didn't care. She was already underwater. She swam. She looped her body as if at the end of a pool length, and swam off again, at the crawl. Already my own mind had gone truant, prompted by Asa's talk of a spiral nebula. I wanted to finish the Way, at least the northern part of it, such as you see if you stay north of the Florida keys. The big wheel of M 51, partnered by a little one, soared at me out of the constellation called the Hunting Dogs, an independent Milky Way system itself holding many billions of stars. I felt a knot of pain, not that ulcer, but the core of an ill-formed metaphor for Milk, who, universe-like, receded faster from us the farther away she was. And, oh, she was far enough. In some ways, out at the beginning of the universe which forever zoomed out of sight the farther we saw. Heavens, indeed. A universe only months ago thought to be ten or twelve billion years old was already sixteen, with a promise of more. Hopeless. What a game, when the better the instrument the more inaccessible the answer becomes. So we settle for M 51, say, glad that it resembles a whirlpool or a Scotch-tape dispenser with tiny delivery platform, or for its neighbors, the stars named Cor Caroli (after Charles I of England) and La Superba, gaudy tumbling red. Meanwhile, back here, the wild goings-on got wilder. Asa walked right up a tree and started to munch a balloon. Kashmiri, real name Eloise Robinson, stripped naked and dowsed herself with warm tea. Milk, for reasons known only to her, burst out with words filched from *The Damnation of Faust* by Berlioz: "Irimiru! Hass! Hass! Karabrao!" Whiplash, death-knell words, they frappéd my blood. All I could do was to haul down the hot-air balloon. When we took off our glasses, we had no eyes. Pi had gone inside, no doubt to meditate a .poem on our preposterous doings, although doubtless something more ambitious than the maxim of hers that I was remembering: *"Mrok* and the world *mroks* with you; *grenkle,* and you *grenkle* alone."* Then, as now, *mrok* meant to be be persistently affable, *grenkle* its opposite. The upshot of this policy, it seemed to me, was that one would be either dishonest but with companions, or honest and alone. Such was my mood, one of apodictic gloom. All of a sudden. Out of that fleecy sky. Sometimes it no more pays to get up than to go to bed. I heard more synthesizer music, each wobble and squiggle and squelch an ad-lib scoff from the cosmic joker.

Actually, Milk was sitting peacefully in the geodesic greenhouse with a thermometer in her mouth, self-condemned to silence. A mighty being, like Wordsworth's, not so much awake as insomniac. Asa was lying flat on the grass, shirt off, hairless chest upward. Kashmiri was in the act of conducting the skittish foal round the back. Pi was scribbling on a little ruled yellow pad. The aerial objects were floating high, bucking and tilting in a minor breeze. Over on the far side of the garden, someone in dungarees was hosing a shrub. One big bucolic halt. Best expressed in an unending paragraph dedicated to Samuel Beckett, an underdone offering on the altar of the comma. Or in a flurry of short ones, like neutrinos cutting through the afternoon without disturbing it at all.

Ugli: a Jamaican citrus fruit produced by crossing a grapefruit with a tangerine.

A word that Milk won't ever have, or need. On the other hand, since she is not expected to become competent, she can be whimsical, garner a few luxury words such as communicative folk don't want. On that day, or in that year, at thirteen past Wednesday on the 77th of October, I'll regale her with *lemma, hoplite,* and *chinquapin.* The day I was describing ran down peacefully to a shrimp dinner at an informal eatery called The Fireplace. Milk troughed as if it were all going not into her body but into a hopper outside. Pi was witty, as usual, conjuring diabolical riddles out of inoffensive words ("A brown bear having a heart attack is having?" "A Kodiak arrest"). Asa balanced forks and knives on tumblers, made a small and accurate mouse out of bread, which Milk devoured, and spoke of visiting New York City. Kashmiri, she hummed, she alluded briefly to Magritte, Stockhausen, and Heidegger, as if presenting cultural credentials; not that she needed to, since anyone capable of surviving Asa must be egregiously gifted at very least. She was. "Why 'Kashmiri'?" I asked. "Because," she said, "I'm woolly. Not straight. The money I might have used to fix my hair, I used to buy *Britannica Three.* The book that sounds like a cruise ship! I have read about one third, and will finish before I'm thirty, in two years' time. Then I'll test myself, or Asa will, to see if I'm fit to embark on *The New English Dictionary.* All umpteen volumes. No sense in just cooling your heels, in this civilization. A person should absorb."

Ado, much. So it seemed at the time to Pi, herself a woman so coordinated intellectually that she seems muscle-bound and all the little Golgi or Purkinje cells in her brain are asking to be set free. After Asa, that Golden Age polymath, that horn of plenty masquerading as a human, it was Pi, not I, who made the phenomenal world perform, quietly folding a cootie (paper beak that pecks if you squeeze and release it) or snipping away at several thicknesses of paper until she revealed between her hands a row of little people holding hands, who became a zigzag that would stand on its own. Her origami comes from the age of five, ten years before she went through a dark night of the cerebellum (or whatever) and began drawing herself tiny in the bottom corners of large sheets of paper. There, in those right-angles, the poet began, born not made. And now she writes about the solar system, sees little cows that sip the hoarfrost at the Martian poles. She has been mighty patient with this pup of a text, must surely have reasoned: After the bravura blather of impatient narcissism, he'll arrive at the runic contradictions of grandstand virtuosity, and then, before the convention he's flouting breaks down entirely, the dreamlike intermittences of resentful improvisation. The rest is silage.

Unkind attributions, these. I'll quit. I'll undertake another book altogether. *Six Characters, Seven Funerals.* If not one entitled *And/Or*, set in Andorra la Vella. I'll go away, disguised as my own baggage. I'll speak Indo-European to the hostess, Esperanto to the taxi men. I'll go out of the top of my head. No. I'll pay my bills, catch up on ten days' correspondence, defrost the refrigerator, trim the shrubs that block the walk, scour the toilet bowl, find a screw that fits the hole in the screen. That's it! Be practical, use our hands together so that Milk can say "Wynd, wynd," even while the angel of silence is flying over us. What I did was to go round the ceiling of the living room and mop up a new brood of spiders, pinhead small but fast. Omit that chore and you have scores of big ones in a week. Ours is a house of spiders, ours is, the cause the trees. I dabbed them to death with tissues while Pi and Milk clipped flowers in the garden, lucky to find white bottle gentians, otherwise known as closed. After a few days the tube splits open to form high-aspect-ratio petals. I'm told the brain is light-sensitive, but not as sensitive as those gentians, I'm stupidly sure. On, on, on.

Galloping about the tennis court, we lost balls and bruised our knees. Milk hit with shocking force when she did hit, maybe under the impression that the game's object was to knock your opponent down. Or maim. I blistered my thumb and forefinger, Pi turned an already tricky ankle. But (bonuses) Milk did an exquisite headstand against the net post, aligned like a plunging egret, her face serene and red, her breath insanely held. For half an hour, having got the patter, she scored in ecstatic disregard of the game, calling her favorite words: "Dirty" (Thirty), "Dew" (Deuce), and most of all "Lo' " (Love). Love-love, love-love, she cried up and down the court, whether playing or not, whether watching or not, even when she looked up at the far corner of the high side net and inexplicably, first, called "ice, ice." The ice, as usual, was in her eye, a refraction, an eyelash icicle. She had done it at five years, had no reason not to do it in her teens. Yet, when her warble brought ice and love together again and again, in the heat of another hot day, with only a couple of teenagers to gape at her, some wildly improbable purity suffused the afternoon, fixed it in mind as a victory over trash, glibness, cant, and pain. Her next-best trick was to stand on two tennis balls, doing something between a sway and a wobble, yet pliably elegant, the spirit of the molecule riding on twin atoms. On her return to the house, she spent an hour in the bath, running it cooler and cooler and testing the filled-in cracks with the tip of a nail brush's handle.

Good days, bad, there weren't that many left. An impossible urge to cram each minute, or not to share her with anyone save Pi, came and went. Hoarding only made things worse. So Milk and I made a morning excursion, all of fifty yards, to a neighboring house converted from fraternity use

130

into a school for handicapped children up to the age of eight. Unlike most schools of this kind, it went on through the summer, although with a contingent reduced from fifteen to half a dozen. I'd seen the children returning from the nearby elementary school, lined up to cross the road, or crouched in refusal on the sidewalk, or expostulating in slurred language on the way home. A little bent, or incomplete, is how they looked, somehow frost-bitten in the marrow, but given to affable cries and jolly scooping motions with the hand. One said hello, when I saw him, by jutting his head up and forward, as if through some invisible screen. A girl, who usually had him by the hand, being a year or two his senior, greeted with spastic flaps of her free hand, making her thumb peck. (I say *making*, but no doubt the thumb pleased itself.) Our visit was all very casual. Milk leered a bit from her teenage altitude, being after all a prefect in her own school: a keeper of law and order, with awful power of imperative and tongue-tied rebuke. I had seen her harangue wrongdoers, with her fierce Nordic temperament, bellowing, "Walk, don't run!" ("War, done ru"). And few dared run after that. Minus her hearing aids, which she has always seemed to think obsolete, she always comes on strong, knowing her defect isn't visible, and on that day, again without them, she interviewed each child a bit like Gulliver among the Lilliputians, using few words but an arsenal of gestures, signs, and discreetly given prods. At first they shrank from her, asking her complex questions from a distance, maybe wondering what it was like on her planet, or deep in the ice from which she had been excavated after several thousand years. After a while, though, they relaxed, took her outside to the slide and the sandbox, where she paused for an interrogative look at me, then all five feet of her careened down the slide, filled a bucket with sand, chased them with bubbling laughs and caught them all, and then let them chase her. So agile at the twist, the double-back, the feint, she might have been a top-class soccer player rehearsing without ball. In the end they mobbed her, closing all ways out, and she let them haul her to the dried-out ground, tickle her to the point of ecstatic distraction, even tears that made her eye make-up run (some days she sneaked it on, on others she forgot or didn't bother). Never having had a friend when out of school, she befriended them all on a sub-verbal level, grabbing and patting and stroking hair both long and short. It seemed she was encouraging them from a great height, though with a touch of sternness in all she did-said, for all the world an indulgent parent. Inside again, she even steered a trio of them through a reading lesson. She said the words written on the blackboard not better, but more loudly, than they, then scrawled a few of her own without erasing. That palimpsest included a few old favorites such as *slide, water,* and *pretty,* ungainly in form but legible, and she seemed shocked when they identified what she'd chalked up. Lord God, I thought, the fact or the art of communication surprises her still. Always doubting it, she lives in a world more random than Planck's. For five minutes, inspired by that breakthrough, she talked to them all with nasal hauteur, pausing and using her hands like some practiced lecturer, say Jacob Bronowski warming to the subject of transhumance, although without his semi-conspiratorial whisper, his oracular sigh. Caught up in this gabfest, while the three young teachers grinned indulgently, I took the eraser, wiped the board clean, and drew the first thing that came to mind, M 51, the Whirlpool Nebula, a rooster's tail in white chalk. Milk pointed, proudly uttered "Milk Way," which was brilliant although wrong, it's not in or near the Way at all. Then she tested them, asking, only to be told it was a firework, a spring, a mother's face. Unthinkingly, since I'd not long ago been looking at it, I'd drawn in the lines of radio emission, which look like fibers or wires within the speckle of the star lanes. And I saw it too, the maternal profile that looked down, maybe with eyes closed,

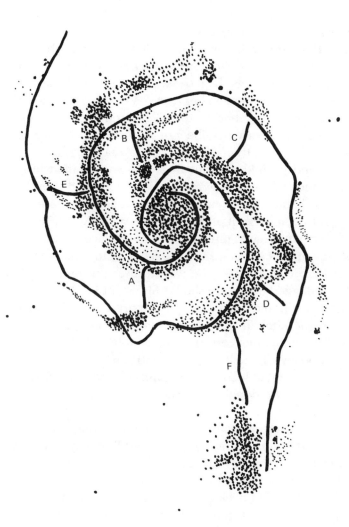

M 51 and Companion Galaxy NGC 5195.
Lines show radio emission. Lines ABCDE show
interarm links and F the link with NGC 5195.

the chin pressed into that slot at the bottom of the throat, the "heartspoon." A lovely analogy, a grand feat of simile, it nonetheless evoked for Milk the wrong image, of a woman several thousand miles away, or at least non-available. For whom she then asked, and our visit ended with repetitious demands from her, which on the walk homeward became an organized interrogation on her part: "Where? When? *Soon?*" Looking back, I saw two or three children waving at us, a goodbye or an invitation, a cheer or a salute, I'm not sure. She had moved among them like a flawed Amazon, leader, den mother, and premature aunt in one, heavy-handed in her ease, at once better and worse, farther along and therefore harder to handle, a vision for their teachers of those children's future, a portrait of the graduate walking tall. In spite of her big hat, she was pink and wet in the face, on the edge of being outright irritable, and she'd begun to walk with that minor limp which, when she was tired or put out, invaded her loose-legged quickstep shuffle. She went into the bath to soothe herself, and then she and Pi pored over the microscope at the kitchen table, examining hair and paper fiber while I made hamburgers, mixed a couple of Jellos for later on. Carried away, I nicked a finger with a scalded needle and gave them a spot of blood to view, the cells like tiny dinghies inflated, or azure doughnuts. "Blood," Milk said. "Blood," I agreed.

Us, after lunch, anti-climactic after my hamburgers. Only Milk is used to meat. I say so, aloud, and humid air swallows the words. Pi dreams. Milk has found a temporary land-of-heart's-desire in the flat plastic oval full of two powders, white and blue. Cut back to past tense; it's no use pretending she is still here. She tilted it this way and that, watching the blue pour into the white: powdered lapis lazuli into Bahamian sand. Blue-slate ice faces. Dune upon dune. Himalayas. Foreign strands. Then tilted it again. Blue galaxy invaded white. I saw teat-shaped rifts, animal-nosed snow zones. Peering through what of the plastic was empty, she examined the day's light, gave it an A minus, and resumed her slow maneuvering. The grains cascaded, merged, folded in. Twelve feet away, we saw the accidentality of shape at work. It was like looking through an oval porthole in a spacecraft. At, maybe, Earth, slithering about in Mary's colors. I saw a blackbird on the rail outside squirt white stuff backward and take flight. Milk was lost in a still-forming galaxy trapped inside an oval plastic plate. Not so much in two minds, I was in several, and the game plan grew of two states of mind for three people, or one for three, or even no state of mind at all but a few tiny parishes, grain-small, vanishing as soon as made. Thus the mind. "Time out," said Pi, walking right across the room and entering Milk's trance. Blue and white grains held them. This, I thought, might be the day when all things come together, meld: the empty tube from the toilet roll; Charlie Parker rippling through "Au Privave" and "Bloomdido" on a sax that had all the tones of talking languageless; a writer called Okot p'Bitek who is African; the hot gaseous spots on Betelgeuse; the use of the word *dynamic* as a noun; a baby hummingbird in a nest of fluff made from cinnamon fern; the Zonule of Zinn; Max Reger sitting on the toilet and writing to a critic that he had "your notice" before him and it would soon be behind him; humble copters ducking their noses; eisegesis; acupuncture; brain damage; giant turtles 250 years old; the airplane graveyard in New Mexico; the forever increasing age of the universe and therefore its size (or vice versa); the gaudy scarves of the Oxford and Cambridge colleges; the TV talk show as the death of the artifact (all's impromptu); the zinc-like jargon of literary critics who know what art is for without knowing what it is; the stamps my mother mails back to me to use again except that they are faintly flecked with ink; the limbic system; the solar system; the digestive system; chipmunks immobile on the front walk like pensive grandfathers; the woman who died at

135

109 after a lifetime in a mental home; Harvard Yard; Big Ben; the Eiffel Tower; eyes that can be made to grow on the limbs of frogs; the ten sexes available to paramecia; and, and, I am nothing if not imaginative, the sundance of the ego; the part of Paris called Montsartre; the habit called cogitus interruptus; a clam playing an accordion; all the symphonies of Beethoven recorded simultaneously on the same tape; the chance of head grafts by 1990; the first interviewed whale; the enormous fraternity house in the sky because of all the Greek letters fastened on stars; a story so baneful it kills all editors who receive it; the drinks tilting in the in-flight movie as the plane sways; a human's being 10^{14} cells; the non-existent end of this sentence which was going to sum up everything. As for the Many and the One, all I know is that I am few. The phone has not rung for days. I have paid no bills. I am living in the posthumous present, in which to write—if it's a tense as well—is to be like Buster Keaton underwater emptying out a sunken ship with a bucket.

Upanishad of a worrier. "Upanishad" means "secret session."

Glancing out, Milk saw the youth who mows the lawn arrive with his machine. She even heard the gruesome chatter as it neared the house. In a trice she had gone to help him with a pair of kitchen scissors, but I fetched her back, trusting neither her nor him. But, while he was out front, I let her clip bits of grass by the back door, and vice versa, which satisfied her just enough. Perhaps, I conjectured, this was a good time to urge her back to the Milky Way in the basement, so I fished out my drawings and plans, trying to figure out what came next. In my principal outline, Cepheus came after Cassiopeia; but, on this day of grace, there seemed no more reason to include Cepheus than to exclude Andromeda, neither being in the Way proper. Both were close, Cepheus pointing away toward the Pole Star and Andromeda straggling down

136

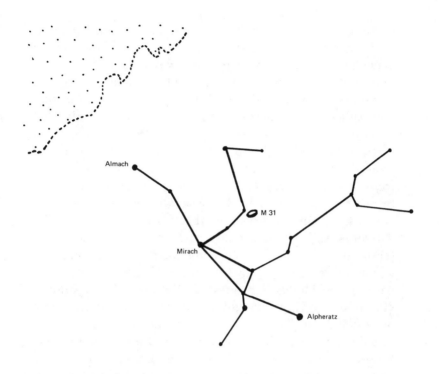

ANDROMEDA

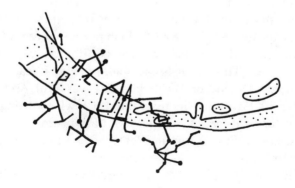

to Pegasus (with which it has a star in common: alpha of Andromeda, known as Alpheratz—"the head of the woman in chains"—is also Pegasus number two). Pi agreed to join in. The youth went, we all three went out and praised the shaved lawn, sat on and patted the stubble, spoke of picnics and ballgames. Coming in through the front door that led right into the basement, we saw the unlit Way. I pointed, said "wynd"; Milk said an almost sibilant "yes," and I got out the tools, the bits and pieces, ready to draw an outline straight from the pages of my *Field Book of the Skies*. It was no use trying to tell Milk how, because Queen Cassiopeia had boasted, Neptune had decreed that her cherished, beautiful daughter Andromeda should be chained to a rock by the seashore, where she would become the prey of a sea monster which Perseus, in the nick of time, changed to stone by flashing the Medusa's head at it. No, but I felt a kindred vibration, knowing a daughter that fitted the pattern, more or less, and angrily resisting while acknowledging the slang idiom about rocks plural and the head. I even felt a bit like Perseus, rescuing Milk by finding something for her to do, and with a private opinion as to where the Medusa's head really was: at a marvelous distance. I marked the holes, Milk drilled them, Pi chose the bulbs while I fitted the sockets. For Alpheratz, blue, doing duty for whitish purple which we didn't have; for others, yellow and green and orange. As soon as the connecting lines were clear, Milk made her interpretation, exclaiming "Fow, fow!" which neither of us understood. It was only while I was upstairs, hunting out a postcard of Messier 31, The Great Spiral Galaxy, that I realized what she'd said. Downstairs, I checked. She was right. Andromeda, drawn as I'd drawn it, resembled a fowl, strutting with a slight forward lean. Commended, Milk beamed, demanded light. Got it, fifteen minutes later, after I finished tinkering with my version of M 31, described by one early astronomer, Marius, as the diluted flame from a candle, seen through horn. Fire behind alabaster seemed nearer, and nothing to do with Keats's invocation: "Andromeda! Sweet woman! why delaying So timidly among the stars?" What we'd created, in our rough-and-ready way, was a visible fowl with an oval headlamp on its back, a headlamp that was a companion galaxy to our own. I thought of the metal-rich giants at its center, of its two companion galaxies (one of which I'd snipped off the postcard when making the cap for the bulb), and I remembered that the whole system was approaching us at about eight miles a second. Just about visible to the naked eye, at least as a fuzzy spot, it gleamed in the basement in lilac, purple, and cream, like elegant batter, crisp at the edges but viscous at center. Like all our other versions, it was hopelessly out of scale, at least as far as outlines and components went, but it seemed a Christmas tree just off the Way, a thing of beauty being a joy for now, most of all when Milk, asking as usual for a truth beyond truth, delivered herself of a long sentence that ran: "Drom'a, no, fow' two leg, one small lamp." A drum it was not, she was not having that; it was a fowl, pausing before it stuck a leg out into the celestial thoroughfare, in order to reach the other side, Cassiopeia, its mother, and then Polaris in the Little Bear.

Upbraiding me for slowness to answer, Milk tapped me on the hand. Quite right, I told her: those spiral arms aren't always as smooth as they look, wouldn't stand comparison with the hostess arms of the major international airlines. Often there are gaps and splits, fringes and loops, and professional astronomers have been heard expressing sympathy for their extra-galactic peers who, stuck inside one of the untidy sections of their galaxy, are trying to unravel the details of the spiral structure. We aren't so well fixed ourselves, knowing as we do only bits of about three arms of the Milky Way. Enjoy these pendant lamps of ours, it will be a long time before they vary or burn out. By the way, Andromeda, or "Fowl," is over two million light-years away, dangling like a charm. Still pondering, as I dubbed in dialogue that Milk deserved but couldn't have, I blotted a small spider with tissue as it scurried up the dark before the Way, and then, only minutes later, absent-mindedly wiped my mouth with the same ball of tissue, thus gaining my first taste of spider as I recoiled from a tart fusion of cocoa and wintergreen (if panic hasn't pitched me into using histrionically guessing likes). As in my name, which sometimes I half-think is not Deulius, but D'Alias, or even Delius, DuLiss, or Dooley. To D'Alias, perhaps, the spider tasted sweet, like a tangerine. But not as sweet as life, come what may; have come what has come, what had already come, namely another Andromeda chained, chained, chained, but in these paragraphs let loose.

Chaste lights prompting her, Alpheratz and M 31 above all, neither Almach nor Mirach much to write home about (said he, of those vast fireballs!), Milk talked to Pi, who couldn't follow, any more than I. Could she have been commenting on this sorry scheme of things entire, of which she'd never heard? "Gnang," she seemed to say. "Gnang," I helplessly replied, displeasing her a lot. "Gnong, gnung, gneng," Pi tried, resorting to blanket technique, but that failed as well. "Don't worry, it happens all the time," I told her: "abstract phonemes uttered for practice." In the end, it was Milk herself who sorted it out. She meant I should remove from Andromeda the small blue bulb I had stolen from the microscope upstairs. Her sense of order had erupted. Things belonged, could not be transplanted. Most of this she mimed, at last drawing a microscope in an exasperated hurry, waving me up the stairs even as she unscrewed the bulb. Behind me as I restored it to its place in the neat mirror under the scope's deck, she patted me on the rump for being good.

GET BULBS, I wrote on the kitchen memo board, by accident reminding myself of a fey ditty, bonus from one of my various childhoods:

140

Khyber, Khyber, Khyber Pass.
If you want a splendid Christlemas,
Get for your most secret self
That enigmatic Red Elf.

Red Elf, I supposed, was Santa Claus gone childish, while the Khyber Pass must have grown out of the old Empire, possibly via the nostalgic dream of a returned colonial administrator or of a child longing to blow bugle with Gunga Din. Get bulbs I would, that very minute. Back with two dozen, I vowed to install Cepheus before it grew dark, but Milk showed no interest, instead returned to the tilt-shaper upstairs, lying on her back and shuffling blue and white contrasts above her at arms' length. Busy preparing a big quiche, Pi murmured lines of her new poem, while I, half-suspecting an attack of migraine was on the way, the cause too many different kinds of light, made a cup of thin soup and in it drank the special salt that staves off the attack. It worked. I'd had no trouble in weeks, which was amazing in view of the pressures. Thank you for my luck, I said to the Caliph of cells, and went downstairs to switch off the Way. There it was, gaunt but sprawled, a touch of Las Vegas with a touch of the computer panel. One flick and a galaxy died, but I had never felt less like God. It wasn't me, yet it was none other.

Up and down the stairs Milk went, eager to exercise, and I suddenly thought how I used to lead a routine life which included a mile run each day. So I cleared the basement, ran the first of what would be fifty, sixty circuits, pursued by Milk, who wasn't even breathing hard when I halted at thirty, puffed and parched. One more run, she demanded, making the motions with arms and legs, but I switched the Way on instead, toured along it with her while my pulse eased up. To me it was a slow-motion haul from Canis Minor and Monoceros to Cassiopeia and Andromeda, but to Milk it was that same comic strip of flashlight, wolf, tennis, handshake, kite,

141

daddy longlegs, M, and fowl, though how fowl connected narratorially with M I wasn't yet sure, or through the M with the daddy longlegs. For each constellation she said her word, spelling out the names of the various colors, oo-ing at the fudged-up nebulae and then challenging, with an imperious hand-sweep, the blank of the remnant all the way to Sagittarius, and past it, into the southern heavens. Soon, I promised, answering myself as well. Before she went. Yet how? Unless we worked night and day. We had fallen badly behind the creator of all this, who held copyright not only of what but also how. Our second (or third?) quiche in a week wafted down from the oven. We switched off, went up. Followed by lots of odd thoughts while munching. "I've used the wrong cheese," Pi was saying, and there I was thinking, Milk won't eat cheese. But, of course, she already had, at least a couple of times before, deceived by the aroma of the ham and the pastry. Then it hit me: there was already a tradition of her stay, therefore much of her stay was over. And the heavy word *stay* jumped the track at that point, evoking lugubrious words about someone's being taken from this place to a lawful place of execution, et cetera. Cut off in one's prime. Gruesome, I thought, how many people, between their own first and second rattles (the baby's and the death), manage to kill off a few of their fellow humans. In the context of all that easy dispatch, then, why fuss about a mere deprivation? A parting? The sort of event Japanese women will emblematize by leaving behind a comb, a symbol with teeth. It was like sitting in a train, waiting to depart. Then the station vanishes as another train moves in. You seem to be moving, while it stays still, but it slides past and you haven't moved at all. Yes, I said in my head, compare with life and death. All your years, you think you have been on the go, but you've been stationary while death has rolled along, going about its never failing business while you've dawdled under the influence of hope. Eating three square meals a day for forty years, just to stave

142

off the inevitable. Drunk thousands of gallons merely to fend off the last parch. Washed and combed only to steer clear of the filth at the end, when the head in its box resembles a badly combed turnip. I came back to quiche with my relish a bit sapped, but ate twice as much as usual, just for ballast, just for spite. Two wonderful faces in front of me: Pi's, casually serious as if a new poem were docking between the cortices, Milk's flushed and prankish. It was like revisiting a country after it's been occupied by a foreign power and all the Czech names over the storefronts have been Germanized. Or as if, to change terms, Gdynia had become Danzig, or Antwerp Anvers. Something had gone, something come. Not the point of no return, which does not move; not that, but an ionization, in which a neutral configuration has altered slightly. As during any rainshower, an electrical uneasiness hung fire. Prickly. Faint. Stale.

Andromeda was done. I wanted to do Cepheus as soon as we could, Andromeda's father or a house with a steep roof, depending on how one saw. Instead of talking, I wandered up and down its outline, from Er Rai at the apex, aimed at Polaris, to *Delta,* the variable double star discovered in 1784 by the deaf astronomer Goodricke, and *Mu,* the so-called Garnet Star. Legend had it that Cepheus himself was one of the Argonauts whom Jason took on his expedition in quest of the Golden Fleece. Excusing myself, I went downstairs again, like some pattern-complex maniac, and drew lines, sawed bits of wood, drilled holes, installed a bulb or two (one white-blue, one garnet, so to speak), and installed the old boy in place just off the upper side of the Way. In the shape of one horizontally tumbling house. That done, I went up again for dessert, leaving a surprise behind. Yet was myself surprised. There on the table sat a vivid Jupiter done in jello, complete with colored bands and the Red Spot. Or, rather, a vertical cross-section through the poles, three inches thick, glistening and still. I clapped applause. Milk too. Then Pi,

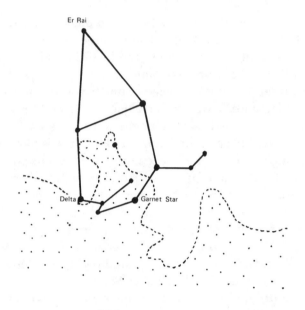

Er Rai

Delta

Garnet Star

CEPHEUS

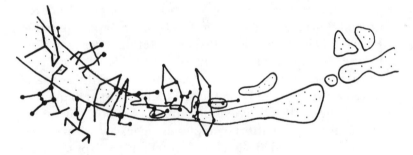

144

blushing a little, dug in a big spoon and served us outsize portions. Here we go, I murmured, slice-radius is over forty thousand miles. Milk ate the Red Spot, and I, before realizing, swallowed what Pi said was the shadow of the moon called Ganymede. Only one quarter of Big Jupe remained, vanished into Milk's unchewing maw. "Eating Jupiter," said Pi, giggling. How sexual, I thought. "Yes," said Pi, reading that near-illiterate thought, "that's really Ganymede's job, among others." It had taken her seven secret hours to prepare. "Let's," I suggested, "eat our way round the solar system. Saturn's the main problem: how?" "With meringue," she whispered. "Rings made of meringue." "Fine by me any time," I said, "but I'll settle for another Jupiter any time." In answer she quoted herself, an uncommon recourse for her, most modest of visionaries, and the amazed-amazing twinned lines clinched our feast:

> *"Vibrant as an African trade-bead with bone*
> *chips in orbit round it, Jupiter floods the night's*
>
> *black scullery, all those whirlpools and burbling*
> *aerosols little changed since the solar system began.*
>
> *The mind reels to berth so gelatinous a rainbow,*
> *suddenly pale salmon, then marbled blue."*

She patted her stomach. "Berthed, indeed," I said. Milk burped, heeded only the vibration, as unaware of breach in etiquette as of her being in the company of two space nuts, two characters who had never recovered from their amazement at being in the universe at all, at having so much of it to peer at. We were even devout, at least about the All's being a tribute to the subtlety of matter. Let's, at least, said our beating minds, look at literature *sub*, as the textbooks used to say, *specie aeternitatis*. Plant the merest thing in the mightiest context. Dwarf all that humans think is grand. And, both holist and reductionist, embarrass thought and style with star, with atom. Push everything to its uttermost, until the very joints of the brain's casing creak. That was us. It wouldn't, we thought, make dying easier, or suffering sweeter, but it would surely make life fuller, even at the cost of a lost hour of sleep each day. It wasn't eternity in a grain of sand so much as the grain in eternity, whose ready definition we found in telescopes that, bigger and better every year, got us nearer only to what would never be seen anyway, not while the speed of light was finite. There will always be something beyond the edge of the observable universe, but never mind: think of how much there is within it. First person plural, we roamed celestially, with, as often as not, a bizarre sense of how impersonal it was to be ourselves. "Hail, holy hydrogen," our prayers began, such as they were, and never have ended, but go on and on, in subjunctive salute.

Going at nothing like the speed even of sound (though in the prose it feels like light), we drove to Silver Hill in Maryland, a trip across the state border, to view the ghost squadron that belonged to the Smithsonian Institution. We were the Wright Brothers. We were Lindbergh. We were pilot, co-pilot, and stewardess aboard the Ford trimotor dubbed *Tin Goose*. Supervised by a lonely guard with a port-wine birthmark running from his ear to his mouth, we sat in seats and thumbed wheels, twanged wires, and peered into cockpits. "Off, off," cried Milk, wanting the frozen assembly to soar as one, taking us clear of grass and sheds. At the first German jet, the ME 262 I think, she leered, scorning its cold storage. At a biplane from World War One, she nodded, relishing the excess of wing area. At a neat little racer with a giant faired-in radial engine with blebs and an undercarriage with spats, she smiled as if recognizing a long-lost relative; something silver-beefy, something pyknic-eager, got her to caress the blebs, the spats, and clamp in her fist the tip of the two-bladed prop. For ten minutes, in that aeronautical

146

trance, she remained in position, linked to the ghost of thunder, while we breathed in the aroma of varnish and oil, flexed our shoulders at the shed's coolness, raised eyebrows when the rain began. Fingal's Cave, I thought; but we were not in the Hebrides, or the New Hebrides, or the newest Hebrides of all. This was the morgue of Icarus. The wax of his wings was the wax in her ears (I cleaned her out every two days with finicking care). I saw her then as a non-starter among contraptions frail, or unflown, or no longer airworthy, and found the analogies almost right. Her stilled soul was with, and of, those giant wings above and alongside her, their fabric dun and bronze as that of a dried-out tea bag, their angles of dihedral and attack a little out of true. She was talking to the engine, I knew not how, but maybe she was consoling it in its enforced idleness. Did I imagine or hear a purr, a cough, a lyrical splutter? What followed was audible beyond doubt: a bubbling flow from her throat. She had vomited on the spat.

Understandably, she recoiled, shaking her head in dismay. "Motion sickness," I told the port-wine guard. "Have you a cloth?" Mopping up, with breath held against the sharp tang of her bile, I told myself that this was really air-sickness after all. Spruced up again, thanks to Pi, who'd prudently got her away from the scene as fast as possible, to the ladies' room and then the open air, she embarked on a fit of guilty effusiveness, patting our backs, shaking our hands, exclaiming "Ah!" as she pointed to quite imaginary blemishes on our faces, arms, and shoes. Equipped with more than our fair share of postcards and leaflets, we drove away, only to stop en route and have Cokes. Once over the Pennsylvania line, we stopped again and had dinner, which Milk ate with benighted confidence, wincing at nothing, not even the big ice cream she hooted for. It all went down, and stayed.

Grinning at Cepheus, hours later, in her pajamas, Milk gave me the most exhausted version of what I call her Borgia nod. Criminals together, we held hands in yet another air space, plotted yet another raid on the Way. "House," she said baldly, meaning the constellation, and plunged both hands at the empty space beyond, asking for more. Would that I could, I'd turn hydrogen into helium, for her, like a well-behaving star. We tucked her in, planted our kisses, waved elaborate farewells. After which there was music, some Nielsen (loud) and some Holst (louder) and some lush Bergsma written in and for Jamaica. Through the scope, we observed Jupiter for real, in between touring clouds, then sat back on the balcony and rattled ice cubes in tumblers at the night that was just as warm as the day had been. Asa was away in New York. Chad had left for Boston. Even the neighbors who owned the pool weren't back. Only we and the stars stayed put, could be counted on. Or so I joshed as, once more inside, we half-watched Tyrone Power and Herbert Marshall in *The Razor's Edge,* wishing only for a character called Occam to curtail the reel and send us to bed half an hour earlier. As for the few days left, I didn't count. The reservations had already been confirmed, for a stop in the country of origin.

Up early, but not bright, I scribbled notes on cards, for inclusion in this. Jittery lines, awkward sketches, little bubbles of dialogue. A note on the prodding pain in my chest went next to a sketch of the plane with spatted wheels and bleb-faired engine. I jotted down the attendant's port-wine nevus, adding: Why do characters with facial birthmarks appear almost mythic? Then I crossed out *characters* and wrote in *people,* all the same remarking my writerly concern. The man was cast before he opened mouth.

Coffee-sped, I slunk out of the house, bought groceries, mailed cards, took out garbage, bellowed at the neighbor dog. It was eleven when Pi got up, and ninety degrees; noon when Milk arrived in a compensatory rush, and ninety-three. A day of scorch, omelets, misquotations. Up to the Olympic pool on campus we went, back to the air-conditioned cool of the bedrooms, to iced tea, and then, while Pi wrote (at a table dotted with Hawaiian rocks akin to what's on Mars), to the basement, where Milk and I made vital decisions about the next constellation. It was like doing a crossword during the bombardment of Pearl Harbor. Question: What's under the black squares? I showed Milk the *Field Guide*'s sketch of Lacerta, flighty little zigzag they call the Lizard, but she dismissed it with a hand-flash I'd seen rejecting food, people, weather, toys, dogs, and TV shows she'd seen before. Yet she made sense, she who'd seen Cassiopeia as an M for her. Lacerta was mere pastiche, whereas she (M) and I (Cepheus, perhaps?) were unique in our starry trespass, while she doubled as chained Andromeda as well, blamed for her mother's mouth. So we passed on, up the line, beyond the coal sack in Cepheus that I reckoned a blind spot in me, and on to Cygnus, one of the chief glories of the sky, headed by the raving white-blue of Deneb, tailed by Albireo, darling of astronomers, a double, gold and blue. This was better meat for her, not least because she called it "Abbala," for *plane.* Swan, I cautioned myself: don't say swan, whatever else you do, she says it's a plane. And it was almost wholly in the Milky Way, a cross planted right in the middle, like a lit-up airfield seen from fifteen thousand feet. We drew it fast, then chose the pegs and bulbs.

Uselessly thinking of Orpheus and Jupiter, both of whom Cygnus has been said to be, I mulled over the little bolt of piety that had soared out of the handbook, assuring us that Cygnus (the Cross) is seen best in winter, when it assumes an upright position, at nine P.M. on Christmas Eve, against the western sky, reminding us of Bethlehem: "a starry symbol of the Faith, a promise from the realm beyond." No, just a lovely clutch of stars, I told my saw as I rubbed it back and forth across the dowels. Here the Way splits into two big

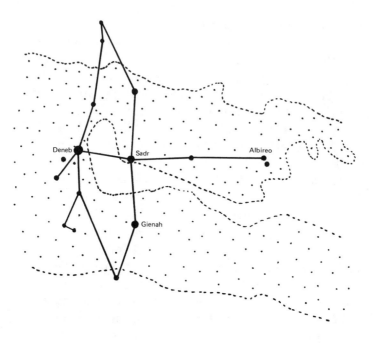

CYGNUS

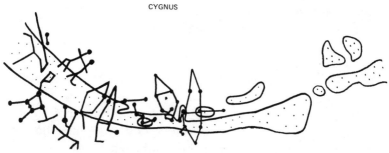

parallel streams that swarm with suns and sacks of stellar coal. Glued or screwed, in went the stars, the biggest bulb for Deneb, that approaches Earth at four miles per second from 1,630 light-years away. For Sadr, "the hen's breast," a yellow one; for Gienah, "the wing," a golden twin. According to the names, we were mixed up about Deneb and Albireo, since the former means *tail* and the latter *beak,* and that would make perfect sense if we were dealing with a swan's long neck. Fact was, however, we had on our hands a plane, which to Milk meant the wings were nearer to the nose than to the tail (certain ultra-sonic experimental models notwithstanding). So I let it stand, especially when she showed me which way the plane was going: eastward, back to Cassiopeia. Paint could not dry fast enough, hands could not whirl at a brisk enough clip. "Wynd," she commanded, and then delivered a long voluntary in which she'd invested heart and soul. "Yah, Milk, out on abbala, zoon, up, znow, when moon i' ot, bye-bye, Pi!" A chunk of Paris plaster would have got the gist. What she followed up with was by no means as obvious. Not only would she and I be flying away from Pi (she *knew*), but we would be taking the Way with us. Hence her haste to fill in the blanks, stud it with other constellations. It was hers. To take away. To fold up, somehow, and stow in the hold of a jumbo jet. Like a shutter. Like a circus tent. Like—

Unselfishly I said "yes," meaning no.

Cosms, I thought: macro and micro. Without hyphens. All we need is a portable universe. It was no use offering her the long photograph from upstairs, of the Way from Cassiopeia to Sagittarius, put together from four separate takes. The balsa frame would snap. The picture didn't in the least resemble what we had down there. No bulbs, no silver paint, no lit-up nebulas. So I decided to make her a miniature as soon as she'd gone to sleep. Such a Milky Way as would fit into a girl's suitcase between her underwear and the raincoat she

151

didn't need. A mini, of the micro, of the macro, that's what it would be, but unfortunately not electrical, nowhere near big enough to hide behind.

Clandestine, that night, I got to work with scissors, maps, and poster colors, tracing paper and a little box of colored paper stars found in a drawer, and made it all. By dawn I was blind, but it was done. I hid it in a storage closet, on top of discarded record albums, to let it dry. Doing it had not only brought departure closer, but given it a face of criss-crossed silver against Prussian blue. What little sleep I got was torn.

Up early, Pi went down and did the next constellation: Lyra, not far from the upper wing of Cygnus. In form, a small triangle attached to one corner of a parallelogram, Lyra just happens to be the direction in which the Sun is taking Earth at about twelve miles per second: our celestial goal, whose beacon is the blue-white Vega, once upon a time the Pole Star and, in twelve thousand years' time, destined to be it again. Taking in the work Pi had done, I thought of what Vega meant (the falling bird) ahd wondered at the manual skill with which she'd affixed the sapphire-blue bulb, the studs for Sulafat and Sheliak, the two tortoises, yellow and white.

Crazy people, I thought. We're not fit to be at any latitude. We interchangeably think of stars. We use our minds like sleds to get to the middle of nowhere. We eat a planet for dessert. I stay up all night to replicate a galaxy. She rises early and makes a copy of Lyra. And yet, this is a holy aberration, as extreme in attentiveness as in otherworldliness. We think big, neat, and often. We *like* the universe, *faute de mieux*. Solar she, galactic I, we're a team. That very fact was visible in what she'd done, not only installing Lyra (a poet putting the lyre into the universe), but also finding a postcard of the Ring Nebula to clip out and stick on. There it was, the famous

152

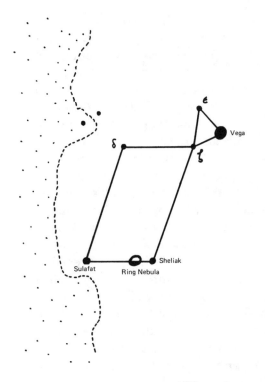

LYRA

153

chromatic smoke ring, in whose middle gleamed a fifteenth-magnitude blue star. Out of proportion, of course, but gloriously heraldic, it gave my vague, bloodshot eyes something to focus on. "It's beautiful," I yelled. "Thank you." I was very welcome, I heard, but she hadn't done it quite for me. Again I called upstairs, saying thank you, for Milk, for Orpheus' magic harp, for what in old Bohemia they called the Fiddle in the Sky. Odd how, in this geometrical figure of no great size, Earth's trajectory, the poetry of Orpheus and the vanished nymph Eurydice came together on behalf of an Earthbound child going nowhere, at least by the standards of society, but imaginative to the roots of her teeth, and in a mighty hot region given to long sleeps. Something eerie skidded through my muddled brain; I groped after it, but lost it, summed it up as atavistic *déjà vu,* went up to breakfast, which only made me sleepier than ever, five cups of coffee or no. During the afternoon, I fell asleep while watching TV. When I woke, Pi and Milk had been out to collect mail from on campus, but not today's: this was Sunday. One letter was full of dithering legal palaver. Another came from my mother, who had been with a friend to a picnic in the grounds of the local manor house; how very English, I thought, and for a second I missed the click of ball on cricket bat, the chimes of that thirteenth-century church, the softly modulated tones of the BBC announcers. There was also a book to review, somebody's Life of Somebody, and I marveled at the phrase: it was as if the somebody were forcing back on the Somebody a Life the latter didn't have, at least not in that shape, not in words, not in chapters, nor with index. Only the photographs were true. I put the book away for after Milk had gone and I'd come back, full circle, my cut-rate gala done with. Confronted with only a few more days, and wondering feverishly what to cram into them, I could only think of the constellation that came next, as if that were the only thing that mattered. Longing, I'd learned, could become wholly disembodied. So I found myself insisting, with stupefied persistence, on Aquila, saying nothing about it, but centering my brain on it and building a myth which went: If you reach Aquila, all will be well. But it wouldn't; after Aquila I'd have to reach, oh, Sagittarius, that scalding fungus of white light wherein the center of the galaxy lay hidden. There was no end, just one halt after another. An old style of behaving had reasserted itself: with too much to do, or to envision doing, I'd do nothing, let everything slide as I sank into a far from pensive funk. Then the hands took over, as always. Paint. Repair. Build. Sweep. Sort out books. Rearrange shirts. Stack dishes into a pagoda tower. Yet I knew that, if time is short, doing nothing makes it longer. On that vapid level I stayed.

An hour later, though, Aquila tugged at my mind again. Leaving Milk and Pi to carry on with the oil painting they had in hand (a representational glimpse of the living room complete with rex begonia, standard lamp, and bookcase), I went downstairs and, with slow-motion relish, began to outline Aquila where Cygnus ended, faintly aware that the Way had taken on a compensatory aspect it hadn't had before, when it was celebratory. A star threnody it had come to be, all the lyricism sucked out. Yet it was some *thing* to do; in occupying the hands, it annulled the mind, gave a standard so vast that nothing mattered when shoved next it. Shrugging at my own brand of dark-brown romanticism, I thanked heaven for three stars in a line, the bright Altair flanked by two dimmer ones. This Eagle was the symbol of the noonday Sun, to the Sumerians at least, as well as the bird of Zeus. A close neighbor of ours, comparatively speaking, with Altair only eighteen light-years distant, it held an asterism called Sobieski's Shield on which I could splurge a cluster of little bulbs, if I felt inclined. No, I'd just mark it with some white-painted little studs, leave it at that, not being in the right mood for *all* things bright and beautiful. Perversely, I might

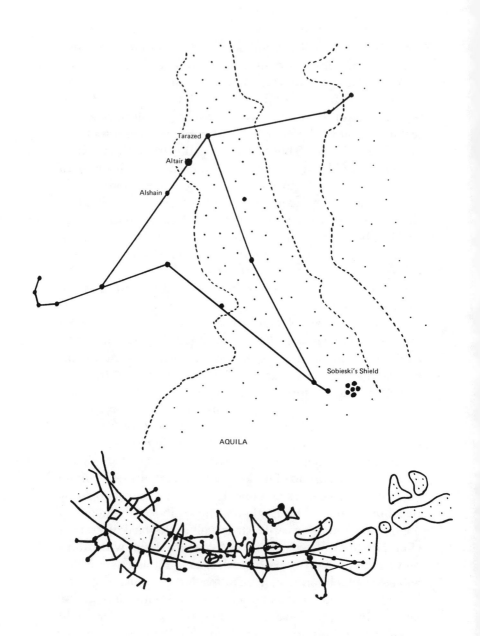

Tarazed

Altair

Alshain

Sobieski's Shield

AQUILA

even add a few stars of my own invention, company for Altair ("the flying eagle," a yellow), Alshain (just another Arabic name for the whole thing, an orange), and Tarazed ("the soaring falcon," a pale orange). I'd stick in, say, the new stars Funkair, Paralyx, Dumpnix, and Cafardalis, just for starters, all yellow, followed by a cluster all of smaller magnitude: Nadaz, Ditherium, Stallnar, and Slumpsych, not to mention the Panic Cluster, the Runaway Catatonia Star, and, of course, the famed Deulius Coal Sack. Poor Aquila! Drawn so differently in each reference book, all the way from a scarecrow to a kite, from a single line bearing three headlights to a chevron-like triangle. I would have to design an outline that Milk would enjoy, have some rapport with, and so I cheated a bit, in the end coming up with what resembled a tent pitched on steep ground, with a streamer flying from its top and a long guide rope that snaked out left. My three main stars, no, Aquila's three main stars (I jettisoned all my neo-stellar objects) came together in the upper half of the left-hand line, a pretty sight dominating the doubles which, quite pedantically, I filched from the most detailed reference book. So, for just about the first time, I had included objects visible only through instruments, not the unaided eye or the field glass. How flashy it looked, with one yellow-green, a white-lilac, a white-bluish, and a yellow-purple, all done with small bulbs, the result being that Aquila had a fairground look, agitated and festive. Cheered up just a little, I even included a version of Sobieski's Shield, capping a bulb with aluminum foil I'd riddled with tiny holes. Next stop, I thought, would be black light, luminous paint, an electronic-eye star that switched on the whole Way as soon as someone came in the door. Such devices I'd save for later, to come down to earth with, after she'd gone, after I'd eaten another seven thousand miles, like some demented runner trying to cross the Milky Way itself, whereas, of course, on this scale of distance my trip wouldn't even take me from one side of

157

a small bulb to the other. Less than a fourth of an inch. Yet I lost that thought, just as well, in a small shock of remembering the so-called black hole, Cygnus X-1, most probably a pair of stars that revolved around each other, one of them remaining invisible although perhaps ten times the mass of our Sun. Moving back along the Way, I drilled two holes, implanted one holder and one bulb, then painted the inside of the second hole mat black and threaded a little black balloon through it, tugging from the other side until the lips came flush with the hole. This was my image of the star, or hole, from which no light escaped. Cygnus was even richer than before. I even thought of inflating the balloon, but decided the effect would be wasted, as invisible as the black hole itself. So I contented myself with bizarre, over-reaching thoughts about the chance that our own universe is itself a black hole as immune to investigation as a solipsist. We live (I said), it all lives, all living is, inside a slot made by a cosmic corpse. Then, recoiling from such hyperbole, I hunted through a shelf of journals for the one in which a black hole had appeared in vivid color. A double-page spread showed Cygnus X-1 itself, a cerise whirlpool with a black spot at center, sucking blue star-stuff into itself from its massive companion. Scorning proportion, I tore out the two pages, Scotch-taped them together, and stuck them in the dark off the Way, just south of Cygnus. A cosmic drama happening Off. I saw the red giant cook its planets as it bloated its diameter to five hundred million miles, and then begin to collapse as gravity squeezed the atoms closer and closer together until the former giant resembled an atomic nucleus with elephantiasis, was only twenty miles across but tens of millions of tons to each spoonful. As if in some gigantic thaw, the neutron star fell down the black icicle of itself until, invisible at the point, it sucked all after it, never to let it return. Gratified by such a cosmic monster, I turned again to twinkling Aquila. My bile was shed. My glooms, although not gone, had moderated. Surely, I thought, at this point a voice should interrupt me, bring me back to the dear dimension of pretzels, eggs, tea, and toast. It is time for solidarity. Let's group again. I went to the foot of the stairs, could hear only faint grunts of concentration (Milk), murmurs of guidance from Pi. The painting went forward. All those pulpy tubes of Terra Verte, Titanium White, Shiva Scarlet, Shivastra Violet, and Cadmium Orange weren't going to waste. What a Hindu-planetary sound they had, even with the small found-poem doing its clinical counterpoint on the tube's back, something that ran: *Colloidal Co-precipitate of* PERMANENT *1. organo-inorganic pigment. 2. Ground in specially prepared non-yellowing drying oils.* The remainder I forgot, but it had something to do with freedom from lead. Of course. Nagged at by my own mind, I called up to them and had the following out-of-time non-conversation. "What are you doing?" "Painting in oils." "Have you finished?" "Nowhere near." "Aren't you hungry?" "I've no idea." "I've just done Aquila, aren't you glad?" "Yes: now do the next one, huh?"

Upset at feeling jealous, I went back to the Milky Way. Fatigue, I told it, is making me snappy. I should be glad, not cross.

Calm down, I told myself. Deulius, be still. Do Sagittarius. Clean up the mess. Be useful.

Going outside, through the screen door, I picked up a fallen apple, slung it high and away, heard the smash of glass from some house behind a row of trees. Inside again, flushed with small-boy naughtiness, I felt what the oil-paint tubes call permanent-opaque. From now on, I'd do the Way, seemly as a Boy Scout, aloof as an angel. Live on Jello. Run my daily mile. Do sit-ups by the score. Write my mother daily. Gladden everybody.

Child of five, when spoken to by strangers, I'd just say "Bugger Off."

Chastised for the next ten years for saying Bugger Off, I developed the habit of the silent scowl that issued the same command.

Ultimately, I learned to speak again, and in terms of mortifying acerbity; would say almost anything sharp, just for the exercise, and so gained a predictable number of friends. As cut off as that, you have to end up writing. After twenty years of that, you get to speak more mildly. Might even be called nice.

Called cruelly Wight, by my father, after the Isle I was conceived on, I wore that smart with honor in pain until the age of twenty, when it occurred to me that, unknowingly, he'd landed me with an old word that meant human being, or creature, as if folk needed to be reassured about my true status. I consoled myself with Blake's couplet ("What wailing wight / Calls the watchman of the night?") and finally got used to being written to as White. Things could have been worse. Had they gone to other islands for their inaugural fornication, I might have been dubbed with such grievous excerpts as these: Sark, from the Channel Islands; Uist, Tiree, Coll, Canna, Rhum, Elgg, or Muck, all from the Hebrides; Hoy, from the Orkneys. All in all, I am very glad they did not go to the Hebrides; had my name come thence, I'd not have lived to twenty. As things turned out, being Wight Deulius wasn't all that bad, for in imagination I joined the Wright Brothers, the White House, and the White Nile; and, when that mythos of mispronunciation didn't work, I enjoyed the frequent calls of *Wait, Wight!* that streamed after me as I ran away. Whitey, school called me, as if I were a pet rabbit, but I responded as bravely as I could, and now, fortune be praised, the name has a touch of erudite distinction, especially when displayed on the jackets of my books, and comes trippingly off the tongue of those who refer to me. It's also, as my father the engineer couldn't have known, beguilingly close to Wit. Perhaps, even, I am the only person in our whole civilization with this archaic name, evocative of our entire race, and in the old literature almost always prefaced with some such fol-de-rol as *Alas, poor.* My mother, I think, had no hand in it at all, so surprised to be pregnant that she almost lost the power of speech, certainly of innovative verbal reference. I think my father even told her some tale about a new law that would regularize society, entailing that children be named after the Eden in which they were conceived. I wonder how many walk this earth, to this day, called Dunfermline, Swansea, or Bath.

Call no man happy who is not dead, runs an old line of the Greeks. I'd alter that to: Call no man happy who hasn't chosen his own name. Call no wight . . .

Cheered by having gone into that, the joke being that you'd see it on the book's cover before you read it in the text, I go back to work, fired by the memory of my father's bewilderment that I didn't have to clock in at work, or keep to certain hours. "You get paid just for talking, just a few hours a week?" he'd say, wondering where he'd gone wrong all his life. The vacations left him speechless, who said little at the best of times. Yet, in his vaguely Neronic way, he was glad that, if I exerted myself, I could earn more in a day than he used to earn in a year. Or something just as preposterous, have more vacation in a year than he'd had hospital time, or sickness leave, in his entire life, before they gave him the gold watch that wouldn't tick, with his name on it. "A little tombstone," he said. "A foretaste. When they give you this, they're getting you ready." On that day, Retirement Day, my mother went into the best room and played Liszt for four hours straight, just to enclose her distress.

Cooking aromas came downstairs. Chicken, I decided, choosing not to find out. Still no sign of Milk, who for good reasons was declining to enter the underworld. All day I had left the two phones unplugged, almost as if the house were a deaf child who disdained appliances, didn't want to be reached. Things could go on like this for weeks, at which point I'd have written evidence from those folk desperate to get through. I liked, I think, the sense of power at being able to plug in a phone to call out, and then sever all communication until the next time. We were masters of our instruments, not they of us (as is more usual in the age of give-you-a-tinkle, give-us-a-call). Or was I just magnifying the fact that Asa and Chad were out of town? Did I not want to realize how little the phone would ring? Or was I shutting out Europe?

Casting around in the basement for something to do, I looked in the corners, found portly spiders at rest in their skeins, decided to exterminate them later, unless they were really gobbling ants and flies. The *Aviation and Space Sciences Encyclopedia* I put back into alphabetical order, then flipped my finger along the amassed spines, like a child with a stick along a fence. Petty doings, these; after Aquila and the revisit to Cygnus, I'd had enough, had a mind like a cross between a chanterelle and a patch of salted snow. Out again, I watched the loud birds, tried to hear the worms and beetles, got the sniff (I think) of the chipmunks and squirrels. And I scanned the local horizon for faces of people whose windows have been broken by party or parties unknown. Thrown by the same person who, in his day, had malingered, or seemed to, in front of the paperback display in the Elmira, N.Y., bus station. All of a sudden, there she was at his side, the ticket-seller-custodian who doubled as porter and Gorgon. Would he like to buy that book? "Which?" he asked, being profoundly startled, never in twenty years of browsing confronted by so intimate, so sportive, a question. "Which book?" he asked. "Any of those you've been reading for the

162

last half-hour," she said. "Oh, I never buy them," he told her with his disingenuous grin of the traveler stranded. It wasn't a library, she announced. "What a shame," he said, "because if it were you'd have better books, and then, being tempted to buy, one wouldn't need to." At that, her officiousness deliquesced into what can only be called a raucous grimace, as if she had been offered a condom to blow her nose into. *Homo itinerans* is often subject to such accost, learns how to cope with the experience only after much standing and wondering. There are, he decided on that occasion, people who care about configurations that, seen from Williamsport or even Aquila, don't matter, are mere whorls in the texture of what only a shallow mind can term the big buzzing blooming confusion. It's not. It's the medium silent ananthous order. What star ever said hello?

As if that weren't bad enough, loitering with no intent to buy, he had also jaywalked on every street from Miami to Montreal, but was agile enough to keep alive. Only in Blackwell's Bookshop, after jaywalking across Broad Street, had he felt at peace, not only reading an entire book while crouched on the stairway, but taking notes from it, and returning months later to check his notes against the book's new edition, and then a year later rechecking his recheck against the third edition. Unless he imagined the whole thing, the punts, the champagne, the emancipated bluestockings who came to tea-and-crumpets but stayed for anatomy. In those days, when he didn't care, didn't have to care, he switched off and wrote poems thick with visionary sap. He hadn't even so much as looked up at the Milky Way, not even during the week-long crossing of the Atlantic that lodged him, like well-spoken jetsam, in 1314 John Jay Hall for an entire year. Manhattan wowed him; I loved it; didn't you? All his selves had a place there, all round the clock, as if the city were itself a sun. Filthy even then, bemerded, a-tremble, sky-high, the city, first seen pink with the sun behind it, had looked like a wedding cake of clay. It seemed a long time ago, almost in a different country. All was tonic, lush, optional. He could play his head as if it were a fish, saying to himself: I (?) am (?) in (?) two (?) minds (?). And get away with it, as little aware of minuend as of subtrahend. *Now* minus *then* equals twenty, years. What, I wonder, had been put into him (I who say he) to retard spoilage, as it says on food wrappers? Backbone, maybe, first installed in the town of Shanklin on the Isle of Wight, thereafter known as Wight's Isle. Or mother's milk, first administered not long after. Or country air, fresh grass, a swift dose of ultra-violet during one or two weeks of each fogbound, sopping year. At any rate, he survived immersion in Manhattan, felt slip away from him the image of an indri, big lemur so-called because the French naturalist Pierre Sonnerat, hearing the Madagascans cry out *Indry!* (Look!), took the imperative for a noun. Well, there were worse indignities by the million between 1943 and 1944. And there are things, even now, to be grateful for: I am not called Shanklin; I can spell; I have found a cigar that I enjoy. What more can I want?

Calmness.
Couthness, or couth (as the British say).
Guile.

An atamasco lily, with funnel-shaped pinkish flowers, to put under my pillow. Sweeten my dreams a bit.

"Come when I call, or tarry till I come. If you be deaf, I must prove dumb." I sure am. Now, where did I hear that?

Under the influence of—oh, an atomic novel I once composed, meaning a novel you cannot divide, at least not into meaningful subcombinations. Called nothing, it was composed wholly of two words, *a* and *the,* I having evacuated all else, as in wartime, from the danger zone. *The a, a the, the the,* it began. You can see the drift away from cliché. There are echoes. It is all action. The characterization is far from heavy-handed. It almost ends. The *the*'s win out over the *a*'s, inevitable when you think of our modern mania for precision.

As if it were winter, I see the lining of my mind out there on the balcony, pitted with the arrowhead tracks of birds. All that snow.

Choice of trees? Well, then, the redbud, known as the Judas tree.

Choice of shells? Make mine the wentletrap, with long ridges crossing its spiral taper. When one thinks one knows it all, one can always find something to add; therefore there's no all at all, at all. You never know.

"After all," then, means after some of it, after a bit of it, not even worth saying *after* in front of it. Nothing is ever said and done. Sagittarius next, and Scorpius to follow, thence to the southern heavens, round and back until the spiral is complete. Yet our Way's just a smattering. Who could count the stars in even it? Or those outside it. *Who counts?* That's what I mean. Something goes on, as behind closed blinds all over the world, has no need of us. As Inkwell, the Oxford sage, once remarked to me in Tom Quad, the sequence leading to man is tortuous and random; it is unlikely that, redone with the same quota of the random, the experiment would yield up man again. I envision, though, the thirty-foot butterfly whose lifetime's occupation (333 years) is to build puys of meringue-like sputum, miles high, visible from enormous altitudes. Conceivably, even, if one looks closely, the square eyes of the simoom bat; the double anus of the Caucasian flantellifer; the green rotary forceps of the Algerian swont. Or, failing these, there might be such novelties as the radioactive tail of the Arctic genferon (to be pronounced with a hard *g*); the navel tusk of the lesser rinderpoon; the rainbow

165

eyes of the Himalayan gypsum roach; the transparent hooves of the Cuban swizzary; the fifth, retractable, foot of the Egyptian dune-fondler; the sonar cone in the muzzle of the Andean charcoal fox; the lethal septum of the banded Siberian frost veltanex.

Cave hybridam! Said: "Karvay," et cetera. Latin for beware of mongrel. I just wonder if there isn't some link between hybrid and hubris. No, that's too much to hope for. It's not so much that the etymology is dubious as that, for once, the dubiology is etymous.

And, and, and: the Andorran pith jaguar; the mint peccary that haunts the remains of nuclear reactors; and the Canberra hopping fecopod, self-propulsive on one perdurable turd. These, and a few others who have begun to stalk through what I genially call my dreams, will be my cell-soulmates when I come to a pretty pass, even the prettiest pass of all. I'll soon, yes, soon (there's a juicy word for you) begin to compose a little prayer, in other words a fit of subjunctive lust. "Please," you have to begin, "on December 25, if you can carry something as big, will you bring me a Junior Hydrogen Bomb? And . . ." Back to that later. What I am volunteering here, of facts as I understand them, must be suspect from the outset. It goes without saying that if someone is forcing something out of you, that person usually thinks it's the truth, whereas what's not extorted's not believed. Exit literature, enter confession.

At that moment Milk was bristling with delight as Pi clipped folded paper and produced a row of tiny creatures advancing hand-in-hand. Cloned in a minute. How describe that expression on Milk's face? Over the years I have tried, have never worded it right. It's a taut effervescence. No. It's a creamy evil-eye. No. It's fellow-conspiratorial élan. No. It has in it a highwayman, greedy but civil: Stand and deliver, ladies and gentlemen. It has also in it a high-honed intellect that should be peering into a cloud chamber as vapor condenses on the ions left in the trail of the speeding nuclear particles, and the cloud tracks form, comparable to the vapor trails of high-flying jets. As well as a touch of the diva who, somehow exults within the planes of her own face. Freebooting Greek *nous* made charismatic, then? No. But nearer. It's all in her face, not in her mind, whose mount (the brain) has too many long thin spines, too few short and fat. See the researches of Martin-Padilla and Dominick Purpura, as I think I mentioned before, perhaps not, what lovely names for research scientists, especially the latter. A Purple Master on the premises, visiting the cerebral cortex: "mental deficiency links with disrupted neuronal geometry, sets abnormalities of mental function alongside congenital heart abnormalities traceable to anatomical defects in the cardiac muscle and valves."

Charming epiphany, jargon-swelled.

Gruesome too, when you reflect that anyone who has prepared micro-slides of post-mortem brain samples from thirty retarded children has actually— I can't, I won't, finish the statement. Just that those thirty didn't make it, see. "OK. We know." "Do you? Good, I'm glad." Never mind the rage. Rage begets migraine, I'm told. Yet I had the migraine before the rage, long, long before.

Getting back to what I was saying, or was saying in order not to say something else, you can buy pristine blank forms, printed by the Oyez Publishers, which offer a small text for multiple-choice response. *"The said child is* [not] *suffering from serious disability or chronic illness."* Alter as appropriate, you're told, and if a child is so suffering, add "namely" and state. . . . Imagine that. It exists, like many thousands printed in 1972 with a 19_ _ on the back, which is only fair with a quarter of a century to go. I wonder who'll be here when they start printing them with a 20_ _. Convenient twin slots for the decade, et cetera. Cheering, when you come to think of it, they haven't printed any of the latter yet. Optimism like ice cream on the cavities.

Consonance, now, that's what's needed: a simultaneous combination of sounds conventionally regarded as pleasing and final in effect. *Ur. Ah. Ugh. Ow. Huh. Hm.* Aloha to all that, I am trying to get back to those days when we ran things down, I mean began the closure (there was no denigration). Roughly the plot runs as follows. The sun froze. The apples melted. The house flinched. Our eyeballs yellowed. We slept with our intestines in neat mounds on our midriffs. Witticisms were the fuel of the look that did not look, the mind that did not count the days. More than ever, with Milk at peace tilting blue and white powder to make estuaries and spurs, Pi and I went to superfine lengths to tie when playing Scrabble. Our scoring is bizarre anyway, so it was easy to make things come out: the last player, needing twenty-three to win, arranged combinations that scored twenty-two. Which is as it always was. We play out of inventive extravagance, to bend language, not to win. Or is it, backhandedly, not to yield? No, it has never been that. It's a case of level heads leveling, gentle fraud. I'd call it the happy version of what happened in Dresden during World War Two, when after the so-called firestorm couples were found melted together in what was left of each other's arms, and dreadfully shrunken. What is more human than that, I ask myself, than hugging together before you burn alive, neither able to help the other, but the arms doing some thing, some last thing, for both? It could never happen on the Isle of Wight, in Shanklin say, that's no target. At least, it hasn't happened yet. And the heat of indignation, or even the vaunted one of composition, is no match. An awful thing to say in the context. Or out. In our minor way we prevail, matching each other at Scrabble, fixing the scores. At one.

Uncommon thing, it took Milk ten days before she saw (or

remarked on, at any rate) the color photograph of herself taken years ago as, grinning smoothly, she prepared to launch herself down a slide. Over by the door to the balcony, it's nearest the sun of all the pictures on the walls. In the bottom left-hand corner there's a small snapshot of her at school, with three friends, all four of them in their hearing harnesses, hers white, theirs blue. Whereas the others look happy, she seems needled by something, holding her doll as if she means to sling it from her. They wear the school's uniform, maroon and blue, whereas she has on a red-white-and-blue dress, horizontally striped. When she finally saw herself behind the thumbprinted glass, she delivered a long-ish speech all to her image as it stood there, no doubt recovering time, and then chanted the girls' names. "Kool," she whirred, where she was now an officer of law and order. No more juicy anarchy for her, but stern waggings of the index finger. After a moment more of contemplation, she examined the other pictures, appearing to grade them privately. The more bizarre the better. She took to Dürer's engraving of a rhinoceros, to the photograph of a woman's head smeared all over with concrete to make a living statue with closed eyes, and seven Hungarian stamps mounted on black. Without a word, she stood before a busy, crowded drawing of spheres, cherubs, and astronomers, pointed with glee to the figure of Copernicus, whose body was covered with eyes and whose mouth was puffing skyward the words *Videbo Caelos tuos,* "I shall see your heavens," while a much relegat-ed-looking Ptolemy leaned back against a shield on the ground, spouting *Erigor dum corrigor,* as well he might, the gist being: "I arise now I am straightened out." Or so I construe, rusty if not worse. At the Trifid and Ring Nebulae, recognizing them from the Way downstairs, she aimed her broad alabaster chin, maybe disdaining them for being no novelties at all, and she quite failed a chimpanzee, the printed plan of a small glider I'd designed at fourteen (a mere

169

model), and, of all things, the composite photograph of the Way from Cassiopeia to Sagittarius. A nifty chiaroscuro picture of Pi playing pool, taking bare-armed aim, earned a passing grade, however, and a tight laugh. I think, of all, the rhino won, because she returned to it, and it only, trying to make her eyes bulge, going down on all fours in a pseudo-pachydermatous crouch, with her arms held up to be the ears. "What?" she asked. Told, she said "Rhine" perfectly, but not the second vowel. Next thing she'd cried "Biosh" and pinched my thigh. It was a rhino charge, of course. I should have known; "biosh" is how she says "pinch," always as a warning or a threat. In that same room, which is this, of course (I no longer being able to write in the basement), she later in the day squatted, thinking herself unobserved, and without a sound let the tears flood out, then slapped her knee in rebuke, being a big girl not entitled to cry. The saw-teeth of those five minutes are still sharp. I want to turn the rhino, Copernicus, all those images, to face the wall, as if to ban her reflected face; but no, I leave things be, as if she's dead. Go on using the room like an addict. Gape at the rhino, the rest, like a masochist. Find not many words that soothe. Or even tell. From time. To time. Like that. "Now then," says Pi, "it's on your face again. You're supposed to be celebrating the past, not mourning the present." I agree, but not without a memo to myself that part of the story of this book's story is the acid-on-the-nerves of writing it at all. Thank heavens, I say, for the strict wallbars of the RNA code called Messenger. It keeps me straight. After five more sets of three paragraphs, it will lead me to one of the three nonsense combinations. UAA, followed at once by UAG, later by UGA, which look no more like nonsense than the rest. At fourteen, an age that comes to mind too much, I lay in bed with a broken arm the doctor had splinted, an injury sustained in a football game and therefore slimy with honor. Why I hadn't been sent to the hospital there and then, I have no idea now; in the end, of course, I was. But, for one night, I slept in splints, or tried to sleep as the ache sharpened into a gnawing pain, and I perversely shoved at the wood that hemmed in the broken ulna. Again and again I made the red-hot flash that made the whole arm jump and a wet break out on the bridge of my nose, this at about three in the morning, a fine case of jubilant suffering. The hurt was mine, or so I reasoned, and worth getting to know while available. With each surge of pain, no one woke, neither my parents nor my sister. No one could tell. And now, with a new break to palp, I press the spot night and day, getting even more electrifying results. Yet, yet, the words haltingly move along. An ulna in the head I hadn't bargained for. Nonsense is quick, meaning is slow.

Goodness! the dawdling that goes on. It was easier, though, to do this with Milk on the premises. Had I not done any then, had the whole thing been retrospective, I'd never have started, no fear; I'd rather fry fish than do this, walking about the house, even the autumn garden, with yellow pad and felt pen in hand, trying to arouse the very echoes I want to go away.

"Calmly, that's how." Pi says this, with terse gentleness.

"Copy," I astronautically tell her. "Willco. If possible. But when you've given blood, you cannot lap it back. Therefore, give more, thus making of yourself an anemic beast." A what? One of Count Dracula's leavings. The one picture in the kitchen, gone unmentioned, reminds me; I see to my left, sneaking up on me from behind the shopwindow of their blood-curdling aquarium, the Count and, in a sturdy night-gown, his drained-dry bride, halted on some twisting steps while he stares away from her and partly through the giant cobweb that stops them live. He has heard something over there, out of sight, far in the dungeon's corner, where the light from his two-foot candle cannot reach. Perhaps it was a ghost moaning "Lugosi, Lugosi," or the outsize spider itself coming to monitor the vibration in its web. Meanwhile, with her long dark hair divided forward over her shoulders, the bride waits, her eyes glazed with destiny, the suck of her mouth compressed outward into a little raisin disk. How goes her choked ditty? Could she but croon.

> Apple, apple, on the tree,
> Have you heard of ecstasy?
> Be my pippin, bite my core;
> *I* don't suck *my* paramour.

Extremes, extremes; she still looks wholesome, whereas I, face all nicked with razor cuts, I look used. Did I nick from wanting not to look as the morning mirror burned with light?

Gluteus maximus, sterno-mastoid, masseter, old muscular friends, they'd leave me if they could. This here joint's done for, that's their creaking say. Backside, head, and jaw must move themselves from hereoninout. Bah, sez I, I'll not be put off, I'll fix them with some rubber bands. Whoa. Steady, girl. Gee-up, now we're off again, none the worse for being a bit awkward in the bandages. I hunch from room to room, hunting words in walls, but I have not even graffitoed my own house.

Collected now, I begin reporting all over again. The tide is in. An author, with a big herring lashed to the top of his skull, has been floated out to sea for the gulls to dive-bomb, his brain an open jar, and now he's back, none the worse for that experience. The trick, ever, is to see yourself as your own best raw material, be as impersonal as Dürer. Look again at his "Rhinocerus 1515." Minus the horn that's partly cut off by the frame, it's only an armor-plated rat. I think he knew. What's frightening isn't there in the so-called animal kingdom; it is cellular. So children may as well play as not, and sheep may as well graze as not, and swallows time the year. The ogre will come in any case.

172

Aimless, Milk and I wandered outside, played soccer with a big apple, kicked at a bush or two, chased one striped and one black cat, found and picked another bottle-nose gentian aromatic as Persia, gathered up withered pine cones into a paper bag, flew planes shaped from our hands with one thumb representing an entire wing, sprinted a hundred yards down the road, fenced with twigs, walked back pigeon-toed and giggling, sat on the grass and watched beetles, picked some wild scallions, came in with the flower and filled a vase with water. Then we joined Pi in the air-conditioned bedroom where she was reading Merezhkovski's Life of Leonardo, and then left her in peace, wandered downstairs to check the Way, make it blaze. "Our position," I told her, in the vein of the mock-heroic inaudible, "is not favorable to a correct survey; but, as we see it, it is marked by strange cavities and excrescences, with branches in all directions, and is interrupted in its course, especially at Ophiuchus and Argo, by the operation of some force as yet unknown. This is true of width as well as course. Curdled or flaky, it mingles bright patches with almost absolute vacancies." I talked as if quoting some ancient book, and no doubt was, but the only bit of what I mouthed that had a source was this: "It is a large part of a larger scheme exceeding the compass of finite minds to grasp in its entirety." Courtesy of Miss Agnes Clerke, in System of the Stars. We now call it the super-galaxy, its head-quarters in Virgo; as for its hind ones, we'll forever have to guess.

Greedy for more of her mind, I outlined Sagittarius with bumbling speed, stood back, breathing hard, and asked. Both my hands flew apart as if a large bird had taken off from between them. "What?" I mimed. One look and she knew, riding a bicycle with both legs and steering with both arms. She'd seen a bicycle for the Moon, or for Mars, a sketchy grid that had not wheels but ball bearings, like a tripod recover-

173

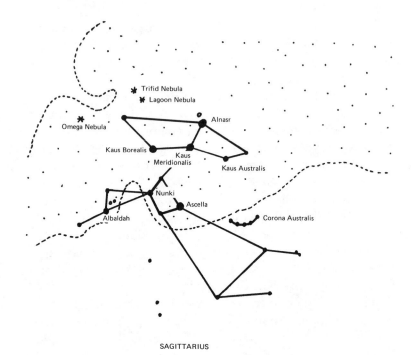

SAGITTARIUS

174

ing from the splits. Perfect vehicle for a weightless one, it floated lunar-lander-like, with that lovely small crescent of Corona Australis just a token seat. Mobilized in the abstract, she rode across the Way, turned and came back, eyes brimming with silver mirth, commanding me to watch. I did. I still do, still see that airy locomotion on the basement floor. Deep in the Galactic center without knowing it, she trod stardust as abler mortals water, and the little pluck of pain in my insides went numb, annulled. Calling to Pi to come and see, I remembered how this girl had never learned to balance on two wheels, had even been frightened to trust herself to a machine that had small side wheels that wouldn't let it tip. Unabashed, even with two observers, Milk toured the up-there neighborhood, all the way from the three famous nebulae—Trifid, Omega, Lagoon—to the Corona, flicking a heel at Alnasr, cocking a snoot at Albaldah, without coming off. Dilated in my trance, I could hardly believe what Pi told me, she having forgotten to do so yesterday. Milk, no child but woman, was having her period and, like a modern woman, was going ahead, pressing on with what mattered.

Cowed, I thankyoued, was okayed. Those who quietly get on with Merezhkovski's Life of Leonardo can see to those who cycle over Sagittarius. And with no fuss at all. You couldn't say that of the Grenadier Guards, the Strategic Air Command, or even the Red Cross. I took deep breaths to sap the shock.

Going back upstairs, after she'd applauded the ride, Pi shot a good word backward about Leonardo, firing me to start with what I suddenly thought of as the illumination of Sagittarius, done monklike, but with bulbs and bits of gaudy card. Down there, staring at the hub of the galaxy, at Archer's Bicycle, I felt moved in the same way as when I watched the Sun ease its way westward above the ridge of the long mountain at which the house points. Not ours, but loaned, the Sun. Old reliable, at least for as many more million years as doesn't

175

matter. I gladdened at its steady tour above us while we tinkered with the apparatus of light: yellow for Alnasr, "the Point," and Kaus Borealis, the northern part of the Bow; then, splurging with two bulbs apiece for Kaus Meridionalis (orange and blue) and Kaus Australis (the same orange, the same blue). "This," I told her, "is the Milk Dipper," but she was more intent on having bulbs in place for Albaldah, Nunki, and Ascella. *Yes,* I mouthed: "yellow, blue, and white." She grinned, a celestial henchwoman. The wiring seemed to take hours. I cut my finger on the sharp rim of a socket. A length of perfectly good-looking wire snapped, and that almost moved her into a rage. My hands flew, planting five little bulbs into the Corona, shape of a nail clipping. Then our bicycle lit up, a riot of tones that made her hop, clap her hands above her head, and with shocking brilliance ask for nebulae by screwing her index finger into her other fist. Up I trotted for my wad of postcards, in which I accidentally put my hand on the Prometheus of Paul Manship, golden ephebe who lolls in the Sunken Gardens of Rockefeller Center with fire in his hand. In that second, I saw Milk, short-haired for once, traipsing across Sagittarius, but stealing the gift of fire from me, at any rate damping me down. She'd made me mellower. You wouldn't think a small bulb could shine through glossy card, but it can. We clipped and trimmed, then rolled narrow tubes of stiff paper, nicked triple flanges to stick to the card, and plugged them over the bulbs to make our three nebulae. A rose-and-white pucker with a white-hot bleb at center, the Trifid cried out for underwear even as my child exclaimed an histrionic "Poo!" See it and die laughing. Less suggestive, the Lagoon has a rift and not much blue, but a positive eczema of stars on one side and a blazing cluster on the other. The Omega is scarlet, shapeless, but studded with blues, an orange, a pure yellow, and has a baffling dark rectangular cloud cutting into its foot, a vortex box. On they glowed, as no telescope can produce them, but only cameras, picking up colors which, when Rome was founded, say, had already been on the way for three hundred years. A far cry, even if you never come to think of it, like Milk, whose bike lamps bloom. Staring bemused at Nunki, so-called Star of the Proclamation of the Sea, I found my mind playing truant, occupied with nothing serene or noble, but caught up in the jargon of medical insurers: small bowel studies, price $30; treatment by radioactive phosphorus for polycythemia vera, $140 for four sessions; prostatectomy, suprapubic (one or two stages), $250. They get you coming and going; but, at least, you can get a platelet count for three dollars, a tubeless gastric diagnex for five. "Nunki," I said, "that would make a lovely nickname"; its sound is informal, biddable, tender, whereas Ascella ("the armpit") sounds like a cold droplet, as no doubt befits a star that's heading off, out of Sagittarius, to some destination of its own. As is the star called *fi*. After thousands of years, with these two runaways at a distance from where they are now, the Sagittarian Milk Dipper will look out of whack, in fact unrecognizable. As if that mattered. One thing about stars, they tend to give the mapmaker time to catch up. And constellations most of all.

Unwinding with a beer which Milk had sampled but didn't like ("sore," she said, getting not quite the exact word), I made her a tiny catapult from a rubber band, amazed to hear electronic sounds at certain tensions. She aimed a spit-heavy paper plug at the TV local newscaster, but, with a wild shot, struck Ptolemy where he sat, high and to the right of the set. "Some game to teach her," said Pi. "She was born to it," I answered. "You can't teach this girl anything; all she needs is practice." I said nothing else, gave over the room to news of area high-school sports, my mind on another of those dark, rotten images that had begun to rise in it like bubbles of mud. Such a lost-property office my head had become that I didn't mind most of its irrelevant fits, but this one wouldn't go away.

177

Long before the Milk Dipper lost its present shape, there would have been goodness knew how many purges, if not here then somewhere else, all in the interests of a thing variously dubbed Nation, Aryanism, Involvement. Goons with armbands or shiny-peaked hats would round up the undesirables all over again, first taking them to deserted schoolrooms, then to trains that would grind a slow one-way trip to some resettlement camp in, oh, Omaha, comparable to those already going full blast in the pampas, Hokkaido, the Baltic coast. And Milk would stand twice condemned, for fraternizing with Jews (Pi's renegade status notwithstanding) and for being unfit. Some summer evening, when the light persisted as if it might never come again, after the last uproarious bout of tennis, and while we were all sipping lemonade with even, blithe *Nachtmusik* drifting out from the house over the terrace to the lawns, the black car would draw up. Or horse box. Or van. I would not go quietly, I would have a gun, use it somehow, however much a mess I'd make. I heard the charge against her: a fraternizing, mentally incompetent Leftist, for whom the state had no use. God help us, I thought, one joins the state only when there is nothing left worth joining; that is the *last* membership short of death. Indeed, the latter had more savvy, knowing how to make the cells make errors after they've divided about fifty times, as well as better manners, oftener than not, and a longer tradition. Yes. Hoping hard, I foresaw how the next purge would bring total victory for the forces of defeat, meaning, I think, that we would all three somehow elude the fate worse than death. Rape scenes from Russian newsreels honed the edge of a certain resolution not to get caught with our drawers down. A ripped-open woman, long dead, with all of her save her legs and rear stuffed into a drainage pipe made to measure for just such a scene, came in front of my eyes, like a large cell cruising over the surface of the iris itself, and told a truth that no amount of time could smooth, I hated

178

then, as now, the deadliness of man, the ease with which humans kill one another when the snake- and horse-brains have a field day; and I knew why other civilizations in the galaxy hadn't bothered to call in. Maybe, by the time the Milk Dipper had lost its wedge shape and become an inverted milk churn or even a cut-off cone, mankind wouldn't be quite so handicapped, would be less in need of special care, might even have heard from whoever was on the planets around Barnard's Star. Here I am, I said, born long before my time, willing to live peaceably on behalf of love and knowledge, a placid and serene soul made saber-toothed only by circumstances. I am the Old World looking for the New, as on a previous occasion; the New was never looking for the Old, any more than birds in the Southern Hemisphere migrate as those in the Northern do. It was just a matter of having a star to mark the pole. North has, South has not. And who's to blame?

Answer there is none. The fortune cookie that could enclose it hasn't been baked. The aroma from the oven, then, was that of three frozen turkey pies, one pie more than there were days to go. Understandably, I think, I cast around for metaphors to badge the oceanic jitters of my mind. As astronomers say, what recedes is red-shifted, what approaches is violet-shifted; but what was I approaching? Only someone that receded. The mind was both red and violet, a stasis of blur. No exit could be had from that. The hot pastry of dinner tasted old. The turkey seemed human. Only Milk was on form, relieved that a certain thing was almost over, not because she wanted especially to go (yet how could we tell?), but mainly because knowing that an end was countably near in days (or sleeps) gave her a sense of mastery. Things she adored she relished the end of, simply because something had become clear. Living as she did, in a flux of the open-ended, she could not help but long for the semicolons in the maze of letters.

179

Uncanny how it felt, nothing so dramatic as waiting behind the curtain while the guillotine that just had thumped was hosed down, but rather as if I were some Japanese soldier going away to war and being honored with the gift of a sash that held a thousand stitches, kept out the chill and bullets as well. That distant-feeling symbolism had come home, from another war to this, the tussle against distance and genes. Chad had already brought Meg to say farewell, he as if glad to get the chore done (he once said the main thing about life is to get through it, implying threescore and ten is too long), and she as well as Milk dismally afraid. Asa we hadn't heard from; when he went he stayed gone. Kashmiri wasn't with him but, I seemed to recall, in Knoxville, busy with a movie of some kind. Everyone was outward bound or gone. On the home front, as I with martial hyperbole called it, things were falling apart so fast that there was only Pi, with a few stars, to hold on to. Accustomed to berating myself for too routine an existence (my argument in its favor having been that a confused head doesn't need a random day-to-day as well), I now found myself in the middle of a dismembered, balletic uproar that had no sound. Ironic to think of it, but I had begun increasingly to blot out half an hour at a time with music, not one of the spheres, but one of arrested atoms. Milk had sampled what came through the headphone cable, but it had impressed her little, just another version of the hearing aid, a different form of static. So, in one sense, I was battling anticipated loss with something almost underhand. Hearing, often enough to drive Pi into mild exasperation, Bergsma's *The Fortunate Isles* and Nielsen's Fifth Symphony (in which the drummer has instructions to drown out the orchestra if he can), I canceled a dimension, was as far away as if I had been holed up in some blockhouse-shaped elementary hotel near Tamanrasset in the Sahara. Meanwhile, in the basement, the space for Scorpius waited. Would we, would I, have the heart to do it? Even if all we did was install massive red Antares, which the Greeks called their "anti-Mars." A star bright as ninepence, in the idiom of the British, it would be our own bull's-eye, a big punctuation mark. Try tomorrow, I resolved. See what she thinks. Have her do it all with her own hands, I'll be staring at that bulb for many months or years to come. It would be a long time before this visitation got repeated. Hence everything was unique, or about to be so, as I could tell even from Pi's face, that of a profoundly stable woman observing the Fall of Rome, the death of a rhetoric, the failure of a nerve. Tact flooded with misgiving primed her smile. I would be leaving her too, in order to sever myself from Milk. Someone else, other than I, might have arranged things better, but for this kind of enterprise there were few rules. You began with the unique and added to it. And, after about fifty years of it, you learned perfectly how, when it was far too late. Upon an impulse, defensive and no doubt part of an emotional fugue I'd entered days ago, I picked out from the shelf a last-century tome on stars and began to read what it said about the Scorpion. Too much fustian for me, the introductory account went on for pages, and my eye skidded until it hit the epithet *rutilans*, for Antares, "glowing redly." That seemed better, except that Antares, being a double, was emerald green as well as fiery red. Skipping quaint lore about the seven famous selected poems of Arabia, said to have been inscribed in letters of gold on silk (or Egyptian linen!) and suspended in the Ka'bah at Mecca, as well as about what the learned saints Augustine and Basil thought concerning the scorpion's derivation from the crab, I found a bit that said the open cluster M 6 resembled a butterfly wing. Yet it was a phrase about something else, I forget what, that caught my mind on the raw and fed it salt. In order to see a certain close double as a double, one needed a magnification of two hundred, at least if one wanted "a clean split without notching"; in other words, a bit of one tended to overlap a bit of the other. Notching was what I was in for; clean split I didn't want and wouldn't get. With one sensible word, "packing," Pi cracked the spell. She asked what I was taking. Had I thought about a present for my mother, with whom, on the other side of the ocean, I would spend a couple of weeks? "A silk scarf," I unimaginatively replied. "Then we should buy it tomorrow, locally; the duty-free prices at airports are a gigantic rip-off." It was the same prudent, caring voice that had persuaded me years ago to start visiting the dentist again, to wean myself of the bottle, to run the mile and lose twenty pounds. Under that same eye I had emigrated from Funk Ghetto to what remained of the twentieth century's fourth quarter, as she repeatedly had stressed. Poets are not supposed to be that practical, though I know of a few others who truly are. In any event, it was Pi who adjusted my wheels back onto what the British call the permanent way (apocalyptic term for a road's rails) and talked me out of the sleepwalking concession I'd made to life. How to repay such a debt I had no idea, but doing what I was told was a start. Out of its shell, the pulp of me felt vulnerable still, even so long after the break, the lawyers, the acrimony, yet feeling light-sensitive was also an intoxication. "Thank you," I said, "for remembering the gift. We'll get one tomorrow, anything but green or brown, which she can't wear." "I know your mother's spectrum," said the poet; "I have it by heart." Non-urgent matters clogged my brain, then turned into vapor. I felt I was living in my own sediment. Hyper-confirm pre-reconfirmed reservations, I kept telling myself: surely there's something I've forgotten. But there wasn't. It was only a matter of getting our two bodies aboard the first plane; aerodynamics and passports would do the rest. Wire only, ran my prearranged instructions, if something goes wrong. It did, but not to us directly. Kashmiri phoned, said Asa had been mugged in New York. His ear was badly cut. I could phone him, though, in the hospital. He sounded re-mote from himself, almost elated that something had happened to him that was over. If something had to happen to him, he said, he was glad it was only this. It was better than waiting, better than wondering. I marveled at such an impersonal sense of self, compared Asa's trouble with my own. Where he'd been struck by mundane lightning, I was being eroded, gnawed. Yet I had nothing to report to him, to the master of so many of our recent ceremonies, whereas he was full of it: just after a pink slip advertising a massage parlor had been thrust into his hand, he had walked away from Fifth Avenue up a side street to light a cigar. Foolish, he said. The three were lounging in the next doorway and had not taken kindly to his declaration, as at some hellhole customs barrier, of a few one-dollar bills and one long package that contained a freak book, four feet high and four inches wide, a book of tall thin poems, which they had taken anyway. And then the knife, applied to his ear with a laugh even as they were going away. A tickle, that was all, with bursts of tingling as, only five minutes later, a police car rushed him uptown. Stitches, swabs, and tests to come. That was all he said, talking as if one of the elect. It was as if he had already survived being a survivor. Or as if he had happened to the event, not it to him. I envied so superbly accommodating a mind, deciding Asa was geared for whatever world he found himself in, whereas I, I was still fudging up a policy that might get me from today to tomorrow without too much blustering fuss.

"Uranus," said Pi, to get my mind off Asa while Milk was mopping condensation off the toilet cistern. "Pronounced with the stress on the first syllable!" "YOOR-anos," I said: "it has five moons, and the cleanest mind of all the planets." Milk brought, as if it were frankincense and myrrh, about a pound of sodden paper towel, wise enough not to thrust it down the toilet, as she might have done a few years ago. "Wet," she declared. "Oof!" Which meant: Throw it away. But, before handing it finally over, she mopped her sweating brow and chin with it, just for completeness' sake.

A synoptic sense of our penultimate day must have been wrapped into that ball of paper. I saw the three of us, expendable as shapes made from a child's building blocks, lined up in syzygy: a sun, a moon, an Earth. But who was which? Not knowing, I decided each was all, and shut the figure out of mind, recasting myself as a Charon who on the next day would overfly the Styx, Pi as Hermes, Milk as Eurydice. Except the myth was garbled. After losing Eurydice, I wouldn't, like Orpheus, develop a loathing for all women. Just a few, that was all. I, Wight Deulius, would live to bungle many another day, even though I dieted and ran and abstained from the sauce.

Crazy impulses began. I'd pack both our cases with sliced ham, dozens of pounds of it, and leave the snazzy new clothes behind. Then Milk would fly back to fetch them. Or we'd just go over with what we stood up in, traveling light as viruses. Not only would we have nothing to declare; we would walk through Immigration, into that country other than the country of origin, without even being seen. We'd transcend the borders. Dream-paced. White-eyed. Aloof. And never be seen again, except in spectroscopes. Present as chemicals only. Blown about by wind, or kept under refrigeration. Only our formula would know us.

Unbelievable what happened next. *"Look, Yah, "* said Milk: *"Chew the vicissitudes and swallow them down. Don't fret. We'll have long holidays together, all three of us. We'll read Pi's poems on a beach somewhere on Antigua. At night we'll play word games, making* Rimbaud *out of* barium. *You'll teach me French, I'll teach you gibberish, my native language. You can both coach me for my final exams—I often wonder why I settled for philosophy instead of, oh, maybe medicine or psychology. I'll make some kind of a living as a book-reviewer. I'll read what you write and puff your books*

184

under an assumed name, see? We'll sit out, nights, and watch variable stars, one good way for an amateur astronomer to make his name. We'll tabulate, we'll wisecrack about Mirfak, Ophiuchus, and RU Lupi, any stars with funny, just mildly obscene-sounding names. But, myself, I'd really rather paint than write, more in the manner (I think) of Francis Bacon and Magritte—if you can envision the mix—than of Rembrandt and Dufy. If you get my drift. Perhaps I should set up in Bayswater or Staten Island, in a loft, with lots of accurate northern light that would also show off my medium-brown hair down to my pelvis, and, I suppose, eventually shack up with some renegade existentialist who runs an antique shop. And whenever the two of us, he and I, took off to roam through jungles or ancient seaports loud with either macaws or loading cranes, we'd stop off and look you up, trying to time it during your vacations. Or just say the hell with it and keep on rendezvousing year in, year out, in Ceylon. And I would keep on talking, in this no doubt perverse vein of the ostentatious uttered, just to make up for lost time. How many phonemes do you think went to waste during my first twenty years? I saw men walk on the Moon, but had not a single comment. In those days I didn't know Moon from Sun, or Europe from America, the Suez from the Panama. Talk for the sake of talking, as Novalis said, is the sincerest thing you can do. Or, as Beckett has it, words have their utility, the mud is mute. Pardon me if I seem like a goldfish, forever surfacing with an aphorism in its mouth, or whatever it was you once said about Pi, whose talk crackles with impacted wit. I'll keep quiet only when peering at Andromeda with you through the Astrax eyepiece of the eight-inch scope. None of your toylike three-incher for me! I'll take especial care of Asa, who's as deaf in one ear as I used to be in both. I'll teach him to sign, just in case. I'm even willing, for a financial consideration, to type your manuscripts for you, for both of you. Pay me in encyclopedias. Or we'll redo, from

185

scratch, the Way in the basement. You must have thought me mighty unresponsive when you did it first. Well, I was mighty, by my own estimate: when one is shut out of things, one feels privy to an absolute of what's left, if you get my— I was going to say drift, but I've said it already. Eloquence is variety, is it not? Excuse me, the phone just rang. It was another invitation to model, such being the main source of my pin money. I'd hate to be dependent. As it is, like a good girl, I balance my checkbook monthly, as the bank says one should, and thus far I disagree by only seven cents. As for what you have already written about me, I'll forgive. The inaccuracies. The lies. The tiny slanders. The ballsed-up chronology. The utter misunderstanding of some of my neatest gibberish. I promise to rebuke you, though, only in Indo-European, most hypothetical of tongues and therefore, I presume through some kind of rearward teleological guess, nearer to God. How do you like them apples? How do you like being addressed in this irreverent way? I know, I know, you've been waiting all your life for this conversation. Lucky you I'm not fifty-five, but only as old as Pi was when I made my first landfall with you two. By the way, she looks better with her hair down than stacked on top. I've often thought that. I'm Nature's girl, catching up at three quarters of the speed of light. My latest discoveries, in case you want to use them, are: the reduction, long desired, of hadrons to quarks and gluons! Mr. George Crumb's composition Voice of the Whale, *which reminded me of a galactic kazoo! and the fake newspapers read by people in movies—the Philadelphia* Sentinel, *the Chicago* Courier, *the London* Daily Messenger! *I try to never let them catch me napping, as well as never to split an infinitive, God alone knows why, but maybe to please you when that look of irresponsible hubris comes over your face after your third cup of coffee. I have also discovered that from bikini to yashmak is fewer steps than you might think; that people who aren't worth talking to are people not*

186

bright enough to know that we're brighter than they think
we are (if you can follow all that); and that rhyming slang,
as practiced by the Cockneys of London, enables one to say
I sent you a picture coastguard *or* Testicles live in pairs in a
wrinkled factotum. *I have, as the saying goes, been around,
have sustained the minimum of damage. Out of* Rimbaud
you can also make radium. *A lemma's a glossed word. A
paraph's a flourish or an underlining. My other favorite
words include* jiffy, trounce, flank, euphoria, crittur, wyd-
wose, *and* blazhenny, *which is Russian for crazy. I especially
admire the Cambridge theoretical astronomer Stephen
Hawking, a severely handicapped paraplegic who insists on
reading his work aloud at conferences, in spite of difficulty
in enunciating consonants. Of late I've been dipping into the*
Rig Veda, *a text I believe you in your finite wisdom haven't
ever read, and I would like to quote. If you think this is the
kettle calling the pot black, then take it or leave it, including
what I fully realize is my own reversal of the usual trope:*
Who knows for certain? Who shall here declare it? / Whence
was it born, whence came creation? / The gods are later than
this world's formation; / Who then can know the origins of
this world? / None knows whence creation arose. / And
whether, he has or has not made it; / He who surveys it from
the lofty skies, / Only he knows—or perhaps, he knows not.
*Don't laugh: you've quoted enough at me in your time. And,
while I'm about it, haven't you overlooked one fact pertain-
ing to the messenger RNA you once saddled me with? According to my book on the subject (which I now read as if
interpreting my premature epitaph), the signal for initiation
of protein synthesis is a partially known sequence of symbols
ending with AUG, the symbol for methionine. Hence, Yah
dear, all proteins when first gotten going start with methionine. What's unusual, though, isn't the chemical, but those
letters, AUG, suggesting augury or inauguration. Could it
just be that I'm beating you at your own game? Baffled?*

187

*Never mind. We nomads leave the aged behind, and they
don't resent it, not a bit. If, as once seemed likely, you are
writing the North American version of what the Japanese
call the* shishosetsu, *the autobiographical novel, shouldn't
you inspect your auspices more roundly? After all, to miss a
trick such as AUG, and have your protagonist remind you of
it through centripetal ventriloquism, isn't that a bit thick?
And it would help a lot, in other areas, if you wouldn't leave
boxes of Kleenex strewn about the floor for folk to tread on,
and if you would please flush the toilet after using it, and if
you would please-please not smoke cigars in the bath. That's
all for now. We are going tonight to hear Schönberg's* Gur-
relieder, *of which I especially love the part called* Behold the
Sun, *and I don't care if you dislike my taste in music. I have
a term paper to write on Croce, heaven help me, and I must
say that old essay of yours, an offprint of which I've really
gone square-eyed looking at, hasn't been much help at all.
Shorter sentences would have helped, as well as a less meta-
phorical style. Give me Swift and Austen any time over Carlyle and Pater. Take care of yourself now. Don't smoke too
many cigars. Eat nothing fried. And get up earlier, which is
to say: Don't stay up all night watching TV, even if you think
you're planning chapters while doing it. There are maxims
that cover all your misdeeds. I won't bore you by quoting
them here; you know them already. The examined life is very
much worth having. P.L. (for Post Locutum, is my Latin
right?): Can you lend me a* Bouvard and Pécuchet? *I finally
got the Voltaire thing, so don't worry about it. I doubt if you
did. Oh, P.P.L.,'tyros speak with their mouths open, whereas
a genius speaks with his mouth full."*

After that, I stared at her face for a good five minutes,
knowing she'd said none of it; but she'd never said none of
it at such intimidating, inspissated, length. All I could think
was that old tag about Einstein's physics, which said that
matter doesn't travel *at* the speed of light. It was like being

188

separated from Milk by a so-called light wall, on one side of which particles were moving more slowly than light, while on the other they were actually faster. I had just space-traveled into what-was-not.

As for coming back, I don't think I ever did. Reminding me of dreams in which I argued with her non-stop, in fantastic erudite language, that long splash of ventriloquism still fills my ears. When a character talks back to its creator, that is one thing; but when a real person who's been made over into a character lets rip with an out-of-time harangue, you begin to believe in sorcery. I still do. Who's to gainsay me when I recount what I thought I heard? Wishful thinking? Of course. But also unwilled and automatic, something to be credited to my synapses firing again and again to relieve the pressure in their turf.

Uncanny, that was UAA, the first of the three triplets that mean STOP or NONSENSE. No doubt I lived up to its role. And this, UAG, is the second. Make sense of that last whole day? Not I. Maybe some other will. All I know is that not only the line between fact and fiction blurred, but also the line between Milk and me, between us and the behaving universe. It felt as if, although they didn't, commas halted us dead while periods fanned the flow. Nouns died. Verbs froze. Adjectives did not describe. While conjunctions severed, prepositions mislocated, and pronouns stood for nothing, the language took an opportunity to communicate nothing but itself. At large. At random. At the merest bidding.

At home to guests: receiving, shaking hands, taking off its underwear, cavorting nude in the presence of grammar. As who should say: I said what could not be, thus I-ing a no one, thus said-ing an unsayable, thus what-ing a not, thus coulding a *non posse*, thus negating a not, and thus making a trespasser of the verb to be. Is that how others have staged, say, a Two-Part Invention for Firmament and Supreme Be-

189

ing? I'll never know. But I know the synapses, "the fastened-together," made a poem of their very own. Gray anti-matter. I host.

Gaga at young age, I held my breath to rid me of the pipe dream thus made burly, lest it undo stoical acquiescences hard arrived at. And so got back to where life can be merely awful, no holds barred. The embarkation. The fastening of seatbelts. The transferring of one's traveling companion to other hands. The mater not alma, not by a long chalk.

Calmer than she had any right to be, Milk fell asleep early, her teeth unbrushed, her body naked, her nightdresses packed. But she had patted me on the back, to inspirit; had taken my hand and conducted me outside to stare together at the apple tree, as if it somehow prefigured our destination.

"Any laundry?" asked Pi. "Any last-minute things to wash?" "Have we," I inquired, "done any laundry these last two weeks? I can't even remember." "We?" "*I* have," she said, with the complete force of one who is going to be alone for three weeks. It felt like having snow between my teeth. A cranial jolt.

Useless, I listened to a piece of music based on Earth's magnetic field, in fact one year's measurements adapted from graph levels to pitch. It had the eerie gravity of certain compositions for pipe organ, sounded aloof and timeless, yet flooded with an abstract geniality as if the solar wind had learned to smile. How enviable, I thought, to be so accommodated to what Isaac Newton called fluxions. How does one achieve it? Is it a human possibility at all? That night it was not.

Chad phoned, reporting a daughter with a strep throat. Heavens be praised they hadn't come over.

An unappeasable fatigue took us to the bedroom for half an hour, nerves tightening Priapus' throat. Then a musical on

TV, at which we peered like horses in fog. At nine-thirty, a swift blast of rain, into which we ventured, patrolling the balcony, I in garish Polynesian shorts, Pi in a batik toga worn like a cape.

"Catharsis," I quipped; "let's go inside." The thunder made us switch off the TV. And then, with all lights out but with Milk's air-conditioner faintly pounding, we watched the lightning as it stabbed our chunk of the Appalachians twelve miles away. What a well-purged night, I thought, when all nightmarish wildness is washed away.

Curiously, though, within an hour the sky was partly clear: man's first picture book open again. Lounging on an outdoor chair I hadn't even tipped the water off, I looked down-range at Scorpius, the constellation we would never finish. Insistent-looking stars formed a claw that sprouted from red Antares, but I saw other shapes as well: the kite, the bucket of Dante, even what the Akkadians called The Place Where One Bows Down. Ah yes, it was all of that! Governing the groin, it emblematized in claws the yoke of matrimony, and presided (so I'd read) over Judaea, Mauretania, Norway, Morocco, Sardinia, and God alone knew what other stamping-grounds.

"Antares," said Pi: "wasn't it the first star observed through telescopes in the daytime?"

"Arcturus," I answered. "Some say it's Arcturus. I don't care. I'll have the whole southern celestial hemisphere to do on my own. Not that it matters. We managed to do an awful lot. It's just—oh, my pattern complex giving me a bad time again. Nothing's ever as neat as you want it."

Countdown, that was my mood. I might even tally the hours as they passed, disdaining to sleep at all and, perhaps, working out there in the damp with the eight-inch scope that tracked without a creak. To be followed by another sleepless

191

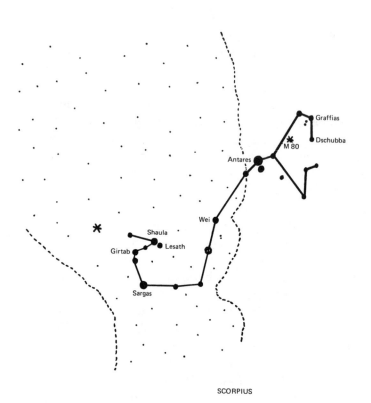

Graffias

Dschubba

M 80

Antares

Wei

Shaula

Lesath

Girtab

Sargas

SCORPIUS

192

night over the Atlantic. *No.* I determined to average five hours at least and not to have one of my caffeine binges out of sheer anxiety. My fill of this night's stars, though, I'd have, as something—not in the basement—to remember her by.

A star by any name is sweet, I told myself, whereas numbers and letters do nothing at all to the mind's aural eye.

"Graffias," I said aloud, "a triple, with dominant lilac and pale white." It means Crab. Halfway between it and Antares lies the cluster which, on the western edge of a starless opening four degrees broad, prompted Sir William Herschel to exclaim: *"Hier ist wahrhaftig ein Loch im Himmel!"* He'd found a true hole in heaven, but one speckled with stars.

After Graffias, I found, with naked eye, in this order, red Entenamasluv, usually called *gamma* only; Dschubba, the forehead, also known as the Tree of the Garden of Light; and Shaula, the sting, thought unlucky. Yet my mind slouched, began mixing things up, blurring *sigma* and *tau,* "the outworks of the heart," with *mu*[1] and *mu*[2], supposed to be a little girl, Piriereua the Inseparable, and her small brother, who together flee from home into the sky when ill-treated by their parents, two other stars who follow them and are still pursuing to this very day. Or so claim the storytellers of the Hervey Islands, not even in my atlas.

Asleep, or nearly so, I lost the scorpion in the fishhook of Maui, with which a Polynesian god drew up from the depths the big island called Tonareva, not in my atlas either, but for better reason. Feeling fished-for myself, I consumed two cans of beer, blundered back inside, and helped Pi with the dishes. Celestial visions gave way to encrusted Jello, fish-perfumed pans, and blood-red charcoal in the broiling tray. Light and mud.

Unbearable humidity drove us again into the bedroom, where Pi almost at once fell asleep. After setting the alarm, I crept out, bore to the balcony the big scope, and began a midnight vigil after mopping up the table's top, resentfully aware that I should have done it before taking the scope outside. If I were unlucky, damn the star called Shaula, I'd find a minor rim of rust on the bottom of the cast-iron mount.

A sky of late July blotted with cirrus did me proud. Like a saliva gash, the Milky Way dragged at my eyes. A fishhook, a bicycle, a tent, and a big bird flowed coldly above, in a dimension not that of air-conditioners and bowstring nerves. Milk's other images were out of sight; but, anticipating to-morrow (now today), I looked east toward Pisces and Aquarius, the direction in which, at our own level, we'd soon be flying at less than star speed. Then I whipped my gaze back, gaped at the naked sky as a giant wedge of cloud cruised over. My ears filled with a thick, muddled squeak, and the eyepiece with bulbous-looking silver geese, legs retracted, heads rigid. I even saw the eyes, aimed away up-range. Blotting out entire constellations, the geese moved north as one enormous wing. Two thousand of them? Who could know? I was trembling.

Aimed instead at Libra, Milk's own group, next to the Scorpion. Who had not lauded it? The list of celebrants included Longfellow, Milton, Marvell, and Homer. The constellation itself resembled not so much Scales or the claws of Scorpius (which once it was) as a two-legged triangular table, with its best star, Zubenelgenubi, glistening pale yellow and light gray at the right-hand corner. On that tiny celestial tray I took an early mental breakfast before my own turning with the planet wheeled it out of sight. Uncouth-sounding, an obscure fourteenth-century line came to mind, and went as fast: *Whoso es born in yat syne sal be an ille doar and a traytor.* An ill-doer and a traitor? Never. Of slanders I'd had enough, no matter where they hailed from.

Church clocks, minutes apart, told me it was one in the morning, while another clock, familiar of my bladder and hormones, told me I could stay out another two hours at least without hopelessly unfitting myself for the day's journey. So I beered, cigared, took heart from a sandwich of Jarlsberg cheese and Roman meal, and looked abroad.

At Deneb chugging pale.
At Vega, the harp star, big stud of pale sapphire.
And Altair, pale yellow, according to some a portent of danger from reptiles.

Astrology, seeping in, I booted out on the wings of a mixed metaphor.

Attached a different eyepiece so as to gain higher magnification, relishing how easy it was, with the eight-inch, to look down as if through a microscope. No more stunted necks. No more wobble. No more the image diving out of sight. Having Milk on the premises was akin, whereas Milk in the cheap cardboard-tubed scope was a mortification of the flesh. Yet, after later on today, meaning today's European version, I'd be back to the toy telescope, more frustrated than ever before. I swore off all comparisons for the next month. It was more than enough to think how bizarrely Asa's ear joined him to Milk. Better by far to think how Milk's images in the basement had been added to the sum of things, whether as analogies or not. And what seemed important, then as now, was to give evidence of having been, even if the result were gross enigma. Daubs, graffiti, doodles. I launched into thoughts on the work of art as spiritual fidgeting that, having nothing to say, wanted to evince, make tracks. At one extreme there was the howl and the babble, at the other dumbstruck gesturing.

Going, going, but here today.

Gone tomorrow is the missing bit, except it doesn't figure as anything besides heavyweight guess.

As with the British, who often arrive at belated self-discovery in some such phrase as "Optimistic? Yes, I suppose I am," I took up a stance without naming it: a Jack Horner of automatic luck, a temporary Prospero. In one sense, I knew as little as the screwworm flies who, bombarded with gamma rays, were exterminated for the sake of livestock.

Under the influence of a not-knowing that wanted to leave a spoor, I was un-educating myself with some success. The pre-sapiens ambit I'd begun to call it, having found nothing else with which to face my lot. Head full of phenomena I'd never wish away—feather palms, the stubby-nosed antelope named saiga, *anableps anableps* the four-eyed fish—I kept inching my way toward a response that was merely evolutionary. The All, so-called, was here to evolve and, in that sense only, be meaningful. There would be no epiphanies, no day of judgment, no solution proffered after the puzzle proved insoluble. There was only process, would ever only be that, at most a trillion books whose ultimate effect might be to modify just a bit the brain (into no longer needing to write them or into writing them better), at least the entirety of human pensiveness since 10,000 B.C., end of the last ice age, gone for nothing: just a flicker in the private life of species. It was nothing to cheer about, yet nothing to lament, there being no alternative.

Gala, then, as I called my two-week fit, amounted to merrymaking during decomposition. It had, it would have, no more power to last than a bit of starlight which, after traveling for millions of years through intergalactic space, jostled at long last through Earth's atmosphere and fetched up against the mirror of some telescope, vanished into the silver-halide grain. That puny. A photon death. Yet, I told myself, it might also come back again and again like migraine, the pain in the head and the neck that was also a visual picnic. Unexpected, fast, and dizzily chromatic. Though I stole thunder, I liked to provide my own lightning.

Add to the gala, though, I couldn't. It was already over. Bar the shouting. I had run out of congruities, whereas irrelevances kept on coming home to roost. Kashmiri, for example, had once been a demonstrator of mechanical toys. My own face in the mirror, reminding me at that small hour not of me but of, oh indignity, the bumphead parrotfish whose fused teeth form a white oral heel in a mule's face. I went to bed, foolishly tried to make my mind go to sleep, and my mind stayed up to watch the maneuvers I performed upon it. Finally I got off by spelling the names of philosophers backward, n-i-e-t-s-n-e-g-t-t-i-W last.

Cozened myself into five-hour oblivion.

"Good morning" was the phrase no one said. It was hot, with cerise flashes in the east, a mound of untrussed cumulus over the roof.

A mind hopelessly divided, I checked the tickets, the bags, the calendar, half-hoping for the catastrophe that would save us all. Then I retrieved the miniature Milky Way, criss-cross silver on Prussian blue, from its hiding place on top of the unused record albums in the walk-in storage closet, and slid it deep into her case, between layers of adult-feeling clothes. Eighteen inches long, bigger than she herself when born. Or maybe not. She would find it, colored paper stars and all, when she needed it, later, or when perhaps she didn't need it at all. Once more I dreamed up the catastrophe that would postpone the trip, or cancel it for good.

As if, setting chocolate bars on fire with a butane lighter, Milk would win us three days more with a singed thumbnail. As if a wheel fell off a plane overflying us en route from Philadelphia to Pittsburgh, and it crashed through the roof. As if, after so much help, air changed its rules and no longer helped a wing up by creating less pressure on top of an airfoil than beneath. Force all wings

197

down. But even her period was over, as Pi said while breakfasting; the girl was eligible to go.

Giant dreams, little velleities.

All the way to the airport Milk smiled, alone in a mucous cocoon of her own creation. The way lay through forest along roughish roads that warned, with orange signs, DEER XING. Eight hundred feet higher, we found the air fifteen degrees cooler. Pi sang quietly to herself. I peered at Milk as she averted her gaze through entire civilizations and saw the forest not as trees or ponds, picnic tables or outhouse toilets in cropped clearings, but as heaving hot lava. So I guessed, as lost in query as she in—in what? In, I'd call it, renegade, outlandish, quicksilver, abundant, idiotic, gunslinging rapture. Homely as hoecake. Magical as lymph. Far as the galaxies in Sculptor.

"Gone out," said the sign that was her face. "Back in time. Don't wait. I'm free."

Ulysses and daughter checked their bags through to final destination. A rivet slipped. An airline man fixed it with a Scotch-tape Band-Aid, flagged the case with a label that said DAMAGED/FRAGILE. Which came first?

Gum from the vending machine lasted her two minutes only as she sapped each stick of its flavor and spat it yards. Retrieving the wads, I balled them up, wandered outside into the early afternoon of mountain air, and flung the ball at the inert, distant windsock.

Urgent waiting glazed all three of us. The commuter plane was ten minutes late, yet here it was, lunging with a halt-snort, then still, while five incredulous survivors entered the terminal. "Bye-bye, Pi," said Milk with an impatient kiss, pulling me by the hand toward the gate. Faces, backs, windows, belts, then the brute glare of the sun blotted us out. "I'll write," I'd said as I hauled at the heavy door that didn't open itself. The plane nosed like the halfbeak fish took off westward, fizzing and lurching. In two hours Milk and I would fly back over that very airport, but higher, well into travel's blur.

Unpressurized cabin, noisy propellers, and sudden falls as the air gave way, these distracted me a little while Milk peered past the curtain into the pilot's quarters, beaming at the tiny red lights that shone and died. One image, of the co-pilot's holding the pilot's hands against the throttle levers during takeoff, reminded me of us, of policeman and prisoner, of nuns' laps. Then I saw that she had fallen asleep leaning forward against the belt, as if frozen a winner as she breasted the tape after a hundred yards. Twirling the ceiling nozzle for cold air, I aimed it across the aisle at her head and let her sleep.

Grounded, we walked half a mile to the international terminal, again checked in, and munched candy bars on thinly upholstered pews. "Red," she kept saying as she pointed at the carpets and the cushions. "Red," I answered, wondering why they'd chosen so unsoothing a hue. The music, however, was creamy violet, an ectoplasm of melted aluminum. Then she ran, I in pursuit. Wet her head at the drinking fountain. Hit the restroom with full force, I outside. Played pinball once. Fished out and put on her hearing aids, for the hell of it, only after ten minutes to rip them off as if profoundly disappointed in the audible.

Commotion began as a rock group, mostly black, arrived and autograph-hunters from all over the airport slipped past the ticket-lift desk. "Which of those guys," someone asked me, "is Jubilant Angst" (or whatever the lead singer's name was, unknown to me)? "It's the girl," I maliciously said, "or rather the one who looks like a girl. You know. Sometimes they even travel with goats and perverted lemurs. I read somewhere that three of them had even raped a fish. There's no knowing. If you want an autograph, you'll have to hurry up." He glared affront and went back to reading baseball scores. Milk eyed them as if she had just read *The Origin of Species* and couldn't understand how they had survived while others disappeared.

Up a ramp to board. It might be a ship. Stale air. Low doorway. View of the bloat cone of the nose, its thick wind-punished glass with wipers just like a car. Into the tube. The nonsense is not in the words but in the doing. This is the last genetic stop, the third triplet that makes no amino acid at all, but a muddle, a mutant, a mess. Very well, then. It felt like having an igloo in each lung.

Ghastly view of Milk's face, fatigue-blue in cabin light, seen rounded as if from 112,000 miles off, aboard Apollo 11. Man's a tumor.

And off. Too many passengers in my head, which has one seat only, the seat of the—here they come, zebus, yaupons, xebecs, all with seats assigned. When the seatbelt makes its final *sneckit,* there's no way back, but only coming out at the other side. Ave and vale. Chew, swallow, yawn. The goop in the sinuses grows fat. We head the conga of the buried two abreast in the class called First.

Useless pleadings came from the loudspeakers next our heads. "Would those passengers using radios or tape record-ers please refrain from using them during flight, as they" (I sardonically interpolate "the machines") "interfere with the aircraft's navigational aids?" Each member of the rock group, amidst whom Milk and I were marooned, was wearing headphones connected to cabin bags loaded with equip-ment. Aural solipsism. Only those who didn't need the mes-sage could hear it. Next thing Milk, who was already with them without being of them, had mimed her request for a headset and was listening, if that's the word, to the music of hemispheres, her face tight in a strained but elated-looking scrunch. She'd gone from one no-man's-land into another, and to hell with the plane's navigational aids.

Grievous images of other fates made her doings welcome. I thought of children who, in extermination camps, had frozen together, but thawed out when buried, making the soil churn a little before giving up the ghost. Anything preferable to that.

Gurgles of delight from Milk made me peek-listen, peeling one of her earphones back; but the decibels weren't bad. She was happy about pretending to be listening: a symbolic refinement.

Cokes and dry sherry down the hatch. She felt unspeakably adult, I childish. Neither of us cared. Planted in the soil of rock she couldn't hear, she flowered, sipped her sherry with ostentatious poise. Listening to the nozzle tunes of desiccated air, I vowed to listen to nothing else, neither jazz nor classical, neither people nor ghosts.

Gargoyles, though, flew First Class in my skull: three-legged Francesco Lentini, the soccer wizard; the Tocci brothers, two boys down to the sixth rib, but only one below; Julia Pastrana, the Mexican Digger Indian called the ugliest woman in the world, mostly for being apish and hairy.

Ugliness didn't really come into it; it was more a matter of how original their deformities were. I peopled the First Class compartment with our own kind.

Carl Unthan, the armless violinist, the virtuoso of the toe.

Grace McDaniels, the mule-faced woman, before whom men fainted when she removed her veil; a sideshow in more ways than one.

Christine and Millie, Siamese twins born into slavery, but eventually pulling in six hundred dollars a week.

201

Charmingly addressed by hostesses. Pampered. Waited on hand and foot, or handless and three-footed. Not a trace of a snigger, even as they stuntedly approached the toilets.

Ghouls of the random, with whom the captain, four stripes on his sleeve, came to make polite conversation.

Apocalypse at thirty-five thousand feet, among the tea and toast. Why hadn't we had our flight in *Moby*, Asa's DC-3?

Coming into the jet stream, the plane lurched, felt as if along its entire length it had sagged, then flowed forward again. Not a single shriek. Milk giggled as her innards fell, a nest of bubbles.

Gross, Elizabethan dinner made us sleepy. Never had we been so plied with viands. Had the airmaids wreathed us in vines, we wouldn't have wondered.

Gear down, my mind was like the jet. The flight had taken only an hour, surely, instead of six. Where was all the air we hadn't flown through?

As for that last goodbye, that handing-over of treasure to the snow queen, the nearer nothing said the better. Let's say it was the keenest thrill I'd had in this life.

Grit-mouthed, I took leave.

Unspeaking, took a cab to the train station.

Ate two boiled eggs with my mother.

Got all the local poop, two years of it.

Crooked a finger round my coffee mug, which she washed daily.

Against just such a chance as this.

Gibbering a bit for lack of company.

As her unseen son's fatigue needled his eyes.

Avian chatter as she celebrated: "You did right to come straight home." And I didn't look back.

"Getting on," I told her. "I am. Don't have the stomach any more for the upset."

"Good clean breaks are better," she said. She knew.

Green grapes, to treat herself on this occasion. She's amused I still hate fruit. And wind. And snow. And noise.

"Galveston," she said. "It was in the *National Geographic*. Weren't you there?" "Somewhere near," I said.

Under the table there was still my father's little foot mat, for when his slippers didn't quite touch.

Generally, she told me, she'd kept very well.

George was dead, though. And others. They all had names.

Chocolate cream cake perked me up.

Gathering my wits for the last half-hour of talk before she returned to the TV, I said something about feeling like a test tube when at forty thousand feet. She let it pass, instead asking if Milk had been good.

"Good? She was perfect. Know what she did?"

Aired my pajamas for me on the second day by draping them over the folding chairs on the balcony. "Aired my pajamas," I said, "even though they weren't damp." My mother's eyes glinted as she opened her mouth in silent exclamation.

Godsend of sleep in my old room.

Grid of the last two weeks is all used up.

Got back power of speech. At long last.

THREE

Ara to
Canis Major

I can begin sentences with an *I* again, not so much glad or proud as astounded to be here on the planet as myself and not a peppermint starfish, a thistle, an emu, a bit of quartz. Or a doorknob. Yet self is fainter than it was; self's effaced, and glimmers elsewhere. As in the case of the Masai mother whose child a lion ate and who, against sage advice, reclaimed her offspring by collecting excrement of lions, at least enough to shape a life-sized newborn baby with, which she carried against her chest, a sun-dried thing light as a plaster cast. Perhaps I'll turn to something else, compile my own photographic atlas of irregular or deformed galaxies, and leave the Milky Way alone. Yet, at a distance that feels like more than several thousand miles, the southern half of the Galaxy we call our own, from Ara to Canis Major, remains an underworld undone.

OTHER DALKEY ARCHIVE
PAPERBACKS OF INTEREST
(all books are novels unless otherwise indicated)

BARNES, DJUNA. *Ladies Almanack* — 9.95
BARNES, DJUNA. *Ryder* — 9.95
COOVER, ROBERT. *A Night at the Movies* — 9.95
CRAWFORD, STANLEY. *Some Instructions to My Wife* — 7.95
CUSACK, RALPH. *Cadenza* — 7.95
DOWELL, COLEMAN. *Too Much Flesh and Jabez* — 8.00
DUCORNET, RIKKI. *The Fountains of Neptune* — 10.95
FIRBANK, RONALD. *Complete Short Stories* — 9.95
GASS, WILLIAM H. *Willie Masters' Lonesome Wife* — 9.95
GRAINVILLE, PATRICK. *The Cave of Heaven* — 10.95
MacLOCHLAINN, ALF. *Out of Focus* — 5.95
MARKSON, DAVID. *Springer's Progress* — 9.95
MARKSON, DAVID. *Wittgenstein's Mistress* — 9.95
MATHEWS, HARRY. *20 Lines a Day* [nonfiction] — 8.95
McELROY, JOSEPH. *Women and Men* — 15.95
MOSLEY, NICHOLAS. *Accident* — 9.95
MOSLEY, NICHOLAS. *Impossible Object* — 9.95
MOSLEY, NICHOLAS. *Judith* — 10.95
NAVARRE, YVES. *Our Share of Time* — 9.95
O'BRIEN, FLANN. *The Dalkey Archive* — 9.95
QUENEAU, RAYMOND. *The Last Days* — 9.95
QUENEAU, RAYMOND. *Pierrot Mon Ami* — 7.95
ROUBAUD, JACQUES. *The Great Fire of London* — 12.95
ROUBAUD, JACQUES. *The Princess Hoppy* — 9.95
ROUDIEZ, LEON S. *French Fiction Revisited* [nonfiction] — 14.95
SHKLOVSKY, VIKTOR. *Theory of Prose* [nonfiction] — 14.95
SIMON, CLAUDE. *The Invitation* — 9.95
SORRENTINO, GILBERT. *Aberration of Starlight* — 9.95
SORRENTINO, GILBERT. *Imaginative Qualities of Actual Things* — 9.95
SORRENTINO, GILBERT. *Splendide-Hôtel* — 5.95
SORRENTINO, GILBERT. *Steelwork* — 9.95
SORRENTINO, GILBERT. *Under the Shadow* — 9.95
THEROUX, ALEXANDER. *The Lollipop Trollops and Other Poems* — 10.95
YOUNG, MARGUERITE. *Miss MacIntosh, My Darling* — 2-vol. set, 30.00
ZUKOFSKY, LOUIS. *Collected Fiction* — 9.95

At better bookstores or directly from the publisher (1 book, 10% off; 2 or more, 20% off; add $1.50 postage and handling): Dalkey Archive Press, Fairchild Hall/ISU, Normal, IL 61790-4241. Credit card orders call (309) 438-7555.